The Crisis of Will in
Piers Plowman

In som seson whan softe was the sunne
I shoop me in to shroudes / as y shep were
& heute Apryle . i pis worlde / woundres to here
how gaily / mostke / on malberue hillis
By felt me a ferly / As fayrye me thoughte
was weey of wandrynge / & wente me to reste
vpon a brood banke / be a borne syde
& as y lay & lened / & loked on pe waters
I slubbede in to slepyng / it swyzede so merye
pat gat y to mecte / A merbelous sweuene
y was in a wyldernesse / wiste y neuer where
I beheld in to pe eest / an heyz to pe sunne
Seyz a tour on a tuft / tryaliy y tymbryd
a deep dale be nethe / a dongon per inne
wt depe dyches & derke / & dredful to syghte
& a fayr feeld ful of folk / y fond per be tweene
Of all mañe of me / pe mene & p ryche
wyrkynge & wandrynge / as this worlde asketh
sume putte hem selue to plowh / & pleyede seldyn
& in settynge & in sowynge / wey swonken ful harde
& sume putte hem to pide / & apurled hem ser after
In contynaunce of clothynge / comen desgysed
& mouwen p peep wastours / wt glotenye dystroyen
In preyrs & in penaunce / putte hem selue mauye
For p loue of oure lord / pei lyueden ful streyte
In hope to habe to hyre . heuen, ryche blysse
As Aubrys & heruytys / pt holde hem selue i celles
& coueyte noust / in autres / to fayren abowte
For no likorous lyflode / here lykium to plese
& sume chesen chaffare / to cheuen pe bettre
As it semep to oure syght / pt swiche me thryuyn
& sume merthis to make / as mynsels y seie
But japers & jangeleris / ben judas chyldryn
pei feynen hem fantasyes / & folis hem maken
& hebben wit at wille / to worche what pei sholde
wat poul seiep of hem / y seil not pue it heere
Quy biuerys & beggerys / faste a bowten wentyn
& fele fyrres for here fausd / & fayten at p ale

MS. C. C. C. O. 201 fol. 1ʳ.

John M. Bowers

The Crisis of Will in
Piers Plowman

The Catholic University of America Press
Washington, D.C.

Library of Congress Cataloging-in-Publication Data

Bowers, John M. 1949–
  The crisis of will in Piers Plowman.

  Bibliography: p.
  Includes index.
  1. Langland, William, 1330?–1400? Piers the
Plowman. 2. Will in literature. 3. Scholasticism
in literature. 4. Laziness in literature. I. Title.
PR2017.W54B6 1986 821'.1 85-25498
ISBN 0-8132-0614-6

For My Mother and Father

Contents

Acknowledgements

This book is the chronicle of a wandering scholar who has left a trail of indebtedness spanning great distances. In Oxford, Rosemary Woolf and John Burrow offered a wealth of suggestions for my early researches, as well as setting for me their absolute standards of exacting scholarship and humane criticism. The Rhodes Trust, under the stewardship of Sir Edgar Williams, opened its coffers to provide generous financial support, while for three years I enjoyed the conviviality of the fellows and students of Merton College amid authentically medieval surroundings. I am also grateful to the president and fellows of neighboring Corpus Christi College for their permission to reproduce the illuminated initial from C.C.C.O. MS 201 as the frontispiece for this volume. In Charlottesville, V. A. Kolve earned my deepest gratitude for his untiring counsel and detailed supervision of this book in its first draft. Hoyt Duggan, Thomas Reed, and Roger Hillas also gave me guidance and useful criticism at this important stage of composition. Many early errors were detected and expunged with the aid of other readers: Ronnene Anderson, Mark Peppler, John Robertson, Susan Russ, and most especially Elizabeth Lehman—first among helpmates. In Pasadena, I was able to complete the final revisions with the financial support of an Andrew W. Mellon Fellowship which came to me through the good offices of Jerome J. McGann, John Benton, and E. Talbot Donaldson. The Division of Humanities and Social Sciences at the California Institute of Technology provided almost limitless resources as well as an array of genial colleagues, among them Daniel Kevles, Rod Kiewiet, John Sutherland, and Susan and Lance Davis, who lavished me with encouragement and friendship throughout my two-year stay. My special thanks go to Terry Atwell and Susan Cave for typing the entire manuscript onto diskettes, and in particular to Joy Hansen for teaching me the microcomputer skills that so hastened the project through its final stages.

The trail ends in Princeton, where I would like to express my gratitude to my new colleagues Peter Allen, John Fleming, and Seth Lerer for their willingness to read the manuscript in its final form. No scholar can neglect the staffs of the libraries where he has invested so much time, for me the Bodleian, the libraries of the University of Virginia and the University of California at Los Angeles, and last but most pleasantly the Henry E. Huntington, for making less arduous the taxing labors of research. At the Catholic University of America Press, I am deeply indebted to David McGonagle for taking the initial interest in my manuscript and to Rita Watrin for her careful copyediting. There are others who have contributed generously and steadily along the way—Mary Carruthers, Richard Osberg, John A. Alford, and Judson Boyce Allen—and the pleasure of acknowledging their contributions makes more complete my satisfaction at reaching an end which, for every reader of Langland, is always to begin again with a renewed sense of wonder. *"The end is where we start from. . . ."*

My final thanks—which should have come first—go to my parents, to whom this book is dedicated.

Princeton   J. M. B.
April, 1985

Introduction

This book had its genesis during my first bewildered attempt as a student to make sense of a poem that seemed like a mystery wrapped in layer upon layer of enigmas. At the beginning of the *Vita de Dowel*, however, I came upon a brief passage that struck me as odd but possibly explainable. Will meets two friars who give him the following advice:

> "God wole suffre wel thi sleuthe, ȝif thy-self lyketh.
> For he ȝaf the to ȝeresȝyue to ȝeme wel thi-selue,
> And that is witte and fre wille, to euery wyȝte a porcioun."
>
> (B. viii. 51–53)

Skeat offered no note to the first line of the passage, and J. F. Goodridge's translation of the B-text failed to provide its normally helpful guidance through its literal meaning: "If you choose to do that, God will not hinder you. . . ." The crucial but elusive term seemed to be *sleuthe*. If Chaucer's Pardoner preached against avarice with the aim of securing a donation from his listeners, why have Langland's two friars lost a golden opportunity by singling out sloth as the deadly sin most threatening to Will? And why have they encouraged a reliance upon free will and intelligence rather than confession to one of their confreres? *And* what is the connection, if any, between the free will which is necessary for virtuous living and the vagabond Will who is searching after Dowel? From these first groping inquiries, much followed.

As it now stands, this study draws together two issues related to two root meanings of the word *crisis* in its title. It offers a "critique of will" insofar as it concerns the fierce fourteenth-century debate over human volition vis-à-vis the poem's protagonist, Will. Unlike previous critics who have been quick to apply a Thomist, Ockhamist, or other single theory of *voluntas*—if indeed any is called to witness—I explore the controversy itself as the context in which Langland placed a dreamer-narrator who often comes close to becoming a psychological personification. And it deals with the "crisis of Will" insofar as it concerns the paralysis of human will in the midst of urgent circumstance of moral choice, which in popular theology was identified as the sin of *acedia* or

sloth. This moral and psychological construct, so narrowly defined to-
day, was sufficiently comprehensive in Langland's day to include most
of the social and spiritual problems which his poem addresses. Dis-
cussed in tandem, these two critical issues go far toward offering a
sense of artistic unity and authorial purpose which has previously
eluded readers of *Piers Plowman*—and certainly eluded this reader
during his earliest efforts.

Critics generally agree that a theological poem can only be under-
stood within the theological context of its age. While our knowledge
of the Latin sources and the exegetical traditions behind Langland's
scriptural quotations is becoming remarkably complete, too little at-
tention has been paid to the scholastic controversies which reached be-
yond the fourteenth-century universities, even as far as the Malvern
Hills, and contributed strongly to an atmosphere of religious skep-
ticism throughout late medieval England. My first chapter deals with
the most unsettling questions of speculative theology and suggests
ways in which the debated topics trickled down from the academic
summits to the lower slopes of the laity. The discussion naturally raises
the question of Langland's own education, and I suggest a level of at-
tainment which was short of the *studium generale* of a university but
still far enough along for the poet to know something about the topics
disputed among the masters and students at Oxford. The chapter con-
cludes by considering various ways in which Langland's skeptical out-
look is reflected in his poem's handling of imagery, its unstable genre,
and its maddening evasion of clarity and certitude.

Chapter II focuses on the controversy over human will or *voluntas*.
The theology of the will has a long and complicated history which
reached a point of dramatic crisis in Langland's century. Not since Au-
gustine's attack on the Pelagians in the fourth century had Christian
philosophers argued so fiercely over the faculty of the soul which al-
lows a man to choose a course of action, determines the moral value of
that action, and may (or may not) require divine grace in order to win
salvation. Far from embracing a single doctrine, Langland emerges as
a religious poet who responded to the broadly felt anxiety which this
controversy created. A full survey of debated issues therefore becomes
the starting point for a proper assessment of this fourteenth-century
allegory whose principal character, quite deliberately, is named Will.

Some theologians such as John Buridan argued that the will had the
power, and indeed the obligation, to suspend its judgments until the
correct choices could be determined with absolute certainty. In a
simpler moral context, however, a man whose indecisiveness prevented
him from engaging in any fruitful endeavors could be considered guilty

of slothfulness. There are two reasons why *acedia* is a particularly troublesome sin and yet, for Langland's purposes, a remarkably useful moral category. First, sloth resulted from a deficiency of the will rather than its perverse or excessive movement. This unique cause gave it an ambiguous status, since its symptoms could be attributed variously to organic melancholy, a venial passion, or the spiritual dryness following in the wake of a mystical experience, none of which could properly be blamed as sinful. The second complexity involves its theological history. In the beginning of the Christian tradition, *acedia* was an eremitic vice analysed almost exclusively in terms of its victim's spiritual condition. Although it never lost this psychological aspect, the concept of sloth was drastically expanded in the fourteenth century to include an impressive range of social abuses: failure to learn a trade, to serve one's master, to pay employees on time, to return borrowed objects, to keep promises, to fight in the army, and to earn a livelihood that would support a family. Chapter III discusses sloth as a sin which had generated such a vast array of spiritual and physical signs that it could serve as a unifying construct for most forms of corruption held up for censure in *Piers Plowman*, suggesting also why Langland had good reason to suspect that *acedia* was the most dangerous sin, not merely because it eluded precise kinds of learned analysis, but because it could appear to be no sin at all.

The poet's clearest examination of vice comes in the five catalogues of deadly sins, reflecting as they do the popular traditions of the pulpit. As a first application of the previous chapter's information and a test of its implicit assumptions, Chapter IV focuses on these catalogues to determine whether the poet has altered traditional materials to grant priority to one particular sin. Two conclusions emerge. Langland has departed from the standard arrangements of Gregory and Cassian to place *acedia* last in each review, in a privileged position made even more conspicuous by the length of each treatment in relation to the other vices. What is more, the features highlighted in these sloth-figures, especially in the Confession Scene, turn out to be similar to many of the features used in portraying Will the Dreamer.

Chapter V focuses upon the poem's first two visions in an effort to perceive social corruption, spiritual laxity, and political neglect within a single moral perspective. Homiletic and penitential writings offer corroborative testimony that the community's disorderly members—wasters, false beggars, priests who desert their parishes, pilgrims who grow tired of their journey, a king who is not vigilant enough in his maintenance of justice, and generally all those who are lured by Lady Mede into neglecting their proper estates within society—are guilty of one specific brand of sinfulness. The Dreamer embodies much of what is wrong in the Fair Field, even from the opening lines when he is introduced "in the habit of a hermit unholy of works." Is he a hermit who is unholy because he has abandoned his cell? Or is he a wanderer who deserves blame for disguising himself as a hermit to beg for alms? These two possible interpretations in fact point to the twin faults found throughout society at large. The King is introduced as the embodiment of an absolute legislative will, the power behind the enforcement of law, although he himself is negligent at first when he tries to force Conscience to marry Lady Mede. When counseled by Reason, however, he sets about guiding his subjects according to the divinely ordained code of duty and estate.

The King may have the power to command, but the people must decide whether to obey. Since society's problems can only be confronted on this level of the individual will, the poem begins to focus more and more upon a protagonist who had largely been the passive narrator up to the end of the second vision. Chapter VI shows how the poem's succession of waking episodes are crafted with a studied ambiguity allowing the reader to reach a pejorative interpretation of Will's actions and reactions. Since so many of his traits can be construed as symptoms of *acedia*—idleness, sorrow, wandering, dozing during prayer, falling asleep in church—Langland raises the serious suspicion that the Dreamer never fully profits from the teachings of his visions and never truly embarks upon the life of Dowel.

The question of autobiographical authenticity becomes more pressing once the characterization of Will is shown to be deeply influenced by commonplace writings on *acedia*. This is especially true in Passus V of the C-text where the Dreamer is labeled with so many readily identifiable traits of slothfulness. He is also placed within the conventional literary form of a debate between Wit and Will which makes him seem more a personification than a faithful reflection of the author. Chapter VII reaches the conclusion that Langland, far from rendering a literal *apologia pro vita sua*, offers us a confession of his inner life only, of his potential for willfulness and his temperamental inclination toward sloth.

Respect for the power of language runs very deep in *Piers Plowman*. While Langland takes every opportunity to condemn those who corrupt language and praise the authors of moral literature, he was left with the disturbing knowledge that words, like works, were no sure reflection of a man's intentions or a sound will. Despite his steady care to discover and communicate truth, he must have worried that his hard poem might be misunderstood and, even worse, that the unorthodox notions voiced by certain of its characters might lead some members of his audience into error. *Piers Plowman* is also charged with anxiety concerning the actual writing of poetry, an occupation that could be confused with both physical idleness and mental vagrancy. On one level, the entire poem is an exploration of that perplexity, which is never fully resolved. But one fact is clear: Langland devoted most of his life to writing and rewriting his poem. Perhaps he engaged in the task as a spiritual exercise to relieve his slothful temperament, or perhaps he persevered in his efforts as a simple act of faith that "making" with words was the one possible form of Dowel that he did best. Chapter VIII brings my study to its conclusion by speculating about the poet's artistic temperament and his motives for writing so doggedly at his poem.

As the aforegoing synopsis suggests, my historicist method involves recovering medieval contexts which are by no means as clearly defined as those supporting, for example, a patristic or iconographic analysis. This method requires the steady introduction of a variety of historical testimony—from scholastic commentaries, devotional manuals, sermons, mystical writings, religious poetry, secular poetry, and even accounts of events in the streets of Oxford—to establish philosophical, political, and moral contexts which the poet himself most likely found complicated and disturbing. I try as far as possible to consign these citations to the notes, although they are presented in the text whenever the precise language or emotional tenor of a passage makes a powerful claim for our attention. It is important to hear witnesses such as Thomas Wimbledon and Julian of Norwich, for instance, speaking in their own voices.

My work has been greatly assisted by several magisterial studies of medieval philosophy and religion. In particular, Vernon J. Bourke's history of the will in Christian thought has made it possible to trace the psychological, moral, and political strains in the scholastic discussions which did so much to unsettle fourteenth-century thinking about the nature of man's soul. And Siegfried Wenzel's detailed analysis of *acedia* has served as an unfailing guide to understanding this complex moral category. I have added a good deal of new material and constructed each discussion in ways most illuminating for my later arguments and explorations. For the sake of economy, separate chapters have been devoted to will and sloth so that the complexity of the two concepts can be most justly represented. Other scholars have contributed substantially in other areas—Heiko Oberman on speculative theology, Ernst Kantorowicz on political theory, and Morton Bloomfield on the seven deadly sins, to name only three—and I have applied these background materials as they were meant to be rather than attempting in every case to re-invent the wheel.

There is a second dimension to the historical method of this study. While the fourteenth-century context of Langland's poem has been carefully respected, I have also tried to draw into discussion the traditions that have emerged in twentieth-century criticism. *Piers Plowman* has provoked more diversity of professional opinion than perhaps any other major work so widely read and so often written about. While minority voices as well as dissenting opinions have been duly noted, my implicit aim has been to delineate two major approaches that have dominated Langland studies and medieval literary studies in general over the past three decades. New Criticism found an eloquent spokesman in E. Talbot Donaldson, whose study of the C-text in 1949 was followed in England by the work of John Burrow and David Mills and in this country by impressive books from the hands of his students, notably Elizabeth Kirk and Mary Carruthers. The case for Exegetics was begun in 1951 by D.W. Robertson and Bernard Huppé, whose reading of *Piers Plowman* through the scriptural tradition has been deepened by Robert Kaske and Joseph Wittig, and continues to be elaborated by Judson Boyce Allen. I have not always agreed with my critical progenitors—Chapter II takes issue with Robertson and Huppé on Langland's doctrine of the will, and Chapter VII responds to Donaldson on the subject of autobiographical authenticity—but these specific disagreements might best be viewed as features of the family romance so typical in the history of scholarship. My larger goal has been to map out as much common ground as possible for New Criticism and Exegetics, not really to effect a synthesis between the two contending schools of thought (a far more challenging task recently taken up by Lee Patterson) but to draw attention to the areas where some consensus has been reached and where separate contributions are to some degree complementary. To that end, I have drawn into discussion the discoveries and insights of many scholars who began their work earlier in the vineyard of Langland studies, preferring to risk the appearance of consistent indebtedness than to obscure the consistency that I hope is growing in our understanding of the strange, haunting poem that is the common subject of our labors.

In accord with most published criticism, I have chosen the B-version as the basis for analysis. Consequently, whenever a passus is cited without reference to version, the B-text should be understood. Interesting passages which exist only in A or C have also been taken into consideration, since I have proceeded upon the assumption that the poet's growing awareness of the meaning and intentions of his poem can often be charted when a line or larger passage is traced diachronically from one version to the next. While no single motive can account for the whole complicated process of revision, the changes that a certain passage undergoes—its alteration, growth, deletion, or transposition from one part of the poem to another—can often serve as evidence of Langland's heightened awareness of such matters as the poem's impact on its audience and his own status as a poet. I have also engaged in many close readings, particularly in Chapters VI and VII, whenever a passage has demanded precise linguistic, stylistic, or moral explication.

Any reading of *Piers Plowman*, close or otherwise, raises the question of editions. Walter W. Skeat's heroic parallel-texts edition of 1886 remains the basis for much published criticism, but it is now being replaced by new critical texts with different readings and different lineation. George Kane's A-text appeared in 1960 and was quickly accepted in preference to the 1952 edition by Thomas A. Knott and David C. Fowler. The B-text co-edited by George Kane and E. Talbot Donaldson arrived in 1975, although its controversial editorial methods have not won universal approval. And at the moment of this writing, G.H. Russell's new edition of the C-text still has not appeared. To complicate matters even more, George Rigg and Charlotte Brewer have published an edition of what they have designated as the Z-text. Because scholarly opinion (including my own) remains deeply divided on whether this represents the author's first draft or a scribe's intriguing alteration of the poem, the relevant testimony of the Z-text has been accepted only provisionally and consigned to the appropriate notes.

In the pages that follow, I have consistently used Kane's A-text, with occasional mention of interesting readings found in Skeat or in Knott and Fowler. For the C-text I have followed Derek Pearsall's edition of 1978 (with the new passus numberings) since it is based upon two superior manuscripts—Huntington MS 143 and British Library MS Add. 35157—not available to Skeat but now serving Russell in his critical edition. Citation from the B-text is more complicated. While I have used Kane and Donaldson as the base edition in all cases, in a few lines I have reverted to Skeat, or chosen one of J.A.W. Bennett's readings, or preferred an appealing variant noted by Kane and Donaldson themselves. Whenever I have departed from their text, the phrase or line has been enclosed in brackets. I have also departed from Kane and Donaldson in matters of capitalization and, less often, punctuation. As a further aid for the reader, most of the personifications, proper names, and names for the Deity have been capitalized.

As this study was making its way through three distinct stages of composition, I recognized that its disposition of materials, its formal proportions, and even its pacing were developing in ways vaguely (and unintentionally) resembling the poem that it addresses. It is therefore sobering to recall Morton Bloomfield's observation that the structure of *Piers Plowman* has been subverted by the fallacy of imitative form: "spiritual confusion demands to some extent artistic confusion." Here I hope any resemblance ends. This study strives to bring greater clarity to our understanding of Langland's wayward masterpiece by showing that his spiritual confusion can be related directly to certain unresolved issues in fourteenth-century theology, and that what seems like artistic confusion is often the result of the poet's thorough, wide-ranging examination of sloth as a concept which in fact draws together and renders intelligible so many of the otherwise disparate features of his poem. Thus I hope that this book, despite its occasional heuristic excesses, will unravel some of the enigmas that surround this allegorical vision while respecting the special beauty of its mystery.

I

Langland in an Age of Crisis

Piers Plowman depicts a world in turmoil. Although Langland offers a vision not shared by all his contemporaries, the briefest look at fourteenth-century England shows how a writer might have felt that his country had suffered more upheavals than in previous ages. Recurrent outbreaks of plague carried off as much as a third of the population, a subsequent transformation of the economy caused widespread social unrest, political turmoil culminated twice in the murders of kings, and religious dissension bred heresies among learned theologians and spiritual doubts throughout the hierarchy of the Church. The Black Death, the Great Schism, the Hundred Years War, Lollardy, the Peasants' Revolt—an historical index of the century forms a litany of disasters.

Langland's poem reflects this prevailing climate of anxiety by enumerating problems, brooding over them, and railing against those felt to be responsible, but almost never does it offer any solid solutions. The poet seems to have discovered during the process of composition that complex problems have even more complex remedies. His struggle came to bear increasingly upon the twin realizations that ideal solutions can seldom be determined with absolute certainty and that these solutions are unlikely to be discovered and enacted by the individual, much less by Christian society as a whole.

The quest of an inquiring mind begins with wonderment, when a man is faced by a phenomenon whose nature or cause he does not understand—the Dungeon of Falsehood, the spectacle of Lady Mede, the tearing of the Pardon—so that he continues his quest until he discovers the truth. The protagonist Will searches after Dowel, but his inquiry really involves the challenge of deciding what it *means* to do well. His is ultimately a crisis of judgment. It is significant, therefore, that judgment was described by many fourteenth-century philosophers as a principal function of the human will that precedes all other actions, spiritual as well as physical, and determines their moral worth. We have every right to expect the influence of these voluntarist theories on an allegory whose central figure is named Will. Yet Langland seems to have felt that the will (*voluntas*) was a faculty ill-equipped by itself to discharge the duties attributed to it by recent theologians. These inherent deficiencies are carefully embodied in Will the Dreamer, in his inability to make correct decisions and to assert himself in the performance of what is right.

If Dante's *Divine Comedy* enshrines the ideals of the thirteenth century with its sense of Thomist certainty, *Piers Plowman* contrasts those ideals with some of the harsher realities of life in the fourteenth century. Charles Muscatine has summed up the feelings of most readers when he stated that an investigation of the poem "in terms of the literature of an age of crisis would seem to be almost redundant."[1] Indeed, Langland looked his world straight on and saw the worst. The choice for him was between a set of glowing ideals that belonged to the past and a set of present realities that were manifestly wrong. Such a dilemma created a crisis for the will, the human faculty charged with choosing between alternatives. While a degree of doubt might be needed to avoid error when authority or cogent evidence was lacking, the will could be placed in the position of being unable to decide, of suspending judgment and potentially falling prey to thorough-going skepticism and despair. Simply avoiding evil was not enough. The will had to turn toward the good and act upon it. To do nothing over an extended period was itself morally wrong, because it led a man into the state of *acedia*, the deadly sin of sloth.

---

1. Charles Muscatine, *Poetry and Crisis in the Age of Chaucer* (Notre Dame: University of Notre Dame Press, 1972), p. 34. Joining in a careful return to the cultural outlook offered by Johan Huizinga in *The Waning of the Middle Ages*, trans. F. Hopman (1924; rpt. Harmondsworth: Penguin, 1955) are S. Harrison Thompson, "Pro Saeculo XIV," *Speculum*, 28 (1953), 801–07; Norman F. Cantor, *Medieval History: The Life and Death of a Civilization* (New York: Macmillan, 1963); Robert E. Lerner, *The Age of Adversity: The Fourteenth Century* (Ithaca: Cornell University Press, 1968); Jeffrey Burton Russell, *Medieval Civilization* (New York: John Wiley, 1968); Sidney Painter and Brian Tierney, *Western Europe in the Middle Ages, 300–1475* (New York: Knopf, 1970), pp. 381–463; and even F.R.H. Du Boulay, *An Age of Ambition: English Society in the Late Middle Ages* (London: Nelson, 1970). Of course the popular revival of Huizinga has been championed by Barbara W. Tuchman, *A Distant Mirror: The Calamitous Fourteenth Century* (New York: Knopf, 1978). D.W. Robertson, Jr., and Bernard F. Huppé, *Piers Plowman and Scriptural Tradition* (Princeton: Princeton University Press, 1951), pp. 234–36, have gone so far as to refer to *Piers Plowman* as "the epic of the dying Middle Ages."

An undercurrent of skepticism had run throughout the Age of Faith. Its roots can be traced back to Augustine, who rejected to some degree the ephemeral world of things as incapable of yielding any sure knowledge. Since no pure truth could be expected from sensory experience, he turned instead to self-knowledge and the discovery of spiritual truths through the aid of divine illumination. The doubts encountered in this internal quest presented no hindrance in the attainment of certainty, since by doubting a man at least became more keenly aware of himself.[2] Just so, a turning inward to study one's own psychology became a trait common to this confused age's writers, although none more persistently and over a longer period of time than Langland.

But not all medieval skepticism was philosophically positive or artistically fruitful. As in every age, a variety of forces were at work to shake men from their faith. Different sorts of skepticism followed from the hardships of daily life, the crass hedonism of youth, and the involuntary doubt of previously secure souls. Abundant testimony to skepticism and even agnosticism comes from writers who either criticized the faithlessness of others or confessed to their own prior doubts and presumptions.[3] Yet a sense of doubt was not always useful in preventing error, and it did not always ease with the passage of years. Caesarius of Heisterbach offers this story illustrating the dangers of intense emotional skepticism:

A certain nun, a woman of advanced age and, as it was reputed, of great holiness, was so disturbed by the vice of sorrow and vexed by the spirit of blasphemy, doubt, and distrust, that she fell into despair. Concerning those things which from infancy she had believed and was bound to believe, she began to doubt completely and could not be induced by anyone to take part in the holy sacrament.[4]

The nun never recovered from her crisis of faith and eventually threw herself in the Moselle River.

The late Middle Ages shows a widespread and more acute sense of

2. Gordon Leff, *Medieval Thought: St. Augustine to Ockham* (Harmondsworth: Penguin, 1958), pp. 34–35 and 39, citing Augustine, *De Trinitate*, X, 10 (*PL* 42:981).

3. Mary Edith Thomas, *Medieval Skepticism and Chaucer* (New York: William-Frederick, 1950), pp. 10–18 and 34. For a range of medieval testimony, see Giraldus Cambrensis, *Gemma Ecclesiastica* (II, xxiv), ed. J.S. Brewer, 2 vols. (London: The Rolls Series, 1862), vol. II, pp. 281–85; Philippe de Navarre, *Les Quatre Ages de l'homme*, ed. Marcel de Fréville (Paris: Firmin Didot, 1888), pp. 80–83; and Jean de Joinville, *Histoire de Saint Louis* in *Recueil des Historiens des Gaules et de la France*, vol. XX (Paris: Daunou et Naudet, 1840), p. 197.

4. Caesarius of Heisterbach, *Dialogus Miraculorum*, ed. Josephus Strange, 2 vols. (Cologne: Lempertz, 1851), vol. I, p. 209 (dist. IV, cap. xl). This story and others follow as *exempla* under the heading "*De accidia*"—"quae viris religiosis solet esse satis importuna" (p. 197).

uncertainty stemming from a variety of causes, most of them centering on the question of God's will. A new kind of religious doubt swept Europe after the crusades, when the men who had marched off full of confidence that God would give them an easy victory over the Saracens returned home defeated and perplexed over God's will and even His power to enact it.[5] Matthew Paris writes poignantly of the soldiers disillusioned after the debacle of Louis's 1250 crusade:

Then many, whom a firm faith did not fortify, began to be wasted as much by desperation and blasphemies as by hunger. And the faith of many—alas, alas—began to waver as they said to one another: "Why has Christ abandoned us?"[6]

The crusades had more than one effect upon the latent skepticism of medieval Europe. Closer contact with the East aided the recovery of classical learning, although greater knowledge did not bring with it greater certainty. On the contrary, skeptical thinking at the universities can be traced to the introduction of the study of natural philosophy during this period.[7]

Skepticism would not be a subject of such general concern if it had been restricted to a few disillusioned crusaders and the occasional mad nun. But in the late Middle Ages a host of problems came to be discussed by laymen and clergy alike, by city folk as well as cloistered theologians:

These [skeptics] dared question the state of affairs into which they had been born, expressing perplexity about the heaven they had been taught to hope for, the hell they had learned to fear; rationalizing the sacraments they had grown up to reverence; exercising their minds over problems of determinism and man's free will which baffled even the churchmen; protesting against a sea of troubles by opposing God's justice—or injustice—with common sense.[8]

Thomas Walsingham went further in accusing the Londoners of 1392 of the most severe sorts of disbelief:

Indeed, among nearly all nations they were then the most haughty of peoples, the most arrogant, and the most avaricious, as well as the worst believers in God and ancient traditions. . . . For certain of them believed, as it was asserted, that there was no God, there was no sacrament of the altar, no resurrection after death, but as a beast of burden dies, so too does a man meet his end.[9]

5. Thomas, *Skepticism*, pp. 34–43.

6. Matthew Paris, *Chronica Majora*, ed. Henry Richards Luard, 7 vols. (London: The Rolls Series, 1872–83), vol. V, p. 108.

7. Thomas, *Skepticism*, pp. 44–57.

8. *Ibid.*, p. 84.

9. Thomas Walsingham, *Historia Anglicana*, ed. Henry Thomas Riley, 2 vols. (London: The Rolls Series, 1863–64), vol. II, p. 208.

Complaints against apostasy were not directed against the laity alone. John Wyclif addressed himself to the disturbing fact that theologians were using scholastic techniques to reach conclusions which either questioned or contradicted the basic beliefs of Christianity.[10] These theologians, mostly members of the voluntarist movement, did indeed raise issues concerning divine will, grace, determinism, and revelation, but often they were refining difficulties which were already centuries old and translating into the language of scholastic philosophy some of the doubts felt throughout society.

If English theologians had limited their discussions to problems of logic—those discussions, that is, for which they are usually called Nominalists—their influence might have been slight. But logic has to do with reason and deals with the ways that things are perceived, named, and then fabricated by the mind within itself. A growing distrust of reason's ability to confirm religious truths was one of the hallmarks of the age, and Roger Bacon was one of the first to press the issue:

Reasoning draws a conclusion and makes us grant the conclusion, but it does not make the conclusion certain, nor does it remove doubt so that the mind may rest on the intuition of truth, unless the mind discovers it by the method of experience.[11]

Robert Grosseteste's study of optics showed that many perceptions could not be trusted unless they conformed with well-established empirical generalizations. His theory is summed up in the *Oxford Commentary*: "one who knows by experience knows infallibly that things are thus, always thus, and thus in all."[12]

While accepting this principle provisionally, Duns Scotus discarded Grosseteste's doctrine of illumination and, more importantly, denied the Thomist analogy between the created and the divine. Thus he made possible the momentous conclusion that a man can have no cer-

---

10. John Wyclif, *Trialogus*, ed. Gotthard Lechler (Oxford: The Clarendon Press, 1869), p. 384: "And there is no doubt whether our religious people are in private so unbelieving, preferring their own signs on certain topics. For all such men are disobedient to the law of the Gospels, since they value their own adulterated signs more than the fruit of faith which is taught in Gospel law." The possible influences of Wycliffite thought upon *Piers Plowman* have been capably assessed by Pamela Gradon, "Langland and the Ideology of Dissent," *Proceedings of the British Academy*, 66 (1980), 179–205.

11. Roger Bacon, *Opus Maius* (VI, i), ed. John Henry Bridges, 2 vols. (Oxford: The Clarendon Press, 1897), vol. II, p. 167.

12. A.C. Crombie, *Robert Grosseteste and the Origins of Experimental Science, 1100–1700* (Oxford: The Clarendon Press, 1953), pp. 169–71, translating from Grosseteste's *Commentaria Oxoniensia*.

tain knowledge other than that derived from experience.[13] To make even sharper his departure from Aquinas in the field of theology, he admitted limits to the power of reason to confirm the revelations of God, since all revelation was a matter of faith and not necessarily of rational or perceptual experience. A brief look at Duns Scotus and his successors shows that the core issue was not nominalism against realism, but the question of how much reason and experience could know about God's plan for salvation.[14]

Men who had inherited a Thomist confidence in the reason's ability to elicit and confirm the teachings of the Church were staggered by the questions raised by the voluntarists. So too were those who had come to expect a perceptible analogy between God's intentions and their manifestation in the world which He had created. Central to medieval culture had been the belief that the divine was manifested in the physical, that the Word had indeed been made flesh, and this belief made possible man's fundamental view of the world as a creation mystically charged with meanings that conformed to revealed truth. If the natural and supernatural were indeed different realms that failed to share a common border, the mystic unity of the cosmos was undone and the created world became a jumble of confused and senseless images. Reason could conjure with these images, piece together ideas, bicker over bits of doctrine, but reason by itself could not re-assemble a perceptual world shattered by the denial of correspondences.

Duns Scotus began this revolution in thought by discounting the causality of Aristotle and Aquinas while seeking to restore to God the illimitable powers that these philosophers had qualified through their metaphysics. Where William of Ockham and his followers made the truly radical break was in their discussion of the absolute power of God's will and the limits of human freedom. When the theory of God's absolute power (*potentia absoluta*) was applied to questions involving free will, grace, merit, and future contingents, a grave problem arose. Matters of revelation were also subject to interpretation from practical experience, and this meant that authority and experience could offer two different answers to the same question.[15] God's absolute power was invoked to solidify this philosophical position, and as Gordon Leff has remarked, Ockham and his followers used scholastic tools not so much to elucidate doctrine as to insist on mystery:

13. Gordon Leff, *Paris and Oxford Universities in the Thirteenth and Fourteenth Centuries: An Institutional and Intellectual History* (New York: John Wiley, 1968), p. 295.
14. Leff, *Medieval Thought*, pp. 260–64.
15. *Ibid.*, p. 290.

. . . where probability simply questioned, God's absolute power destroyed. Where reason ended, God's *potentia absoluta* began, taking charge of what was not subject to verification and showing how uncertain and unknown it was. It removed all effective standards of judgment. In that sense, the God of skepticism ceased to be the God of tradition: He was so unknowable that His attributes melted in the blaze of His omnipotence, leaving no certainty.[16]

The *voluntas Dei* became the subject of the most urgent theological discussion during the first half of the fourteenth century. The absolute power and freedom of His will had never really been in question, but these commentators pursued the implications of that absoluteness to ask what was the sphere of its activity, whether certain past decisions could be superseded, and how man might understand the workings of Heaven's will. Was it outside time and space, wholly withdrawn from any action within the created universe? Or did God continue to assert His will in the on-going governance of the world? Was the covenant of creation by which all things are ruled, as well as the message of redemption expressed by Christ in the New Testament, fixed and unalterable according to God's *potentia ordinata*? Or can God change His mind according to a *potentia absoluta*? And if so, how would He choose to tell us about His altered intentions?[17]

Ockham himself argued that God's will was so completely free that nothing at all was certain and therefore matters of faith could not be discussed. By liberating God from the necessity of following a set plan laid down by the Bible, these propositions could be seen as making mockery of revelation, since Christ's teachings might no longer be valid. A man might be allowed to hate God, grace might bestow no merit, a man's will by itself might determine his reward, grace and sin might exist together, and God might damn a virtuous man while saving a reprobate. By granting the unbridled freedom of divine will, Ockham needed to acknowledge the possibility of a divine caprice wise beyond man's power to comprehend, overturning the established categories of cause and effect, will and deed, good and evil.[18] Only unshakeable confidence in divine benevolence saved these religious phi-

16. *Ibid.* See also Marie Anne Pernoud, "Innovation in William of Ockham's References to the 'Potentia Dei'," *Antonianum*, 45 (1970), 65–97.

17. Leff, *Medieval Thought*, p. 288; F.C. Copleston, *A History of Medieval Philosophy* (New York: Harper & Row, 1972), pp. 253–59; William J. Courtenay, "Covenant and Causality in Pierre d'Ailly," *Speculum*, 46 (1971), 94–119; and Courtenay, "Nominalism and Late Medieval Religion" in *The Pursuit of Holiness in Late Medieval and Renaissance Religion*, ed. Charles Trinkaus and Heiko A. Oberman (Leiden: Brill, 1974), p. 47.

18. Leff, *Medieval Thought*, p. 289.

losophers—and Langland, too, as we shall see—from the despair of even trying to search after truth.

Wyclif's absolute claims for the Bible as revelation and the fervor of his following in England are evidence for the continued prevalence of the skepticism encouraged by Ockhamist debates. The appearance of Bradwardine's *De Causa Dei* with its proof that faith is independent of metaphysics and philosophy does not mean that the "modern Pelagians," against whom it was written, had retreated from their unorthodox speculations about grace, free will, and future contingents. Nor had they ceased to exert influence.[19] Two of the most extreme Ockhamists survived Bradwardine, and their writings circulated alongside his for the remainder of the century, carrying forth Ockhamism's most radical views on the freedom of man's will and its involvement in the unfolding of future events. Thomas Buckingham (c. 1290–1351) granted so much freedom to human will that he speculated God Himself could not be certain of contingencies, since He played no part whatsoever in determining the choices a man might make. The implications of this and other of Buckingham's arguments in his *Sentences* would unsettle the most liberal Christian: God's revelation through the word of Christ may no longer apply; God can deceive and be deceived; the criteria for salvation may no longer be valid; and revelation, in respect to future world events, may never come to pass. The Augustinian view of history could be pushed aside, an eternal verity reduced to a vast tangle of contingencies. Following Buckingham on the complete freedom of human will, Adam of Woodham (d. 1357) proclaimed the absolute power of God's will and entertained the same possibility that God might be free from the obligation of accepting His own revelations.[20]

The aforegoing review of Ockhamist propositions has been based largely on the work of scholars such as Gilson, Leff, and Knowles. As specialists in the field already know, a revisionist movement among more recent historians of medieval philosophy has modified and in some cases overturned many of these earlier understandings, particularly in the case of fourteenth-century skepticism.[21] William of Ockham is no longer thought to have undermined the established order, engaged in the wholesale destruction of natural theology, or pushed for a

19. *Ibid.*, p. 297.
20. *Ibid.*, pp. 292–93.
21. Valuable descriptions of the shift are offered by two scholars instrumental in the movement: William J. Courtenay, "Nominalism and Late Medieval Thought: A Bibliographical Essay," *Theological Studies*, 33 (1972), 716–34; Heiko A. Oberman, "Fourteenth-Century Religious Thought: A Premature Profile," *Speculum*, 53 (1978),

divorce between the realms of reason and faith.[22] His arguments are carefully constructed to limit skeptical implications and stop short of skeptical conclusions, especially in the handling of epistemological problems.[23] Even Gordon Leff has recanted, confessing his earlier tendency to view Ockham from the false perspective of radical Ockhamism and to see in his extant writings the "speculative extravagances" of his followers.[24]

The arguments of the radical or "left wing" Ockhamists have also come under careful review. We are now told that Robert Holcot pursued a logic which merely seemed to lead to skepticism, when in fact he held with Augustine that the Church and divine creation provided a sound basis for understanding God's transcendent truths. The *potentia absoluta* refers only to those possibilities which were initially available to God. Some of those possibilities were realized at the moment of creation, while others are now merely hypothetical and should not concern mankind. By embracing the belief that God does not deny grace for those trying their hardest—*facientibus quod in se est Deus non denegat gratiam*—Holcot held that man's natural powers could acquire sufficient knowledge about faith to insure salvation.[25] Therefore, although he might risk the accusation of Pelagianism, he avoids being indicted as a skeptic.

Historians on both sides of the skepticism issue agree that their differences arise not so much from the facts as from the interpretation of

---

80–93. David C. Steinmetz, "Late Medieval Nominalism and the *Clerk's Tale*," *ChauR*, 12 (1977/78), 38–54, warns against literary interpretations based upon the older understandings of Ockhamism. Sound application of these materials is found in the work begun by Russell A. Peck in "Chaucer and the Nominalist Questions," *Speculum*, 53 (1978), 745–60.

22. Heiko A. Oberman, "Some Notes on the Theology of Nominalism, with Attention to Its Relation to the Renaissance," *HTR*, 53 (1960), 47–76; Oberman, *The Harvest of Medieval Theology: Gabriel Biel and Late Medieval Nominalism* (Cambridge, MA: Harvard University Press, 1963), pp. 42–52; and Courtenay, "Nominalism and Late Medieval Religion," *The Pursuit of Holiness*, pp. 26–59.

23. R.C. Richards, "Ockham and Skepticism," *New Scholasticism*, 42 (1968), 345–63; Marilyn McCord Adams, "Intuitive Cognition, Certainty, and Skepticism in William of Ockham," *Traditio*, 26 (1970), 389–98; and William J. Courtenay, "The Critique on Natural Causality in the Mutakallimum and Nominalism," *HTR*, 66 (1973), 77–94.

24. Gordon Leff, *William of Ockham: The Metamorphosis of Scholastic Discourse* (Manchester: Manchester University Press, 1975), pp. xiii and xxi.

25. Oberman, "Some Notes on the Theology of Nominalism," 54–63; Oberman, "'Facientibus Quod In Se Est Deus Non Denegat Gratiam': Robert Holcot, O.P., and the Beginnings of Luther's Theology," *HTR*, 55 (1962), 317–42; Oberman, *The Harvest of Medieval Theology*, pp. 235–48; and William J. Courtenay, "Revisions in the Understanding of Late Medieval Thought," *The Pursuit of Holiness*, pp. 32–54.

facts.[26] Moreover, these differences tend to be readjustments rather than outright rejections of earlier interpretations. Yet how much more radically would all these interpretations differ if the facts themselves were differently received? This is a crucial question. Years ago, Konstanty Michalski reminded his readers that every historian's analysis will differ greatly from the apprehension, formulation, and resolution of problems by the actual citizens of a past epoch. This reminder was issued in conjunction with a plea for scholars to provide themselves with complete, carefully edited texts of philosophers such as Ockham and Holcot.[27] This noble aim, while doing proper justice to individual thinkers and facilitating truer internal interpretations such as those sought by Courtenay and Oberman, nonetheless distorts the ways in which these ideas were actually introduced and received during the fourteenth century. Those contemporary misconceptions, however remote from what the philosophers might have written and meant, must be taken into fullest consideration by a literary critic who would understand the role of a poet like Langland in an age that included so many non-academic thinkers trying to deal with scholastic controversies.

Though far from complete, our best evidence suggests that the issues debated within the universities were exaggerated, poorly understood, and grossly distorted even within the confines of the academic community. Manuscript transmission of texts was a major hindrance to the clearest possible understanding. The flourishing *pecia* system at Oxford meant that larger works such as Holcot's Commentary on the *Sentences* might be encountered in piecemeal fashion.[28] A partial reader might not be aware, as was the case with John of Mirecourt's inquisitors, that certain dangerous statements did not represent the author's conclusions or even his actual thoughts, but rather the positions of some imaginary *adversarius*.[29] Ernest Moody has summed up the difficulty by stating that "the inexact or outright corrupt transmission of an author's text could muddle his argument or, as in the case with Holcot, attribute to him a position exactly opposite to the one

26. Oberman, *The Harvest of Medieval Theology*, p. 30; Beryl Smalley, "The Bible and Eternity: John Wyclif's Dilemma," *JWCI*, 27 (1964), 73–89.

27. Konstanty Michalski, "Le Problème de la volonté à Oxford et à Paris au XIVe siècle," *Studia Philosophica: Commentarii Societatis Philosophicae Polonorum*, 2 (1937), 234.

28. Graham Pollard, "The *Pecia* System in the Medieval Universities," *Medieval Scribes, Manuscripts and Libraries*, ed. M.B. Parkes and Andrew G. Watson (London: Scolar Press, 1978), pp. 145–61.

29. William J. Courtenay, "John Mirecourt and Gregory of Rimini on Whether God Can Undo the Past," *Recherches de Théologie Ancienne et Médiévale*, 39 (1972), 255. Elsewhere Courtenay notes that an author was invariably quoted in a piecemeal fashion

which he in fact held."[30] Even when whole texts were completely read, the manuscripts rarely offered the author's final *ordinatio* or revised edition of his work. An author such as Ockham may never have brought his analysis to a definitive stage, since most writers constantly refined and altered their positions through the exchange of ideas with contemporaries over a number of years.[31]

The condemnations brought to bear upon various schoolmen offer valuable evidence of the distortions to which philosophical discussions were open. Editors of Bishop Tempier's condemnations of 1277 have observed that "many of the propositions represent at best a crude version of the genuine Averroistic teaching" without coherent order or any immediate context.[32] In the articles brought against Ockham in 1326, only selected passages from his Commentary were quoted, while crucial words and phrases were routinely omitted so that the author's original thoughts and intentions became hopelessly blurred.[33] During the condemnation of John of Mirecourt in 1347, the philosopher himself complained that the examiners had misquoted his thoughts and misinterpreted his intentions. Indeed, a close examination of the relevant texts indicates that he never taught the accused doctrines and actually constructed his *Sentences* Commentary directly against the condemned positions.[34]

Written texts tell only part of the story, masking what was probably the larger threat to which these official condemnations were responding. The oral disputations in which masters and students engaged seem to have provided a forum for the expression of far more dangerous extremism. Bishop Tempier prefaced his Condemnation with a complaint against students who "are exceeding the boundaries of their own faculty and are presuming to treat and discuss, as if they were debatable in the schools, certain obvious and loathsome errors."[35] Even a strictly orthodox master might be obliged to debate dangerous issues, since

---

and in whatever manner suited the writer who was quoting him; see *Adam Wodeham: An Introduction to his Life and Writings* (Leiden: Brill, 1978), p. 115.

30. Ernest A. Moody, "A Quodlibetal Question of Robert Holkot, O.P., on the Problem of the Objects of Knowledge and Belief," *Speculum*, 39 (1964), 54–55.

31. *Ibid.*, 56; Richards, "Ockham and Skepticism," 345–63; and Courtenay, *Adam Wodeham*, pp. 2–3.

32. Ralph Lerner and Muhsin Mahdi, *Medieval Political Philosophy: A Sourcebook* (New York: The Free Press, 1963), p. 336.

33. Auguste Pelzer, "Les 51 Articles de Guillaume Occam censurés en Avignon en 1326," *Revue d'Histoire Ecclésiastique*, 18 (1922), 243–44.

34. Courtenay, "John Mirecourt and Gregory of Rimini," 226–28. J.A. Robson, *Wyclif and the Oxford Schools* (Cambridge: Cambridge University Press, 1966), p. 35, reminds us that Nicholas of Autrecourt was similarly condemned for erroneous opinions which he had not claimed outright in his writings.

35. Lerner and Mahdi (eds.), *Medieval Political Philosophy*, p. 337.

the rules of a quodlibetal disputation required him to address whatever questions were raised by his colleagues.[36] Richard Fitzralph complained about the Pelagian arguments which he heard constantly elaborated, while Bradwardine lashed out against a similar radicalism that he had encountered as a student:

In the philosophical faculty I seldom heard a reference to grace, except for some ambiguous remarks. What I heard day in and day out was that we are masters of our own free acts, that ours is the choice to act well or badly, to have virtues or sins, and much more along this line.[37]

Although this is typical of Bradwardine's attack, the heresies themselves are not apparent in the written works of the theologians who were his targets.[38] It is therefore more likely, as the above passage suggests, that Bradwardine was responding as much to what he heard as to what he read, that is, those debates which have not come down to us in any manuscript form.

Besides the waywardness of lecturers, Bradwardine complained about the naiveté and rashness of listeners.[39] The audience of a scholastic disputation would have included many who were quite young, and even if they could understand the technical Latin, they might not properly discriminate between posing a question and consenting to the answer which the question seemed to imply. To ask "Can God change the past?" leads to many provocative topics, but it does not mean the speaker believes, or will eventually conclude, that God can and probably has altered history. It had been the earlier concern of Bishop Tempier that unregulated academic debate might lead simpler minds into theological error.[40] A young cleric who, like Langland perhaps, ran out of money and left school far short of the fourteen years necessary for a Master's degree probably took with him just such a distorted sense of the inflammatory questions debated in the schools, but with-

36. P. Glorieux, *La Littérature Quodlibétique* (Paris: Vrin, 1925), pp. 45–47.
37. Cited by Heiko A. Oberman, *Forerunners of the Reformation: The Shape of Late Medieval Thought*, trans. Paul L. Nyhus (New York: Holt, Rinehart and Winston, 1966), p. 135. Oberman, *Archbishop Thomas Bradwardine, A Fourteenth Century Augustinian* (Utrecht: Kemink & Zoon, 1957), p. 122, quotes Fitzralph's complaint from *De Summa de Erroribus Armenorum* (II, 34.630 A). The audacity of lecture-hall debates has been discussed by Damasus Trapp, "Augustinian Theology in the Fourteenth Century: Notes on Editions, Marginalia, Opinions and Book-Lore," *Augustiniana*, 6 (1956), 147–231.
38. Oberman, "Some Notes on the Theology of Nominalism," 60.
39. Robson, *Wyclif and the Oxford Schools*, p. 37. William J. Courtenay, "The Effect of the Black Death on English Higher Education," *Speculum*, 55 (1980), 707, suggests that undergraduates were even less skilled in Latin and critical thinking by the time Langland would have been a student.
40. Lerner and Mahdi, *Medieval Political Philosophy*, p. 337.

out a subtle understanding of the development and resolution of these questions.[41]

The dissemination of disputed propositions in simplified form was no doubt facilitated by sermons, whether the academic sermons such as Bradwardine's *Sermo Epinicius*, which students attended, or the parish sermons which these same students, who later became priests, delivered throughout England. This pastoral clergy probably provided the link between the schools and the lay populace, since there is no doubt that thornier theological issues involving free will, good works, and the role of God's foreknowledge began to concern both the literate upper class and the simpler laity.[42] Whereas Ockham and Holcot complained that theologians were stopped in the streets and pressed by tradesmen and housewives to resolve such issues,[43] the second half of the century witnessed a continuing ferment which is evidenced by the Lollard movement. As K. B. McFarlane has noted, "a logical system of the most academic ingredients was so speedily vulgarized that within a couple of decades this gospel of the schools had become widely diffused among the laity as well as the non-graduate clergy, right across the English midlands from Kent to East Anglia to the marches and mountains of central Wales."[44]

It is hard to gauge this popular reaction, hard even to find evidence that the common folk knew specifically about the difficulties created at the universities, except for rare references such as Ockham's and Holcot's complaints that "laymen of modern times" expected theologians to supply rational supports for their faith. Yet it is clear that profoundly disturbing questions were sometimes discussed by the century's least serious thinkers as well as the scholastic experts. When in the *Miller's Tale* Nicholas, the Oxford clerk, convinces his simple-minded landlord that a second Flood is on its way, or in the *Nun's Priest's Tale* Pertelote alludes to Bradwardine's doctrine of predestina-

41. H.G. Richardson, "An Oxford Teacher of the Fifteenth Century," *Bulletin of the John Rylands Library*, 23 (1939), 436–57, esp. 456–57; and Thompson, "Pro Saeculo XIV," 807.

42. Important preliminary work has been begun by Janet Coleman, *Medieval Readers and Writers, 1350–1400* (New York: Columbia University Press, 1981), and more specifically *Piers Plowman and the "Moderni"* (Rome: Edizioni di Storia e Letteratura, 1981).

43. Beryl Smalley, *English Friars and Antiquity in the Early Fourteenth Century* (Oxford: Blackwell, 1960), p. 29, quotes from Ockham's *Tractatus contra Benedictum* and, pp. 186–87, cites Holcot's complaint against the "laici moderni temporis" from his Commentary on the *Sentences*.

44. K.B. McFarlane, *Lancastrian Kings and Lollard Knights*, ed. G.L. Harriss and J.R.L. Highfield (Oxford: The Clarendon Press, 1972), p. 142. See also Claire Cross, "'Great Reasoners in Scripture': The Activities of Woman Lollards, 1380–1530," *Medieval Women*, ed. Derek Baker (Oxford: Blackwell, 1978), pp. 359–80.

tion, Chaucer is making fun of the common folk who had caught wind of these academic controversies:

> Witnesse on hym that any parfit clerk is,
> That in scole is greet altercacioun
> In this mateere, and greet disputisoun,
> And hath been of an hundred thousand men.
>
> (*CT*, VII, 3236–39)[45]

What gradually emerged was an anti-intellectual spirit that took many forms—a return to monastic theology, Bradwardine's attack on radical speculation, and Wyclif's insistence on the supremacy of Biblical authority[46]—but this spirit manifested itself most clearly in the age's fideism and blind trust in the teachings of Holy Church, the figure of authority encountered and then left behind by Will the Dreamer at the beginning of his wanderings.

The radical theories of fourteenth-century voluntarists and the widespread abuses of dialectic deepened an antagonism toward philosophical inquiry that had existed from the dawn of Christianity. Paul first warned against the dangers of philosophy when he wrote to the Colossians: "Beware lest any man cheat you by philosophy and vain deceit, according to the tradition of men, according to the elements of the world and not according to Christ."[47] Dame Study voices the prevailing sentiment of Langland's age:

> Ac Theologie haþ tened me ten score tymes;
> The moore I muse þerinne, þe mystier it semeþ,
> And þe depper I deuyned, þe derker me þouȝte.
> It is no science, forsoþe, for to sotile inne.
>
> (B. x. 185–88)

The poet must have been reporting a relatively common occurrence when he described the arguments heard at the tables of wealthy men who refused to accept God's will:

---

45. *The Works of Geoffrey Chaucer*, ed. F.N. Robinson (Boston: Houghton Mifflin, 1957), p. 203. This edition is used throughout.

46. Morton W. Bloomfield, *Piers Plowman as a Fourteenth-Century Apocalypse* (New Brunswick, NJ: Rutgers University Press, 1962), pp. 48–49.

47. Col. 2.8, quoted in English from *The Holy Bible: Translated from the Latin Vulgate* [Douay-Rheims] (London: Catholic Truth Society, 1956). All Latin verses are quoted from *Biblia Sacra* (Madrid: Biblioteca de Autores Christianos, 1965). Tertullian launched a venomous attack on Aristotelian dialectics in *On Prescription Against Heretics* (vii) in *The Ante-Nicene Fathers*, ed. Alexander Roberts and James Donaldson (Buffalo: The Christian Literature Publishing Co., 1885), vol. III, p. 246. For a fuller discussion, see Etienne Gilson, *Reason and Revelation in the Middle Ages* (New York: Scribner, 1938), pp. 9–11.

I haue yherd heiȝe men etynge at þe table
Carpen as þei clerkes were of Crist and of hise myȝtes,
And leyden fautes vpon þe Fader þat formede vs alle,
And carpen ayein clergie crabbede wordes:
"Why wolde oure Saueour suffre swich a worm in his blisse
That bewiled þe womman and þe wye after,
Thoruȝ which werk and wil þei wente to helle,
And al hir seed for hir synne þe same deeþ suffrede?
Here lyeþ youre lore," þise lordes gynneþ dispute,
"Of þat ye clerkes vs kenneþ of Crist by þe gospel:
Filius non portabit iniquitatem patris &c.
Why sholde we þat now ben for þe werkes of Adam
Roten and torende? Reson wolde it neuere!"

                                                    (B. x. 104–16)

Augustine had established the proper medieval response to this rational vexation: "Understanding is the reward of faith. Therefore do not seek to understand so that you might believe, but believe so that you might understand." [48] Augustine's advocacy of a faith free of philosophical elaboration can be found in many of his writings, but perhaps the most memorable passage comes in his *Confessions* at a moment in the midst of his conversion crisis when he considers the example of Anthony of Egypt, a man whose holiness was unaided by learning:

What is the meaning of this story? These men have not had our schooling, yet they stand up and storm the gates of heaven while we, for all our learning, lie here grovelling in the world of flesh and blood! [49]

Of course the most famous English echo of Augustine is found in the lines spoken by Will at the conclusion of the A-text:

Arn none raþere yrauisshid fro þe riȝt beleue
þanne arn þise kete clerkis þat conne many bokis,

48. Augustine, *In Joannis Evangelium Tractatus*, XXIX, 6 (*PL* 35:1630). This injunction was often repeated by later Augustinians such as John Scotus and Anselm; see Etienne Gilson, *History of Christian Philosophy in the Middle Ages* (New York: Random House, 1955), pp. 114 and 129.

49. Saint Augustine, *Confessions*, trans. R. S. Pine-Coffin (Harmondsworth: Penguin, 1961), p. 170. Gilson, *History*, pp. 72–73, cites other instances from *De Genesi Contra Manichaeos*, I, ii, 4 (*PL* 34:175–76); *De Diversis Quaestionibus LXXXIII*, q. 28 (*PL* 40:18); *De Civitate Dei*, XI, xxiv (*PL* 41:337–38); and *Epistola*, 166, v, 15 (*PL* 33:727). See also Gilson, *Reason and Revelation*, pp. 17–24. Complaints against the insufficiency, even the danger, of philosophy were especially common among Franciscans who were faithful to the ideals of their founder and among later mystics who longed for a direct worship of God unimpeded by the rational intricacies of philosophy. For example, Agnellus (c. 1195–1236), founder of the Grey Friar's School at Oxford, mourned over the futile dialectics he heard carried on in the disputations of his brethren: "Simple brothers enter Heaven, while learned brothers dispute whether there be a God

No none sonnere ysauid ne saddere of consience
þanne pore peple, as plouȝmen, and pastours of bestis,
Souteris & seweris; such lewide iottis
Percen wiþ *paternoster* þe paleis of heuene
Wiþoute penaunce at here partyng, into þe heiȝe blisse.

(A. xi. 307–13)

As much as *Piers Plowman* suggests an acquaintance with the language and methods of scholasticism, Langland seems disaffected in his hope of reaching the goal of discovering the religious truths for which these techniques had been developed. Here, too, he shows the long-term effects of Ockhamism:

. . . in the circumstances of the time, there could be no simple return to a more direct faith. For better or for worse, the full-fledged body of metaphysics and philosophy that had grown up could not be summarily dismissed: to leave it free to follow its own course was ultimately to concede to the natural standards of Averroism. It put theology in the same danger as that constituted by Averroism—of being toppled from its pedestal by those uncommitted to its laws.[50]

He emerges as an intellectual poet uncommitted to the laws of scholasticism, the worst faults of which are dramatized in the *Vita de Dowel* as part of a psychological allegory showing the soul crippled by the conceits of the intellect. Only after the vision of the Tree of Charity does the poem begin to rise out of the tedious tangle that dialectic had become for most of Langland's contemporaries.

Some understanding of the religious debate throughout the land helps to explain the popularity of *Piers Plowman*, but it leaves unanswered the questions of where Langland figured in the intellectual hierarchy and, specifically, the manner and extent of his education. Since the pioneering work of Mabel Day and Greta Hort, critics have placed the poet nearer and nearer to the center of scholastic contro-

---

at all!"; Charles Edward Mallet, *A History of the University of Oxford*, 3 vols. (New York: Longmans, 1924–28), vol. I, p. 61, which also notes that the question "Utrum sit Deus?" was a favorite of the schools. Langland's distortion of Augustine's statement has been discussed by Mary Carruthers, *The Search for St. Truth: A Study of Meaning in "Piers Plowman"* (Evanston: Northwestern University Press, 1973), p. 93; and C. David Benson, "An Augustinian Irony in *Piers Plowman*," *N&Q*, n.s. 23 (1976), 51–54. In a highly significant article, Judson Boyce Allen, "Langland's Reading and Writing: *Detractor* and the Pardon Scene," *Speculum*, 59 (1984), 342–62, has argued persuasively for Hugh of St. Cher's commentary on Romans 2 as the poet's source for this Augustinian echo (344–45).

50. Leff, *Medieval Thought*, pp. 271–72. Konrad Burdach, "Der Dichter des Ackermann aus Böhmen und seine Zeit," *Vom Mittelalter zur Reformation: Forschungen zur Geschichte der Deutschen Bildung* (Berlin: Weidmannsche, 1932), vol. III, pt. 2, pp. 140–371, sees in Langland's poem the drama of the human will liberating itself from the morass of dialectic.

versy.[51] One critic writes about Langland's response to Ockhamist logic, another studies the poem in terms of Nominalist epistemology, another argues that Langland's theological position in the *Visio* is close to that of Aquinas, while yet another explicates the Pardon Scene in light of the debate between Nominalists and Augustinians over the need for grace in performing good works.[52] A recent study by Janet Coleman reviews the prominent university topics of the day—a day which was actually three decades before Langland wrote the opening lines of the A-text—while driving hard at the conclusion that his poem responds to the specific theological issues of the *moderni* which he knew as an insider.[53] The fact that these various critical arguments reach conclusions which do not always agree with each other, and have not won universal acceptance, should on the face of things give us cause to suspect their common assumptions about the poet's scholastic background.

The greater Langland's learnedness is thought to be, the greater has been the temptation to place him squarely in Oxford as a student or even a member of a faculty. The nineteenth century found some support for this view in an early manuscript inscription which identified the poet as the son of a certain Stacy de Rokayle who lived in Shipton-under-Wychwood in Oxfordshire.[54] In more recent years, David Fowler has gone so far as to argue that the author of the B-text was a deeply committed member of the arts faculty in its struggle with the friars for

51. Mabel Day, "Duns Scotus and *Piers Plowman*," *RES*, 3 (1928), 333–34; Greta Hort, *Piers Plowman and Contemporary Religious Thought* (London: S.P.C.K., 1938). Although Hort makes considerable claims for the poet's scholasticism, her chapter "Langland's Knowledge of Theology" (pp. 28–59) argues that his Latin quotations were largely drawn from the Breviary, the Missal, and miscellanies of authorities. Allen, "Langland's Reading and Writing," has narrowed the source-search to the commentaries of Hugh of St. Cher.

52. John F. McNamara, "Responses to Ockhamist Theology in the Poetry of the *Pearl*-Poet, Langland, and Chaucer," Doctoral dissertation, Louisiana State University, 1968; Britton J. Harwood, "*Piers Plowman*: Fourteenth-Century Skepticism and the Theology of Suffering," *Bucknell Review*, 19, no. 3 (1971), 119–36; Bloomfield, *Apocalypse*, p. 165; Willi Erzgräber, *William Langlands "Piers Plowman": Eine Interpretation des C-Textes* (Heidelberg: Carl Winter, 1957); and Denise N. Baker, "From Plowing to Penitence: *Piers Plowman* and Fourteenth-Century Theology," *Speculum*, 55 (1980), 715–25. Other studies arguing in favor of Langland's familiarity with particular scholastic thinkers include Oscar Cargill, "The Date of the A-Text of *Piers Plowman*," *PMLA*, 47 (1932), 354–62; A. V. C. Schmidt, "Langland and Scholastic Philosophy," *MÆ*, 38 (1969), 134–56; Willi Erzgräber, *Neues Handbuch der Literatur Wissenschaft*: vol. 8, *Europäisches Spätmittelalter* (Wiesbaden: Athenaion, 1978), pp. 231–39; and Daniel Maher Murtaugh, *Piers Plowman and the Image of God* (Gainesville: University Press of Florida, 1978).

53. Coleman, *Piers Plowman and the "Moderni"*.

54. Skeat, II, p. xxviii.

control of Oxford.[55] Of course, Professor Fowler would like for us to believe that the B-poet was not Langland at all but rather John Trevisa. Not that he actually states that Trevisa wrote the poem: "I suspect the B-poet was in all probability a man very much like John Trevisa."[56] Yet in the subsequent description of this distinguished Oxonian's career, the reader of *Piers Plowman* is forced to conclude that the poet was very much *un*like John Trevisa, a relatively long-time fellow of Queen's College who traveled extensively on the Continent, became chaplain to Thomas Lord Berkeley, and was the indefatigable translator of such massive works as the *De Proprietatibus Rerum* of Bartholomeus Anglicus and the *Polychronicon* of Ranulf Higden. By contrast, the B-poet shows no signs of being a foreign traveler, admits to behaving contemptuously to social superiors such as Lord Berkeley would have been, and betrays little of the encyclopedic lore to be gained from Bartholomeus or the historiographical method to be found in Higden— even if such an obsessive writer and reviser had time to translate these vast works into English. By themselves, these considerations argue against Langland's having been anything like the sort of man who would have felt at home in a medieval SCR in Oxford.

Why then have we been so eager to place Langland in a *studium generale* and specifically at Oxford? The substance of his learning and the methods of his poem indicate that he must have been familiar with the subject matter as well as the methods of the schools. His writing shows a clear debt to university categories such as *quodlibet, quaestio,* and *distinctio.* He explores the favorite academic topics of free will, grace, and good works as they relate to the winning of salvation.[57] He introduces allegorical figures such as Dame Study, Clergy, and Theology, and he even includes a colorful scene in which a gluttonous don gorges himself at high table (B. xiii. 22–102). If modern critics review these facts and conclude that Langland must have been a university man, I think it is largely because Oxbridge scholars over the past hundred years have provided such an inviting historical context by chron-

55. David Covington Fowler, "Poetry and the Liberal Arts: The Oxford Background of *Piers the Plowman*," *Arts libéraux et philosophie au moyen âge* (Paris: Vrin, 1969), 715–19.

56. David C. Fowler, *Piers the Plowman: Literary Relations of the A and B Texts* (Seattle: University of Washington Press, 1961), p. 186, with a review of Trevisa's remarkable career, pp. 186–205.

57. Gervase Mathew, *The Court of Richard II* (London: Murray, 1968), p. 86. Bloomfield, *Apocalypse*, pp. 161–69 (Appendix II), endorses the opinion that Langland "had a university education or its equivalent" (p. 63). Janet Coleman's book *Piers Plowman and the "Moderni"* offers a wide-ranging review of these topics, although her interpretative argument focuses only on the Pardon Scene and the salvation of Emperor Trajan.

icling their respective *almae matres* so abundantly back to their medieval beginnings. While monastic and fraternal schools have produced few (if any) alumni-historians in modern England, the two universities have enlisted the efforts of Montague Rhodes James, F. M. Powicke, A. B. Emden, Roger Highfield, J. A. W. Bennett, Gordon Leff, and others who have provided such a detailed picture of the intellectual and institutional life of Oxford and Cambridge that it is hard to imagine a man of elevated education, not to mention a major theological poet, who did not fit neatly into that picture.[58] Oxford is probably favored by Langland scholars because it was the center for more heated controversies, it produced four times as many students as Cambridge, and it was closer to Langland's reputed home whether in the Malvern Hills or at Shipton-under-Wychwood.

The internal evidence that forces us to acknowledge Langland's concern with scholastic topics also forces us to admit he probably had not read the major schoolmen, so many of them native Englishmen. Although Beryl Smalley has remarked that by the late fourteenth century Bradwardine's name had become a household word in England,[59] it is not a household word with any currency in Langland's poem. Chaucer might casually allude to Oxford scholars such as Bradwardine, Strode, and Gaddesden—all of them specifically Merton men[60]—but while today's critical commentaries on *Piers Plowman* are filled with references to the works of Thomas Aquinas, Duns Scotus, William of Ockham, Robert Holcot, and Thomas Bradwardine, Langland shows no familiarity with these theologians even as names. And he was not a writer who disdained a showy allusion. The absence of these names is evidence on a par with the dog that did not bark in the night. In part, it helps us to set an upper limit for Langland's educational attainments.

What then should be considered the lower limit? While the pastoral clergy had brought to the lay populace an unsettling, if nodding, acquaintance with the thorniest theological issues, Langland's Latin literacy raises him above the level of these befuddled laymen. Latin

---

58. M.R. James has chronicled the early histories of several Cambridge colleges and libraries: St. John's, Trinity, King's, Christ's, Clare, Jesus, Pembroke, Peterhouse, St. Catharine's, Magdalene, Corpus Christi, Gonville and Caius, and Queens'. See also Frederick Maurice Powicke, *The Medieval Books of Merton College* (Oxford: The Clarendon Press, 1931); A.B. Emden, *A Biographical Register of the University of Oxford to A.D. 1500*, 3 vols. (Oxford: The Clarendon Press, 1957–59); Roger Highfield, *The Early Rolls of Merton College* (Oxford: The Clarendon Press, 1964); Gordon Leff, *Paris and Oxford Universities*; and J.A.W. Bennett, *Chaucer at Oxford and at Cambridge* (Oxford: Oxford University Press, 1974).

59. Smalley, "The Bible and Eternity," p. 77.

60. Bennett, *Chaucer at Oxford and at Cambridge*, "The Men of Merton," pp. 58–85.

served as the basis of instruction in the grammar schools, of course, where a few classical texts, the Scriptures, and passages from the Church Fathers were adapted for the purposes of oral conversation and public disputation, in line with the long-established Trivium of grammar, rhetoric, and logic.[61] Grammar school students read Aesopic fables, to which Langland seems indebted for his fable of the belling of the cat (B. prol. 146–209), and Cato's *Distichs*, which Langland quotes a bit too ostentatiously in judging the validity of dreams and endorsing the need for relaxation (B. iv. 155; xii. 20–22). Graduates of grammar schools who proceeded to a university were usually very young, and few of them could afford to stay long enough to take a degree. Langland is usually classified as one of those who left early for financial reasons. In the C-text, the narrator says that when he was young, his father and relatives sent him to *scole* until he had a firm grounding in *holy writ* (C. v. 35–41), but his backers died and he was left incompletely trained for any advanced clerical vocation. Commenting on this passage, J. A. W. Bennett has decided that *holy writ* implies the study of theology and *scole* means a university.[62]

Yet the word *scola* in the Middle Ages represented a very broad generic term, which could refer equally to a university or a grammar school, but could also refer to a monastic school, a chantry school, a guild school, a hospital school, and a collegiate church school.[63] If the internal evidence of the poem suggests that Langland did not climb to the highest rung of the university ladder, it also indicates an attainment beyond the grammar school level. If he does not refer to Bradwardine, he does cite with some ease (if not perfect accuracy) the Bible, Augustine, Ambrose, Jerome, Isidore of Seville, and other authors avail-

---

61. G.R. Potter, "Education in the Fourteenth and Fifteenth Centuries," *Cambridge Medieval History*, ed. J.B. Bury, *et al.*, vol. VIII (New York: Macmillan, 1936), pp. 688–717. Nicholas Orme, *Education in the West of England, 1066–1548* (Exeter: University of Exeter, 1976), p. 22, offers a detailed description of the texts used in grammar education. James A. Weisheipl, "Curriculum of the Faculty of Arts at Oxford in the Early Fourteenth Century," *MS*, 26 (1964), 143–85, and "Developments in the Arts Curriculum at Oxford in the Early Fourteenth Century," *MS* 28 (1966), 151–75, gives a descriptive catalogue of the texts used in the Trivium and Quadrivium. These syllabi suggest that Langland had an acquaintance with authors only in grammar, rhetoric, and logic.

62. Bennett, p. 14. Orme, p. 4, notes that a university was generally referred to in the plural as "the schools" in medieval times. G.H. Russell, "The Salvation of the Heathen: The Exploration of a Theme in *Piers Plowman*," *JWCI*, 29 (1966), 116, includes a well-balanced assessment of Langland as neither "semiliterate" nor "a learned and finished theologian."

63. John Nelson Miner, "Schools and Literacy in Later Medieval England," *British Journal of Educational Studies*, 11 (1962/63), 16–27.

able to a reader of Lombard's *Sentences*, and he shows at least an arm's-length acquaintance with the major scholastic controversies of his day. For the present purposes, I would suggest it is worth considering that Langland reached the last stage of his formal education at a center of learning about which too little is now known, namely the late fourteenth-century cathedral school.

The rise of these schools in the thirteenth century followed in the wake of the Fourth Lateran Council, which required every cathedral church to have a master of theology to teach its clerks as well as other poor scholars.[64] Besides canon law, these schools offered instruction in theology with the aim of giving its students a thorough grounding in *sacra pagina*, which was normally translated as "holy writ," the same term used by Langland to describe the substance of his own schooling. The cathedral chancellor, as a master and sometimes doctor straight from a university, normally delivered the same lectures according to the same schedule as he might have delivered at Oxford, and we know that theologians of prime importance went out to the provinces. Thomas Buckingham, for example, served as Chancellor of Exeter Cathedral from 1340 until two years before his death in 1351.[65] Thus in a sort of ripple effect, scholastic controversies might have emanated from the epicenter at Oxford until reaching the cathedral schools throughout England.

The immediate question that arises is which cathedral school the young Langland might have attended. A variety of evidence suggests that the most likely candidate would be Worcester.[66] The opening lines of *Piers Plowman* place the action in the Malvern Hills which lie to the west of Worcester, and poetic convention typically required that a wanderer in search of marvels must travel to the west, as does Gawain when he passes near Angelsey in Wales. The linguistic evidence of the C-text manuscripts, studied by a team of researchers under Angus

64. Two extremely useful studies of the cathedral schools are presented by Greta Hort, "Theological Schools in Medieval England," *Church Quarterly Review*, 116 (1933), 201–18; and Kathleen Edwards, *The English Secular Cathedrals in the Middle Ages*, 2nd ed. rev. (Manchester: Manchester University Press, 1967), "The Cathedral Schools," pp. 185–205.

65. Robson, *Wyclif and the Oxford Schools*, pp. 45–46.

66. Hort points in this direction in her article "Theological Schools." The suggestion is taken up by Joseph S. Wittig, "*Piers Plowman*, B, Passus IX–XII: Elements in the Design of the Inward Journey," *Traditio*, 28 (1972), 212–13. A contrary view on Langland's education was voiced by G. G. Coulton, "Theological Schools in Medieval England," *Church Quarterly Review*, 118 (1934), 98–101, although he accounts only for the poet's knowledge of the Bible and the Breviary, not for the knottier issues of scholastic theology.

MacIntosh, indicates that all these manuscripts can be located in a tight cluster centering on Worcestershire, suggesting that the final version of the poem did not travel far from the site where it was written and where perhaps the poet had labored for most of his life, including his students days.[67] Worcester Cathedral had a regular chapter, and a letter written in 1305 by the president of the Benedictine Order in England to the prior of Worcester indicates that instruction at the cathedral school was in the hands of the Benedictines.[68] The letter also makes clear that the school was attended by both regulars and seculars. Since stipulations still held that lectures be delivered by trained theologians, it is reasonable to speculate that these masters came from Gloucester College or Durham College, the two Benedictine foundations in Oxford. A letter sent in 1381 to the prior of Worcester from the prior of students at Oxford, requesting contributions, suggests that a bond of obligation had developed between the two places.[69]

Monks had been studying at Oxford since the 1290s, and the practice was encouraged by Benedict XII's *Summi Magistri* (1336) which called for one out of every twenty monks to study at a university. The aim of such an education was to produce better preachers, although the lure of the schoolmen appears to have become very strong for some of these regulars. One Westminster monk by the name of Langham (c. 1340) owned a library containing works by Aquinas in addition to *quaestiones* and sermons by Fitzralph.[70] The manuscripts preserved in Worcester Cathedral Library provide even fuller evidence of the theological interests of the brothers in this particular chapter. MS Worcester Q46 contains sermons delivered by John of Dumbleton at Oxford around 1293, and MS Worcester Q99 offers a long list of *quaestiones* predominantly concerned with the problems of speculative theology. The list includes questions such as "an voluntas sit potentia passiva" and "an voluntas in suo actu presupponat actum intellectus" and "an ad certitudinem fidei magis operetur ratio vel voluntas"—that is, ex-

67. Angus MacIntosh has not yet published the results of this research, though his methodology is used in a variety of articles such as "Word Geography in the Lexicography of Medieval English" in *Lexicography in English*, ed. Raven McDavid and Audrey Duckert (New York: New York Academy of Sciences, 1973), pp. 55–66.

68. *The Liber Albus of the Priory of Worcester*, pts. I and II, ed. James Maurice Wilson (London: Worcestershire Historical Society, 1919), no. 315, pp. 54 ff.

69. *Documents Illustrating the Activities of the General and Provincial Chapters of the English Black Monks, 1215–1540*, ed. William Abel Pantin, 3 vols. (London: Camden Third Series, nos. 45, 47, 54, 1931–37), vol. III, pp. 142–44.

70. Barbara F. Harvey, "The Monks of Westminster and the University of Oxford" in *The Reign of Richard II*, ed. F.R.H. Du Boulay and Caroline M. Barron (London: The Athlone Press, 1971), pp. 108–30, also presents valuable material on monastic colleges in fourteenth-century Oxford.

actly those sorts of questions involved in the scholastic debates over human volition in the first half of the fourteenth century.[71]

This speculation focusing attention on the Worcester cathedral school would account for many of the scholastic features and intellectual prejudices found in *Piers Plowman*. It would place Langland beyond the educational level of a grammar school but short of the *studium generale* of a university. It would explain how a member of the secular clergy should have such a deep familiarity with Benedictine theology, not to mention sympathy with the monastic life, that Morton Bloomfield has felt that Langland was quite possibly a member of that order.[72] And it would account for Langland's acquaintance, albeit second-hand, with the major scholastic issues of his century and yet his simultaneous hostility, maybe encouraged by Benedictine teachers, toward the fraternal orders whose members had been so instrumental in pushing forward the frontiers of theological speculation.

Whether taught at an early age by a provincial monastic master or a mediocre university don, a religious thinker like Langland would not have failed to be provoked by concepts filtering down from eminent schoolmen such as Buckingham and Woodham. A conservative in most matters, Langland tended to settle finally upon the orthodox, but not with any quick or lasting assurance. The influence of the voluntarists is to be found not so much in the theology that he proposes as in the way his poem goes about proposing it, in the topics that arise, in the action of the allegory, even in the poem's visionary mode. When the Four Daughters of God debate the prospect of the Harrowing of Hell, for instance, Truth and Justice maintain that for any souls to be taken from Satan would be against divine law (B. xviii. 110–424). Subsequent events show—and it is significant that Will's perceptual experience confirms the words of Book (the Bible)—that God has worked according to His own loving wisdom and has willed a New Law. From the limited point of view of the devils and of some men, God has changed His mind. The failure of the poem to continue its narration of sacred history to the final event in time, the Day of Judgment, departs from the practice of other works like the *Cursor Mundi*

---

71. *Oxford Theology and Theologians, c. A.D. 1282–1302*, ed. A.G. Little and F. Pelster (Oxford: The Clarendon Press, 1934), pp. 151–52 for the sermons and pp. 303, 318 and 333 for the *questiones* cited.

72. M.W. Bloomfield, "Was William Langland a Benedictine Monk?," *MLQ*, 4 (1943), 57–61. The poet closely associates his praises for the cloister and for the school (B. x. 305–10); see Elizabeth M. Orsten, "'Heaven on Earth': Langland's Vision of Life within the Cloister," *ABR*, 21 (1970), 526–34. Wittig, "The Inward Journey," p. 211, argues for Langland's indebtedness to monastic moral psychology rather than to scholasticism.

and the Corpus Christi plays that presented their audiences with a complete picture of the divine artifact called history. With the attack of Antichrist and the profusion of apocalyptic features in the poem's last passus, it is indeed remarkable that Langland mentions the Doom only once, in a context remote from the main action (B. xx. 293). If he does not endorse the Ockhamist position that future contingencies cannot be known, he leaves room for doubt. And in a universe where God might supersede what He had once ordained and where truth might no longer reside in the old authority of the New Testament, some men may have thought themselves once again in an age of prophecy when the visionary poet, like the inspired lunatic, might prove to be the messenger of God's latest decree.

It is not my intention to trace the precise ways in which Langland reacted to the great theological controversies of his century —how he seems to have accorded with Ockham in one place, with Wyclif in another—but rather to point out some of the intellectual cross-currents that surface from time to time and thereby contribute to the general turbulence felt throughout *Piers Plowman*. Nor is it my intention to insist that the poem's confusion is the result of utter theological befuddlement in Langland's own mind. Compositional difficulty is suggested by the poet's apparent inability to complete the A-version, perhaps because the world that had at first seemed remediable with the proper corrections had become more problematic in the poem's second vision.[73] If Langland became unsure how to proceed, he made the right artistic decision. He stopped writing, and took up the continuation of the B-version only after coming to terms with his problems—or rather discovering a way to integrate his sense of the problematic into the structure of the poem.

A major part of that artistic solution was to make the Dreamer, up to this point largely a passive observer, into the central actor, with *his* mind mirroring the confusions and contradictions of a world filled with too many plausible choices and too many contending claims—of society and the individual, of lofty learning and simple piety, of grace and free will, of this world and the next. If a portrayal of his mind's halting progress does not always result in satisfying poetry so that even an admirer like John Burrow admits that "Langland can be boring,"[74]

73. G.H. Russell, "Some Aspects of the Process of Revision in *Piers Plowman*" in *Critical Approaches*, ed. Hussey, p. 30; and A.C. Spearing, *Medieval Dream-Poetry* (Cambridge: Cambridge University Press, 1976), p. 145.

74. J.A. Burrow, "Words, Works and Will: Theme and Structure in *Piers Plowman*" in *Critical Approaches*, ed. Hussey, p. 124. Rosemary Woolf, "Some Non-Medieval

what does result is probably the first instance in a major English poem of the fallacy of imitative form. As Morton Bloomfield puts it, "spiritual confusion demands to some extent artistic confusion."[75]

The Middle Ages did not lack a sense that an artistic creation should have a planned and orderly arrangement. Augustine taught that the rules governing human institutions and creations would, ideally, be dominated by the same transcendent law that is manifested in number, weight, and measure. In *The City of God* (XI, 30) he uses a verse from the Wisdom of Solomon (11:21)—"omnia in mensura, et numero, et pondere disposuisti"—to proclaim number as the form-bestowing principle in the divine work of creation; few verses were quoted so regularly in medieval Latin texts.[76] Langland seems well aware of these standards when he has Conscience criticize the disarray of the Friars:

> And if ye coueite cure, Kynde wol yow telle
> That in mesure God made alle manere þynges,
> And sette it at a certain and at a siker nombre,
> And nempnede hem names, and noumbrede þe sterres.
>
> (B. xx. 253–56)

Guided by authorities such as the Bible and St. Augustine, as well as Boethius and Macrobius, medieval writers developed a sense that poetry should be an orderly creation whose structures, determined by the

---

Qualities of *Piers Plowman*," *Essays in Criticism*, 12 (1962), 124, is also stern in her judgment that in some parts the poem's style seems "matted, turgid or flat." C.S. Lewis is even more severe in his rebuke that Langland is "confused and monotonous, and hardly makes his poetry into a poem"; *The Allegory of Love: A Study in Medieval Tradition* (Oxford: Oxford University Press, 1936), p. 161.

75. Bloomfield, *Apocalypse*, p. 6. Agreement with this claim has been voiced by George Kane, *Middle English Literature: A Critical Study of the Romances, the Religious Lyrics, "Piers Plowman"* (London: Methuen, 1951), p. 244; John Lawlor, *Piers Plowman: An Essay in Criticism* (London: Edward Arnold, 1962), p. 233; Charles Muscatine, "Locus of Action in Medieval Narrative," *Romance Philology*, 17 (1963), 115–22; David Mills, "The Role of the Dreamer in *Piers Plowman*," *Critical Approaches*, ed. Hussey, p. 181; Barbara Palmer, "The Guide Convention in *Piers Plowman*," *LSE*, n.s. 5 (1971), 13–28; and Muscatine, *Poetry and Crisis*, pp. 79–80. The poem's chaos is viewed as "strategic incompetence" by Priscilla Martin, *Piers Plowman: The Field and the Tower* (New York: Barnes and Noble, 1979), p. 2, while Joseph S. Wittig, "The Dramatic and Rhetorical Development of Long Will's Pilgrimage," *NM*, 76 (1975), 52–76, argues that the poem describes the will's resistance to affective reform without reflecting the poet's own doubts or confusion.

76. This appraisal comes from Ernst Robert Curtius, *European Literature and the Latin Middle Ages*, trans. Willard R. Trask (New York: Pantheon Books, 1953), p. 504. Gilson, *History*, p. 595, n. 35, comments on the same aesthetic sensibility, using as testimony Augustine's *Epistola*, 140, ii, 4 (*PL* 33:539–40); *De Libero Arbitrio*, I, viii, 18, and I, xv, 32 (*PL* 32:1231 and 1238–39); and *In Joannis Evangelium*, xix, 12 (*PL* 35:1549–50).

faculty of reason, paid tribute to the analogy between human and divine creation through number.[77]

In sharp contrast to works like *The Divine Comedy* and *Pearl*, however, there is no sign of artificial construction in *Piers Plowman*. Langland's method of composition ignores proportion and shows no regard for numerology. The passus divisions are arbitrary and frequently jar with the action. Our poet does not even show an internal concern for demarcation equal to that of *Wynnere and Wastoure* where the first division concludes with the half-line "for here a Fitt endeth."[78] This lack of structural self-consciousness carries with it implications that reach to the heart of Langland's poem. If the formal orderliness of *The Divine Comedy* emphasizes the harmony of the universe that Dante the pilgrim traverses from bottom to top, the structural irregularity of *Piers Plowman* accords with Will's experience of the disarrayed world in which he wanders.

Though indebted to a variety of formal resources—debate, sermon, satire, theological commentary, quest romance, and even apocalyptic literature—*Piers Plowman* is not finally controlled or explained by any of them.[79] Yet the traditional genre to which Langland's poem most obviously belongs, the dream-vision, is also the form best able to create ambiguity and sustain a sense of uncertainty without any need of final resolution. Langland's contemporaries believed in unseen realities that framed and sometimes impinged upon their own: the Fair Field is bounded by the Dungeon of Hell and the Castle of Heaven, and from that castle a pardon is sent down to Piers and his followers. Dreams—though this point was constantly debated —might afford one way of seeing further, more deeply, more truly:

77. Edgar de Bruyne, *Etudes d'esthétique médiévale*, 3 vols. (Brugge: De Tempel, 1946), vol. I, pp. 9–26; and Robert M. Jordan, *Chaucer and the Shape of Creation: The Aesthetic Possibilities of Inorganic Structure* (Cambridge, MA: Harvard University Press, 1967), pp. 10–14 and 20–43 *passim*. Jordan, pp. 40–43, draws attention to the concern for "management and disposition of fixed elements constituting a preconceived whole" in treatises such as Vinsauf's *Poetria Nova* collected by Edmond Faral in *Les Arts Poétiques du XIIe et du XIIIe siècles* (Paris: Champion, 1924). Generous documentation is also presented by Russell A. Peck, "Numerology and Chaucer's *Troilus and Criseyde*," *Mosaic*, 5 (1972), 1–29.

78. *Winner and Waster*, ed. Israel Gollancz (London: Oxford University Press, 1930), p. 28 (l. 217).

79. Muscatine, *Poetry and Crisis*, p. 74. Hort, *Piers Plowman and Contemporary Religious Thought*, p. 39, makes an unconvincing argument that the poem as a whole represents a vast polyphonic disputation in which each debate is mapped out as a scholastic dialectic. Bloomfield has suggested the hybrid genre of "apocalypse" in *Piers Plowman as a Fourteenth-Century Apocalypse*, pp. 8–10. Carruthers, *The Search for St. Truth*, p. 171, comes closer to the heart of the matter in maintaining that the poem "consciously rejects every possible informing structure."

Visions erased the sheer line between the known and the unknowable, the discoverable and the revealed. They interlocked the simultaneous realities; they made visible the unseen; they clarified the hidden shape of truth . . .[80]

This ingrained belief in the potential of dreams to open a portal into an invisible spiritual realm was inherited from the ancient world and granted special sanction in Macrobius' commentary on part of Cicero's *De Re Publica* ("The Dream of Scipio"), but inherited also was the suspicion that many dreams were empty and worthless.[81]

Joining and mixing with the classical tradition was the Biblical account of how God had spoken to men in their dreams, as well as examples of how men like Joseph and Daniel correctly interpreted the dreams of others. With the large number of divine visions granted men in their sleep—the *Apocalypse of St. Paul* and the *Dream of the Rood* are two widely separated examples[82]—it should come as no surprise to find such dreams discussed by later writers whose larger concern was mysticism. Working from the *Liber de Modo Bene Vivendi*, attributed to St. Bernard in the fourteenth century, Richard Rolle enumerates the various types and causes of dreams, again allowing for mixed visions:

. . . þer er sex maners of dremes. Twa er þat na man, haly ne oþer, may eschape. þei er if þair wambe be ovre tome or ovre full; þan many vanitees in seer maners befalles þam slepande. þe thrid es of illusyons of oure enmy. þe ferth es of thoght before and illusion folouand. And þe fyft, thorow þe revelacion of þe Hali Gast, þat es done on many a maner. þe sext es of thoghtes before þat falles to Criste or hali kyrk, revelacion comand after. In þus many maners touches þe ymage of dremes men when þai slepe. Bot sa mykell we sall latlyer gyf fayth till any dreme þat we may not sone wyt whilk es soth, whilk es fals, whilk es of oure enmy, whilk es of þe Hali Gaste.[83]

With so many kinds and causes of dreams, the reader of a dream-poem might never be sure exactly what sort of vision he confronted, a per-

80. Carolly Erickson, *The Medieval Vision: Essays in History and Perception* (New York: Oxford University Press, 1976), pp. 28 and 30.

81. Macrobius, *Commentary on the Dream of Scipio*, trans. W.H. Stahl (New York: Columbia University Press, 1952), pp. 87–92; C.S. Lewis, *The Discarded Image: An Introduction to Medieval and Renaissance Literature* (Cambridge: Cambridge University Press, 1970), pp. 60–66; and for a fuller discussion of other medieval commentaries on dreams, Walter Clyde Curry, *Chaucer and the Mediaeval Sciences*, 2nd ed. rev. (London: Allen & Unwin, 1960), pp. 195–240.

82. *The Apocalypse of St. Paul* in *The Apocryphal New Testament*, trans. M.R. James (Oxford: The Clarendon Press, 1924), pp. 525–55, and other early Christian visions are discussed by Spearing, *Dream-Poetry*, pp. 11–16.

83. *The English Writings of Richard Rolle*, ed. Hope Emily Allen (Oxford: The Clarendon Press, 1931), p. 93. This passage from *The Form of Living* is translated with various changes from *Liber de Modo Bene Vivendi*, lxviii (*PL* 184:1300–01).

plexity made unusually acute in *Piers Plowman* where there is not a single dream but rather eight separate visions in the B-text, with two more dreams-within-dreams—a complication unique in all medieval literature.[84]

Since so much uncertainty was possible, poets often provided themselves with various defenses for the truthfulness of their visions. Guillaume de Lorris begins his *Roman de la Rose* with a defense based casually on the authority of Macrobius. Relying on the Biblical tradition, the author of *Mum and the Sothsegger* responds to Cato's skepticism about dreams by asserting the positive example of Daniel. Other fourteenth-century poets, however, though appearing to follow a similar strategy, achieve quite a different effect. Chaucer prefaces *The House of Fame* with a rambling discussion of the nature of dreams in which he skeptically refuses to take a stand on either side of the question, and only hopes for the best.[85]

Langland's passage on dreams (B. vii. 154−72) creates a comparable sense of ambiguity. Although it discredits Cato's *sompnia ne cures* (*Distichs*, II, 31) by adducing the same Biblical authorities as *Mum and the Sothsegger*, it does not mention, as does *Dives and Pauper*, that many Scriptural passages also reject the interpretation of dreams as a form of witchcraft.[86] Furthermore, the contents of the dream are approved not by Langland but by the Dreamer, whose judgments are always open to suspicion. It is also worth noting that Will does not use these authorities to endorse the entire dream, only its conclusion— namely, that doing well is better than receiving a pardon from Rome (B. vii. 173−76). And finally, Will's approval applies only to this individual dream, the second vision of the poem, and not to any others before or after. The reader is placed in the uncomfortable position of having to remain alert for evidence with which to evaluate *each* later

84. The peculiarity of Langland's multiple visions is remarked upon by Spearing, *Dream-Poetry*, p. 141, and by S.S. Hussey, "Introduction" to *Critical Approaches*, pp. 17−18. Robert W. Frank, Jr., "The Number of Visions in *Piers Plowman*," *MLN*, 66 (1951), 309−12, reviews the disagreement that exists among critics over how many different dreams there actually are.

85. Chaucer, *Works*, ed. Robinson, p. 282. Sheila Delaney, *Chaucer's "House of Fame": The Poetics of Skeptical Fideism* (Chicago: University of Chicago Press, 1972), offers an insightful study of the medieval skeptical tradition and, specifically, the ways in which Chaucer has incorporated this sense of uncertainty into his dream-vision. Debates over the trustworthiness of dreams are also inserted into *Troilus and Criseyde* (V, 358 ff) and *The Nun's Priest's Tale* (*CT*, VII, 2921 ff). See also Guillaume de Lorris and Jean de Meun, *Le Roman de la Rose* ed. Félix Lecoy, 3 vols. (Paris: Champion, 1970), vol. I, p. 1 (ll. 1−20); and *Mum and the Sothsegger*, ed. Mabel Day and Robert Steele, 1936, EETS o.s. 199, p. 52 (ll. 871−75).

86. *Dives and Pauper*, ed. Priscilla Heath Barnum, 1976, EETS o.s. 275, pp. 177−78.

vision, evidence that does not always point to the same conclusion. When Will swoons for joy at hearing Piers' name (B.xvi.18–22) or has a dream "as Crist wolde" (B.xiii.21–23), we feel that the dreams may well be sanctioned from above. But when the visions are described with phrases like "a ferly of Fairye" (B.prol.6) or "as it sorcerie were, a sotil þyng wiþ alle" (B.xv.12), then there is cause for doubt. The cumulative effect is one of pervasive uncertainty about the trustworthiness of these dreams, a sense of skepticism ably summed up in *Dives and Pauper*: "But forasmychil as dremys comyn on so many dyuers maner and it is wol hard to knowyn on what maner it comyn, weþer be God or be kende or be þe fend or be ony oþir wey, þerfor it is wol perlyous to settyn ony feyth þerynne."[87]

There has been a growing consensus among critics that a narrator's eye-witness account of the events in his dream serves as an authenticating device, suspending disbelief and lending credence to what he tells. However weird and fantastical the dream, it really happened—the narrator really saw it in his mind's eye.[88] Yet if the dreamer's testimony in poems like *Pearl* and *The Book of the Duchess* gives us the sense of a coherent visionary experience, the same cannot be said of *Piers Plowman*. Langland is masterful in his ability to weaken the integrity of the dream, blurring the distinction between dream and reality that otherwise gives the vision its special power to dazzle and convince. By moving between dreams and waking life, between dreams and dreams-within-dreams, the poem breaks down the familiar boundaries between types of experience, each with its own rules of action and perception. The audience is left confused as to where things happen, when and why.

The vision even ceases to be a vehicle for allegorical action. Familiar scenes from daily life occur in the first vision, and allegorical characters, like Need (B. xx) as well as Reason and Conscience (C. v.), appear in waking episodes. The warped logic of the dream—sometimes a mental wilderness where everything is slippery, everything problematic, nothing what it had seemed to be—begins to assert itself in Will's waking life, which comes to be equally characterized by abrupt shifts of time and place. Years pass in a few lines, a flash-back becomes the

---

87. *Ibid.*, p. 177. The difficulty in distinguishing among the causes of dreams and telling the true from the deceptive, the good from the evil, was a cause of one more kind of medieval skepticism according to Thomas, *Skepticism*, p. 17, and J.A. MacCulloch, *Medieval Faith and Fable* (Boston: Marshall Jones, 1932), pp. 183–200.

88. Spearing, *Dream-Poetry*, p. 75; Larry D. Benson, *Art and Tradition in "Sir Gawain and the Green Knight"* (New Brunswick, NJ: Rutgers University Press, 1965), pp. 180–81; and Morton W. Bloomfield, *Essays and Explorations* (Cambridge, MA: Harvard University Press, 1970), p. 184.

new present-moment of the action, and the Dreamer falls asleep in Malvern and wakes up in London.[89]

If the conviction of the dream is based upon our confidence in the narrator as eye-witness, we grow increasingly uneasy with the inability of the poem, purportedly Will's attempt to set down his experiences in writing, to keep these experiences distinct. While the Dreamer is coping with his most important crises in private dreams, his life in the wide world of God's creation becomes vaguer, more confused, more and more dream-like.[90] Rather than use the *visio* merely to give authority to his poem as a real experience, Langland adapts the conventional features of this genre to create a sense of epistemological uncertainty, so that the reader comes away bewildered, unable to recall exactly what happened and in what order.

Another reason why the reader fails to form a clear recollection of the poem, and therefore comes away with the sense of having shared in a life of mental confusion, is the remarkable lack of visual imagery. Contrary to the various literary traditions to which *Piers Plowman* is otherwise indebted—sermons, personification allegory, and the poetics of the Alliterative movement[91]—there is a general absence of visu-

89. Many have commented upon the especially confusing movement of Will's dreams, among them Spearing, *Dream-Poetry*, p. 142; Woolf, "Non-Medieval Qualities," 117–18; and Constance B. Hieatt, *The Realism of Dream Visions: The Poetic Exploitation of the Dream-Experience in Chaucer and His Contemporaries* (Paris: Mouton, 1967), pp. 89–97. Langland even uses linguistic tricks, taking advantage of the two meanings of the verb *mette* to create ambiguity as to whether Will meets a character in the waking world ("wiþ Nede I *mette* [OE *mētan*]," B. xx. 4) or dreams about the encounter (I "*mette* ful merueillously [OE *mǣtan*] Antecrist cam þanne," B. xx. 52–53). The apparently plotless sequence of events, whose causality is hidden even from the narrator, is taken into valuable account by Mary J. Carruthers, "Time, Apocalypse, and the Plot of *Piers Plowman*" in *Acts of Interpretation, The Text in its Context, 700–1600: Essays in Honor of E. Talbot Donaldson*, ed. Mary J. Carruthers and Elizabeth D. Kirk (Norman, OK: Pilgrim, 1982), pp. 175–88.

90. A.C. Spearing, "Verbal Repetition in *Piers Plowman* B and C," *JEGP*, 62 (1963), 722–37, concludes that the poem's vagueness is a "reaction against the clear-cut systems and distinctions of late scholasticism." *Anecdotes Historiques d'Etienne de Bourbon* (IV, 226) ed. A. Lecoy de la Marche (Paris: Renouard, 1877), pp. 195–96, records one instance in which medieval doubt over the reality of the created world expressed itself through the image of the dream: "utrum mundus aliquid esset nisi sompnium."

91. G.R. Owst writes at length on the highly visual quality of late medieval sermons in *Literature and Pulpit in Medieval England* (1933; rev. Oxford: Blackwell, 1961), pp. 149–209. Woolf, "Non-Medieval Qualities," 116–17, remarks that this absence of visualization sets *Piers* apart from other allegorical dream-visions like *Pearl* where sensual images are heightened beyond nature. Spearing, *Dream-Poetry*, p. 139, notes that the sparseness of detail found in Langland's waking prologue and generally throughout *Piers* is unusual among all the extant poems of the Alliterative Revival. Elizabeth Salter, "Piers Plowman and the Visual Arts," *Encounters: Essays on Literature and the Visual Arts*, ed. John Dixon Hunt (New York: Norton, 1971), pp. 11–27, notes Langland's lack of indebtedness to painting and sculpture for his poetic imagery.

alization resulting in a shadowy drama of characters without attributes and names without faces. This lack of imagery would have seemed just as strange to a medieval audience—and probably more so.

From Aristotle onward, men understood that "it is impossible even to think without a mental picture."[92] The scholastics transmitted and elaborated Aristotelian theories such as this for the later Middle Ages, and in doing so, commentators such as Albertus Magnus and Thomas Aquinas affirmed an ancient observation common enough in anyone's personal experience: unusual, grotesque, and especially vivid images are the easiest to remember.[93] Thomas Aquinas repeats the Aristotelian axiom that mental images (*phantasmata*) are necessary for the operation of the mind—"Nihil potest homo intelligere sine phantasmate"[94]—and enlarges upon Albertus to suggest that images (*imagines*) be designed for the recollection of spiritual information:

Lighting on such likenesses and images is necessary, because simple and spiritual ideas (*intentiones*) slip somewhat easily out of mind unless they are tied, as it were, to bodily images (*similitudinibus corporalibus*); human knowledge has more mastery over objects of sense (*sensibilia*).[95]

Although heir to scholastic as well as homiletic traditions which endorsed the use of *imagines* to imprint spiritual lessons, Langland resists the conventional wisdom, seldom enforcing his teachings with poetic images that can be easily remembered, with certain arguable exceptions such as the Rat Parliament, the Castle of Caro, and the Confession Scene. Where he does introduce an important image, however, it is likely to be remarkable only in its commonness: a field, a plowman, a tree, a barn.

No true poet works without images, of course, especially one still writing in a Western tradition that harkens to that Horatian dictum *ut pictura poesis*.[96] Yet when Langland invokes visual images in his use of simile or in his invention of allegorical figures like the Half Acre and

92. *De Anima*, 432a, and *De Memoria et Reminiscentia*, 450ab, are contained in Aristotle, *De Anima*, trans. W.S. Hett (Cambridge, MA: Loeb Classical Library, 1957), pp. 180–81 and 290–91. A concise discussion of Aristotle's theory of memory is offered by Frances A. Yates in her fascinating study *The Art of Memory* (1966; rpt. Harmondsworth: Penguin, 1969), pp. 46–49.

93. *Ibid.*, pp. 74–75 and 84–85.

94. Thomas Aquinas, *De Sensu et Sensato* and *De Memoria et Reminiscentia* in *Opera Omnia*, 25 vols. (Parma, 1852–73), vol. XX (1866), pp. 145–196 and 197–214. Also see *ST*, 1a, q. 84, art. 7 (vol. XII, pp. 38–43).

95. *ST*, 2a2ae, q. 49, art. 1 (vol. XXXVI, pp. 62–63) forms the first part of a discussion of prudence.

96. Horace, *Ars Poetica* (361) in *Satires, Epistles and Ars Poetica*, ed. and trans. H. Rushton Fairclough (Cambridge, MA: Loeb Classical Library, 1929), pp. 480–81. A

Christ the Knight, he does so with scant regard for their integrity. They are likely to be juxtaposed with other images that jar with one another, or they are simply forgotten once the more important spiritual sense is revealed. David Mills points out that in Holy Church's explanation of love (B. i. 148–62), "she is compelled to use images, but shifts reference so frequently that the image breaks down."[97] And John Burrow has observed that the typical piling up of similes, as in the description of Gluttony, creates a dizzying, phantasmagoric effect with shapes melting into shapes. Langland is no less cavalier in the way he abuses images which were initially invoked as vehicles for allegorical actions. Rather than sustain a coherent literal level, he creates constant interference that results in the disintegration or fading out of the image, to be replaced by the naked significance of the allegory or by a second image destined to suffer the same fate. When the Crucifixion is presented as a joust fought by Christ the Knight at Jerusalem (B. xviii), so much interference from the Biblical account creeps into the narrative that the joust is nearly forgotten, and the few remnants of the image that are left strike the audience as sustaining a metaphor rather than staging an allegory.[98]

Even more confusing is Langland's habit of transforming and discarding images that had been part of the allegory. When he allows Piers to alter the notion of pilgrimage in the Half Acre—going on a pilgrimage is transformed into the act of plowing a field—the result is a characteristic fusion of images that destroys our mental picture, not only of the current images but also of allied images, in this case the Tower of Truth to which the pilgrims had been heading. Burrow sees all this as

---

caveat against the facile use of this phrase is issued by V.A. Kolve, "Chaucer and the Visual Arts" in *Writers and Their Background: Geoffrey Chaucer*, ed. Derek Brewer (Athens, OH: Ohio University Press, 1975), pp. 290–91. The entire subject is elaborated in brilliant detail in his later book-length study, *Chaucer and the Imagery of Narrative: The First Five Canterbury Tales* (Stanford: Stanford University Press, 1984), pp. 1–84, with rich documentation, pp. 373–408.

97. Mills, "Role of the Dreamer," p. 200; and John Burrow, *Richardian Poetry* (New Haven: Yale University Press, 1971), pp. 135–36.

98. John Burrow, "The Action of Langland's Second Vision," *Style and Symbolism in Piers Plowman: A Modern Critical Anthology*, ed. Robert J. Blanch (Knoxville: University of Tennessee Press, 1969), p. 226. On the lineage of this figure, see Wilbur Gaffney, "The Allegory of the Christ-Knight in *Piers Plowman*," *PMLA*, 46 (1931), 155–68; Rosemary Woolf, "The Theme of Christ the Lover-Knight in Medieval English Literature," *RES*, n.s. 13 (1962), 1–16; Woolf, *The English Religious Lyric in the Middle Ages* (Oxford: The Clarendon Press, 1968), pp. 44 ff; Raymond St-Jacques, "Langland's Christ-Knight and the Liturgy," *Revue de l'Université d'Ottawa*, 37 (1967), 146–58; and Douglas Gray, *Themes and Images in the Medieval English Religious Lyric* (London: Routledge & Kegan Paul, 1972), p. 131. Langland's suspicions of the allegorical mode have been more fully discussed by Martin, *The Field and the Tower*, pp. 71–90 and 111–29.

an entropic process in which images like the Half Acre, which seemed so full of all the right meanings at first, turn out to be too restrictive, merely provisional, "a way of putting it—not very satisfactory." As he says elsewhere, "It is as if the images which carry Langland along are consumed in the process."[99] A certain amount of destabilization is inevitable when an allegorist tries to force a finite image like plowing to accommodate a rich spiritual meaning like pilgrimage, but Langland shows greater contempt than perhaps any other writer of the period for the limitations of images, specifically their inability to contain and communicate an elusive spiritual reality.

Langland's skeptical regard for images is evident in the ways he avoids concrete descriptions. When he does resort to imagery, he tends toward three major responses. First, as already mentioned, he moves away from the image and supersedes it with a statement of the naked spiritual truth—the jousting in Jerusalem becomes a narration of the Crucifixion—thus replacing the literal sense with the allegorical, directly stated. Next, he becomes dissatisfied with the fitness of an image and substitutes another which seems closer to the sense he is trying to establish: the pilgrimage to Truth becomes a season of plowing in the Half Acre. And thirdly, Langland capitalizes on the native ambiguity of images by creating figures whose quality *in bono* or *in malo* cannot be determined. The Dreamer himself is the supreme example of this studied ambiguity from the very beginning, as I shall explain at length in Chapters V and VI. When he describes himself dressed as a "*sheep*," for instance, are we to understand that he is a real shepherd, a pastor carrying on the work of the Good Shepherd, one of the lost sheep, or a wolf in sheep's clothing?[100]

David Mills has also registered the ambiguity in Will's initial entry— "Is he a sinner, a guide to salvation, or both?"—and has felt that it contributes to the general sense of uncertainty in the poem.[101] It is hard to know which, if any, of Empson's types of ambiguity best describes

---

99. Burrow, "Second Vision," p. 226, with the previous citation from "Words, Works and Will," p. 120, quoting T.S. Eliot, *East Coker* (II, 18). The broader implications of such an aesthetic are explored by Rudolf Arnheim, *Entropy and Art: An Essay on Disorder and Order* (Berkeley: University of California Press, 1971).

100. Skeat, II, p. 2, takes pains to define *shepe* as shepherd, but the difficulties of this gloss are raised by J.A.W. Bennett (ed.), *Piers Plowman: The Prologue and Passus I–VII of the B Text as Found in Bodleian MS. Laud Misc. 581* (Oxford: The Clarendon Press, 1972), p.80. It is possible that the Dreamer resembles a sheep because he is actually wearing a sheepskin. John Cassian prescribes that hermits should wear sheepskins in imitation of Old Testament ascetics; see *De Institutis Coenobiorum et De Octo Principalium Vitiorum Remediis Libri XII*, ed. Michael Petschenig (Vienna: Corpus Scriptorum Ecclesiasticorum Latinorum, no. 17, 1888), p. 13 (I, 7).

101. Mills, "Roles of the Dreamer," p. 186.

Langland's practice, whether an intention to mean several things or an indecision as to what he means, but since in subsequent waking episodes the Dreamer is described with details suggesting irreconcilable qualities of virtue and vice, I am tempted to place him in Empson's last and most disturbing category:

. . . when the two meanings of the word, the two values of the ambiguity, are the two opposite meanings defined by the context, so that the total effect is to show a fundamental division in the writer's mind.[102]

Insofar as a word can be used to elicit an image in the reader's mind, it is flawed in being unable to insure that the image and its *intentio* will suit the meaning in the poet's mind—if indeed that mind is made up— and frequently it will be deficient since it cannot, by itself, embody and guarantee a spiritual lesson. I believe that the character of Piers the Plowman represents such a name, with elicited image, developed for the sake of just this limitation—Langland's fourth way of responding to the inadequacy of images—since no one can say clearly or indisputably who he is or what he symbolizes. Mills phrases it more grandly: "Piers Plowman stands as the assertion of the nominal, himself an infinite in whom all triads meet and who unites time and space and defies change."[103]

The poet's foredoomed hope of embodying all the spiritual meanings of his poem in the figure of a plowman finds its parallel in the Dreamer's error of thinking that Dowel is a man who resides in some inn beside the highway. Will confuses the verbal with a nominal. Irreducible in their capacity for meaning, Piers and the Three Do's are never meant to be fully knowable through the words used to describe them. Mary Carruthers is altogether convincing when she argues that while *Piers Plowman* may be ultimately concerned with the moral application of knowledge, its primary problem is epistemological rather than moral—and specifically that Will's mental quest is bedeviled by "the fluid, partially understood, inadequate verbal signs of an insufficient rhetoric."[104]

Not only is Piers a nominal whose image is protean and whose essence unascertainable, he also embodies all of Langland's hostility to-

102. William Empson, *Seven Types of Ambiguity*, 3rd ed. rev. (London: Chatto and Windus, 1953), pp. 5 and 192.

103. Mills, p. 199.

104. Carruthers, *The Search for St. Truth*, p. 25. And yet Anne Middleton, "Two Infinities: Grammatical Metaphor in *Piers Plowman*," *ELH*, 39 (1972), 183–85, notes that the inner structure of language, namely grammar, provides "one of the least unreliable explanatory models" as opposed to the distortions of personification allegory.

ward the types of external show that contribute to a hollow formalism usurping the place of the inner spiritual reality and cluttering rather than illuminating the life of man. Piers sides with spirit against body, content against form, meaning against sign. His antagonism shows itself in the second vision through his work as the great substituter: he rejects the pilgrimage in favor of plowing, then tears the pardon in preference for the life of penance. In neither case does he reject the theory, only the debased form of its practice. Piers stands for a mode of perception that looks beyond the external and into the secret heart of things. Anima later explains more precisely the object of Piers' vision as the *wil* behind words and works, with another swipe at the scholastic method:

> "Clerkes haue no knowyng," quod he, "but by werkes and wordes.
> Ac Piers þe Plowman parceyueþ moore depper
> What is þe wille and wherfore þat many wight suffreþ:
> *Et vidit deus cogitaciones eorum. . .*
> Therfore by colour ne by clergie knowe shaltow hym neuere,
> Neiþer þoru3 wordes ne werkes, but þoru3 wil oone,
> And þat knoweþ no clerk ne creature on erþe
> But Piers þe Plowman, *Petrus id est Christus.*"
>
> (B. xv. 198–200 and 209–12)

Langland is concerned with a problem that had vexed Englishmen from the dawn of the Christian tradition. Bede had said that the quality of a man's will could be known by his deeds—"Per arborem intelligimus seu bonam seu malam voluntatem"—but elsewhere admitted to the impossibility of judging man's will and intent by external acts like the giving of alms.[105] This doubt is echoed by a fourteenth-century mystic quoting St. Gregory: "Mani semes gode dedes & are noght gode, for þai are noght done with a gode wille."[106] We find an enlargement of Augustinian skepticism, resembling Wyclif's own, applied to all human acts and institutions, as well as the transitory objects of the created world, that is, all the objects of human perception. "Because people cannot directly perceive the inner world of the spirit and the will," says Burrow, "they are inclined to forget about it, and become preoccupied with forms of words and external observances which in themselves have no value."[107]

---

105. Bede, *In Matthaei Evangelium Expositio*, I, vii (*PL* 92:38) and I, vi (*PL* 92:31).

106. "Our Daily Work" in *Yorkshire Writers: Richard Rolle of Hampole and His Followers*, ed. C. Horstman, 2 vols. (London: Swan Sonnenschein, 1895–96), vol. I, p. 141.

107. Burrow, "Words, Works and Will," p. 114.

Langland's personal solution could have been the same one chosen by other souls beset by this crisis. He might have turned to a life of austere piety, devoid of ritual and occupied by a continual meditation according to the *via negativa*, looking beyond the jig-saw world of images and into the wordless purity of God's will. Fortunately for later generations of readers, this is not the alternative he chose. While he approves the life of the ascetic and the contemplative, he realizes that the vast majority of men must follow the active life of this world and struggle with all the encumbrances it imposes. To them he offers his poem.

Haukyn stands as the archetype of the active man whose soul is constantly soiled by contact with the world:

"And kouþe I neuere, by Crist! kepen it clene an houre
That I ne soiled it wiþ si3te or som ydel speche,
Or þoru3 *werk* or þoru3 *word* or *wille* of myn herte
That I ne flobre it foule fro morwe til euen."

(B. xiv. 12–15; emphasis mine)

Surely part of the solution to Haukyn's problem has already been included in Langland's previous discussion of the Three Do's. Patience, quoting a definition given by Charity, says that Dobest means to love God and keep His Commandments:

"Wiþ *wordes* and *werkes*," quod she, "and *wil* of þyn herte
Thow loue leelly þi soule al þi lif tyme.
And so þow lere þe to louye, for þe lordes loue of heuene,
Thyn enemy in alle wise eueneforþ wiþ þiselue."

(B. xiii. 140–43; emphasis mine)

This adds to Clergy's earlier definition of Dobet as acting in strict accord with one's intent:

"Loke þow werche it in *werk* þat þi *word* sheweþ;
Swich as þow semest in si3te be in assay yfounde;
Appare quod es vel esto quod appares;
And lat no body be by þi beryng bigiled
But be swich in þi soule as þow semest wiþoute."

(B. x. 260–63; emphasis mine)

And even earlier, the two friars had told the Dreamer that his wit and free will needed to work according to Dowel's instructions:

"God wole suffre wel þi *sleu*þe if þiself likeþ,
For he yaf þee to yeres3yue to yeme wel þiselue
Wit and *free wil*, to euery wi3t a porcion,

To fleynge foweles, to fisshes and to beestes.
Ac man haþ moost þerof and moost is to blame
But if he werche wel þerwiþ as Dowel hym techeþ."

(B. viii. 51–56; emphasis mine)

In all four passages, and in many others that could be cited,[108] Langland emphasizes the need for man to have a virtuous will and to act well according to its choices and assertions. A discrepancy between will and action would generate many of the difficulties already listed, such as focusing attention, ordering mental images, deciding, and actually doing. Yet the failure of the will, even a good will, to fulfill its duty in directing the actions of the body raised a problem of special concern to Langland: the problem of *acedia* or sloth, which the two friars in the passage quoted above have singled out as the Dreamer's most prominent vice.

I have sought in the preceding pages to expose some of the tangled roots of fourteenth-century skepticism and to discuss some of its ramifications, both philosophical and artistic, as they appear in *Piers Plowman*. As later chapters will show in detail, most of the poem's changes in direction, as well as its tensions, are created by the multiplication of alternatives, because instead of choosing among the possible precepts for moral action, Langland moves on to refine or redefine the alternatives without ever making clear-cut decisions. His sense of crisis would not have been so severe if he had accepted a basic "double-truth theory" as did Aquinas, so that the discoveries of the intellect could be considered merely provisional, forever open to revision if new evidence or a clearer theory were found, while the tenets of faith were left undisturbed.[109] But Langland insists that there *is* a single Truth and that all the tools of the inquiring mind must be used in searching for it, for better or worse, even if the mind risks becoming so intent on inquiry that it loses sight of its goal.

Langland's opening vision shows the whole of humanity poised between the great alternatives of Truth and Falsehood—God and Satan, Heaven and Hell. Although the Dreamer is told that the foremost representative of falseness is Lady Mede, we later discover that there are

108. For example, B. iii. 238–39, v. 502–05, xiv. 137–39, and xv.44–46.
109. Lewis, *The Discarded Image*, p. 16, quotes from the astronomical writings of Aquinas as part of a fascinating glimpse into the medieval "theory of the nature of theory." In a related discussion, Copleston's *History of Medieval Philosophy*, p. 7, explains how a double-truth theory could still generate a sense of crisis for the Christian thinker. Sheila Delaney, p. 21, sees "skeptical fideism" as a way of saving both the conclusions of reason and the tenets of faith.

two types of meed and that virtue lies in choosing the right one and rejecting the wrong (B. iii. 231–33). Later the people set out on a pilgrimage toward a destination called Truth, which had been defined by theologians as the accord between human will and the will of God, but the collective will of the folk wavers in the Half Acre, where all concludes in wrangling and despair.[110] In the second vision we expect that the stalemate over the best way to reach Truth will be dispelled by the arrival of a pardon sent to Piers and all his followers. Instead of a resolution, however, the pardon gives rise to another conflict and another set of alternatives: the invalidity of the document argued by the Priest as opposed to the value of the message endorsed by Piers. Langland's skill in making the outcome ambiguous is evidenced by the heated debate among modern scholars. What has seldom been appreciated is that Langland chooses this episode to bring Will into the action and position him, significantly, midway between the Priest and Piers so that he can read over their shoulders. And Will remains suspended between these two alternatives even after he has awakened. Although he inclines toward Piers' position, he does not act upon it. Nor does he wholly reject the Priest's argument. He merely decides that trusting in pardons "is noȝt *so siker* for þe soule, certes, as is Dowel" (B. vii. 186). Relative sureness is not tantamount to certainty, only to a refinement of doubt.

In setting off to search for Dowel, the Dreamer has made a choice of sorts, though it is no more successful than the decision of the folk to set out on a pilgrimage to Truth's Tower. In neither case is the chosen alternative completely known, and in neither case do the arbiters act fully upon their decisions. Both failures can be attributed specifically to the will, whose main function after judging between alternatives is directing the soul and body to act in favor of that choice. The search for Truth and the quest for Dowel are finally problems for the will— for the communal will of the folk and, more specifically as the poem

---

110. Frederick Copleston, *A History of Philosophy*, rev. ed., 8 vols. (Westminster: Newman, 1950), vol. II, pp. 51–67. Augustine, *The Teacher, The Free Choice of the Will, Grace and Free Will*, trans. Robert P. Russell (Washington: Catholic University of America Press, 1968), p. 146, says this about the relation between *veritas* and *voluntas*: "What we call a separation from truth . . . is a perverse will which makes inferior things the object of its love" (*Free Choice of the Will*, II, 14, 37). Edward Vasta believes this definition of Truth comes closest to Langland's meaning, in "Truth, the Best Treasure, in *Piers Plowman*," *PQ*, 44 (1965), 23–24. Martin, *The Field and the Tower*, pp. 12–13, maintains that "the poem is constructed on a series of dichotomies" of interpretation, such as the one produced by the tearing of the pardon, and no such dilemma is ever fully resolved so that one anti-climax follows another until the "climactic anti-climax" of Conscience's final quest after Piers.

progresses, for Will the Dreamer. And these problems were made more complicated for Langland and his audience by a host of conjectures raised during a fierce fourteenth-century debate over human volition, its powers, its limitations, and its role in the salvation of man's soul. The scope of that debate, along with some ways it touches upon Langland's poem, forms the subject of the following chapter.

II
Complexities of the Will

D. W. Robertson, Jr., and Bernard F. Huppé have offered the first full-length study of *Piers Plowman* to recognize that Will the Dreamer represents to some extent the faculty of the human will, the power of the soul responsible for moral choice and moral action. Choosing, consenting, intending, desiring, enjoying, and loving are all activities belonging to the will, which needs regenerative grace to help it to perform good works. Unless guided by reason and conscience as well, the will strays from the true goal and falls prey to cupidity.[1]

Robertson and Huppé refer to these central doctrines as a standard by which to judge Will's actions, but in doing so, they fail to mention that during the hundred years preceding Langland's career, the human will had become the focus of an intense debate involving the main issues of moral theology. Not since Augustine's attack upon the Pelagians in the fourth century had theologians argued so heatedly over the faculty which determines the extent of man's power to act, the ethical nature of his actions, and his dependence upon divine aid to accomplish what is right.[2] Of all the contending voices in this scholastic debate, Robertson and Huppé choose as their sole witness Godfrey of Fontaines (d. 1306), an extremist who argued the passivity of the will and its subjugation to the intellect—a position opposing Bishop Tempier's condemnations of 1277 as well as the mainstream of later English

---

1. Robertson and Huppé, pp. 13, 34, 240 *et passim*. This general view of the will is also set forth by V.J. Bourke's "Will" in *The New Catholic Encyclopedia*, vol. XIV, pp. 909–13; Archibald Alexander, *Theories of Will in the History of Philosophy* (New York: Scribner, 1898), pp. 76–157; Gilson, *History of Christian Philosophy*, pp. 78–79; and Leff, *Medieval Thought*, pp. 37–38.

2. Gordon Leff, *Gregory of Rimini: Tradition and Innovation in Fourteenth Century Thought* (Manchester: Manchester University Press, 1961), p. 155.

thought deriving from Duns Scotus, who held that the entire cause of volition rested with a free and wholly independent will.[3] The following synopsis of will in the history of philosophy is designed partially to show the bewildering complexity of the problem that Robertson and Huppé passed over in silence and partially to show the difficulty of deciding exactly where Langland might have stood in terms of a debate that had largely subsided before he began writing his poem, with the victory going to the moderate voluntarists. He is typically ambivalent, even eclectic in his treatment of these doctrines. But there can be no doubt that his concerns with *voluntas* were considerable and contributed to the sense of anxiety that surrounds the central events of his poem. He insisted upon establishing *Will* as the name of his protagonist in all three versions, and his revisions suggest a growing preoccupation with the powers and limitations of the will.[4] Yet rather than try to deduce Langland's concept of the will by applying

3. Leff, *Medieval Thought*, p. 270. For a fuller exploration of Godfrey's psychology of the will, see Odon Lottin, "Le Libre Arbitre chez Godefroid de Fontaines," *Revue Néoscolastique de Philosophie*, 40 (1937), 213–41; and Robert J. Arway, "A Half Century of Research on Godfrey of Fontaines," *New Scholasticism*, 36 (1962), 211–17. Several recent critics have also applied this rationalist theology or detected the influence of other individual authorities: Erzgräber, *Langlands "Piers Plowman"*, draws upon Duns Scotus; Wittig, "The Inward Journey," 226, follows Bonaventure; Elizabeth D. Kirk, *The Dream Thought of "Piers Plowman"* (New Haven: Yale University Press, 1972), p. 161, finds Bernardine views; Carruthers, *The Search for St. Truth*, p. 93, refers back to Robertson and Huppé in conceiving *voluntas* as merely an appetitive faculty; Martin, *The Field and the Tower*, pp. 5–6, considers only the pre-fourteenth-century line from Augustine to Aquinas in fixing the poem's theology of will; and Janet Coleman, pp. 31–33, sees Langland as a strict student of *Moderni* psychology.

4. George Kane, *Piers Plowman: The Evidence for Authorship* (London: The Athlone Press, 1965), pp. 58–64, discusses the occurrences of the name *Will(e)* in all three versions: A. v. 43–44, viii. 42–43, ix. 117–18; B. v. 60–61, viii. 128–29, xv. 152–53; C. i. 3–6, vi. 1–2, x. 68–71. The C-revisor has taken care to establish Will as the Dreamer's name from the moment he first enters the visionary action. Also in the C-text, Anima becomes Liberum Arbitrium (C. xvi. 157), a figure who also replaces Piers as the guardian of the Tree of Charity (C. xviii. 105). Donaldson writes at length on this latter substitution in *Piers Plowman: The C-Text and Its Poet* (1949; rpt. London: Frank Cass, 1966), pp. 180–98, bringing to bear Bernardine concepts to show that Liberum Arbitrium was understood as "that part of man which bears the impress of the image of God to which man was created" and which might be restored through proper spiritual exercise (p. 189). George Sanderlin, "The Character '*Liberum Arbitrium*' in the C-text of *Piers Plowman*," *MLN*, 56 (1941), 449–53, responding to Mabel Day's Scotistic analysis of the Tree of Charity in "Duns Scotus and *Piers Plowman*," draws upon John Damascene and Hugh of St. Cher to show that *liberum arbitrium* was widely regarded in the thirteenth century as a universal power to be identified with *all* other powers of the soul. Sanderlin's position has been challenged by A.V.C. Schmidt in "Langland and Scholastic Philosophy," and both Schmidt and Donaldson have been corrected by Britton J. Harwood in "*Liberum-Arbitrium* in the C-Text of *Piers Plowman*," *PQ*, 52 (1973), 680–95. The obvious lack of consensus among these able scholars should suggest the limited hope for success in providing similar, but necessarily lengthier, glosses on Langland's passages dealing with matters of *voluntas*.

lengthy commentaries to dozens of passages—and thereby demonstrating more than anything else the non-systematic nature of his thought—I intend in this chapter to suggest the difficulty of the problem he inherited and the wide range of current theories he might have waded through.

The Christian doctrine of the will first emerges from the Letters of Paul, who discovered the phenomenon in his turning from the Old Law of "thou shalt do" to the New Law of "thou shalt will."[5] While he agreed with the Greek ethical schools in his desire to make men virtuous and holy, he departed from the post-Socratics in his belief that the human faculty of desire—Jerome's translation introduces the word *voluntas*—was corrupted by original sin and therefore unable by itself to achieve the good, even if guided by right knowledge.[6] The human soul is in bondage to sin. What is worse, man alone cannot liberate himself because he requires the gift of God's grace to remove original sin and unbar the access to faith.[7] In an unregenerate state the will is predetermined to sinful acts, but in a state of grace it is inclined toward a holy life.

Continuing in holiness, however, was not easy. Paul learned through personal experience (the path to self-knowledge to be followed by later voluntarists) that the will is never wholly fixed in righteousness, because the flesh is hard to subdue and the impulses of good and evil continue to war with one another, even in the soul of a man who has been pardoned. Paul gives voice to his frustrations in his Epistle to the Romans:

For I know that in me, that is, in my flesh, no good dwells, because to wish is within my power, but I do not find the strength to accomplish what is good. For I do not the good which I wish, but the evil that I do not wish, that I perform.[8]

The meaning of this passage, like the experience itself, is not easy to grasp. There is the possibility that Paul sees himself as a man in a state of sin struggling to obtain grace for the first time, but Archibald Alexander suggests that we are given the picture of man who has already known grace, but is struggling to attain holiness by overcoming the corrupt principle that constantly rebels against his changed character.[9] Paul is saying, then, that sin continues to reside in man's fleshly nature

5. Hannah Arendt, *The Life of the Mind: Volume II, Willing* (New York: Harcourt Brace Jovanovich, 1978), p. 68.
6. See Rom. 1.18–32, 3.9–18, and especially 12.1.
7. Rom. 5.1–11 and Eph. 2.8–10.
8. Rom. 7.18–19.
9. Alexander, *Theories of the Will*, pp. 84–85.

even after grace has been bestowed, a predicament touchingly drama-
tized by Langland when he invokes the figure of Haukyn the Active
Man, whose cloak of baptism, once clean, is continually soiled anew
by the seven sins:

> "And kouþe I neuere, by Crist! kepen it clene an houre
> That I ne soiled it wiþ si3te or som ydel speche,
> Or þoru3 werk or þoru3 word or wille of myn herte
> That I ne flobre it foule fro morwe til euen."
>
> (B. xiv. 12–15)

Paul's emphasis on grace was challenged by the followers of Pelagius,
a fourth-century British monk whose writings, totally unknown dur-
ing the Middle Ages, elicited a series of responses from Augustine that
established the standard doctrine of the will for the next eight cen-
turies. The Pelagians believed that there was no original sin and that
Adam's fall was personal, having no effect upon his descendants. All
acts were the result of a will that was completely free because each
man's will was undetermined toward good or evil. Since grace was
therefore the reward rather than the cause of merit, man could avoid
sin without God's help.[10] Augustine countered by arguing that man's
will, while essentially free to turn toward good or evil, was not able to
secure salvation without divine grace.[11] In writings such as his *Confes-
sions* and *Concerning Grace and Free Will*, he insisted upon the radi-
cal insufficiency of man's will to earn even the first advent of grace
without the aid of God.

Partially in response to the Pelagians and partially out of a need to
understand his own conversion experience, Augustine took a new ap-
proach when he chose to investigate the will not in isolation but in its
interconnection with the soul's other powers of understanding and
memory. Within a triadic scheme analogous to the three indivisible
members of the Trinity, *voluntas* became nothing less than the whole
soul in action.[12] Langland shows his familiarity with this tradition by
fusing the members of the Augustinian analogy and having *Fre Wille*
instead of the Holy Spirit proceed from the Father and the Son of his
Trinity (B. xvi. 220–24). Augustine altered Paul's concept by locating
the trouble not in the dual nature of man, half carnal and half spiritual,
but in the will's own inner action toward or away from the good.[13]

10. *Ibid.*, pp. 108–09; Leff, *Medieval Thought*, pp. 52–54.
11. Bourke, "Will" in *NCE*, p. 912, drawing upon *Retractationum*, I, ix, 1–6 (*PL*
32:595–99). Other anti-Pelagian tracts are listed by Leff, *Medieval Thought*, p. 38.
12. *De Trinitate*, X, xi–xii and XV, xi (*PL* 42:982–84 and 1089).
13. Arendt, *Willing*, p. 93.

Thus the moral quality of the soul was determined by a will that could approach God by believing and loving the truth, or could fall into sin by refusing to conform to divine law. Sin was defined by Augustine specifically as a perverse movement of the will.[14]

While the will's movements could be in different directions, they could also be of various kinds—intellective, affective, physical. A man must know the good before he can act upon it, but ignorance could itself be blamed on the will:

Not to know is one thing, unwillingness to know is another. The will is surely at fault in the kind of man of whom it is said that "He would not understand that he might do well." (Ps. 35.4)[15]

Unlike the Platonists who considered the acquisition of knowledge as an end in itself, Augustine believed that knowledge was needed to make possible the choice of the good, but that even an informed inclination toward virtue was worthless without a determination to act. It is not enough to amass bits of intellection as Will the Dreamer does throughout the most laborious stretches of *Piers Plowman* (B. x–xv).[16] A man must choose to do what is right, and Holy Church makes this knowledge readily available to all. Augustine did not, however, set up the will as a cold calculator of alternatives and enforcer of actions. Will was the soul in the act of loving, and Augustine went so far as to define will as love in its strongest form.[17] Even the worst appetitive impulses of the soul—sensual desire (*cupiditas*) and lust (*libido*)—were movements of a loving will.

All three aspects of the Augustinian will—learning, feeling, and acting—were transmitted by major theologians like Anselm and were, I believe, incorporated into the structure of the *Vitae* sections of *Piers Plowman*. The intellectual phase covers the entry of Thought to Anima's discourse on charity (B. xiii–xv), the affective journey begins with the Tree of Charity and lasts till the end of the poem (B. xvi–xx), and physical actions fall in those waking moments when Will has the opportunity to translate into deeds what he has learned in his dreams.

14. Bourke, "Will" in *NCE*, p. 912, referring to passages in *De Trinitate*, X, xi (*PL* 42:982–84); *Retractationum*, I, xv, 3–4 (*PL* 32:609–10); *De Duabus Animabus*, xi, 15 (*PL* 42:105); *De Civitate Dei*, XIV, vi–vii (*PL* 41:409–11); and *Confessions*, VII, 3 (trans. R. S. Pine-Coffin [Harmondsworth: Penguin, 1961], pp. 136–37).

15. Augustine, *Grace and Free Will* (3, 5), trans. Russell, p. 256.

16. Donald R. Howard remarks upon Will's excessive curiosity and deficient action in *The Three Temptations: Medieval Man in Search of the World* (Princeton: Princeton University Press, 1966), pp. 181–82.

17. Augustine, *De Trinitate*, XV, xxi, 41 (*PL* 42:1089); and *Concerning the City of God against the Pagans* (XIV, 6), trans. Henry Bettenson (Harmondsworth: Penguin, 1972), pp. 555–56.

If this analysis is valid, the reader must decide whether Will's intellectual quest amounts to anything other than a futile exercise of curiosity, whether his affective experiences do not end in a harmful sorrow described by Augustine as "an act of will in disagreement with what we reject,"[18] and whether Will performs any worthy actions—*any*—in his waking life.

The doctrine of the will remained relatively unaltered from the death of Augustine until the twelfth century, when Aristotle's psychological writings began to surface in Western Europe.[19] Thereafter, many Christian thinkers became dissatisfied with a simple triadic division of the soul and began to attribute man's actions to a plurality of operative powers. Other writers sought to redefine the roles of reason, intellect, and will in ways allowing for the superiority of man's rational parts.[20] This rationalist movement culminated with Thomas Aquinas, although his exaltation of reason does not mean that he neglected the will. Indeed, Vernon J. Bourke has proclaimed Aquinas' study of volition as one of the most rigorous analyses in the history of Western thought.[21] Such an extensive and subtle analysis does not permit brief summation, but there are several obvious points that distinguish the Thomist doctrine from Augustine's theory, not to mention the approaches of later English commentators such as Duns Scotus and William of Ockham.

First of all, Aquinas saw will and reason as separate faculties and not merely aspects of the soul in action,[22] and he assigned to the will a lesser role in the operation of the soul. Two apprehensive faculties, intellect and reason, had their corresponding appetitive faculties of will and *liberum arbitrium* (free choice). The will was completely subject to the intellect because the object to which the will inclined was always presented to it by the intellect, since the will was not thought to be

18. *Ibid.*

19. Gilson, *History*, pp. 136–39, discusses the elaboration of an essentially unchanged Augustinian doctrine by prescholastic theologians like Anselm.

20. Vernon J. Bourke, *Will in Western Thought: An Historico-Critical Survey* (New York: Sheed and Ward, 1964), pp. 55–76; Pierre Michaud-Quantin, "La Classification des puissances de l'âme au XIIe siècle," *Revue du Moyen-Age Latin*, 5 (1949), 15–34; Odon Lottin, *Libre Arbitre et liberté depuis saint Anselme jusqu' à la fin du XIIIe siècle*, *Psychologie et morale*, vol. I (Louvain: Abbaye du Mont César, 1942), 11–389.

21. Bourke, *Will in Western Thought*, p. 69.

22. For a fuller discussion of Aquinas' debt to John Damascene for his faculty and appetitive theories, see Bourke, *Will in Western Thought*, p. 59, and "Will" in *NCE*, p. 912. Damascene's consideration of the will is found in the third part of his *Sources of Knowledge* (*PG* 94:943–46), whose medieval translation by Burgundio of Pisa, called *De Fide Orthodoxa*, provides the basis for study by Odon Lottin in "La Psychologie de l'acte humain chez saint Jean Damascène et les théologiens du XIIIe siècle occidental," *Revue Thomiste*, 36 (1931), 631–61.

endowed with any cognitive powers.[23] The intellect, not the will, enabled a man to have his greatest happiness in knowing God through contemplation, and the will's loving, which was so important to Augustine, would be forever imperfect if it were not for the intellect's guidance. After Aquinas, however, many of his scholastic *defensores* such as Godfrey of Fontaines tended to select only extreme propositions such as these, so simply put here, to serve as the basis for their theories of the will's radical passivity.

The supremacy of Aquinas' doctrine did not go unchallenged for long, however, and within a decade after his death in 1274, attacks were launched that would eventually culminate in a movement rivaling his own and doing much to sweep aside the claims he had made for human reason. He had never enjoyed the support of all thirteenth-century theologians—Grosseteste, for one, emphasized the active role of the will in *De Libero Arbitrio*[24]—but perhaps the greatest blow came in 1277 when Bishop Etienne Tempier of Paris officially condemned the doctrine of the passive will. Reasserting Augustinian principles, the Bishop prohibited anyone in his diocese from teaching that the human will was in any way subject to rational coercion or simple appetitive urges. It was false "that the soul wills nothing unless moved by another" and "that the will of man is necessitated by cognition, as is the appetite of a brute."[25] Many theologians who might have been leaning toward Aquinas, especially at the University of Paris and later at Oxford, were swayed by this ecclesiastical act, while others began to insist that the human will was indeed a completely self-determining agent and that the cause of volitional acts lay exclusively in the will itself.[26] Shortly after Tempier's condemnation, for example, Peter John Olivi used his *Quaestiones in II Librum Sententiarum* to initiate an

23. Alexander, *Theories of Will*, pp. 132–33; and Gérard Verbeke, "Le Développement de la vie volitive d'après saint Thomas," *Revue Philosophique de Louvain*, 56 (1958), 5–34.

24. Lottin, *Libre Arbitre et liberté*, 183–97; Daniel A. Callus, "Robert Grosseteste as Scholar," pp. 28–30, in *Robert Grosseteste: Scholar and Bishop*, ed. D.A. Callus (Oxford: The Clarendon Press, 1955); and James McEvoy, *The Philosophy of Robert Grosseteste* (Oxford: The Clarendon Press, 1982), pp. 234–35. Bonaventura, who died in the same year as Aquinas, also made generous allowance for the will; see Etienne Gilson, *La Philosophie de Saint Bonaventure* (Paris: Vrin, 1924), pp. 325–46.

25. Bourke, *Will in Western Thought*, pp. 174–75. For a fuller account of the circumstances leading to the articles, see A.J. Denomy, "The *De Amore* of Andreas Capellanus and the Condemnation of 1277," *MS*, 8 (1946), 107–49. The articles themselves are printed in *Chartularium Universitatis Parisiensis*, ed. H. Denifle and E. Chatelain (Paris: Delalain, 1889), I, 473, pp. 543–55.

26. Bourke, *Will in Western Thought*, p. 84. For the details of the thirteenth-century voluntarist movement, especially Henry of Ghent and Godfrey of Fontaines, see Antonio San Cristóbal-Sebastián, *Controversias acerca de la voluntad desde 1270 a 1300* (Ma-

orderly philosophical offensive against the Thomist doctrine of volition. The debate had begun.

Before proceeding to the complications of that debate, we would do well to recall the principal tenets that were to be disputed by fourteenth-century voluntarists and rationalists. Most authorities throughout the tradition believed that the will was naturally infirmed. Aristotle taught that it encompassed lower appetites that could overrule reason, and Paul and Augustine agreed that *voluntas* was corrupted by original sin. Aquinas accepted these positions and decided that the will must be subject to *intellectus* and must follow the dictates of this apprehensive faculty in order for the soul to function virtuously. Augustine had defined sin as the perverse movement of the will against the rational laws of God, and in his polemics against the Pelagians, who believed that the free will by itself could win salvation, he maintained that divine grace was necessary for the will to complete its choice of the supreme good and thus to insure redemption. Augustine followed the Stoics such as Cicero in considering the will essential to the acquisition of knowledge by focusing the senses, deciding among *ficta*, and judging what information to consign to memory, but he felt that the nature of the will was ultimately affective and not intellective: the will was the soul in the act of loving, whatever the object of that love. And finally, Paul and Augustine established the practice of examining the will personally and not abstractly, by prolonged and careful introspection. Understanding that practice of self-examination is crucial to our understanding the method of the fourteenth-century voluntarists. Here again, Peter John Olivi stands as a pioneer of considerable importance.

While Olivi proved to be the most influential pre-Scotian proponent of will, he deserves further mention for at least two other reasons. First, Olivi was a member of the Franciscan Order, whose hegemony in the fourteenth century was such that Heiko Oberman has recently suggested that the later Middle Ages might well be called the "Franciscan Middle Ages." [27] Almost all the major schoolmen who would enter the debate on the side of the will were Franciscans—Roger Bacon, Duns Scotus, William of Ockham, Adam of Woodham—and they all shared the profound interest in man's affective life that characterized nearly all

---

drid: Editorial y Librería, 1958). Leff has more to say about the impact of Tempier's condemnations on the universities in *Paris and Oxford*, pp. 229–38.

27. Oberman, "Fourteenth-Century Religious Thought," p. 81, and for further remarks on Olivi, pp. 89–90. So great was the weight of Franciscan scholasticism that John V. Fleming's *Introduction to the Franciscan Literature of the Middle Ages* (Chicago: Franciscan Herald Press, 1977) seeks to restore some balance in the direction of the order's vernacular writings.

Franciscan thinkers.[28] And second, Olivi subjected all arguments to the test of personal experience—the *experimentum suitatis* or experiment of the mind with itself—saying that we can feel within our consciousness the will stirring itself to action and asserting complete volitional control over the other functions of the soul.[29] This appeal to direct experience became the hallmark for other Franciscan psychologies of volition.[30] The increased subjective awareness produced by these studies encouraged an intense inwardness among other fourteenth-century thinkers[31] and probably afforded a model for Langland's introspection: to search within himself, to feel moving within his soul a free and head-strong agent, and to give that active force its proper name—Will.

Scholasticism in the first half of the fourteenth century was characterized by this emphasis on the will rather than reason. Freedom, determinism, predestination, merit, habit, original sin, the effects of grace were all pressing issues which centered upon the question of will. So decisive was the shift that all dominant schools remained strongly voluntaristic until the end of the Middle Ages. But this does not mean that a consensus was reached even among the followers of a prominent spokesman like Ockham, and certainly not during the debate's most heated period around 1339 to 1347.[32] The rationalists could boast many distinguished members, among them John Quidort, Nicholas Trivet, Thomas Sutton, and (of course) Godfrey of Fontaines, but the more provocative and ultimately more influential theories were those proposed by Englishmen like Duns Scotus and William of Ockham who stressed the free and self-activating character of the will.[33]

Different writers concentrated on different topics, depending upon their scholastic or mystical interests, but the debate generally centered

28. David Knowles, *The Evolution of Medieval Thought* (Baltimore: Helicon Press, 1962), p. 306, says that emphasis on the will was only natural with Friars Minor "whose first inspiration came from one whose life was a response to the love of God as seen in the Incarnation and Passion of Christ."

29. Bourke, *Will in Western Thought*, pp. 83–84 and 175, citing Peter John Olivi's *Quaestiones in Secundum Librum Sententiarum*, q. 57 (Quaracchi: Ex Typographia Collegii S. Bonaventurae, 1922–26), vol. II, pp. 332–33.

30. Bourke, *Will in Western Thought*, pp. 86–87, discusses how Ockham claimed that a man can directly experience his ability to will or to refuse a suggestion from reason.

31. For a discussion of this sort of introspection (*experientia interna*), see Béraud de Saint-Maurice, "The Contemporary Significance of Duns Scotus' Philosophy" in *John Duns Scotus: 1265–1965*, ed. John K. Ryan and Bernardino M. Bonansea (Washington, D.C.: Catholic University of America Press, 1965), p. 354; and Ephrem Longpré, "The Psychology of Duns Scotus and Its Modernity," *Psychology and the Franciscan School*, ed. Claude L. Vogel (New York: Bruce, 1932), pp. 19–77, esp. pp. 27–28.

32. Michalski, "Problème de la volonté," p. 235; Bourke, "Will" in *NCE*, pp. 912–13.

33. Bourke, *Will in Western Thought*, p. 35.

on five major questions: (1) Does the will preserve any freedom in spite of its dependence on God? (2) Does the will have a cognitive function? (3) Does the will have the tendency to create purely semantic distinctions? (4) Is it possible to gauge the intensity of the will when it loves? and (5) Can the will have an experiential knowledge of God through mystical acts of love?[34] These questions elicited a wide range of speculation even from the main voluntarists, but one thing seems clear for the purposes of this discussion. These endless definitions, restrictions, claims, and qualifications of *voluntas* would have made it impossible for a writer with Langland's education to give the name *Will* to the protagonist of a theological allegory without the most careful consideration, if not deliberate intent.

Duns Scotus, the first great voluntarist, espoused a concept of the will's preeminence that was closely related to his belief in the uniqueness of the individual. All *rationes* might be identical in their determination toward absolutes, but every single *voluntas* is unique: it moves differently and it has its own *haecceitas*. Unlike the Thomists who taught that the intellect moves the will, Duns Scotus offered this remarkable dictum: "causa totalis volitionis in voluntate nihil aliud a voluntate est"—"nothing other than will is the total cause of volition in the will."[35] Being completely free, the human will is capable of acting in accord with reason or in opposition to it. The will may not be able to respond without intellectual information about its object, but knowledge is the condition and not the cause of volitional activity.[36] While the will depends upon the intellect for its cognitions (only later did philosophers attribute cognitive powers directly to the will), the will itself determines the choice of cognitions. The intellect needs the will to direct its attention and can function properly only when its object is confirmed by the will. Without this confirmation, the intellect ceases to operate. The will is therefore superior to the intellect both in its full control over decisions *and* in its ability to choose what knowledge will serve as the condition of those decisions.[37] Here, Duns Scotus accords with Augustine's belief that the will tells the intellect what to choose for its understanding and tells the memory what to retain and what to forget.

34. Michalski, p. 255.

35. *Opus Oxoniense*, ed. M. F. Garcia, 3 vols. (Quaracchi: Collegium S. Bonaventurae, 1912–14), I, 8, discussed by Leff, *Medieval Thought*, p. 270; Knowles, *Evolution of Medieval Thought*, p. 307; and Gilson, *History*, p. 463.

36. Bourke, *Will in Western Thought*, p. 85, citing John Duns Scotus, *Opus Oxoniense*, vol. I, pp. 348–50 (I, iii, q. 3) and vol. II, p. 698 (II, xxv, 1).

37. Gilson, *History*, p. 463, relying upon Duns Scotus, *Reportata Parisiensia*, IV, d. 49, q. 2, n. 11–12, and *Commentaria Oxoniensia*, lib. II, d. 25, q. 1, n. 20–23.

Scotus further secured the primacy of the will by introducing the notion of indifference (*prima indifferentia*). The Augustinians had taught that when a sound will was presented with an alternative between good and evil, it was powerless to resist choosing the good. Duns Scotus, on the other hand, believed that when the intellect presented some object to the will for its judgment, the will could be indifferent toward the object and have no predilection to move one way or another. The will possessed a perfect freedom to accept or reject any object presented to it by the intellect. What is more, it could direct the intellect to consider one object or another—and then pause, deciding whether or not to act.[38]

Even from this bare summary, it is plain to see that Scotus' doctrine by itself, without the complications added by later theorists, could have offered Langland three essential notions: (1) the will can operate independently of reason; (2) it can determine how much knowledge to accumulate in advance of a decision; and (3) in the face of many contending alternatives, the will can suspend judgment and, in effect, decide not to decide.

Like Scotus, William of Ockham proclaimed the will as the supreme power of the soul, totally free and thus superior to the intellect, but his extension of this belief to the subjects of virtue, merit, grace, original sin, and the sacrament of penance drew into question his orthodoxy and resulted in his condemnation by a papal commission in 1326.[39] Since an urgent ecclesiastical move of this sort is usually a sign that the object of criticism has already established a strong influence, it should come as no surprise that this condemnation's fifty-one articles contained all the germs of Ockhamism to be developed later in the century, especially in Paris during the 1340s.[40] For example, Ockham proposed that the will was the sole determining agent in a moral act; reason might set the worth of the deed, but the will still had complete control in deciding whether to conform with reason. The will even had the freedom to reject absolute good, once it had been recognized as such, and to choose evil instead.[41] This stress on the greater importance of the soul's inner activity led to heightened suspicion of outer acts and experiences, resulting in some extreme speculation. In opposition to

---

38. Bourke, *Will in Western Thought*, p. 85, calls to witness two passages from Scotus—*Opus Oxoniense*, vol. II, p. 704 (II, xxv, 1), and *Quaestiones Quodlibetales*, in *Opera*, ed. L. Wadding (Paris: Vivès, 1891–95), vol. XXVI, xxi, n. 14. For a fuller account of indifference theory in fourteenth-century philosophy, see Edward J. Monahan, "Human Liberty and Free Will According to John Buridan," *MS*, 16 (1954), 72–86.

39. Pelzer, "Les 51 Articles de Guillaume Occam," 240–70.

40. Leff, *Paris and Oxford*, p. 251.

41. Leff, *William of Ockham*, pp. 486–87.

Scotus, for example, he argued that the sacrament of penance alone could not, without contrition and a good impulse of the will, result in a remission of sin.[42] It is clear that Langland's suspicion of formalism, so nicely registered by John Burrow, finds a correlative in the writings of Ockham, who saw virtue as intrinsic to an interior relation between will and reason that is ideally, but not necessarily, realized in exterior acts—works and words.

Ockham's theory of the primacy of human will was complicated by his doctrine of the *absoluta potentia* of God's will. To his statement that the merit of an act depends on its acceptability to God must be added the disturbing reminder that man cannot be sure what is and is not pleasing to God in the incomprehensibility of *His* will.[43] The theology that Ockham constructs upon this dual concept is tame by comparison with what his followers proposed, namely, that if God so wished, a man could be free of original sin, his private will could earn salvation without grace, and he could know and do God's will without the guidance of Bible or Church.[44] Whereas Ockham had made free will a prerequisite in any act of merit, Robert Holcot ceded so much power to divine volition that he removed from man's will almost all dignity of action and merit. Gordon Leff summarizes Holcot's radical theology:

Not only is there no order between grace and glory, but God can love the sinner more than one in grace; there is no need for free will to do anything to gain divine acceptance: "one loving God less [than another] can be loved the more by God;" a man can merit by false faith and, conversely, can receive no reward for fulfilling God's precepts. God Himself "can deceive and lie," and in the case of His knowledge of future contingents, God could cause Christ to deceive His disciples.[45]

In matters of allegiance to school and doctrine, a religious writer like Langland is seldom easy to pin down. Virginia Woolf's observations on Chaucer as a philosophical poet apply nearly as well to the author of *Piers Plowman*: "Questions press upon him; he asks them, but he is too true a poet to answer them; he leaves them unsolved, uncramped by the solution of the moment, and thus fresh for the generations that

---

42. *Ibid.*, p. 511. Similarly, Langland writes that a penitent soul might receive God's mercy on the basis of his intention to make satisfaction, even if he is unable to accomplish the deed (B. xvii. 241–42).

43. Leff, *Ockham*, p. 476, quoting *Reportatio Super IV Libros Sententiarum*, III, q. 5, art. I.

44. Leff, *Gregory of Rimini*, p. 156.

45. Leff, *Medieval Thought*, p. 292, drawing upon Holcot's *Commentary on the Sentences*, I, 4 and II, 2.

come after him."[46] Moreover, signs of radical Ockhamism in Langland's poem must always be judged carefully, since they can often be explained by recourse to traditional, entirely orthodox authorities. The fact that divine visions come to Will when he seems least deserving, for example, may indicate the influence of Holcot's proposition that God could love a sinner more than a soul in grace *or* these visions may simply conform to Augustine's belief that signs of God's grace were not always given according to one's merit: "We see, in fact, that [grace] is given, and continues to be given daily, not only where there are no good merits, but also where there are many previous merits that are evil."[47]

Such is the subtlety of Ockham's thought that *voluntas* does not need to be described as prime, since will and intellect are not ultimately different powers of the soul. The consequence of this view had an important impact on later psychology, because the will could be seen as having its own cognitive powers independent of the intellect.[48] This tendency to fuse volition, affection, and cognition was not completed until later in the fourteenth century when a group of Oxford scholars sought to attribute to the human will a wide variety of cognitive activities that included judgment, evaluation, and a sort of discursive reasoning.[49] Against heated objections from rationalists such as Gregory of Rimini and Pierre d'Ailly, arguments were put forth by Robert Holcot and Adam of Woodham stating that since the will judges objects and then moves knowingly toward or away from those objects, it must be endowed with some sort of cognition. How else could the will weigh alternatives and make value judgments?[50] Their

46. Virginia Woolf, "The Pastons and Chaucer" (1925), reprinted in *Geoffrey Chaucer: A Critical Anthology*, ed. J.A. Burrow (Baltimore: Penguin, 1969), p. 125.

47. Augustine, *Grace and Free Will* (6, 13), trans. Russell, p. 265.

48. Bourke, *Will in Western Thought*, pp. 83–84, discusses how this notion was anticipated by Olivi. On Ockham, see pp. 173–74 and 86–87, citing *Super IV Libros Sententiarum Subtilissimae Quaestiones* (Lyons, 1495), Bk. II, 2 K: "Intellectus et voluntas sunt idem realiter in se et cum essentia animae."

49. Bourke, *Will in Western Thought*, p. 134. Reason still played its traditional role in supplying correct knowledge for moral conduct; see David W. Clark, "William of Ockham on Right Reason," *Speculum*, 48 (1973), 13–36.

50. Michalski, pp. 262–64 and 267, with reference to mystical cognition, p. 261; Leff, *Gregory of Rimini*, pp. 163–65; and Bourke, *Will in Western Thought*, p. 36. For discussions of Holcot's remarkable career, see Emden, *A Biographical Register of the University of Oxford to A.D. 1500*, vol. II, pp. 946–47; Gordon Leff, *Bradwardine and the Pelagians* (Cambridge: The University Press, 1957), pp. 216–27; and Oberman, *Archbishop Thomas Bradwardine*, pp. 43–46. Beryl Smalley pays special attention to his non-scholastic writings and allegorizations in "Robert Holcot, O.P.," *Archivum Fratrum Praedicatorum*, 26 (1956), 5–97, and in *English Friars and Antiquity*, pp. 133–202. For a brief survey of Woodham's thought, see Oberman, *Bradwardine*, pp. 46–48.

conclusion was to invest in the will the powers of cognition and reasoning in addition to its usual acts of wishing, intending, choosing, and moving of man's other potencies.

The possible effect of such speculation upon *Piers Plowman* might be quickly noted. Without a prior tradition crediting *voluntas* with cognitive and rational powers, Langland probably would not have been able to conceive of a psychological allegory built around an active, argumentative, multi-faceted character named Will. But to the Dreamer's powers should be added his limitations. While he may have cognitive experiences as shown when he reasons, wrangles, weighs, judges, and does all the other things attributed to the will by advanced voluntarists at Oxford, Langland's Will may not in fact perform his prime intellective duties: to choose and consent and command and conclude.

We cannot say with any certainty that Langland took sides in the theological debate concerning the will. All evidence indicates that he was neither systematic nor doctrinaire. He seems to have been largely a theological conservative who was much unsettled by the religious dissension of his age, a man who tried to follow the old Augustinian tradition on *voluntas* while mingling with it, without careful regard for clarity, certain new theories that had been discussed at Oxford a single generation earlier—theories that he probably knew only partially or indirectly, in the same way most modern writers know about the psychologies of Freud and Jung. Part of the confusion in Langland's thinking may be explained by his fragmentary knowledge, but part may be due to the confusion of the debate itself, a tangle only now being unknotted by diligent scholars like Gordon Leff, Heiko Oberman, and William Courtenay who have access to a wide range of texts spanning almost a century of development.

Just as Langland was not doctrinaire, he was not consistent even in his adherence to fundamental Augustinian doctrines. For example, when Anima explains his many names in terms of his different functions (B. xv. 23–39), Langland is following Augustine, who had identified the soul with its powers so completely that these powers came to be regarded as mere names given to the soul according to its various actions—a position also endorsed by many Franciscan voluntarists.[51] But Langland is not faithful to a single theory. When in the C-text (v. 1–106) he presents Will and Reason as two separate allegorical

51. For comments on the Augustinian position, see Bourke, "Will" in *NCE*, p. 912, and Gilson, *Bonaventure*, pp. 325–34. The operation of the will is high on Anima's list of activities: "And whan I wilne and wolde, *animus* ich hatte" (B. xv. 24).

characters, he seems to incline toward the theories of Albertus Magnus and Thomas Aquinas, who followed John Damascene in regarding the powers of the soul as discrete faculties, with will and intellect as the two most important. Langland's inconsistency can be interpreted in many ways, as carelessness, confusion, skepticism about which theory made the stronger claim, even as evidence for the case of multiple authorship. But if we assume a single poet, it largely suggests the wide-ranging interest and inquiry of a poet whose concerns with the problems of man's soul were obsessive, yet never finally resolved—the myriad-mindedness of a theological poet.

All this controversy over the will's cognitive and intellective aspects should not draw attention away from its other powers, less hotly contested but no less important: the will's affective impulses and its power to command actions. A key part of Duns Scotus' discussion pertains to the nature of human deeds so that for him the will always involves an action (*praxis*) either elicited or commanded. An elicited act is begun and completed within the power of the will internally, and a commanded act is initiated within the will but completed outwardly in other human potencies—senses, limbs, speech —that are directed in their movement by the will. Since the act of commanding (*imperium*) is volitional, Scotus extended his line of thinking to conclude with a legislative theory. To make a law was to will.[52] The distinction was upheld even by a fifteenth-century Thomist like Reginald Pecock:

Mannys wil haþ ij maners of deedis, fforwhi he haþ inward priuey deedis whiche he may hide and kepe pryuey fro ech oþir man, as ben summe willyngis and nyllyngis, chesyngis and refusyngis . . .
And also mannys wil haþ outward deedis comaundid to be do bi þe same wil, as ben seyng, heeryng, spekyng, walkyng, smytyng. . . .[53]

This division of the will's acts goes back at least to the twelfth century when theologians tended to make a two-fold distinction slightly different from that of Duns Scotus: the effective will (*voluntas effectionis*) directed exterior human actions under the control of volition, and the affective will (*voluntas affectionis*) produced interior feelings of love and other emotional impulses.[54]

---

52. Bourke, *Will in Western Thought*, p. 176, citing Duns Scotus, *Ordinatio*, "Prologus," pars 5, q. 2 ("Quid Sit Praxis"), in *Opera Omnia* (Civitas Vaticana: Typis Polyglottis Vaticanis, 1950), vol. I, pp. 155–60: "praxis ad quam extenditur habitus practicus non est nisi actus voluntatis elicitus vel imperatus" (p. 156).

53. Reginald Pecock, *The Folewer to the Donet*, ed. Elsie Vaughan Hitchcock, 1924, EETS o.s. 164, pp. 126–27.

54. Bourke, *Will in Western Thought*, p. 133, with particular attention to Alanus de Insulis, *Regulae de Sacra Theologia*, lxxix (*PL* 210:661–62), and Simon de Tournai,

This attention to the affective side of the will retains a pure Augustinian principle often neglected by later commentators, rationalists and voluntarists alike. The highest form of love, of course, is the love of God, which nonetheless exists in various degrees of perfection depending on the will's ability to join mystically with the will of God. Psychological voluntarism in the fourteenth century, even when heavily cloaked by scholastic procedures, was fundamentally a Franciscan movement which had been provided with an important stimulus by the Cistercian Bernard of Clairvaux with his emphasis on the primacy of volitional experience in the soul's loving union with God.[55]

Despite his advocacy of *voluntas* as the prime agent in mystical devotion, Bernard placed limitations on the will's power to know God in the same way as the intellect could. Love was able to raise the will toward God, give it a certain resemblance to Him, and kindle in it a sentiment of God, but its affective experience was different from the cognitive processes of the intellect with its ability to assimilate an object known by its species.[56] During the thirteenth century, however, Franciscan thinkers like Bonaventure and Olivi began to remove Bernard's objections by asserting that the human will should not be distinguished from the general power of the soul that achieves its ultimate fulfilment in the mystical love of God.[57] Indeed, Bernard's own qualifications of the will's powers hardly seem to matter when we hear him speak with such lofty exuberance of its union with God's will at the height of contemplation:

Just as a little drop of water mixed with a lot of wine seems entirely to lose its own identity while it takes on the taste of wine and its color, . . . and just as air flooded with the light of the sun is transformed into the same splendor of light so that it appears not so much lighted up as to be light itself—so it will inevitably happen that, in the saints, every human affection will then, in some ineffable manner, melt away from self and be transfused into the will of God.[58]

This is the Bernardine rapture echoed in Dante's *Paradiso* and down through later mystical writings such as John Ruysbroeck's *Love's Gradatory*, where the contemplative at the height of ecstasy is described as someone who "thus acquires one and the same will with the Divine

Disputationes (51, 3), ed. Joseph Warichez (Louvain: Spicilegium Sacrum Lovaniense, 1932), pp. 149–50.

55. Etienne Gilson, *The Mystical Theology of Saint Bernard*, trans. A. H. C. Downes (London: Sheed and Ward, 1940), pp. 85–118.

56. *Ibid.*

57. Bourke, "Will" in *NCE*, p. 912.

58. Bernard of Clairvaux, *On the Necessity of Loving God* (X) in *The Wisdom of Catholicism*, ed. Anton C. Pegis (New York: Random House, 1949), p. 256.

Will, so that it is no longer possible or lawful to desire and will any-thing but that which God wills."[59] The consistency of the mystical lan-guage from Bernard of Clairvaux to John of the Cross makes it all the more remarkable that Langland offers a poem relying so frequently upon this tradition—its language, its visions, its intimations of mysti-cal transport—but never allowing for the protagonist Will to draw anywhere near an actual union with God.[60] Piers is the one rendered mystically coincident with Christ, while the Dreamer remains alien-ated as a distant observer even during the grandest visions in Passus XVIII.

If perfect union with God's will is the highest goal of the human soul, it is an experience impossible to write about, as Bernard says, and not the true stuff of poetry according to one modern authority.[61] Far easier to discuss and much more relevant to the good life in this world is the *opposite* experience, the isolation of man's will and its separation from the divine will. In his classic analysis, Augustine defines sin wholly in terms of some movement of the will:

. . . when it turns away from the changeless good, common to all, and turns towards a good of its own, or to an external or lower good, then the will sins. It turns toward a good of its own whenever it wants to be its own master. . . . Thus, a man who becomes proud, curious, and sensuous is delivered over to another kind of life which, in comparison with the higher life, is a death.[62]

This standard formulation was passed along through the centuries by Augustinian theologians, all allowing for the solipsistic turning of the will into a world of its own causes, designs, and ends.[63]

Even mystics were not blind to the worldly implications of such willfulness. One fourteenth-century writer (whether Richard Rolle or Walter Hilton is uncertain) devoted a treatise to the problem of the iso-lated or "propyr wille" that opposes all standards for conduct—God's will, the common will of the people, and the governing will of a ruler:

59. John Ruysbroeck, *Love's Gradatory*, trans. Mother St. Jerome (London: R & T Washbourne, 1915), p. 71. John of the Cross, *Dark Night of the Soul*, trans. E. Allison Peers, 3rd ed. rev. (New York: Doubleday, 1959), pp. 167–75 (II, xix–xx), elaborates the ten steps on the mystical ladder of divine love according to Bernard.

60. Elizabeth Salter, *Piers Plowman: An Introduction* (Oxford: Blackwell, 1962), pp. 58–62, attempts to compare Will's dreams to the visions of mystics like Bernard and Walter Hilton, but is forced to admit that his visions "are not identical with those high intimations of 'heavenly fairhead' made to the mystic."

61. Cyril Connolly recalls a remark made by Auden over dinner in New York in 1946: "Mysticism and fucking . . . are the two extremes where man forgets himself and art consequently can't be made;" see "Some Memories" in *W.H. Auden: A Tribute*, ed. Stephen Spender (New York: Macmillan, 1975), p. 73.

62. Augustine, *The Free Choice of the Will* (II, 19, 53), trans. Russell, p. 161.

63. See for example Anselm, *Cur Deus Homo?*, I, xi (*PL* 158:376–77).

"Goddis wylle, and alle gode mens wille, and principaly ouer alle thynge till our suffraynes wil to whame we ere suget made ry3t als vn-to God."[64] It was specifically this brand of willfulness that inspired the author of *Mum and the Sothsegger*:

> And ther-for I fondyd with all my fyue wyttis
> To traueile on þis tretis to teche men þer-after
> To be war of wylffulnesse, lest wondris arise.[65]

Langland's concern with this problem is voiced early in the poem in Lady Holy Church's sermon where scriptural citations and examples of contemporary social abuses are marshaled to emphasize that man must will the same as God wills. Just as the individual Christian must be guided by the teachings of the Church, kings and knights should execute the law within the limits imposed by God (B. i. 94–104). The central intent of Holy Church's lesson is aptly described by Edward Vasta: "God's will is the absolute rule of action, and to make one's own will one's law is to contradict, rather than to conform to, God's will."[66] The rationalist commentator John Quidort takes the problem one step further by asking what action would be possible if the unrestricted will (*voluntas absoluta*) were cut off from the other powers of the soul? He decided that the will, by itself, could do absolutely nothing.[67] We are, therefore, left to ponder the meaning of Langland's allegory with its multiplication of departure scenes. Will leaves behind Holy Church, then the King, then the people in the Half Acre, then even his own Wit. Is it any wonder that the action of the poem becomes so slow, at times almost static, after Will has retreated from Wit at the beginning of Passus X?

While the voluntarists accorded the will far greater power in carrying out independent actions, they also proposed other conditions when the will could be rendered inactive by its own choice. Duns Scotus had already set forth his "indifference theory," according to which the will was able to suspend judgment, but the eminent Paris philosopher John Buridan—best known for his starving donkey—initiated by far the most extensive analysis of the circumstances under which the will might decide *not* to decide.[68] Since the decision of the

---

64. "Propyr Wille" in *Yorkshire Writers*, vol. I, pp. 173–75.
65. *Mum and the Sothsegger*, p. 2 (Prol., 50–52).
66. Vasta, "Truth, the Best Treasure," p. 22.
67. Bourke, *Will in Western Thought*, pp. 35–36 and 48–49, n. 25, quotes John Quidort as saying that the isolated will "non poterit velle quia deest sibi principium actionis et volitionis."
68. Buridan, who died after 1358, exerted considerable influence in Paris and gained an international reputation within a few years after his death. A full account of his life

will to suspend its own operation can only be the result of volition, the will demonstrates the soul's absolute freedom to avoid all coercion from the outside. Dispensing with Scotus' terminology, Buridan introduced the notion of *libertas oppositionis*, meaning the liberty of the will to act in contrary ways, to move by itself to cause something, not to cause it, or to cause its opposite. The will required this freedom in order to sift through the mass of lesser goods and apparent goods that clutter a man's daily existence. Buridan believed that if an ultimate end were offered to the will in the form of universal good without any semblance of evil obscuring it, the will would automatically incline toward that alternative and assent. But Buridan was also wise enough to realize that life is not so simple. Good is laden with semblances of evil, evil masquerades as good, and some lesser goods obstruct man's grasp of the greater good. The power of *libertas oppositionis* was given to humankind to allow perfection in a world where nothing is immediately certain, through a process which later thinkers might call "methodical doubt" or "vital skepticism." It would be perilous, after all, to accept what appears *prima facie* to be good and reject what at first seems evil.[69] Liberty of opposition was granted to man so that, prior to accepting an object on the basis of appearances, he might make a thorough inquiry concerning the totality of its goodness and finally choose what is really the better.[70]

The impact this thinking might have had on *Piers Plowman* is clear. Buridan argues for the absolute moral necessity of skepticism, basing his defense on the will's need to suspend its operation until a clear judgment can be made. Thus it is possible to see the psychological allegory of the *Vita de Dowel* not as a rambling and purposeless section in which the poet flounders in search of his subject, but rather as a dramatization of Will's suspending of judgment and his weighing of every possibility until he knows *exactly* what Dowel means. It remains to be

---

and writings is offered by Edmond Faral, "Jean Buridan," *Histoire Littéraire de le France*, 38 (1949), 462–605, with more recent reviews of his career from James J. Walsh, "Nominalism and the *Ethics*: Some Remarks about Buridan's *Commentary*," *Journal of the History of Philosophy*, 4 (1966), 1–13; and T. K. Scott, Jr., "Nicholas of Autrecourt, Buridan, and Ockhamism," *Journal of the History of Philosophy*, 9 (1971), 15–41. The best account of his contribution to the voluntarist theory of the will is contained in Monahan's "Human Liberty and Free Will According to John Buridan," which draws generously upon Buridan's *Quaestiones in Aristotelis Ethica Nicomachea*

69. Monahan, pp. 73–74, quoting from the *Ethica*, III, 1, and p. 78, citing *Ethica*, III, 3. Oberman, "Some Notes on the Theology of Nominalism," 68–69, points out that the newly won freedom of the will gave man "the heavy responsibility of guarding against hallucinations."

70. The influence of Buridan's thought in England is suggested by Pecock's *The Folewer to the Donet*, pp. 85–87, with its defense of the will's need to suspend judgment.

decided, however, whether Will falls prey to habitual skepticism by accepting doubt as the final outcome of inquiry rather than the beginning of the long roadway toward Truth.

By choosing in this chapter to survey the history of will in medieval thought, I have intentionally avoided one of the toughest critical difficulties in *Piers Plowman*: the relation between Will the protagonist and William the poet. The amount of information I have offered concerning *voluntas* does not mean that I endorse the position of Robertson and Huppé, who hold that Will is simply a personification of the human will and comes off as "so appealingly human a character" because of the flexibility of the faculty he represents.[71] Nor do I side with those who propose a strictly biographical reading of the poem, for reasons explained more fully in Chapter VII. I believe that the truth lies somewhere in between. Will is meant to be seen as a human character—no reader has ever thought otherwise, certainly at the beginning of the poem—but when the action turns inward and the poet introduces psychological personifications like Reason, Wit, Conscience, Imaginatyf, and Anima, then to Will's character is added another dimension that relies upon what the poet and his audience understood about *voluntas*. This discussion has, therefore, had the central purpose of correcting the impression left by Robertson and Huppé that this theological understanding was clear, uncomplicated, and unanimous throughout the fourteenth century.

Having corrected that impression, I feel obliged to correct another which this chapter may have left—namely, that Will's conduct can be discussed clinically as the operation of *voluntas*, without eliciting moral judgment on the quality of that conduct. Those actions of Will that can be illuminated by recourse to voluntarist commentators take on a different light when judged as the behavior of a real man, a ragged cleric wandering in the Malvern Hills and later begging for his living in London. Although Buridan might defend the need for *voluntas* to suspend its decisions until a true good has been determined, a different judgment might be rendered upon a man named Will who postpones intellectual decisions, delays his affirmation of faith, and neglects good works until he can be absolutely sure what "Dowel" means. All these actions have as their source the will, but there was a special moral term that could be applied to a man's inaction, whether he is reluctant to work, unable to make choices, or slow to love. For Langland and his audience, that term was *acedia*.

71. Robertson and Huppé, p. 240.

III

The Ambiguity of *Acedia*

For a long time it has been the prevailing fashion among cultural historians to look upon the later Middle Ages as a period of stagnation when people endured the constant oppression of tedium and melancholy. Johan Huizinga did much to fix in people's minds this image of a time when immense sadness burdened men's souls and moans of pessimism were regularly heard from chroniclers and court poets alike.[1] Barbara Tuchman's best-seller subtitled *The Calamitous Fourteenth Century* has further popularized this view with chapter-headings such as "Born to Woe," "This Is the End of the World," "In a Dark Wood," and "Danse Macabre." Because extreme generalizations of this sort can never adequately describe the life of humankind in any age, other recent historians have restored some balance by asserting what readers of *The Canterbury Tales* have known all along—that fourteenth-century England was also distinguished for its energy, gaity, and zest for living.[2]

But just as an historian is often inclined by philosophy or personal temperament to view some past age in a distorted mirror, a poet almost always has prejudices that cause him to picture his world in ways neither comprehensive nor well-balanced. Melancholy lyrics such as "*Temps de doleur et de temptacion*" by Eustache Deschamps may not

1. Huizinga, *The Waning of the Middle Ages*, pp. 30–31. Reinhard Kuhn, *The Demon of Noontide: Ennui in Western Literature* (Princeton: Princeton University Press, 1976), p. 64, discusses the nineteenth-century view of the melancholic Middle Ages.

2. The cause of the revisionists has been ably served by F.R.H. Du Boulay, who responds convincingly to Huizinga in "The Myth of Decline," the opening chapter of his book *An Age of Ambition*. Maurice Keen has lodged a narrower complaint in his article "Huizinga, Kilgour and the Decline of Chivalry," *Medievalia et Humanistica*, n.s. 8, ed. Paul Maurice Clogan (Cambridge: The University Press, 1977), pp. 1–20.

accurately represent the spirit of the whole age as Huizinga claims,[3] but they do indicate that a considerable number of late medieval writers were able to look upon their societies with a somber eye and to speak movingly of the sorrow and decline they felt in the world around them. Melancholy, pessimism, ennui, monotony, boredom—all these are modern terms describing a complex psychological condition that usually went under one name in Langland's day—*acedia*, or in Middle English *slouthe*. Considering the large number of French lyrics cited by Huizinga as typical expressions of poetic melancholy, it would seem remarkable that sloth itself was almost never treated as a central theme in larger works of medieval literature.[4] In one sense we should not be surprised, since narrative poetry has to do with action, and sloth is by definition an absence of action. Only the author of a rare creation like *Hamlet* can construct the kind of paradoxical plot in which action centers upon inaction. Yet I believe that *Patience*, for instance, also represents a meticulous study of *acedia* insofar as the condition can be observed from outward symptoms like sleeping, flight from religious duties, irritable outbursts against authority, and cries of self-negating despair. The harder task was undertaken by Langland, who set about to expose slothfulness in *all* its aspects: in society at large, in the conduct of the individual, and in the life of the inner spirit.

There are three main reasons why the modern reader is not likely to take much notice of sloth in medieval literature or to sympathize with a writer's concerns when his subject was *acedia*. First of all, *acedia* was usually shrouded in a specialized terminology that owes much to monastic and mystical commentators. Next, the symptoms of the vice had become so standard that writers felt they had made their point by simply mentioning the symptoms without actually using the word *slouthe* outright. And finally, the complex notion, once so scrupulously expounded by theologians and even village parsons, has grown so narrow over the centuries that today it suggests little more than a tendency to procrastinate. In the fourteenth century, however, those who dealt with questions of morality faced the opposite problem. They had inherited a concept of *acedia* which was already sprawlingly large and which, moreover, was steadily accruing new meanings during their own age. The prime goal of this chapter is to examine that complex theological tradition whose categories and explanations did so much

3. Huizinga, pp. 31–35.
4. *Ibid.*, p. 32. Siegfried Wenzel, *The Sin of Sloth: Acedia in Medieval Thought and Literature* (Chapel Hill: University of North Carolina Press, 1967), p. 127, pauses to remark upon this surprising absence of more intensive poetic explorations of a spiritual state that was always regarded as a source of great annoyance in the didactic literature of the period.

to shape Langland's sense of worldly waste, religious decline, and personal anxiety by accommodating these disparate annoyances within a single moral construct.

Viewed in brief, sloth had been an eremitic and monastic vice that expressed itself in a host of spiritual symptoms—somnolence, boredom, nervousness, sorrow, despair—as well as the rarer complaint of spiritual dryness experienced by mystics after periods of intense contemplation. From the twelfth century onward, however, greater attention was paid to the physical aspects of sloth, such as laziness, sleeping too much, a reluctance to work, wasting of material goods, and even a man's refusal to serve his king. If medieval thinkers were stymied by the bewildering array of this sin's species, which included everything from mumbling prayers to draft-dodging, many commentators also admitted difficulty in explaining its causes. If sloth was a sin, then it must involve a perverse movement of the will and therefore stem from a volitional defect. But *acedia* was unique among the seven deadly sins because it could result from no movement of the will at all. That is, it could result from a volitional deficiency. For this reason, some analysts were inclined to consider sloth as a mere passion and not a sin, unless *voluntas* confirmed itself in the habit of that passion.

The word *acedia* is a linguistic alien to Latin no less than to English. It comes from the Greek ἀχηδία or ἀχήδεια, "lack of care," and was first used widely by desert fathers such as John Cassian (c. 360–433) who were concerned with the welfare of hermits.[5] Holy men who had fled to the desert in search of a more intense religious life found themselves plagued by the effects of continual solitude, heat, silence, and spiritual concentration. All too often they felt themselves under the attack of a foe they called the Noonday Demon, who made them weary, listless, and irritable.[6] Thus affected, a hermit grew unquiet in mind, dejected in spirit, and bored with his cell. He wanted to break his vows and roam about, visiting his fellow anchorites. The reader of Langland's C-text will take note that Will, dressed like a hermit, himself has been visiting "many [sellis]" (C. prol. 5).

John Cassian devotes an entire section of his treatise *De Institutis Coenobiorum* (c. 425) to the assaults made by the Noonday Demon

5. *Ibid.*, pp. 6–12.
6. The Noonday Demon is first mentioned in Psalm 90.5–6: "Scuto circumdabit te veritas eius; Non timebis a timore nocturno; A sagitta volante in die, A negotio perambulante in tenebris, Ab incursu, et *daemonio meridiano.*" This text is discussed by Wenzel, pp. 7 and 17. See also Roger Caillois, "Les Démons de midi," *Revue de l'Histoire des Religions*, 115 (1937), 142–73; 116 (1937), 54–83 and 143–86; and Rudolph Arbesmann, "The *Daemonium Meridianum* and Greek and Latin Patristic Exegesis," *Traditio*, 14 (1958), 17–31.

upon hermits who became weary and dejected at heart as a result.[7] As a certain cure, he prescribes physical work designed to keep the hands busy and the mind engaged.[8] There are many examples of hermits absorbed in manual labor for the sole purpose of escaping *acedia*, but none perhaps more compelling than the story of Paul the Hermit (mentioned by Langland, B. xv. 290–91), who spent his spare time weaving baskets, day after day, only to burn the surplus at the end of each year.[9]

Besides offering practical guides, Cassian probes the pathology of *acedia* as it was explained to him in a series of interviews with the most famous desert fathers. His *Conlationes Patrum* (c. 427) offers this enlarged catalogue of the vice's progeny: "laziness, sleepiness, rudeness, restlessness, wandering about, instability of mind and body, chattering, and inquisitiveness."[10] Besides connecting *acedia* with sadness and wrath, Cassian's most valuable contribution to later theology was the idea of a genetic concatenation of the major vices, with all the sins springing in a specific order from sloth. To eradicate all vices, a man must first destroy *acedia* and then proceed in set order to sorrow, wrath, and so forth until concluding with lechery.[11] Cassian's order of eight vices stemming from sloth, though it did not become standard during the Middle Ages, continued to assert influence among the monastic brothers who best understood the virulence of *acedia*.

Respectful as it was of Cassian's writings,[12] Benedictine monasticism

7. *A Select Library of Nicene and Post-Nicene Fathers*, gen. eds. Philip Schaff and Henry Wace, 2nd. ser., vol. XI, contains Cassian's *The Institutes*, trans. Edgar C. S. Gibson (New York: The Christian Literature Company, 1894), p. 266, rendering *De Institutis Coenobiorum* (X, i).

8. The necessity for manual labor is discussed at length in *De Institutis Coenobiorum*, X, 7–25, especially 17–18, where the authority of Paul the Apostle is brought to bear. Augustine, *De Opere Monachorum* (*PL* 40:547–82) also prescribes manual labor.

9. *De Institutis*, X, 24 (Gibson translation, pp. 274–75). For Langland's treatment, see Samuel B. Hemingway, "The Two St. Pauls," *MLN*, 32 (1917), 57–58.

10. Edgar Gibson, p. 347, translating John Cassian's *Conlationes XXIV*, ed. Michael Petschenig (Vienna: Corpus Scriptorum Ecclesiasticorum Latinorum, no. 13, 1886), V, 16: "de acedia [nascuntur] otiositas, somnolentia, inportunitas, inquietudo, peruagatio, instabilitas mentis et corporis, uerbositas, curiositas" (pp. 142–43). Continuing concern for the threat is discussed by Francis D.S. Darwin, *The English Mediaeval Recluse* (London: S.P.C.K., n.d.), pp. 22–23.

11. Wenzel, p. 21.

12. St. Benedict prescribed the reading of Cassian's two major treatises in the concluding chapter of his *Regula*, ed. Rudolphus Hanslik (Vienna: Corpus Scriptorum Ecclesiasticorum Latinorum, no. 75, 1960). English renderings are drawn from *St. Benedict's Rule for Monasteries*, trans. Leonard J. Doyle (Collegeville, MN: The Liturgical Press, 1948). The standard source for information about Cassian's life and influence is Owen Chadwick's *John Cassian*, 2nd. ed. (Cambridge: The University Press, 1968), where the digression on *acedia* is characterized as a separable "treatise on manual work

differed radically from the spiritual life of the Egyptian hermits—in organization, in practice, and even in response to the climate of the land—and these differences resulted in a considerable transformation of the coenobite's concern with sloth. Since all activities in a Benedictine institution were communal, the monk never had occasion to suffer the pains of solitude. Rather than the hermit's continual meditation, every minute of the monk's life was regulated by a series of varied activities that included liturgical worship, manual labor, and spiritual exercise. The climate in most European countries did not annoy the monk with the daily oppression of heat—except "in a somer seson whan softe was þe sonne" perhaps—and sleep was viewed by Benedict as a natural need of the body that should be satisfied (*Regula*, XXII). Benedict even permitted his monks to nap after lunch, at exactly the time when the Noonday Demon was known to strike.[13]

Boredom over the daily routine of the religious life, however, continued to be a real problem, so much so that Benedict devoted an entire chapter to the subject of daily labor, beginning with the famous apothegm "Idleness is the enemy of the soul."[14] He dictated that the whole waking day outside the performance of the Divine Office should be filled with manual labor and sacred readings. To avoid difficulty during the reading periods, he prescribed that one or two senior monks patrol the abbey so that "there be no lazy brother [*frater achediosus*] who spends his time in idleness or gossip and does not apply himself to the reading, so that he is not only unprofitable to himself but also distracts others."[15] Such brothers were given forms of physical work, even on Sundays.

As careful as Benedict was to prevent the problems of idleness and inattentiveness that had troubled the Egyptian fathers, *acedia* took on a new sense in European monastic communities where physical withdrawal from the world was completed by a more abstract kind of movement: the subjugation of the individual monk's will to the command of the abbot.[16] Absolute obedience to the head of a religious

---

in a monastery" (p. 46). See also Philip Rousseau, *Ascetic, Authority, and the Church in the Age of Jerome and Cassian* (Oxford: Oxford University Press, 1978). Cassian's prescriptions for the contemplative life remained a standard source for mystical and devotional writers even until the fifteenth century, as Wenzel notes, pp. 29 and 214, with special reference to Henry Suso, whose popularity in England is evidenced by William Caxton's translation of "*Orologium Sapientiae*, or The Seven Poyntes of Trewe Wisdom," ed. Karl Horstmann, *Anglia*, 10 (1888), 323–89.

13. Benedict, *Regula*, XLVIII. For further comment, see Vinzenz Stebler, "Die *Horae Competentes* des Benediktinischen Stundengebetes," *Studia Anselmiana*, 42 (1957), 17.

14. *Regula*, XLVIII, 1: "Otiositas inimica est animae."

15. *Ibid*, XLVIII; *Benedict's Rule*, trans. Doyle, p. 69.

16. Wenzel, p. 27.

house as Christ's representative was the fundamental principle of Benedictine monasticism, and its stern command stands boldly writ at the very beginning of the *Regula*: "Receive willingly and carry out efficiently your loving father's advice, that by the labor of obedience you may return to Him from whom you had departed by the sloth of disobedience."[17] This connection between the Fall and slothful negligence (*desidia*) repeats even more forcefully Cassian's conviction that sloth was the source of all other vices. Enshrined at the head of Benedict's *Regula*, this notion became an essential part of the monastic sensibility for the remainder of the Middle Ages.[18]

While the monastic aspects of *acedia* persisted throughout the medieval period, along with illustrative stories drawn from the lives of the desert fathers, a far broader concept of the vice resulted from the general movement toward a popular theology in accord with the Fourth Lateran Council of 1215. Christian society had found its lasting center in the village and the city, not the cloister.[19] Along with the simple necessity of worldly survival through work, there was a deepening religious belief that "man is born to labor" (Job 5.7). God had commanded Adam that "with labor and toil shalt thou eat [of the earth] all the days of thy life" (Gen. 3.17). Biblical passages of this sort were used to preach the lesson that work meant not merely some occupation to keep the body from idleness, but real labors to bring forth material as well as ghostly fruits. By the fourteenth century, the emergent work-ethic had become linked with the duties a man performed as part of his estate within society, a belief vigorously expressed in the following passage from a sermon delivered by Thomas Brinton, Bishop of Rochester (1373–89), a man Langland may have heard at St. Paul's Cross:

Since man is by nature born to work, the army of Christians, which chiefly consists of three degrees, namely of prelates, religious, and workers, must in

17. *Benedict's Rule*, trans. Doyle, p. 1; *Regula*, Prolog, 1: "Ut ad eum per oboedientiae laborem redeas, a quo per inoboedientiae desidiam recesseras." On the Middle English understanding of *desidia*, see *Three Middle-English Versions of The Rule of St. Benet*, ed. Ernst A. Kock, 1902, EETS o.s. 120: "þu mai turne a-gayne to hym by þe labur of obedience, fra whame þu had gane by þe *slewth* of inobedience" (p. 1).

18. An interesting example can be found in *The Dream of the Rood*, 122a–129a, where *langunghwila* has been identified with *acedia* by John V. Fleming in "*The Dream of the Rood* and Anglo-Saxon Monasticism," *Traditio*, 22 (1966), 63–64. Langland would undoubtedly have been familiar with the *Regula*'s cautions against sloth, as well as with Cassian's original writings, if he were a member of the order as suggested by Bloomfield, "Was William Langland a Benedictine Monk?". Caesarius of Heisterbach, *Dialogus Miraculorum*, vol I, pp. 197–98 and 202–06 (IV, xxviii, xxix, xxxiii–xxxviii) offers numerous stories about sleeping monks as dire examples against *acedia*.

19. Wenzel, p. 179.

hope of the kingdom of God be constantly occupied: either in the works of active life (which are the works of mercy, such as feeding the poor, clothing the naked, visiting the sick, and similar things), or in the works of contemplative life (which are praying, keeping vigil, preaching, hearing divine matters, etc.), or in the works of human servitude (such as digging, plowing, sowing, reaping, and working with one's own hands). In consequences, those miserable idlers [*miseri ociosi*] who are not usefully occupied in any of these three degrees and hence are unfruitful, deprive themselves by divine justice of the kingdom of God.[20]

While sloth retained its older meaning to Benedictine brethren, lay folk conceived of a far wider and more pragmatic definition informed by such works of popular devotion as *Handlyng Synne* and *Jacob's Well*. The neglect of religious duties was still preached against, but suddenly a host of worldly faults were crowded under the bold rubric of *acedia*: not keeping promises, not ruling a proper household, not caring for and correcting one's wife, not returning borrowed objects promptly, not paying wages on schedule, not serving one's master loyally, not learning a trade in youth, and not earning one's own daily bread.[21] Common economic problems of this sort, so far from the mind of the hermit in his cave, formed a major part of the new popular morality during the fourteenth century.

Almost paradoxically, the age of Langland also witnessed a great flowering of mysticism. Whether these mystics followed the Franciscan meditational mode or the *via negativa* taught by writings attributed to Dionysius the Areopagite,[22] they found themselves faced with some of the same psychological difficulties as the desert fathers. The vision eventually fades, the feeling of intimate union with God cannot last, and even the most accomplished mystic must descend from the mountain—and there the difficulty begins. Over and over again in the mystical literature of the Middle Ages from John Cassian to John of the Cross, we read of men and women experiencing severe lassitude or "spiritual dryness" (*ariditas spiritualis*) after the periods of contemplation that had given them such great ecstatic pleasure. The desperation of this feeling is effectively conveyed by Cassian:

---

20. *Ibid.*, pp. 91–92, translating from Thomas Brinton, *Sermons. 1373–1389*, ed. Mary Aquinas Devlin, 1954, Camden Third Series, nos. 85–86, *Sermo 20*, vol. I, p. 83. Owst, *Literature and Pulpit*, p. 577, believes that Langland owed a direct debt to Brinton for his "sentiment of the sanctity of productive labour" (p. 568).

21. Wenzel, p. 90.

22. For example, *The Cloud of Unknowing*, ed. Phyllis Hodgson, 1944, EETS o.s. 218, p. 125; and in the same volume, *The Book of Privy Counselling*, p. 154.

. . . for no reason we were suddenly filled with the utmost grief and weighed down with unreasonable depression, . . . so that while we were groaning and endeavouring to restore ourselves to our former disposition, our mind was unable to do this, and the more earnestly it sought to fix again its gaze upon God, so was it the more vehemently carried away to wandering thoughts by shifting aberrations, and so utterly deprived of all spiritual fruits as not to be capable of being roused from this deadly slumber even by the desire of the kingdom of heaven, or by the fear of hell held out to it.[23]

Although commentators vary in their classification of spiritual dryness —some treating it as identical with *acedia*, others claiming it as part of a passion that has only the potential to lead to slothfulness[24]—the mystic felt that the greatest peril lay in his inability to reach again toward God. The feeling of alienation from a divine essence which had been so closely approached, sensed, even tasted, left a contemplative like Walter Hilton feeling "as naked & as pore as a mon þat were robbed."[25]

Because the rigors of *ariditas spiritualis* could afflict the soul for extended periods of time—Teresa of Jesus complained that she suffered for as long as three weeks at a stretch[26]—mystics had ample opportunity to examine their problem, determine its causes, and search for some cure. The remedies that were often recommended included devout prayers, further meditation, and hard work (the hermit's *occupatio*).[27] But this regimen in no way insured that the feeling of emptiness would not return. Bernard of Clairvaux commented on the constant fluctuations in the spiritual life, how one moved "now more

23. Edgar Gibson, p. 331, translates Cassian's *Conlationes*, IV, ii (p 98). For a wider survey of the phenomenon among early mystics, see M. Lot-Borodine, "L'Aridité ou 'siccitas' dans l'antiquité chrétienne," *Etudes Carmélitaines Mystiques et Missionaires*, XXII, 2 (1937), 191–205. The subject is also treated in Evelyn Underhill's chapter "The Dark Night of the Soul" in *Mysticism: A Study in the Nature and Development of Man's Spiritual Consciousness* (London: Methuen, 1930), pp. 380–412.
    24. Wenzel, pp. 61–63, listing symptoms of spiritual dryness which are identical to *acedia*'s, from Bernard of Clairvaux, *Sermones Super Cantica Canticorum*, LIV, in *Opera*, ed. J. Leclercq, C. H. Talbot, and H. M. Rochais (Rome: Editiones Cistercienses, 1957), vol. II, pp. 107–08.
    25. Walter Hilton, *An Exposition of Qui Habitat and Bonum Est in English*, ed. Björn Wallner, *Lund Studies in English*, 23 (1954), p. 56.
    26. St. Teresa of Jesus, *The Life, Relations, Maxims and Foundations*, ed. John J. Burke (New York: The Columbus Press, 1911), p. 221.
    27. See, for example, Nicholas Love's early fifteenth-century translation of Pseudo-Bonaventura's *Meditationes* as *The Mirrour of the Blessed Lyf of Jesu Christ*, ed. Lawrence F. Powell (Oxford: The Clarendon Press, 1908), p. 78, where he writes about the man who has become "som tyme so drie in soule, and as voyde of deuocioun as he were forsake of god": "Wherefore be he not in despeire therby, bot besilich seche Jesu in holy meditaciouns and gode werkes, and specially in deuoute prayeres, and he schal fynde hym at the laste in dewe tyme."

sluggishly, now more joyfully,"[28] but perhaps the most poignant account of the phenomenon is offered by Julian of Norwich:

An after thys he shewde a sovereyne gostely lykynge in my soul. In thys lykyng I was fulfyllyde of the evyrlastyng suernesse, myghtely fastnyd withou3t any paynefulle drede. This felyng was so glad and so goostely that I was all in peese, in eese and in reste, that ther was nothyng in erth that shulde haue grevyd me.

This lastyd but a whyle, and I was turned and left to my selfe in hevynes and werynes of my life and irkenes of my self, that vnneth I could haue pacience to lyue. Ther was no comfort ne none eese to my felyng, but feyth, hope and cheryte; and these I had in truth but fulle lytylle in felyng. And anon after thys oure blessyd lorde 3aue me a3eane the comfort and the rest in soule, lykyng and suernesse so blyssydfully and so myghtely that no drede, ne sorow, ne no peyne bodely ne gostely that myght be sufferde shulde haue dyssesyde me. And than the payne sheweth ayeenn to my felyng, and than the joy and the lykyng, and now the oonn and now that other, dyuerse tymes, I suppose about twenty tymes. And in the tyme of joy I myght haue seyde with seynt Paule: "Nothyng shalle departe me fro the charyte of Crist;" and in the payne I myght haue seyd with seynt Peter: "Lorde, saue me, I peryssch."[29]

Since *voluntas* was the part of a mystic's soul credited with the power to experience God, fluctuations in spiritual strength were inevitably attributed to a "wayke will."[30]

Late medieval analyses made a careful distinction between spiritual dryness and *acedia* on the basis of a person's resistance: sloth if one failed to fight, dryness if the feeling persisted despite all efforts to shake it off. Typical is the distinction made by John of the Cross:

. . . there is a great difference between dryness and tepidity. Because the state of tepidity implies great negligence and slackness in will and mind, without willingness to serve God; but purgative dryness is accompanied by the usual willingness, with concern and sorrow (as I have said) that one does not serve God.[31]

But scholastic analyses of the thirteenth and fourteenth centuries had not achieved this degree of clarity, and for writers in Langland's day,

28. Bernard, *Sermones Super Cantica Canticorum* (XXI) in *Opera*, vol. I, pp. 124–25.

29. *A Book of Showings of the Anchoress Julian of Norwich*, ed. Edmund Colledge and James Walsh, 2 vols. (Toronto: Pontifical Institute of Mediaeval Studies, no. 35, 1978), vol. II, pp. 354–55.

30. See, for example, Richard Rolle, "The Two Ways of Christian Life" in *English Prose Treatises of Richard Rolle de Hampole*, xi, ed. George G. Perry, 1866–1921, EETS o.s. 20, p. 41.

31. *Noche Oscura* (I, ix) in *Vida y Obras de San Juan de la Cruz*, ed. Crisogono de Jesus, *et al.* (Madrid: Biblioteca de Autores Cristianos, 1964), pp. 553–56.

confusion over the will's involvement in the persistence of *ariditas spiritualis* is closely related to a continuing ambiguity concerning the causes of sloth. Was it the result of a defective will and therefore a sin of volition? Or was it an involuntary passion to which no moral blame could be attached?

Thomas Aquinas had confronted these problems in *Quaestio Disputata De Malo* (q. 11) and the *Summa Theologiae* (2a2ae, q. 35) where, in the process of harmonizing Cassian's catalogue of eight vices with Gregory's seven, he took up the vital question of whether sloth is a special vice, a mortal sin, or any sin at all.[32] Having inherited Aristotle's psychology with its elaboration of bodily and spiritual appetites, Aquinas was inclined to speak of sloth in terms of a passion not sinful in itself but dangerous only insofar as it could lead to an evil end (*ST*, 2a2ae, q. 35, art. 1). He defined it as *tristitia spiritualis boni*, with sorrow meaning "the negative reaction of man's sensitive appetite to an object which is either truly evil, or evil only in appearance but good in reality."[33] As in the debate over the will, we are again faced with the problem of judging appearances, whereby *acedia* is the sorrow of having judged wrongly.

While Aquinas spoke of sloth only in terms of an appetitive movement that involved judging, consenting, and feeling, later scholastics made allowance for slothful *tristitia* as a kind of passion independent of man's volition and resistant to it. Guillaume d'Auvergne points out that "this vice is sometimes increased and strengthened by the melancholy humor or vapor." Under these circumstances, there is less sinfulness attached to those melancholic symptoms which could otherwise be signs of sloth: *taedium cordis, timor, instabilitas loci, amaritudo animi*.[34] One thirteenth-century writer, for instance, says that sorrow results "sometimes from the abundance of melancholic humors, in which case it behooves the physician rather than the priest to prescribe a remedy."[35] The need to make the correct distinction, however, was

---

32. The relevant passage from *De Malo* is found in Thomas Aquinas, *Opera Omnia*, vol. VIII (1856), pp. 357–61. For Gregory's replacement of *acedia* with *tristitia* among the capital vices, see *Moralia in Job*, XXXI, xlv (*PL* 76:621).

33. Wenzel, p. 48.

34. *Ibid.*, p. 59, translating from Guillaume d'Auvergne, *Opera*, 2 vols. (Orléans and Paris, 1674), vol. I, p. 174 (*De Virtutibus*, 17), and Alexander of Hales, *Summa Theologica*, 4 vols. (Quaracchi: Collegium S. Bonaventurae, 1924–48), II–II, 566. The fear that mental sluggishness, with an organic cause, might prevent the divine illumination leading to truth is discussed by Steven P. Marrone, *William of Auvergne and Robert Grosseteste: New Ideas of Truth in the Early Thirteenth Century* (Princeton: Princeton University Press, 1983), p. 203.

35. Wenzel, p. 160, rendering David of Augsburg, *Formula Novitiorum* (51), ed. Marguerin de La Bigne, *Maxima Bibliotheca Veterum Patrum et Antiquorum Scrip-*

vital for a man who found himself infected with these symptoms. Should he summon the priest or the physician? A victim schooled only in religious lore might immediately suspect an attack of sloth, while a man trained in physic might realize that his suffering had little to do with external circumstances and his willingness to be happy. A man acquainted with both traditions, however, might linger in a state of indecision.

One of the most penetrating and original analyses from the medieval period is presented by neither priest nor physician, but by the poet Petrarch in his *Secretum* (1342–43), a treatise largely consisting of a dialogue between the author and St. Augustine.[36] The two interlocutors range over a number of topics until they reach a discourse on the seven deadly sins, in which Petrarch departs from the traditions of both Gregory and Cassian by placing *acedia* last and devoting more time to it than to any other vice.[37] Earlier in the dialogue, Augustine had proposed that no man could be unhappy against his will, but the author responded that the desire for happiness was sometimes too weak to overcome the distractions and the plague of phantasms that gripped his soul. Later, he speaks of that weakness in terms of a passion belonging specifically to *acedia*. Other vices might launch frequent assaults, but sloth was a "tenacious plague" that oppressed him for days and nights on end (pp. 83–87). Here we find the poet complaining, it seems, against the mystic's spiritual dryness. Petrarch benefited from the Thomist analysis insofar as he was willing to acknowledge that his sorrow was in part a *tristitia saeculi* caused by having to endure a world which was so corrupt and ugly. Life in a hectic city whose streets were clogged with noisy beggars and tradesmen, and fouled by roaming hogs and wild dogs, nauseated him with a weariness of the world (p. 97). What is remarkable about Petrarch's self-analysis, however, is that his *tristitia* had an ambivalence befitting an emotional response to a world that was corrupt, chaotic, and dung-smeared *but also* lovingly created by the hand of God. With bitter-sweeet disgust reminiscent of Langland's own hearty vehemence, Petrarch presents himself as a man

---

torum Ecclesiasticorum, 28 vols. (Lyons, 1677; Genoa, 1707), vol. XIII, p. 438. Raymond Klibansky, Erwin Panofsky and Fritz Saxl, *Saturn and Melancholy: Studies in the History of Natural Philosophy, Religion, and Art* (London: Thomas Nelson, 1964), pp. 300–304, examine the often overlapping relationships between melancholy and sloth.

36. *Petrarch's Secret, or The Soul's Conflict with Passion*, trans. William H. Draper (London: Chatto & Windus, 1911); page numbers in the text refer to this edition.

37. Wenzel, p. 156, forms part of a larger discussion (pp. 155–63) of Petrarch's original treatment of *acedia*, developing ideas already presented in his article "Petrarch's Accidia," *Studies in the Renaissance*, 8 (1961), pp. 36–48.

who took uncommon delight in the anguish he felt toward a contemptible world and traced these feelings to their psychological root. *Acedia* could also come as a bodily and spiritual inertia such as Petrarch mentions elsewhere in the *Secretum* (p. 118) and acknowledges more broadly in his later work *De Remediis Utriusque Fortunae*, completed in 1366:

> It also happens that this evil has absolutely no apparent cause, neither sickness nor plagues, nor injustice, nor dishonor. . . . it is like a voluptuousness in suffering that causes the soul to be sad, a malady all the more dangerous because its cause is so complex and difficult that it renders the cure equally so.[38]

Among other complaints, Petrarch regrets that this gratuitous assault ruins his powers of concentration, not for praying and meditating on the Passion of Christ, as would a mystic, but for *writing* history and poetry.[39] Despite Petrarch's care to distinguish the artist's feeling of emotional sterility from the spiritual dryness of a contemplative, the modern reader might reasonably suspect that the psychological experiences are basically the same. Like a mystic transported in an ecstasy of contemplation, the poet withdraws into a rapture of total concentration, closed up in the image-packed mansion of his own mind where hours are passed in the all-consuming process of thinking, creating, rewording, and bodying forth the forms of things unknown. When the pleasures of the creative frenzy are at an end, then comes the emotional let-down and the sense of aloneness. The poetical spirit has departed. Emotional lassitude follows.

Aside from Petrarch, medieval poets were not much inclined to complain publically about the debilitating side-effects of their trade,[40] perhaps because they were constantly defensive about the occupation itself—so often attacked by moral conservatives as frivolous, even evil—and were, therefore, reluctant to admit to more dangers than were generally recognized. Nonetheless, I believe that Langland was thoroughly acquainted with this occupational hazard, as he was with the ambivalent disgust over society's corruption, and in the concluding chapter of this book I shall speculate about his personal bouts with poetic *acedia*.

In brief, then, Langland's age had inherited the schoolmen's elabo-

---

38. Petrarch's treatise is quoted in translation by Kuhn, *Demon of Noontide*, p. 72.
39. Wenzel, p. 162.
40. *Ibid.*, p. 127, remarks of the Middle Ages that "one misses more intensive poetic explorations of a personal experience which, in its more 'interesting' spiritual aspects, must have been shared by a large number of lettered men and women capable of expressing themselves in verse and imagery."

rate concept complete with its bewildering sense of comprehensiveness. The first eremitic and monastic writers had viewed *acedia* primarily as a spiritual phenomenon involving laziness and somnolence, and their concept of the vice dominated moral thinking through the eleventh century. With the intellectual wakening of the twelfth century, spiritual writers placed even greater stress on internal phenomena such as mental slackness, boredom, tepidity, and disgust; that is, they began probing the full psychology of the vice, a task both encouraged and complicated by the gradual recovery of classical documents.[41] Alain de Lille pointed the way for future analyses when he identified *incircumspectio* as one of the species of this sin—"a vice of the mind through which one fails to discern the opposition between vices with sufficient caution."[42] By considering an error in judgment a part of *acedia*, Alain moved in the direction followed by later commentators who recognized sloth as a passion that impeded the processes of judgment as an activity increasingly attributed to *voluntas*. The thirteenth-century *Compendium Theologicae Veritatis* considers every sin as a disorientation of the will misguided by an internal good, an external good, or an inferior good.[43] When the disordered will flees from what it should embrace, the movement can be threefold according to the three divisions of the soul—rational, irascible, or concupiscible. If the will shrinks from some good because the impulse of the concupiscible part is defective, the result is *acedia*.

Aquinas developed a more satisfactory theory by recognizing that good and evil can be real, apparent, or mixed, and therefore despite the Thomist elevation of reason, his psychology of moral conduct consists of a grand confrontation of the will with the world of its objects. Although the *tristitia* resulting from the will's withdrawal from anything judged to be evil is fundamental to man's natural appetition, whether the object is real or imaginary, easy or hard to overcome, present or anticipated or remembered, Aquinas finally decided that the sorrow belonged particularly to *acedia*, a theological vice that he traced to the deepest roots of man's volitive and affective life.[44] His ultimate analysis comes in the *Summa Theologiae* (2a2ae, q. 35), of which Wenzel writes:

41. Siegfried Wenzel, "*Acedia*, 700–1200," *Traditio*, 22 (1966), 73–102.
42. Odon Lottin (ed.) "Le Traité d'Alain de Lille sur les Vertus, les Vices et les Dons du Saint-Esprit," *MS*, 12 (1950), 42: "Incircumspectio est animi uitium quo quis minus caute discernit contrarietatem uitiorum."
43. Hugh Ripelin of Strasbourg (d. 1268), *Compendium Theologicae Veritatis*, III, 6, in Albertus Magnus, *Opera Omnia*, ed. Auguste Borgnet, 38 vols. (Paris: Vivès, 1890–99), vol. XXXIV, p. 93.
44. Wenzel, pp. 45 and 55.

From this analysis the vice emerges as a disorder in man's affective life. At the root of *acedia* lies, not physical exhaustion or a weakening of man's will or intellectual darkness, but a disorientation of his affect or, as we would say today, his emotional life. . . . For medieval Christianity *affectus* is, of course, not a matter of sentiment and "feeling" but of will and love resulting in "good works."[45]

The connection between love and will is strictly Augustinian, since will is nothing other than the soul in the act of loving, so that *acedia* as an affective disorder results in the slowness of all three—willing, loving, and acting.

Bertrand Russell is surely correct when he says that "one of the essentials of boredom consists in the contrast between present circumstances and some other more agreeable circumstances which force themselves irresistibly upon the imagination."[46] Centuries earlier Epictetus had spoken of the sorrow arising from the disparity between what a man intends and what he achieves, and this disparity was put in terms of volition: "I want something, and it does not happen; and what creature is more wretched than I?"[47] Medieval writers understood this phenomenon too, since they wrote that slothful sorrow arises when one's desire for some object has been delayed or frustrated.[48] What, then, was the grandest object of man's desire, the most agreeable circumstance that a fourteenth-century Christian's mind might imagine, but his will not possess quickly enough?

The perfect joy of heaven was surely the chief expectation of all believers. In her discussion of Duns Scotus' voluntarism, Hannah Arendt has suggested that even the notion of "eternal peace" or perfect rest itself arises out of man's experience of restless anxiety as the "desires and appetites of a needy being that can transcend them in mental activities without ever being capable of escaping them altogether."[49] In addition to a transcendent realm where the will is united endlessly with God, as opposed to the periodic ecstasies which mystics enjoyed, the coming of a thousand-year kingdom on earth ruled by Christ and inhabited by His martyrs was promised by the Bible (Rev. 20.4–6). Yet

45. *Ibid.*, pp. 64–65.

46. Bertrand Russell, "Boredom and Excitement" in *The Conquest of Happiness* (1930; rpt., London: Unwin, 1975), p. 44.

47. Epictetus, *The Discourses* (II, xvii, 18), trans. W. A. Oldfather, 2 vols. (New York: Loeb Classical Library, 1926–28), vol. I, pp. 342–43.

48. See, for example, David of Augsburg, *Formula Novitiorum*, 51; Henry of Balnea, *Speculum Spiritualium*, I, xvi (Paris, 1510), fol. xiii^r; Denis le Chartreux, *Summa de Vitiis et Virtutibus* (I, 60) in *Opera Omnia*, vol. 39 (1910), p. 115 (Wenzel, p. 246, n. 65).

49. Arendt, *Willing*, p. 144.

millenarians had been expecting the Kingdom for so long that they began to see instead only the prolonged destruction of the Antichrist at work, as at the end of *Piers Plowman*.[50] Others may have tried to believe that they were already living in the Kingdom ordained by Christ at the end of his ministry and presided over by the Church, although they found little in the way of perfection in the daily workings of that grand conception.

Writing of the pervasive pessimism sensed everywhere at the close of the Middle Ages, Huizinga speaks of the despair of men who surveyed the colossal wreck of society: "Institutions in general are considered as good or as bad as they can be; having been ordained by God, they are intrinsically good, only the sins of men pervert them."[51] In such a world where there is no hope of improvement or progress, however slow, those whose imaginations could not stop envisaging a better order of things inevitably faced a gulf. Confronted by crushing realities before his eyes—paradise lost through sin, paradise not yet regained, and the willful perversion of so many divinely willed institutions—the idealist could not be blamed if he complained, inveighed, and sometimes despaired, though always going on, never learning to be patient with the imperfect, never learning to remain silent.

This is not the place to speak in detail about the ways in which *Piers Plowman* responds to the complex tradition of *acedia*, but I think Donald Howard's intuitions are correct when he speaks of Langland's moral reaction to contemporary social problems:

One who wandered in the world of fourteenth-century England, that time of plague, famine, and depopulation, would have been bound to think about economic questions, and a man of theological inclinations would see those questions in terms of human need and human avarice, labor and sloth.[52]

Howard is not the first to notice Langland's special attention to this vice. Commenting on the revision from the A- to the B-text, Nevill Coghill feels an ominous strengthening of *acedia*'s role, particularly in the Confession Scene where Sloth "is greatly expanded by many dark details of contemporary abuse."[53] The sorts of abuses noticed by Cog-

50. Norman Cohn, *The Pursuit of the Millennium*, rev. ed. (New York: Harper and Row, 1961), pp. 13–21, discusses the disillusion when "signs" of the *eschata* were not promptly followed by the Coming of the Kingdom.

51. From Huizinga's chapter "Pessimism and the Ideal of the Sublime Life" in *Waning of the Middle Ages*, p. 36.

52. Howard, *The Three Temptations*, p. 166. Critics such as Murtaugh, *The Image of God*, are thus slightly misleading when they focus solely on *cupiditas* as the great obstacle to society's reformation.

53. Nevill Coghill, "The Pardon of Piers Plowman," *Proceedings of the British Academy*, 30 (1946), 331.

hill—false beggars, wandering clergymen, lax parents—are not things a twentieth-century reader might immediately associate with sloth. Nor would a monastic reader of the twelfth century. But for Langland and other moral thinkers of his day, *slouthe* was exactly the right word. In his valuable treatment of *Piers Plowman*, Siegfried Wenzel focuses on the poet's departures from the popular tradition of confessional manuals and handbooks for preachers, devoting more than half of his discussion to the curious figure Robert the Robber, who follows Sloth in the Confession Scene of the B-text. Wenzel concentrates on Langland's personifications because he otherwise distrusts the poet's grasp of the more complex theories about the vice.[54] While it is true that Langland shuns the neat categories of Thomist thought, in doing so he allows himself greater freedom in examining a single subject in preference to others. Since the inspection of individual types was paramount to Langland, the bold general rubrics that are always so clearly writ by Dante are obscured in *Piers Plowman*. But what Langland loses in formal proportioning, he gains in the artistry of a poet who comes close to fusing his form with his content. Though far from unlearned, Langland recognizes the profound inadequacy of a theoretical synthesis forged by scholastic reason to explain a complex volitional or affective state that he knew from keen observation as well as from personal experience. Thus he brings to his poem the unwieldiness, honestly registered, of a concept that Thomists had tried to argue into orderliness.

Langland placed sloth in the forefront of his concerns from the very beginning, satirizing social and political corruption with the same eye for individual instances as the author of *Wynnere and Wastour*, whereas the need to deal forthrightly with human will arose only after the poem became more psychological and subjective owing to the realization that *acedia*, though visible throughout society, had its roots in the interior life of the spirit. To get at these roots—to feel out the causes and search about for relief—meant turning inward. One of Langland's chief artistic difficulties came in examining sloth as a social sin involving laziness and wastage *and* as a personal sin stemming from spiritual idleness and a deficiency of *caritas*. Whereas a theologian like Grosseteste could designate these two broad divisions,[55]

<hr />

54. Wenzel, p. 135. The full discussion spans pp. 135–47.
55. *Ibid.*, p. 173, notes that scholastic theologians of the thirteenth century typically divided *acedia* into two different aspects —idleness of the body and laziness of a sorrowing soul—and this division is perfectly expressed by Robert Grosseteste in *Templum Domini*, MS. B.M. Burney 356, fol. 25ʳ.

the poet felt the need to relate them and integrate them into his work's structure.

Since the A-text apparently circulated for some years in an unfinished form, we might reasonably infer that Langland had a hard time settling his difficulty and perhaps even recognizing the scope of that difficulty. In the end the problem was to some extent solved—though some would question the aesthetic effectiveness of the solution —by dividing the poem into the *Visio* and the *Vitae* sections. In the first, Will looks upon the social and political corruption of his day; and in the second, his attentions are turned in upon himself, including that part of his mental self given to curiosity, rambling arguments, and irascible disputes. Another part of the solution was to punctuate the dream with various waking episodes in which Will is given the opportunity to enact good works according to his ghostly instruction, or possibly to show all the outward signs of physical sloth.

Wenzel's focus upon Langland's response to the "popular image" of the vice nonetheless deserves our careful regard, because the poet made generous allowance for the homiletic tradition familiar to his audience. Yet while Langland uses catalogues of the capital vices several times, he handles them in ways his audience would not have expected. In the chapter that follows, I shall examine anew the various personifications of Sloth to show how the many alterations of traditional materials, even without reference to the rest of the poem, make clear Langland's special interest in this single vice.

IV

Sloth Personified and Transformed

Langland offers his most detailed examinations of *acedia* in the five catalogues of deadly sins that occur periodically from Passus II to the last passus of the poem. Although these sections rely heavily on homiletic traditions contributing to what Wenzel calls the "popular image" of the sin found in devotional handbooks and didactic poems, they never grant the easy security of *topoi* borrowed without alteration from familiar sources. Langland is never simply derivative. His method here is like that at work elsewhere in that he awakens his audience's expectations, then fails to fulfill them, always with the effect of sharpening our critical senses and forcing us to search for motives. And the answer in this case almost invariably comes to bear upon the figure of Sloth.

The cardinal sins developed early in the history of the Church and came down to the Middle Ages in two principal sequences, one set forth by Gregory the Great and the other by John Cassian. The Gregorian ordering eventually became standard: pride followed by wrath, envy, avarice, sloth, gluttony, and lechery.[1] After the Fourth Lateran Council of 1215 when the Church placed heavier emphasis upon the moral instruction of the lay populace, greater interest was taken in the seven sins by priests whose duty it was to warn their congregations. In

1. Morton W. Bloomfield, *The Seven Deadly Sins: An Introduction to the History of a Religious Concept, with Special Reference to Medieval English Literature* (East Lansing: Michigan State College Press, 1952), pp. 69–80, discusses the development of the two major sequences, each with its own fixed order: Cassian's eight (*gula, luxuria, avaritia, ira, tristitia, acedia, cenodoxia,* and *superbia*) and Gregory's seven (*superbia, ira, invidia, avaritia, tristitia, gula,* and *luxuria*). He goes on to explain the predominance of the Gregorian arrangement and its acceptance by influential theologians and popular writers, pp. 105–21.

order to resist a sin, a man must first know its nature.[2] Tracts on the art of preaching laid stress upon the use of clear schemata and striking images in order to make moral lessons more tangible to a listening audience and more memorable for listeners and readers alike. Thus the fixed catalogue of sins, already long honored among clerical orders, lent itself admirably to the needs of the pulpit.

As understanding of the sins increased and the number of sub-vices grew, a useful mnemonic image was discovered—the allegorical tree-diagram—that served as an organizational scheme and a clearly defined visual image.[3] Yet while the tree-diagram was useful in codifying the deadly sins, it had the critical limitation of preventing any differentiation of one sin from another. The branches of sin were identical as visual images.

To fill the demand for distinct and easily remembered images, homiletic writers widened the practice of rendering the sins in personification. As Owst puts it, "the Vices themselves now strutted upon the scene as well-known types and characters of the tavern or the marketplace." On the most elementary level one finds seven static tableaux, each presenting an isolated sin in the form of a person prone to it. Wrath tears at his clothes, Sloth lies asleep on the ground, and so forth. This sort of presentation was made more dynamic by parading the sins in a procession (*processus vitiorum*) such as one finds in Dunbar's "Dance of the Sevin Deidly Synnis."[4] Next in degree of

2. For a discussion of the effects which the edicts of the Fourth Lateran Council had upon homiletic writing and thence upon popular literature, see D. W. Robertson, Jr., *A Preface to Chaucer: Studies in Medieval Perspectives* (Princeton: Princeton University Press, 1962), pp. 173 ff.

3. In *The Parson's Tale*, for example, Chaucer lays out the tree of sin with its seven major *braunches* and various *twigges* growing from each branch. For further examination of the tree-diagram, see Bloomfield, *Seven Deadly Sins*, pp. 24 and 70–89 *passim*; also, Rosemond Tuve, "Notes on the Virtues and Vices," *JWCI*, 26 (1963), 264–303, and 27 (1964), 42–72, with special attention to Part II, pp. 59–60, n. 93. Yates, *The Art of Memory*, pp. 184–86, discusses occurrences of the tree-diagram in the Renaissance and, earlier, in the writings of Ramon Lull (c. 1235–1315).

4. William Dunbar, *Poems*, ed. W. Mackay Mackenzie (1932; rpt. London: Faber and Faber, 1970), pp. 120–23. Owst, *Literature and Pulpit*, p. 87. For a history of such personifications during the early Middle Ages, see Adolf Katzenellenbogen, *Allegories of the Virtues and Vices in Mediaeval Art from Early Christian Times to the Thirteenth Century* (London: Warburg Institute, 1939). See also Bloomfield, *Seven Deadly Sins*, pp. 100–04, for the iconographic development of the sins. Frances Yates traces the theory of theological imagery in the writings of Albertus Magnus and Thomas Aquinas as well as in the preaching tracts of the friars (pp. 82 ff.). She suggests that strongly visual personifications of the vices developed as memory images in accordance with these psychological doctrines (pp. 92 ff.). Smalley, *Friars and Antiquity*, pp. 165–83, examines the use of verbal "pictures" such as Holcot's picture of *Pigritia* (p. 174). Verbal representation of vice also had an importance to secular writers. As an example of *notatio*, Geoffrey of Vinsauf gives a lengthy description of a slothful man with all the attributes of

complexity comes the confession of the seven vices found in *Cursor Mundi*,⁵ for example, or in the much more sophisticated fashion in Dante's *Purgatorio*. On what might be called the highest level of medieval development, writers began to allow for the dramatic participation of personified sins in the larger moral universe where they engaged with virtues, demons, angels, and men.

These three levels of discrimination—in no way meant to represent a line of chronological development—are important to us because Langland employs all of them in different sections of *Piers Plowman* and, in the process, moves roughly from the lowest to the highest degree of complexity. The ways in which he treats the sins will be discussed in the following pages: how he arranges the order of their appearance, how he focuses on certain vices to the exclusion of others, and how he ends each catalogue and moves into the next scene of action. Two general impressions emerge. The Sloth-figures are always the most prominent in each catalogue, and their attributes are often shared by Will the Dreamer. Elizabeth Kirk has suggested that the Dreamer's parasitic existence is projected into these figures so that the emphasis on this single sin becomes organic to the view of man's corruption and society's degeneration.⁶

The first catalogue of sins is cleverly woven into Lady Mede's marriage contract. Signers of the document become "princes in pride" and owners of certain allegorical lands: the Earldom of Envy and Ire, the County of Covetise, and the Lordship of Lechery (B. ii. 79–92). Langland then moves almost imperceptibly into a true personification of Gluttony, portrayed at first with details appropriate only to that sin (B. ii. 93–96). Yet as Gluttony materializes into a more concrete figure, he begins to assume within his character aspects of the final sin in the sequence:

And þanne to sitten and soupen til sleep hem assaile
And breden as Burgh swyn, and bedden hem esily
Til Sleuþe and sleep sliken hise sydes;
And þanne wanhope to awaken hym so *wiþ no wil to amende*,
For he leueþ be lost, þis is his laste ende.

(B. ii. 97–101; emphasis mine)

The next clause of the charter guarantees the pains of Hell to all those who follow this line of degeneration from pride to deadly sloth. The

---

Sloth personified; see *Poetria Nova*, trans. Margaret F. Nims (Toronto: The Pontifical Institute of Medieval Studies, 1967), pp. 65–66.

5. *Cursor Mundi*, ed. Richard Morris, 1874–93, EETS o.s. 57, 59, 62, 66, 68, 99, 101, vol. III, pp. 1552–59.

6. *The Dream Thought of "Piers Plowman"*, p. 59.

most dangerous of all vices is targeted as wanhope, or despair "wiþ no wil to amende," which belongs to *acedia*.

As in the other catalogues of sins in *Piers Plowman*, sloth is placed last, in the same prominent position given it in the late Ostiensic list to which Langland apparently owes nothing.[7] Indeed, he has consistently avoided all the standard orderings, even altering his own arrangement from one catalogue to the next. He allows for only two constants: the initial placement of pride, and the last position for sloth. Augustine had spoken of *superbia* and *desidia* as the extremes between which men must find a moderate path, but that model does not seem to have lent itself to this situation.[8] Nor does it conform to the order in the *Secretum* of Petrarch, although he had also departed from the major traditions in placing *acedia* last in his discussion of the vices. I suspect that the Italian author and Langland broke with common practice for much the same reason. They wished to arrange the vices in an order that made sense in terms of their personal experience, and therefore *acedia*'s placement last in each case signifies its special threat.

The conjunction of gluttony and sloth reflects in part their frequent classification as corporal sins,[9] but this does not fully explain why Langland so often shows the gluttonous man sliding into a state of sloth. In each case Gluttony is characterized most vividly by drunkenness, and no learned treatises are necessary to explain that bored men often turn to liquor, and the more they drink, the more melancholy they become. Later in the Confession Scene, drunken Gluttony again descends to the state of *acedia*:

> Wiþ al þe wo of þe world his wif and his wenche
> Baren hym to his bed and brou3te hym þerInne,
> And after al þis excesse he hadde an Accidie
> That he sleep Saterday and Sonday til sonne yede to rest.
>
> (B. v. 357–60)

On the other hand, wanhope or "despeir of the mercy of God" (*ParsT*, 692) can beset any sinner who relents in his hope of salvation and is placed upon the same suicidal course as Judas. Avarice becomes such a figure in the sequence of the Confession when he refuses to make restitution and is denied a pardon (B. v. 279–80). Already special emphasis is given to *acedia* as the vice which is placed last in every cata-

---

7. For some discussion of the Ostiensic arrangement, see Bloomfield, *Seven Deadly Sins*, pp. 105–06.

8. Augustine, *Epistola*, 48, 2 (PL 33 : 188): "inter apicem superbiae et voraginem desidiae iter nostrum temperare debemus."

9. Wenzel, p. 88, with special mention of *Piers*, pp. 142–43.

logue and whose branches extend across traditional boundaries to affect the portrayal of other vice-figures.

The Confession of the Seven Deadly Sins (B. v.) is perhaps the most engaging and memorable section of the *Visio*. Langland parades before us the vices vividly drawn and enlivened with many colorful details of current abuse, each personified in the form of a man completely given over to it. Here as elsewhere in the poem, Pride leads the procession and Sloth brings up the rear, occupying the privileged final position.

Although one might assume that placement in the first or last position would lend almost equal force, Sloth emerges as the far more impressive character. Langland devotes uneven amounts of space and detail to the vices. Whereas Sloth's confession extends over 75 lines in the B-text (v. 385–460), Pride is allotted only nine lines, Lechery a disappointing four. The C-poet restores some balance by expanding the description of Pride to 47 lines, though Lechery's portrait is increased to only 26, and Sloth's confession occupies an enlarged 119 lines. Sloth is made even more prominent in the C-text, where his confession is segregated from the others and placed first in the next passus (vii. 1–119). Since in all texts Sloth is the last vice whose image the audience is invited to evoke visually in their minds and the last whose verbal confession we are made to attend, his example is most clearly retained in the memory.[10] Thus, it becomes most immediately useful in judging the next section of the allegorical action—the confused wanderings of the Pilgrims.

The unequal lengths of the seven confessions raise a question worth addressing before we turn to Sloth himself. Why has Langland almost completely neglected Lechery? The answer may involve the vice's venial nature, since Lady Mede is theologically correct when she claims that "it is synne of þe seuene sonnest relessed" (B. iii. 58). But I suspect that the abbreviation of *luxuria* is directly related to the enlargement of *acedia*. Rabanus Maurus, for example, had written that the slothful man grows dull in his carnal desires,[11] and this lack of lust is confirmed

---

10. The motives and mechanics of revision in this passage are also discussed by George H. Russell, "Poet as Reviser: the Metamorphosis of the Seven Deadly Sins in *Piers Plowman*" in *Acts of Interpretation*, ed. Carruthers and Kirk, pp. 53–65. Rhetorical handbooks like the popular *Ad Herennium* (III, x, 18) taught a lesson familiar enough in most people's experience, that what is said last is remembered best: "quoniam nuperrime dictum facile memoriae mandatur, utile est"; in *Rhetorica ad Herennium*, ed. Harry Caplan (Cambridge, MA: Loeb Classical Library, 1954), pp. 188–89. On the influence of this work during the medieval period, see Yates, *Art of Memory*, pp. 20–41 and 63–92.

11. Rabanus Maurus, *De Ecclesiastica Disciplina*, III: "otiosus homo torpescit in desideriis carnalibus" (*PL* 112:1252).

by Sloth when he admits "I am noȝt lured wiþ loue" (B. v. 432). If the pervasiveness of sloth in *Piers Plowman* means the near exclusion of lechery—as Chaucer's favorite vice seldom looms large in Langland's moral cosmos—then deficiency of love in even its lowest form can explain a lot about Sloth, about Will, and about the poem at large.

Bernard of Clairvaux had defended carnal lust as the first degree in man's ascent to higher forms of love, since this passion guaranteed that at least a man would love himself for himself.[12] Only a man lacking this primal lust for self-gratification could fall to such a depth of lovelessness that he could seek his own death through despair. Augustine believed that concupiscence moved the will to choose evil,[13] but if Will the Dreamer is little concerned with lust, this may partially explain why he does not commit more flagrant sins—envy, simony, theft— while still not moving up Bernard's ladder toward higher forms of love. And finally, there is the effect which a lack of love would have upon the poem in general. From Augustine onward, it was understood that love (or desire) resulted when the soul, dominated by the action of the will, engaged in a violent meditation upon some image gathered by the senses from an exterior bodily form.[14] If the force of love is indeed lacking in the psychology mirrored in the poem, whether it be Langland's own psychology or the emotional make-up of the Dreamer he creates, then this could help to account for the sparsity and general instability of imagery throughout the text. A mind lacking the all-binding power of love cannot keep a firm hold on images.

The Confession of Sloth (B. v. 385–460) is the most comprehensive examination of *acedia*'s popular image in any single part of *Piers Plowman*. Langland assembles the standard traits of behavior, physical characteristics, and spiritual shortcomings appropriate to the sin, but without any rigid fidelity to the traditions he draws upon. Sloth enters "al bislabered wiþ two slymy eiȝen," and before he can begin, he must have a place to sit down, whereupon he quickly falls asleep. Repentance then awakens him and sets him to confession. Sloth's shrift runs the full gamut of abuses, those traditionally outlined in monastic handbooks and those cited in current tracts interested in social corruption. It results in a complete portrait of *homo accidiosus*, but one hard to visualize because of the amount of contradictory information.

---

12. Bernard, *De Diligendo Deo*, viii, 23–25 (*PL* 182:987–89).

13. Augustine, *Grace and Free Will*, trans. Russell, p. 259.

14. Augustine, *De Trinitate*, XI, iii, 5 (*PL* 42:975–76). The secular authority favored by modern scholars is Andreas Capellanus, who describes the process in *De Amore*, ed. E. Trojel (Copenhagen: Libraria Gadiana, 1892), p. 3: "Amor est passio quaedam innata procedens ex visione et immoderata cogitatione formae alterius sexus."

Sloth begins by divulging a series of spiritual flaws related to the neglect of religious duties or their forfeiture through improper exercise (B. v. 393–414). He has made forty vows but always forgotten them by the next morning.[15] He is able to repeat idle rhymes about Robin Hood but cannot recite the Pater Noster. He is "occupied eche day, halyday and ooþer, / Wiþ ydel tales at þe ale and ouþerwhile in chirches" (B. v. 402–03).[16] Seldom does he think upon Christ's Passion, and when he does kneel with his prayer-beads, his mind wanders constantly from the sounds that he mutters.[17] The words merely rise from the memory without the assertion of will necessary for their validation. He has not attended confession and has not shriven himself annually as required.[18] He has performed no penance for his sins and, what is worse, has not even experienced the contrition necessary to bring a man to forgiveness.

These omissions relating to the sacrament of penance represent serious faults belonging specifically to *acedia*, but they also imperil the unshriven man who may still be stained by the remaining six sins. Thus, couched among so many other abuses here, the feature of *acedia* that will achieve overwhelming prominence at the poem's end is the lack of contrition, the emotion necessary to begin the rite of confession and the cleansing of sin.

After this survey of Sloth's spiritual neglects, Langland examines the range of his physical symptoms, which center rather interestingly upon wastage and other social abuses not included in the treatises of previous centuries (B. v. 422–40). The subject of idleness is passed over in silence, although Sloth's inclination to sleep (not mentioned outright in the confession) is demonstrated at least once when he falls asleep upon entering, and perhaps again when he swoons after a sharp warning from Repentance (v. 441). The sub-vices which Langland enumerates are remarkably similar to the transgressions against Dowel that he criticizes throughout the *Visio*. Sloth begs and borrows from others

15. For a typical instance of forgetfulness ascribed to sloth, see *Jacob's Well: An English Treatise on the Cleansing of Man's Conscience*, ed. Arthur Brandeis, 1900, EETS o.s. 115, p. 109 ("De Accidia").

16. Compare this with the following admonition against *acedia*, *Ibid.*, p. 103: "þou omittyst & leuyst þi prayerys vnsayd, & lettyst oþere of here prayerys, & fro þe heryng of goddys woord, & fro dyvyn seruyse; . . . þou ȝevyst þe noȝt to lere þi pater noster, aue maria, & þe Crede, ne þe articles of þi feyth, ne þe x. comaundementys."

17. *Ibid.*, p. 104: "þou has noȝt full herd & seyd dyuyne seruyse, but parcellys þerof; þou hast noȝt dewly preyid for þe qwyke & for þe dede, ne dewly thankyd þi god for his gyftes."

18. See *The Book of Vices and Virtues: A Fourteenth Century English Translation of the "Somme le Roi" of Lorens d'Orléans*, ed. W. Nelson Francis, 1942, EETS o.s. 217, p. 28.

only to forget immediately the debt, neglecting then to pay his servants. During his youth he had failed to learn any form of employment and has been a beggar ever since. This statement explicitly links the lazy beggars of the Fair Field with the sin of sloth, just as the following passage places wasters and gluttons in the same group:

> [I, Sloth, have] yspilt many a tyme
> Boþe flessh and fissh and manye oþere vitailles;
> Boþe bred and ale, buttre, melk and chese
> Forsleuþed in my seruice til it my3te serue no man.

(B. v. 435–38)

In the midst of Sloth's confession, between the opening list of spiritual faults and the concluding social offenses, Langland inserts a brief passage exploring another traditional aspect of the sin, a passage that alters in radical ways our visual image of the figure he had invoked at first. Sloth, who had begun by describing himself as a layman, suddenly becomes a cleric:

> I haue be preest and person passynge þritty wynter,
> Yet kan I neyþer solue ne synge ne seintes lyues rede;
> But I kan fynden in a feld or in a furlang an hare,
> Bettre þan in *Beatus vir* or in *Beati omnes*
> Construe clausemele and kenne it to my parisshens.

(B. v. 415–19)

Acedia began its theological life as an exclusively clerical vice, a sin of hermits and monks, and while it never wholly lost this aspect of its nature, Langland focuses upon the particular neglect of a priest for the well-being of his congregation.[19] Later Anima is precise about the cause of such a priest's carelessness, accusing him of performing the service "with ydel wille" (B. xv. 127).

Nor should one fail to register the irony involved here in Sloth's ad-

---

19. In *Cursor Mundi*, vol. III, p. 1556 (ll. 28360–67), Sloth is depicted as a clergyman and makes a similar admission of wrong-doing:

> And i, prest, funden vte of distresse
> In dedly sin has sungen messe,
> Or haue i sungen in cursing
> Or help oþer men to sing,
> In dedly sin I tok vnscriuen,
> Myn orders sua war þai me giuen,
> And did min office na-þe-lese
> þat vn-despensed sang i messe.

Middle English Sermons, ed. Woodburn O. Ross, 1940, EETS o.s. 209, p. 53, includes a passage in which the preacher criticizes himself and his fellow priests for falling prey to sloth and making a bad example for their parishioners. For further comment, see G.R. Owst, *Preaching in Medieval England* (Cambridge: The University Press, 1926), pp. 25 ff.

mission that he cannot gloss *Beati omnes*. This text from Psalm 127 had long been invoked in manuals for the condemnation of sloth, and it is also cited later by Hunger in his condemnation of wasters (B. vi. 250−52).[20] The last two lines of this section of the Confession are also echoed elsewhere in the *Visio*: "I kan holde louedayes and here a Reues rekenyng, / Ac in Canoun nor in decretals I kan noȝt rede a lyne" (B. v. 420−21). In the C-text Langland criticized monks and canons who served as "ledares of lawedayes and londes ypurchaced" (v. 158), as in the B-text he referred to Religion's becoming a "ledere of louedayes" (B. x. 312). These lines from the Confession make clear that secular activities which distracted the clergy were meant to be judged as slothful, even if the poet neglected to say so outright in each instance.

The instability of Sloth's fictive identity, changing from layman to priest and then back to layman again, poses one of the problems of the passage. Owst cites it as an example of the poet's individual clumsiness in adapting his sources, but Wenzel has demonstrated that such transformation or "shape-shiftings" were common in the *acedia* tradition.[21] Another problem is created by the way Langland concludes the confession. In the B-text the puzzling figure of Robert the Robber is introduced and renders his own non-categorical confession. An appealing solution to this problem is proposed by Wenzel, who focuses upon the imperative of restitution and the hope of divine mercy as the two unifying themes:

Hence the passage under discussion expresses a very harmonious psychological sequence: from the confession of sloth to the promise of amendment, including the restitution of wickedly won goods, and thence to the possibility of despair, which is warded off by the saving thought of Christ's mercy. It may very well be that poor Robert stands for three or six or seven deadly sins and not for sloth alone.[22]

This interpretation seems to reflect something of the C-poet's intentions as well. Langland, having transferred much of Robert's testimony to the confession of Avarice, ends Sloth's confession with "þe braunches þat bryngeth men to sleuthe" (vii. 70−119), a long section itself trans-

20. Wenzel, p. 142.
21. Owst, *Literature and Pulpit*, pp. 88−89. Wenzel, pp. 139−40. In an instructive discussion of illuminations in manuscripts of the *Roman de la Rose*, Rosemond Tuve examines the common difficulty artists had in picturing personifications that were meant to be visually apprehensible but, as abstractions with self-contradicting attributes, were actually very hard to visualize in any single bodily form; *Allegorical Imagery: Some Mediaeval Books and Their Posterity* (Princeton: Princeton University Press, 1966), pp. 321−24.
22. Wenzel, p. 144.

posed from the B-text's description of Haukyn's stained cloak (xiii. 409 ff.).[23] The branches do not really represent sub-vices of sloth but rather versions of the other six sins—the avarice of those who will not give alms (C. vii. 73), the lechery of those who give themselves to whoredom (76), the wrathful (78), the flatterers (90), and the proud (96). But this conclusion of Sloth's shrift is not simply a coda to the Confession Scene. If Langland has adopted the traditional tree-image, he is original as well as firm in his statement that these branches lead specifically to sloth. Thus *acedia*, with its species despair, is shown to be the vice toward which all other vices move, if not erased, as their grim spiritual end. As Elizabeth Kirk has noted, "sloth and wanhope are the image of the insubordinate human will losing even its own intrinsic vitality, that responsive individuality which led God to look at creation and call it good."[24]

The confession of Sloth is important because it assembles so many of the traditional traits of the sin, prominent but unnamed elsewhere in the poem, and because it brings into high profile certain moral features shared by the Dreamer. A few brief examples will suffice here since this subject will be more fully treated in later chapters. When Sloth enters, he complains that he cannot "stonde ne stoupe ne wiþoute a stool knele" (B. v. 387), just as the Dreamer himself objects that he cannot stoop because he is too tall (C. v. 24). Once seated, Sloth "bigan *Benedicite* with a bolk and his brest knokked, / Raxed and [rored] and rutte at þe laste" (B. v. 390–91). Although described more coarsely, this is nonetheless reminiscent of the Dreamer who, at the beginning of this same passus, walks less than a furlong, sits softly down, and falls asleep while babbling his Pater Noster (B. v. 5–8). Sloth laments his misspent youth with the line "*Heu michi quia sterilem vitam duxi Iuuenilem*" (B. v. 441); this Latin hexameter, used only twice in the poem, is the same one applied to the Dreamer much earlier by Lady Holy Church (B. i. 141).

The next catalogue of deadly sins comes with Langland's description of Haukyn's Coat of Christendom, "moled in many places wiþ manye sondry plottes" (B. xiii. 273–459). In the poet's exegesis, these spots

23. On the other hand, the proliferation of so many vices caused by sloth might be explained in part by Augustine's *In Psalmum CI*, 10 (*PL* 37:1301), where the man who has fallen into despair knows that nothing can be worse and so he might as well commit whatever sins he wishes. In a similar passage from *In Psalmum CXXIX*, 1 (*PL* 37:1697), the victims of despair are robbers, reminiscent of Robert the Robber, and their example suggests why the branches that bring men to sloth could so easily have replaced the lament of desperate Robert.

24. *The Dream Thought of "Piers Plowman"*, p. 60.

become the capital sins listed in an order that by now has become roughly standard, beginning with Pride and concluding with Gluttony and Sloth. While the vices are presented not always as personifications but more generally as titles under which are listed a series of examples, Gluttony becomes a true personification who, as before, realizes the sinfulness of his life, despairs of God's mercy, and lapses into wanhope. This again serves as a transition to *acedia*:

> That into wanhope he worþ and wende nauȝt to be saued.
> The whiche is sleuþe so slow þat may no sleiȝtes helpe it,
> Ne no mercy amenden þe man þat so deiep.
>
> (B. xiii. 406–08)

Sloth is not rendered in personification, and the passage that follows is the same discussed already as "þe braunches þat bryngen a man to sleuþe." Although these branches spread out in unexpected directions and eventually touch upon sins not typically related to *acedia*, sloth itself is treated in its traditional senses (B. xiii. 411–20). A slothful man has no sorrow for his misdeeds and performs poorly whatever penance a priest sets upon him. He fears no sin, lives against the creed, and adheres to no rule or law. He blasphemes, ignores religious holidays, and hates to hear stories about poverty and the martyrdom of God's saints.

One of the remarkable things about this description is the way in which Langland chooses to focus exclusively upon spiritual dangers. While in the *Visio* most of the discussion was devoted to worldly aspects of sloth—idleness, wasting, forgetting community obligations — in the *Vita de Dowel* the poet explores the sins of the inner man. What is more, the spiritual failings of Will's interior quest seem to form a gloss upon his earlier condition, since the Dreamer of the *Visio* has exhibited the same flaws here attributed to *acedia*. Constrained by no eremitic or monastic rule, he had roamed idly about seeking marvels, and when he finally sat down to say his prayers, he quickly fell asleep.

Langland includes another exposition of deadly sins in one of the didactic speeches of Patience (B. xiv. 201–61), who reviews the "seuene synnes" while relating each vice to his central theme of patient poverty.[25] The general sequence is the one we have seen before —Pride at

---

25. Patience had prior occasion to touch upon *acedia* in familiar conjunction with gluttony, with special reference to the Sodomites who would normally serve as an example against lechery (B. xiv. 75–78). The connection between *acedia* and the sin of Sodom, suggested by Ezech. 16.49, is made also in the *Ancrene Wisse*, ed. J.R.R. Tolkien, 1962, EETS o.s. 249, p. 216.

the head of the list and Sloth at its end—although Langland has made some peculiar alterations. He distinguishes Covetise and Avarice as two separate vices, but omits Envy, a sin against which the poor would seem to require a firm warning. Though Gluttony does not immediately precede Sloth, *acedia* is still made a salient feature of his condition: "So for his glotonie and his greete sleuþe he haþ a greuous penaunce" (B. xiv. 235).

Patience's treatment of Sloth refines earlier admonitions against false begging in the *Visio*. Many poor people must remain idle for lack of gainful employment, but the poor should take no joy in idleness and should look forward instead to the bliss of heaven (B. xiv. 261). We are reminded that Christ in the guise of poverty performed the greatest of works: "And in þat secte oure Saueour saued al mankynde." Langland's discussion moves next to the subject of religious begging and the proper union of poverty with patience, all in opposition to the slothful pursuit of that occupation by greedy friars and false beggars such as the "heremytes on an heep."

By the end of the poem, the catalogues of vices are included not merely for the sake of moral digression. In ways that are utterly original, Langland transforms *acedia*'s popular image with its emphasis on external neglect and not inner attitudes such as insufficiency of love for the divine good.[26] The martial assault on Unity becomes allegorically one of the poem's most inward actions, since the final attack of Sloth succeeds when Flattery has put Contrition to sleep. Thus the listing of vices, which at first might have appeared a simple borrowing from pulpit rhetoric, becomes a crucial part of the poem at its pessimistic close showing a vision of society sunk low in slothful despair because man's spirit, so numb and sluggish, cannot feel the sting of contrition necessary for its repair.

Langland presents this last and most startling assembly of deadly sins in the poem's concluding passus, when the Dreamer falls asleep and has a vision of the Antichrist coming in human form to destroy the crops of Truth (B. xx. 51 ff.). Antichrist has filled his ranks with the sins that have been mankind's strongest foes—Pride, Lechery, Covetise, Envy, and Sloth—in addition to other hostile powers such as Life, False, and Fortune. Although Langland says that the "seuene grete geaunt3" of the deadly sins accompany Antichrist, they are not all described with equal attention to appearance and conduct, nor are they all mentioned by name. Wrath, which had been missing from the A-

26. Wenzel, p. 140.

text Confession Scene, is curiously omitted here too,[27] and Gluttony, which had previously been so closely related to physical sloth, also fails to appear. Here Langland seems concerned more with spiritual sins than with fleshly ones, and it is therefore not surprising that Sloth develops into one of the most fearsome vices. Sloth attains this special stature not merely through a privileged placement in the order of appearance, but also by a ferocity and force of presence unique to all the antecedent traditions of *acedia* and the *processus vitiorum*.

When the siege of Unity commences, most of the vices are less visually precise than in Langland's other treatments. In the case of Sloth, however, his genesis and conduct are described with careful attention to allegorical detail. The figure of Life strides unto the scene and announces that he, along with Health and Pride, will cause men to have no dread of Eld and Death, to put sorrow out of their minds, and to feel no concern for their sins (B. xx. 153–55). Since these spiritual failings are reminiscent of Sloth in the earlier Confession Scene, it should come as little surprise that Life proceeds to mate with Fortune (Will's temptress in Passus XI) and spawn the *new* Sloth:

> This likede Lyf and his lemman Fortune
> And geten in hir glorie a gadelyng at þe laste,
> Oon þat muche wo wroȝte, Sleuthe was his name.
> Sleuþe wax wonder yerne and soone was of age
> And wedded oon Wanhope, a wenche of þe stuwes.
> Hir sire was a sysour þat neuere swoor truþe,
> Oon Tomme Two-tonge, atteynt at ech a queste.
> This Sleuthe wex sleiȝ of werre and a slynge made,
> And threw drede of dispair a doȝeyne myle aboute.
> For care Conscience þo cryde vpon Elde
> And bad hym fonde to fighte and afere Wanhope.
>
> (B. xx. 156–66)

While two capital sins have been dropped, Langland transforms Wanhope, normally a sub-vice of *acedia*, into a "wenche of þe stuwes" and thus a full-fledged warrior. After Life has attempted a flight from Eld toward the false comforts of Physic, Conscience is assaulted inside

---

27. The deletion of Wrath from the A-text Confession prompted J.M. Manly to propose the theory that a page was lost from the proto-A-manuscript, resulting in the omission of this material from all subsequent manuscripts; see "The Lost Leaf of *Piers the Plowman*," *MP*, 3 (1906), 359–66. This hypothesis seems unlikely in the light of what we see later in the B-continuation. Langland apparently did not share with other poets the need for all sins to be described with equal care, or even that they all needed to be included in a catalogue. Typical of the poet's practice is this last passus of the B-text, which neglects *two* capital sins.

Unity a second time by the vices which are now led by the giant Sloth; even prideful priests are under his command:

> Sleuþe wiþ his slynge an hard saut he made.
> Proude preestes coome with hym; passynge an hundred
> In paltokes and pyked shoes, purses and longe knyues,
> Coomen ayein Conscience; . . .

> (B. xx. 217–20)

Sloth appears for the third and last time in the closing lines of the poem where he and Pride make their final assay upon Unity, which is now on the verge of collapse since Contrition has ceased to weep for his sins (371–74). This presentation of Sloth as a fierce warrior is remarkable and probably unprecedented in the *acedia* tradition. In the legion of sins described in *The Assembly of Gods*, for example, "Slowthe was so slepy he came all behynde." In *The Castle of Perseverance*, Sloth assumes a relatively minor role in the battle, where the vice that succeeds in winning Mankind from grace is Covetise.[28] Marking the contrast is the standard characterization found in Huon de Mery's *Tournoiemenz Antecrit*, summarized here by Wenzel:

> . . . the figure of Peresce (*pigritia*) forms the rear guard in the host of the Fiend. She is asleep, prefers to remain in her pavilion, and never leaves the company of Cowardice, Treason, and Despair. When she rides to battle, she drowses on top of a "restful, slothful elephant," and as soon as Prowess brandishes her lance, she runs away for good.[29]

The large and menacing Sloth of Passus XX reveals at last Langland's true realization of this sin's virulence. We are shown vice unmasked, and the figure that had been a comic butt in the Confession Scene is now horrific.

It has been suggested that the attack of the vices upon Unity was influenced by the older notion of a slothful man as an undefended town. This comparison is made by Peraldus and repeated in *Jacob's Well*: "slowthe makyth þe as a cyte vnwallyd, redy & esy for alle synnes & for alle feendys to entryn in-to þi soule."[30] Bloomfield is fur-

---

28. John Lydgate (?), *The Assembly of Gods*, ed. Oscar Lovell Triggs, 1896, EETS e.s. 69, p. 19 (l. 631); and *The Macro Plays*, ed. Mark Eccles, 1969, EETS o.s. 262, esp. pp. 72 and 74. Wenzel, p. 137, notes the uniqueness of the Sloth-figure at the end of *Piers Plowman*.

29. *Ibid.*, pp. 117–18, reading from *Li Tournoiemenz Antecrit*, ed. Georg Wimmer, *Ausgaben und Abhandlungen aus dem Gebiete der Romanischen Philologie*, no. 76 (Marburg, 1888), ll. 1174–1220 and 2454–55. Other contributors to this tradition include Aldhelm, *De Octo Principalibus Vitiis* (PL 89:281–90); and *Songe du Castel*, ed. Roberta D. Cornelius, *PMLA*, 46 (1931), 321–32.

30. *Jacob's Well*, p. 114; William Peraldus, *Summa de Vitiis et Virtutibus*, II, iv (Ant-

ther reminded of the millenarian prediction that in the world's last age all Christians would return to the coenobitic ideals of the early Church, when monks viewed their chapter as a fortress and their brethren as an army in battle against the legions of evil.[31] One of the greatest dangers lurked inside the beleaguered community itself in the form of Benedict's *frater accidiosus*—here represented by Friar Flattery—who corrupts the others, slackens discipline, ruins concentration, and thus leaves the fortress vulnerable to assault.

But the last line of defense in *Piers Plowman* belongs not to the monks' liturgical practice but to the sacrament of penance. Unity is entered by way of practicing contrition and confession (B. xx. 212–13), but once Flattery has caused Contrition to feel nothing, to forget his wicked deeds, and to fall asleep—all, in a literal sense, symptoms of *acedia*—then the sacrament is incomplete and it cannot help. The fortress is assaulted once again by Sloth leading the horde of vices (B. xx. 362–79).

This is not the first time that the sacrament of penance has been frustrated, though the outcome has always been the same. When Covetise was denied forgiveness in the Confession Scene because he refused to make restitution, "thanne weex þe sherewe in wanhope & wolde han hanged hymself" (B. v. 279); Robert the Robber was just barely saved from despair by his promise to amend his life and return what he had stolen.[32] Restitution is a basic part of penance because "to return what one owes" (*redde quod debes*) is visible evidence of contrition, as confirmed in Passus XX (308). One must pay for one's sins and confess to a priest, not a friar, but the first step must be a sincere sadness of the sort described by Chaucer in *The Parson's Tale*: "Contricioun is the verray sorwe that a man receyveth in his herte for his synnes, with sad purpos to shryve hym, and to do penaunce, and neveremoore to do synne."[33] A recurrent complaint in the fourteenth century was that friars did not make strict demands for restitution,[34] but Langland has

<hr>

werp, 1587). Also see John Bromyard, *Summa Praedicantium*, A, viii, art. 4 (Basel, 1484), where the sinful soul is likened to a castle built by Satan where Acedia is the *camerarius*. Richard Rolle (*Yorkshire Writers*, ed. Horstman, vol. I, p. 140) includes this passage against Idleness: "he makis waie to þe fende in him-selfe. þerfore Salomon likyns slike til a Cite with-outen wall: *Sicut urbs sine murorum ambitu: ita vir qui non potest cohibere spiritum in loquendo.*"

31. Bloomfield, *Apocalypse*, pp. 148–49.

32. Wenzel, p. 146.

33. Chaucer, *Works*, ed. Robinson, p. 230. The standard theology is explained by P. Palmer and P.E. McKeever, "Sacrament of Penance," *NCE*, vol. XI, pp. 73–83, esp. 76. The necessary participation of the will is mentioned by John de Burgh, sometime Chancellor of Cambridge, in his *Pupilla Oculi* (1380), transcribed by Hort, *Religious Thought*, p. 153.

34. Bloomfield, *Apocalypse*, p. 131.

pushed aside consideration of the external act, as usual going to the root to determine the quality of contrition and to see whether there is true sorrow. Here he reflects the general concern of an age when followers of Wyclif had argued that contrition *by itself* could delete sin and make even confession unnecessary.[35] While few accepted this unorthodox concept, all would have agreed that without contrition not one sin could be forgiven. No matter what the sin, therefore, man's failure to cleanse it could lead to despair:

> Ac whiche ben þe braunches þat bryngen a man to sleuþe?
> Is whan men moorneþ noȝt for hise mysdedes, ne makeþ no sorwe,
> Ac penaunce þat þe preest enioyneþ parfourneþ yuele.

> (B. xiii. 409–11)

After so many instances in which the thwarting of penance has led to wanhope, it should come as no surprise at the end when the whole community, lacking the safeguard of Contrition, is beset by Giant Sloth.

To succeed in the battle against all the sins, *The Book of Vices and Virtues* offers this typical paradigm for marshalling the weapons of penance:

> For who-so wole not assente to synne, he ouercomeþ þe bataile, þat is a riȝt liȝt to ouercome to a bolde herte, and wel longe and euele to a slowȝ herte and a wery, . . .
> Now schalt þou wite ȝif a man be wel armed to ouercome a bataile, þat is to seye to venquise parfiȝtliche synne, hym bihoueþ haue þre þinges þat ben verailiche in penaunce. þe first þing is repentaunce in herte. þe secunde schrifte of mouþ. þe þridde is sufficiaunt amendes in dede doynge.[36]

Langland has shown the failure of this paradigm inside Unity, where many are *slowȝ* and *wery* and where even the foremost defense of Contrition is lacking. The picture really is as grim as it seems. Although the Christian community is the same as in the Half Acre, its problems are more severe now because Piers is absent and Conscience is no longer advised by Reason, whose aid was proven essential when the King tried to force a marriage with Lady Mede.[37] Conscience tries to marshal the defenses, but he allows into the fortress representatives

35. Gordon Leff, *Heresy in the Later Middle Ages: the Relation of Heterodoxy to Dissent, c. 1250–c. 1450*, 2 vols. (Manchester: Manchester University Press, 1967), vol. II, p. 576, citing *Selected English Works of John Wyclif*, ed. Thomas A. Arnold, 3 vols (Oxford: The Clarendon Press, 1869–71), vol. III, pp. 461–62.

36. *The Book of Vices and Virtues*, p. 171.

37. Charles W. Whitworth, Jr., "Changes in the Roles of Reason and Conscience in the Revisions of *Piers Plowman*," *NQ*, 217 (1972), 7.

from various estates of society—brewers, vicars, lords, and kings—who are unwilling to submit to his rule or, if they do, misunderstand the significance of their decision. The folk in the Half Acre had progressed much further. They had listened to Reason's sermon, Repentance had caused their Will to weep in contrition, the Seven Deadly Sins had confessed, and they had set off on a pilgrimage to Truth to make restitution. Although their sacred journey may have been left unfinished because of uncertainty about the best means for securing their goal, the people inside Unity have not even reached the point of confession. Contrition sleeps while the Sins, so docile during the Confession Scene, are now pressing armed rebellion.

Bloomfield has written that men in the fourteenth century widely believed in the imminent end of the world and the coming of a great new age after a time of troubles.[38] However much Langland may have been affected by this apocalyptic spirit, he never draws back the veil to reveal the coming Golden Age, but instead dwells at length on the signs which were to precede the Second Coming according to the prophetic tradition: "bad rulers, civil discord, war, drought, famine, plague, comets, sudden deaths of prominent persons, and an increase in general sinfulness."[39] By introducing so many of these signs of disintegration and even picturing the assault of Antichrist, Langland leads the reader to expect the sort of apocalyptic ending which Frank Kermode has described as fundamental to the fiction of the Christian tradition.[40] Yet Christ does not return to halt the corruption and punish the evil, Will does not die to face individually the throne of judgment, and the poet does not allude to the death of any well-known person whose name would have fixed the action within history and given events the sense of a definite ending. Instead, *Piers Plowman* concludes upon a note of anxious disillusion, because the secular and spiritual chaos seems never-ending. Since the Dreamer never fully awakens in the last line of the poem, the action is suspended *inter aeternitatem et tempus*, in that fictive time-frame which Kermode traces back to the period of skepticism following the scholastic upheavals of the thirteenth century.[41]

38. Morton W. Bloomfield, "*Piers Plowman* as a Fourteenth-Century Apocalypse" in *Interpretations of Piers Plowman*, ed. Edward Vasta (Notre Dame: University of Notre Dame Press, 1968), pp. 341–42. To the contrary, Robert W. Frank, Jr., "The Conclusion of *Piers Plowman*," *JEGP*, 49 (1950), 314, believes that Langland was interested in the Antichrist's corruptions as problems in themselves, not as signs of the imminent Doom.

39. These standard signs are listed by Cohn, *Pursuit of the Millennium*, p. 21.

40. Frank Kermode, *The Sense of an Ending: Studies in the Theory of Fiction* (New York: Oxford University Press, 1967), pp. 8–17.

41. Kermode, *Sense of an Ending*, pp. 67–74. For further reference to this dreamlike dimension of *aevum*, see Gilson, *History*, pp. 73 and 592–93, n. 23; Ernst H. Kan-

Without referring specifically to Langland, Northrop Frye comes close to describing perfectly the effect of his poem:

The phase of tragic irony is represented by the poem of melancholy in its extreme form of accidia or ennui, where the individual is so isolated as to feel his existence a living death . . . and the theme of death is presented in terms of simple physical dissolution: "earth upon earth," as a medieval poem has it. The appropriate *epos* form of this phase is the *danse macabre*, the poem of the dying community.[42]

That community is again represented by the Dreamer, old and impotent now, whose aged temperament would have rendered him even more susceptible to *acedia*.[43] Conscience deserts the desperate community and sets off on a pilgrimage in search of Piers, although the language he uses to describe his goal—"til I haue Piers þe Plowman" (B. xx. 385)—gives us cause to suspect that, without the aid of Reason, he misunderstands the object of his quest as much as the Dreamer who had set out looking for an inn-dweller named Dowel. And even if Piers should return to Unity, Conscience holds out no perfect guarantee that he can remove the Church's gravest threat. While Piers is said to be able to destroy Pride and the Friars, there is no mention of his power over Sloth (B. xx. 380–86).

In the last passus of the poem, Langland has unmasked the monster *Acedia* to show the truest shape of a vice that has been presented earlier in disguises that were either humorous or familiar—that is, in the most insidious forms of a sin which can thus seem like no sin at all. Yet Sloth's presence in the poem has not been restricted to the five catalogues of sins alone. In the following chapter, I shall explore how Sloth has been lurking in many other disguises, beginning when Will the Dreamer enters "in habite as an heremite vnholy of werkes."

torowicz, *The King's Two Bodies: A Study in Mediaeval Political Theology* (Princeton: Princeton University Press, 1957), pp. 275–84; and Bloomfield, *Apocalypse*, p. 22.

42. Northrop Frye, *Anatomy of Criticism: Four Essays* (1957; rpt. New York: Atheneum, 1969), p. 297. I presume he refers to the Middle English *Erthe upon Erthe*, ed. Hilda M. R. Murray, 1911, EETS o.s. 141.

43. Though *acedia* could trouble a man at any period of his life, it was thought to have an especially firm grip during old age; see "The Mirror of the Periods of Man's Life" in *Hymns to the Virgin and Christ*, ed. Frederick J. Furnivall, 1867, EETS o.s. 24, pp. 58–78, esp. ll. 517–60. Carruthers, *The Search for St. Truth*, p. 164, sees the Dreamer's agedness as mirroring the sapped condition of his will, the prime definition of aridity.

V
Society, the King, and an Unholy Hermit

This is a chapter of parts. It has as its subject the first two visions of *Piers Plowman* (B. prol.–vii), although no attempt is made to take into account everything in those bustling, densely populated pages. My aim is rather to concentrate on four questions central to this study and, if I am correct, to Langland's poem as well. (1) When the Dreamer enters "in habite as an heremite vnholy of werkes," are we to gather that he actually is an unholy hermit, or that he is unholy because he disguises himself as a hermit? (2) If the Fair Field offers a complete view of society with all its estates, what conclusion is to be drawn from the fact that so many people· have deserted their proper status and do not fulfill their assigned duties? (3) What legal theories stand behind the King's role as judge over society's corruption and enforcer of legal remedies? And (4) since public correction becomes a matter of individual repentance and confession followed by an act of satisfaction— symboled by Langland as plowing the Half Acre—how are we to understand man's dual failure to plow *and* do penance?

In the turbulent fourteenth century when English mysticism burst into full flower, we find again the solitary figure whose prominence had waned after the earliest days of the desert fathers. The hermit, never completely submerged by the organizational fervor of the intervening centuries, appeared once more as a major force in society.[1] No

---

1. R.W. Southern, *Western Society and the Church in the Middle Ages* (Harmondsworth: Penguin, 1970), pp. 300–01. For further studies on the resurgence of a fourteenth-century mysticism which so often included solitaries, see J. J. Jusserand, *Piers Plowman: A Contribution to the History of English Mysticism* (London: Unwin, 1894); Anna Groh Seesholtz, *Friends of God: Practical Mystics of the Fourteenth Century* (New York: Columbia University Press, 1934); Greta Hort, *Sense and Thought: A Study*

longer the lone hero warring against the powers of Satan such as Cassian praised in the *Conlationes*, the new solitary became his own author and audience. Dame Julian was a solitary, Richard Rolle was a hermit, *The Ancrene Wisse* and Walter Hilton's *Ladder of Perfection* were written for anchoresses, and *The Cloud of Unknowing* was addressed to a youth intending to become a recluse. As Sir Richard Southern puts it, "the spiritual warrior was out; the critic and contemplative came in."[2]

Yet these new hermits did not busy themselves only with works of literature and meditation. The prevailing notion seems to have been that although they renounced the world, they should not forsake humanity. Their practice was quite different from the famous Egyptians who had hidden under layers of brush or squatted atop columns to insure solitude. Hermits lived in cities like London, Coventry and Durham, and they were encouraged by their bishops to do good works such as administering leper hospitals, repairing roads, taking tolls, maintaining bridges, and tending the fires in lighthouses.[3] The representative of the new type was probably Richard Rolle, who mixed freely in society, called at men's houses, and dined with people regardless of their social rank.

That was the practice. A conservative in so many other matters, Langland disapproved of the modern hermits while heaping praise on the ascetic ideal of the ancient desert fathers. In the B-text (xv. 272–91) he cites the examples of hermits like Anthony, Giles and Paul (the basket-weaver) who did not beg alms in public places, but fled instead to the wilderness where they trusted in God to provide for their temporal needs.[4] And in the C-text (ix. 187–281) he adds a long section

---

in Mysticism (London: Allen & Unwin, 1936); Rufus M. Jones, *The Flowering of Mysticism: The Friends of God in the Fourteenth Century* (New York: Macmillan, 1939); Paul Molinari, *Julian of Norwich: The Teaching of a Fourteenth Century English Mystic* (London: Longmans, 1958); George Wood Tuma, *The Fourteenth Century English Mystics: A Comparative Analysis*, 2 vols. (Salzburg: Institut für Englische Sprache und Literatur, 1977); and Valerie Marie Lagorio and Ritamary Bradley, *The Fourteenth-Century English Mystics: A Comprehensive Bibliography* (New York: Garland, 1981).

2. Southern, *Western Society and the Church*, p. 301; Julian of Norwich, *Revelations of Divine Love*, trans. and intro. Clifton Wolters (Harmondsworth: Penguin, 1966), p. 22. Darwin, *The English Mediaeval Recluse*, pp. 1–7, makes a careful distinction between hermits and ancres which many medieval writers, including Langland, ignored by blurring the two into a single group confined to cells.

3. Rotha Mary Clay, *The Hermits and Anchorites of England* (London: Methuen, 1914), pp. 66–72 and 85–90; Peter F. Anson, *The Call of the Desert: The Solitary Life in the Christian Church* (London: S.P.C.K., 1964), p. 166.

4. Fleming, *Franciscan Literature*, p. 13, writes that "it is a remarkable fact that, of contemporary literary genres of the period, none enjoyed a wider success, apparently among all classes of literate society, than the *vitae* of the great saints of the desert."

contrasting the good hermits of old with the modern ones who crowded the towns and highways and begged among people in churches. Of the many virtues belonging to the good hermits, perhaps the most important is mentioned first in the poem—they did *not* leave their cells:

> . . . Ancres and heremites þat holden hem in hire selles,
> Coueiten noȝt in contree to cairen aboute
> For no likerous liflode hire likame to plese.
>
> (B. prol. 28–30)

If this is a prime virtue, what must the reader think of Will the Dreamer who, dressed as a hermit, makes his entrance while wandering over the Malvern Hills?

Piers Plowman begins with many features that belong to the literary realm of the *chanson d'aventure*—the warm May season, the rolling hills, the bubbling brook, the poet searching for marvels—but the effect is deeply qualified by the third line, where the Dreamer says he is dressed in the habit of a hermit who is unholy of works. This line is explosive. Its reverberations are felt throughout the Prologue and determine the ways we begin to think about the narrator-protagonist. Although Langland is careful not to say that Will *is* a hermit, the fiction invites us to picture him as one initially—to judge his unholiness if he is one, or to wonder why he dresses as a hermit if he is not one. Calling the Dreamer *vnholy* would probably have elicited a specific response, since from Cassian's day onward, the hermit's worst and most frequent enemy was known to be *acedia*.[5] If Will were a hermit and unholy, he would most likely be slothful.

This is the reaction I believe the first readers of *Piers Plowman* would have had, since the poem's earliest manuscripts and the references to Langland's work in contemporary documents suggest that the poem's first patrons were the clergy or members of religious institutions. Only in the fifteenth century did the poem attract a following among lay readers.[6] An unholy hermit's wandering through the countryside and (in Skeat's C-text) visiting the cells of his brethren are exactly the sorts of details that might have been lost on a lay audience but sensitively registered by clerical readers.

Benedict's *Regula*, as we have seen, endorsed the teachings of Cassian and warned that precautions be taken against the *frater accidiosus* who was idle, inattentive to his reading, and distracting to others. Langland's awareness of monastic rules in general is shown by his criticism

---

5. John Cassian, *De Institutis Coenobiorum* (X, 1), ed. Petschenig, pp. 173–74.
6. J.A. Burrow, "The Audience of *Piers Plowman*," *Anglia*, 75 (1957), 373–84.

of those who disobeyed the command forbidding travel outside the cloister (B. iv. 120–21).[7] Since he was familiar with this prohibition against wandering monks, he was probably also aware that such roaming was labeled *accidiosus*. One eleventh-century author makes the same distinction as Cassian:

There are two kinds of sloth: one that compels the monk to sleep and to be lazy in God's service, the other that makes him to wander here and there and urges him to flee from the society of the brothers with whom he lives.[8]

While a hermit was not necessarily constrained by the same obligations as a monk to remain in one place, strict hermits like those praised early in the Prologue were bound by vows and orders, and Langland's conservative opinions suggest that he saw little difference between monks and hermits in terms of their obligation to rules.

Of the four kinds of monks distinguished by Benedict, hermits are designated as the second kind: "those who, no longer in the first fervor of their reformation, but after long probation in a monastery, having learned by the help of many brethren how to fight against the devil, go out well armed from the ranks of the community to the solitary combat of the desert."[9] Hermits continued to be thought of as solitary monks bound to an order, and even when eremitic rules were not designed for associates of a monastic house, they continued to show an indebtedness to the Benedictines.[10] But the monk who kept to no cell and showed no obedience was certainly not a fourteenth-century phenomenon, as Benedict himself shows when he speaks with disdain of the *gyrovagus*:

The fourth kind of monks are those called Gyrovagues. These spend their whole lives tramping from province to province, staying as guests in different monasteries for three or four days at a time. Always on the move, with no stability, they indulge their own wills . . . Of the miserable conduct of all such men, it is better to be silent than to speak.[11]

---

7. A similar complaint is made later: "Ac now is Religion a rydere, a rennere by stretes, / A ledere of louedayes and a lond buggere" (B. x. 311–12). The implications of this sort of disobedience are explored by David E. Berndt, "Monastic *Acedia* and Chaucer's Characterization of Daun Piers," *SP*, 68 (1971), 435–50.

8. *Tractatus de Ordine Vitae*, x, 30 (*PL* 184:579).

9. *St. Benedict's Rule* (i), trans. Doyle, p. 6.

10. Charlotte D'Evelyn, "Instructions for Religious" in *A Manual of the Writings in Middle English, 1050–1500*, ed. J. Burke Severs, The Connecticut Academy of Arts and Sciences, vol. II, 1970, pp. 478–79, quotes from *The Rule of St. Celestine*, showing how monastic imagery was used to explain the hermit's call of obedience.

11. *St. Benedict's Rule* (i), trans. Doyle, p. 7. Bloomfield, *Apocalypse*, pp. 24–25, feels that many of Langland's unholy hermits would fall into the category of the gyrovagus.

These Gyrovagues, who have submitted their wills neither to God nor to an abbot, have therefore not followed Benedict's prime directive for curing the flaw created by "the sloth of disobedience."[12] John Bromyard, using monastic language, speaks soberly of those who refuse to abide according to any *worldly* rule:

The Devil indeed finds a class, namely the slothful, who are in no order, and they do not labor with the rustics, and do not travel about with the merchants, and do not fight alongside the knights, and do not pray and chant with the clergy. Therefore they shall go with their own Abbot, to whose order they belong, namely the Devil, where there is no order except eternal horror.[13]

Bromyard's language is not surprising since monks and hermits were both obliged to do work, whether busying *occupatio* or productive *labor*. And like Langland, as we shall see, he extends the ideal of monastic organization to all the estates of society as parts of a single metaphoric order.

Breaking voluntary oaths of obedience and ceasing to perform good works were consequences that could follow from many causes, even from the direct temptation of the Devil,[14] but Peter Anson in his book on hermits agrees with Wenzel that most causes had a single root:

There were other and even more subtle temptations to be resisted: ostentatious piety, depression, doubts, and apathy. All could be regarded as symptoms of "accidie," the besetting sin of cloistered religious, often due to overwrought nerves and the mental strain of a life in which no real relaxation is possible.[15]

One spiritual species of "accidie" was hatred of one's abode (*horror loci*) which, along with other symptoms such as curiosity, caused the hermit to flee his cell in a gesture that compelled a clear moral judgment. Whereas the slothful monk might escape his brethren, the slothful hermit left his solitude and sought out his neighbors.[16] Having already presented the Dreamer as an unholy hermit, the C-text elaborates the image by offering a new line in which Will reports that he "say many [selles] and selkouthe thynges" (prol. 5). Skeat explains that these *sellis* are the cells of various religious houses which he had

12. Wenzel, p. 27.
13. John Bromyard's *Summa Predicantium*, A, viii, art 6 ("Accidia").
14. A tale from the Vernon Manuscript tells of a hermit tempted by the devil to leave his cell and return to the world; see "Die Evangelien-Geschichten der Homiliensammlung des Ms. Vernon," ed. Carl Horstmann, *Archiv für das Studium der neueren Sprachen und Literaturen*, 57 (1877), pp. 258–59.
15. Anson, *The Call of the Desert*, p. 174.
16. *Ancrene Wisse*, ed. Tolkien, p. 8, speaks of the need for a hermit to remain constant to his abode or to incur mortal sin.

visited. The poet's condemnation of "londleperis heremytes" further emphasized the wrongness of this practice (B. xv. 213). As Skeat observes, the Dreamer is "not like an anchorite who keeps his cell, but like one of those unholy hermits who wanders about the world to hear and see wonders."[17] What Skeat fails to mention—and what Langland did not need to tell his audience outright—is that such roaming by a hermit comes under the heading of *acedia*.

The hermit's habit which the Dreamer wears had a distinctive appearance and, as the mark of a religious vocation, a number of formal meanings. The usual costume in England during the fourteenth century was made of gray or black wool that was poor and scratchy, nearly the same as sackcloth. But some hermits, harkening back to Cassian's instructions on dress, sought to imitate the desert fathers by wearing the skins of goats and sheep.[18] This may explain why Will says "I shoop me into a shroud as I a sheep weere" (B. prol. 2). When a hermit assumed his habit, moreover, he was made to understand that it must be worn day and night for the rest of his life, and that it would become his shroud at burial.[19]

Taking on the habit meant putting off the old man forever. Aware of the special temptations accompanying this new life, the author of the ordination ceremony for the hermits of St. Paul included a special warning against idleness for those assuming the habit.[20] While there were individual understandings that varied from cell to cell, one significance was understood well enough by all hermits: Jesus designated rough clothing as the sign of the penitent who voluntarily applied himself to the life of self-inflicted penance (Mt. 11.21).[21] So prominently did the habit figure in official ceremonies investing a man as a hermit that any variation in dress would have been seen as a violation of vows, a willful desertion of what had been willingly undertaken.

Yet there was a popular saying in the Middle Ages that "the habit

---

17. Skeat, II, p. 2. In *Piers Plowman: The Z Version*, ed. A.G. Rigg and Charlotte Brewer (Toronto: Pontifical Institute of Mediaeval Studies, no. 59, 1983), the Dreamer admits that he wandered about and "sey many *sellys*" (pro. 5) as opposed to the virtuous "hankres ant hermytus that holdeth hem in here *sellys*" (pro. 29).

18. Anson, *The Call of the Desert*, p. 164. Cassian, *De Institutis* (I, vii), trans. Gibson, p. 203, explains why a hermit should wear a sheepskin: "And this garment . . . signifies that having destroyed all wantonness of carnal passions they ought to continue in the utmost sobriety of virtue, and that nothing of the wantonness or heat of youth, or of their old lightmindedness, should remain in their bodies."

19. D'Evelyn, "Instructions for Religious," p. 480, referring specifically to *The Rule of St. Linus*.

20. Clay, *Hermits and Anchorites*, pp. 200–02.

21. P.F. Mulhern, "Penance" in *NCE*, vol. XI, p. 73, and Clay, p. 86.

does not make the hermit,"[22] and the closeness of this phrase to Langland's description of the Dreamer invites a second interpretation. No one to my knowledge has ever thought Will was a real hermit. Not only does Langland fail to renew this initial suggestion, but later details describe other forms of religious employment, especially in the C-text's "autobiography." If not a hermit, the Dreamer wears clothing similar to the disguises assumed by other figures in the *Visio*:

> Heremytes on an heep with hoked staues
> Wenten to Walsyngham, and hire wenches after;
> Grete lobies and longe þat loþe were to swynke
> Cloþed hem in copes to ben knowen from oþere;
> Shopen hem heremytes hire ese to haue.
>
> (B. prol. 53–57)

Anson says that these characters were typical of a class of vagabonds who loitered on the main roads, pretending to have the gift of prophecy and begging for alms:

There were innumerable beggars who found it paid better to pose as hermits. They roamed the countryside, often garbed in a sort of monastic habit. Frequently they were barefoot, with uncut hair and shaggy beards. Their policy was to say that they were on their way to some famous shrine, and so appeal to the charity of the faithful to assist them on the journey.[23]

The Dreamer resembles these false hermits in a variety of ways—in his clothing, his idleness, and his travels—but even more striking is the common physical attribute. In *Piers* the pretenders are described as *longe*, the same adjective applied twice to the Dreamer, first in the cryptic autograph—"I haue lyued in londe, quod I, my name is *longe* Wille" (B. xv. 152)—and later in passages such as the C-text autobiography where he complains that he is "to *long*" to perform jobs that require stooping (v. 24).

There is, in short, an uncomfortable ambiguity surrounding the Dreamer from the very beginning.[24] He might be a hermit who has committed the unholy act of deserting his cell. Or he might just be wearing ragged old clothes that give him the look of a hermit. Or he

---

22. Anson, p. 164. Clay says, p. 165, that "the hermit's garb was a favorite disguise" and, pp. 89–90, that "the habit was assumed by mere beggars" such as one William Blakeney, who was condemned to the pillory for his fraud.

23. Anson, pp. 161 and 167. Bloomfield, *Apocalypse*, p. 185, n. 38, offers several titles for further reading on the problem of false hermits in the Middle Ages.

24. Anson, p. 164, mentions the difficulty of telling sincere ascetics from tramps and vagrants.

might be unholy because he has put on a hermit's habit as part of a disguise to gain an easy livelihood. This last alternative has been favored by many critics who have addressed the problem,[25] and the C-poet strengthens the argument of guilt-by-association by offering his audience a fuller, more memorable view of false hermits:

> Ac thise ermytes þat edifien thus by the heye weyes
> Whilem were werkmen, webbes and taylours
> And carteres knaues and clerkes withouten grace,
> Holden ful hungry hous and hadde muche defaute,
> Long labour and litte wynnynge, and at the laste they aspyde
> That faytede in frere clothinge hadde fatte chekes.
> Forthy lefte they here labour, thise lewede knaues,
> And clothed hem in copes, clerkes as hit were,
> Or oen of some ordre or elles a profete,
> Aȝen þe lawe of Leuey, yf Latyn be trewe:
> *Non licet uobis legem uoluntati, set uoluntatem coniungere legi.*

> (C. ix. 203–12)

The last line of this passage is crucial: "It is not lawful for you to bend the law to your will, but for you to bend your will to the law."[26] It suggests that the two major interpretations of the Dreamer, which seem to point in different directions, actually converge upon a single moral point. The hermit who leaves his cell and the laborer who disguises himself as a hermit both have set their wills against the law. The hermit has broken the oath which he had voluntarily taken; the workman has deserted the profession to which he had been committed by birth or contractual agreement. All these violations of secular duties, as we shall see, were also condemned as forms of *acedia* and required a superior will, ideally embodied in the King, to compel individual wills to conform to the law of order and estate.

In *De Regimine Principum*, one of the major political treatises of the period, Thomas Aquinas offers a formulation for the good life that he applies equally to the individual and to the body politic:

For the well-being of the individual two things are necessary: the first and most essential is to act virtuously (it is through virtue, in fact, that we live a good

---

25. Robertson and Huppé, p. 34; Donaldson, *The C-Text and Its Poet*, p. 128; and Mills, "Role of the Dreamer," p. 186. *Piers the Plowman: A Critical Edition of the A-Version*, ed. Thomas A. Knott and David C. Fowler (Baltimore: The Johns Hopkins Press, 1952), pp. 44–45 and 154, favors seeing him as a false hermit who wanders from his cell.

26. John A. Alford, "Some Unidentified Quotations in *Piers Plowman*," *MP*, 72 (1974–75), 398, finds a similar passage in Innocent III's *De Contemptu Mundi*, II, iv (*PL* 217:718).

life); the other, and secondary requirement, is rather a means, and lies in a sufficiency of material goods, such as are necessary to virtuous action.[27]

What was called a society was a group of men united by a common desire for the temporal goods necessary for life in this world. Obtaining these bodily goods may have had a secondary importance, but without temporal means a man does not have the strength to struggle toward virtue.[28] The action of the poem's first vision (B. prol.–iv) is generally concerned with showing how mankind has confused the two goals, making temporal things an end in themselves so that both virtue and society are corrupted as a result. The answer to this problem is found at the beginning of Holy Church's sermon: render unto Caesar what is Caesar's and unto God what is God's (B. i. 46–57). It is the function of reason and *kynde wit* to distinguish between the two. Actually making the choice between primary and secondary goods is, of course, a matter for the will, but that is only the start. As Langland later realized, deciding in favor of virtue next entailed finding means, which were themselves a matter of choice and therefore voluntary. In the first dream of the *Visio*, however, his attentions were occupied with broader sorts of discrimination.

Complementing the reaction against false hermits and *lolleres* (B. xv. 213–15; C. ix. 213–18) is the persistent work-ethic of the *Visio* voiced by Conscience: "Ech man to pleye with a plow, pykoise or spade, / Spynne or sprede donge or spille hymself with sleuþe" (B. iii. 309–10). In the first place, labor was necessary for survival by providing man's bodily needs—food, drink, clothing (B. i. 20 ff.)—and therefore sloth stood as an enemy to the body as well as the spirit. As Chaucer put it, sloth "ne hath no purveaunce agayn temporeel necessitee." Productive work or "winning" also assumed an air of religious sanctity; "certes," says Chaucer again, "hevene is yeven to hem that wol labourn, and nat to ydel folk" (*ParsT*, 685 and 716). Langland praises both physical and spiritual forms of labor, and his relentless insistence upon right works of both kinds bridges the otherwise dissimilar worlds of the *Visio* and *Vitae*. The appearance of this strong work-ethic in the latter part of the fourteenth century is not surprising since the labor force, previously adequate to the economic requirements of the nation, had been severely depleted by recurrent outbreaks of plague. Owst

27. *De Regimine*, I, xv, in *Aquinas: Selected Political Writings*, ed. A.P. D'Entrèves, trans. J.G. Dawson (Oxford: Blackwell, 1954), pp. 80–81. See also Copleston, *Medieval Philosophy*, p. 299, and "The Individual and the Community" in Ewart Lewis, *Medieval Political Ideas*, 2 vols. (New York: Knopf, 1954), vol. I, pp. 193–240.

28. This is the crux of Need's speech to Will in B. xx. See also Gilson, *History*, pp. 79–80.

does well to correct Huizinga's assertion that *Piers Plowman* was "the first expression to the sentiment of the sanctity of productive labor;" in one sense, Langland was simply adding his voice to a chorus already issuing forth from pulpits throughout England.[29] The concern shared by all these social critics was that men should work "as þe world askeþ," different men faithfully carrying out different tasks, all according to a theory of the division of labor conceived by God.

Medieval society was traditionally divided into a series of well-defined gradations or estates, each of which contributed to the welfare of the whole.[30] Yet even in the early fourteenth century, this revered hierarchy was threatened by growing diversification within individual divisions and by the appearance of new groups that belonged to no traditional categories.[31] A revolutionary such as Marsilius of Padua might propose that the estates had been established by the will of the community and therefore could be altered by communal consent,[32] but the conservative Langland clearly viewed these estates as divinely ordained, with the role of consent restricted to a man's willingness to toil productively at his assigned tasks. Lady Mede arrived on the scene as the great villain because she rewarded a man's labors whatever their propriety—even if there were no labors at all—and therefore she had the power to tempt men into deserting their proper duties. Friars heard confession, pardoners preached like priests, monks owned land and lived like aristocrats, and parsons abandoned their parishioners to live

29. Owst, *Literature and Pulpit*, pp. 568–69.

30. Huizinga addresses this topic specifically in *The Waning of the Middle Ages*, p. 55, and generally throughout his chapter "The Hierarchic Conception of Society," pp. 54–64. For a discussion of Aquinas' belief that "the diversification of men for diverse tasks results primarily from divine providence," see Dino Bigongiari, *The Political Ideas of St. Thomas Aquinas: Representative Selections* (New York: Hafner, 1953), p. ix, translating from *Quaestiones Quodlibetales*, q. vii, art. 17 (*Opera Omnia*, vol. 9 [1859], pp. 565–67). See also Rufus William Rauch, "Langland and Mediaeval Functionalism," *Revue of Politics*, 5 (1943), 441–61.

31. Leff, *Medieval Thought*, p. 255, and May McKisack, *The Fourteenth Century: 1307–1399* (Oxford: The Clarendon Press, 1959), p. 346. Anna P. Baldwin's study *The Theme of Government in Piers Plowman* (Cambridge: Brewer, 1981) offers an entire chapter on "Piers the Ploughman and the Waster" (pp. 56–63) in which she discusses how "Langland's view of social duty . . . coincides closely with that of the fourteenth-century legislators, who for the first time were having to enforce the loyalty and honest work supposedly implicit in the ancient feudal system" (p. 57).

32. Alexander Passerin D'Entrèves, *The Medieval Contribution to Political Thought: Thomas Aquinas, Marsilius of Padua, Richard Hooker* (Oxford: Oxford University Press, 1939), pp. 53–55. Agreeing that Langland held with the traditional view that society existed as a static hierarchy ordained by God are Donaldson, *The C-Text and Its Poet*, pp. 109–10; Bloomfield, *Apocalypse*, pp. 102–03; and David Aers, *Chaucer, Langland and the Creative Imagination* (London: Routledge & Kegan Paul, 1980), pp. 2–3.

comfortably in London.[33] Langland's vision of the ideal society is un-
folded early in the poem:

> The kyng and kny3thod and clergie boþe
> Casten þat þe commune sholde hire communes fynde.
> The commune contreued of kynde wit craftes,
> And for profit of al þe peple plowmen ordeyned
> To tilie and to trauaille as trewe lif askeþ.
> The kyng and þe commune and kynde wit þe þridde
> Shopen law and leaute, ech lif to knowe his owene.
>
> (B. prol. 116–22)

Plowmen are set aside as those who supply man's temporal needs, but
the King and the Commons cooperate in shaping the law by which
each man conforms faithfully to his own estate.

No one has yet to produce an exhaustive study of Langland's politi-
cal theories, although Donaldson, Kean, and Baldwin have made sig-
nificant contributions for the increase of our understanding.[34] All three
scholars agree that Langland accords, though not consistently, with
much of the political thought of his time and that if he did not know
Aquinas and the major Continental theorists directly, there were other
sources that he was certainly drawing upon.[35] One of the basic con-
cepts of medieval political thought, derived ultimately from Aristotle,
was that the human race resembled a single organism whose individual
parts were moved by a common will—*voluntas totius humanae natu-
rae*—emanating to all the members from the king as the head.[36] Lang-

33. B. prol. 83–99; iii. 12 ff.; x. 322 ff. Also see P.M. Kean, "Love, Law, and *Lewte* in
Piers Plowman" in *Style and Symbolism in Piers Plowman*, p. 143.

34. Donaldson, *The C-Text and Its Poet*, "The Politics of the C-Revisor," pp. 85–120;
P. M. Kean, "Justice, Kingship and the Good Life in the Second Part of *Piers Plowman*,"
in *Critical Approaches*, ed. Hussey, pp. 76–110, and "Love, Law, and *Lewte* in *Piers
Plowman*," pp. 132–55; and Baldwin, *The Theme of Government in Piers Plowman*.

35. Kean, "Love, Law, and *Lewte*," p. 138. George Kane, "The Perplexities of Wil-
liam Langland" in *The Wisdom of Poetry: Essays in Early English Literature in Honor
of Morton W. Bloomfield*, ed. Larry D. Benson and Siegfried Wenzel (Kalamazoo: Medi-
eval Institute, 1982), p. 81, states that *Piers* shows an acquaintance with political propo-
sitions going back to Ockham or Marsilius, perhaps by way of Wyclif's *De Potestate
Papae*.

36. Thomas Gilby, *The Political Thought of Thomas Aquinas* (Chicago: University
of Chicago Press, 1958), pp. 259–60. Elizabeth T. Pochoda, *Arthurian Propaganda:
"Le Morte Darthur" as an Historical Ideal of Life* (Chapel Hill: The University of
North Carolina Press, 1971), p. 52, quotes as evidence for the persistence of this concept
in late medieval England a passage by Sir John Fortescue: "In this order, as out of an em-
brio, is formed an human body, with one head to govern and control it; so from a
confused multitude is formed a regular kingdom, which is a sort of mystical body, with
one person, as the head, to guide and govern"; see *De Laudibus Legum Angliae*, trans.
Francis Gregor (London: Sweet and Maxwell, 1917), p. 21.

land himself uses this image in a speech made by the King toward the end of the poem (B. xix. 466–74).

Aquinas made allowance for the power of a communal will,[37] but the authority representing the new voluntarist age was Marsilius of Padua, whose *Defensor Pacis* (1324) stands as a major departure in the history of political thought. Similarities between Marsilius and Ockham are such that it is difficult to decide which influenced the other, but it is clear that more than one fourteenth-century theorist was insisting upon will, not reason, as the constituent element of law.[38] Following Aristotle, Marsilius regarded the state as an organism made up of six parts, each with its own function: *agricultura, artificium, militaris, pecuniativa, sacerdotium,* and the supreme member called variously *iudicialis, consiliativa, pars principans,* and *principatus.* The order has something in common with Langland's society of plowmen, knights, clergy, and king. Whereas Aquinas and others taught that these estates were natural or divine in origin, Marsilius proposed that they were established by the will of man. They were the creation of a supreme human will which he called the *humanus legislator* and which he believed had created, separated, and maintained the various classes of the social hierarchy, including the ruling class or *pars principans.*[39] Marsilius granted the human will, to which others had attributed only the power to consent to externally imposed estates, the extraordinary power to elect the king, make laws, and alter the class structure.

I hasten to add that Langland shows no signs of being this progressive in his political thinking. His king is not elected, laws exist as natural paradigms, and the estates are fixed and in no way open to human tampering. What Marsilius sanctions as alteration by human will, Langland condemns as willful violation: "*Non licet uobis legem uoluntati, set uoluntatem coniungere legi.*" But the strongly voluntaristic spirit of the age would have compelled him to think more carefully about the role of will, whether as creator or consenter, in the workings of human institutions so vital to the production of life's necessities.

Whatever the origins of the world's estates, it was understood that virtue lay in performing one's duties willingly and that the violation of fixed divisions would bring a just punishment. Preaching at St. Paul's Cross in 1388, Master Thomas Wimbledon delineated the main *partes* and warned against man's failure to accept them:

37. *ST,* 1a, q. 81, art. 3 (vol. 11, pp. 210–15).
38. D'Entrèves, *The Medieval Contribution to Political Thought,* pp. 44–48 and 86.
39. *Ibid.,* 53–55.

And o þyng y dar wel seye: þat he þat is neiþer traueylynge in þis world on prayeris and prechynge for helpe of þe puple, as it falliþ to *prestis*; neiþer in fyȝtinge aȝenis tyrauntis and enemyes, as it falliþ to *knyȝtis*; neiþer trauaylynge on þe erþe, as it falliþ to *laboreris*—whanne þe day of his rekenyng comeþ þat is þe ende of þis lif, ryȝt as he lyuede here wiþoutyn trauayle, so he shal þere lacke þe reward of þe peny, þat is þe endeles ioye of heuene. And as *he was here lyuynge aftir noon staat ne ordre*, so he shal be put þanne "in þat place þat noon ordre is inne, but euerelastynge horrour" [Job 10.22] and sorwe þat is in helle.[40]

All that is missing is Bromyard's conclusion, quoted earlier, that such orderless men are slothful.[41]

It is one of the curious things about *Piers Plowman* that Langland does not concern himself more often with crimes of violence. Though frequent enough in the late fourteenth century, murder, arson, rape, armed robbery, and other acts that can be stopped in progress or deterred by threat of punishment are not, in their way, as troublesome for him as crimes of omission. A thief can be made to return stolen goods, but how does one deal with an idler who has deprived society of goods through his failure to produce? Like so many other medieval political thinkers when faced with a problem, Langland turned almost automatically to kingship for an answer.

Legal theory in the Middle Ages was complicated by a multitude of questions converging upon the subject of volition. To what extent was the law a manifestation of God's will and to what extent a product of custom and human design? Was the king subject to the law necessarily or did he submit to it only voluntarily? Is the king's command an act of pure volition or must it also involve the absolute guidance of reason? Can the king, without conducting himself as a tyrant, still govern badly by failing to assert his will in the maintenance of law? To what extent is the will of the people involved in electing the king and thereafter consenting to obey laws commanded by the monarch's will? Just as the image of the body politic would suggest, the conduct of the state was widely viewed as analogous to the conduct of the individual, so that political analyses naturally drew upon the language and concepts otherwise reserved for discussing morality. With Langland no less than

---

40. *Wimbledon's Sermon "Redde Rationem Villicationis Tue": A Middle English Sermon of the Fourteenth Century*, ed. Ione Kemp Knight (Pittsburgh: Duquesne University Press, 1967), p. 66; emphasis is mine. Bloomfield, *Apocalypse*, p. 87, agrees with Skeat that Langland may have known Wimbledon directly.

41. Owst, *Literature and Pulpit*, p. 554.

with Aquinas, politics existed as a category of morality, not as a separate science.

Just as voluntarist thinking became pervasive among theologians from the early fourteenth century onward, there was a growing tendency among legal theorists to conceive of law as the expression of a creative will invested in the whole community. This belief was best articulated by Marsilius, whose doctrine of the *legislator humanus* has been seen as anticipating the modern concept of popular sovereignty.[42] Langland, however, seems powerfully drawn to the older tradition as it was enshrined in the *Policraticus* by John of Salisbury, who hailed law as the eternal pattern of justice and the image of the divine will.[43] The law's source and its sanctity are never questioned in *Piers Plowman*; the poet's central concerns lie with the King's acceptance of his full legal duties and the people's consent to be ruled according to the letter of the law—that is, for the King and Commons to accord themselves variously with God's will, however that might be humanly determined.

Some writers like Grosseteste believed that a king had the right to command nothing except what was established by the law;[44] others contended that whatever the king did, even the cruelest act of tyranny against his subjects, was ultimately an expression of God's will and therefore had the force of law.[45] John of Salisbury endorsed the more common belief that the king was subject to established laws just as all other men are, *non necessitate sed uoluntate*.[46] While Aquinas' legal theory had a strong rationalist flavor throughout, he still held to the prevailing theory that "the sovereign is not exempt from the law's directive power, and he ought to fulfil the law voluntarily and not forcedly."[47]

42. D'Entrèves, *Medieval Contribution to Political Thought*, p. 55; and R.W. and A.J. Carlyle, *A History of Mediaeval Political Theory in the West*, 6 vols. (Edinburgh and London: William Blackwood, 1903–36), vol. VI, pp. 508–11. Baldwin, pp. 13–14, argues that in the Prologue to the B-text, Langland offers a model of limited monarchy, according to which a king "shares with the community the power to make the law."

43. *Ioannis Saresberiensis Episcopi Carnotensis Policratici siue de Nugis Curialium et Vestigiis Philosophorum Libri VIII*, ed. C.C.I. Webb, 2 vols. (Oxford: The Clarendon Press, 1909), iv, 2. W. Ullman, "The Influence of John of Salisbury on Medieval Italian Jurists," *EHR*, 59 (1944), 384, writes that "recent researches into fourteenth-century jurisprudence have shown that the *Policraticus* was one of the most quoted and perused treatises written by a medieval philosopher."

44. *Roberti Grosseteste Epistolae* (CII), ed. H.R. Luard (London: The Rolls Series, 1861), pp. 308–09.

45. Kantorowicz, *The King's Two Bodies*, pp. 87–93.

46. John of Salisbury, *Policraticus*, iv, 6 (vol. I, p. 252). For a closer examination, see Kantorowicz, pp. 104–07.

47. *ST*, 1a2ae, q. 96, art. 5: "princeps non est solutus a lege quantum ad vim directivam ejus, sed debet *voluntarius*, non coactus, legem implere" (vol. 28, pp. 136–37).

English writers, however, show a marked concern for the potential of the monarch's will to corrupt rather than conform to the law, especially after the nation's bitter experience with Edward II and later with Richard II, both of whom were denounced for setting their personal wills above the law.[48] Ockham was careful to distinguish between two types of kings: the one governs according to his own will without being bound by human law and without swearing to preserve law or custom; the other is bound to execute the laws and willingly swears to do so.[49] This latter theme was sounded by Henry of Bracton when he maintained *"non est enim rex ubi dominatur voluntas et non lex."*[50] The Lancastrian apologist Henry Knighton went further in arguing that if the king behaved willfully toward the law and the people, his subjects had the right to depose him.[51] For a king to perform his royal duties correctly—that is, to perform the tasks belonging to his estate—he needed guidance to rule legally and not willfully, and the source of that guidance was reason.

Langland made it clear that for the proper regulation of the realm, Reason must be present in court to counsel the King (B. iv). A strong tradition stemming from Cicero had made no allowance for the will, in fact, and elevated *ratio* as the prime source of human governance.[52] Following in this tradition, Aquinas wrote that law was an ordinance of reason promulgated for the common good by a monarch whose commands were not actions of a sovereign will but were directed by reason. Even Grosseteste felt that reason should be the prime force in the king's rule.[53] The spokesman for this tradition in *Piers Plowman* is

48. Carlyle, *Mediaeval Political Theory*, vol. VI, pp. 70–75. The Coronation Oath was recast in 1307 with the addition of a clause protecting the council of magnates from the arbitrary rescission of rightful laws to which they had assented and, inferentially, from the king's arbitrary and capricious legislation against their will; H.G. Richardson, "The English Coronation Oath," *Speculum*, 24 (1949), 44–75.

49. Carlyle, vol. VI, pp. 44–45, quoting Ockham, *Dialogus*, III, i, 2, 6. Concern for the prince's *privata voluntas*, which might overwhelm his *persona publica* and work against the state, can be traced back to the *Policraticus*, iv, 2. For further discussion, see Kantorowicz, *The King's Two Bodies*, pp. 95–96; and Pochoda, *Arthurian Propaganda*, pp. 41–43.

50. Henry of Bracton, *De Legibus et Consuetudinibus Angliae* (i, 8, fol. 5), ed. George E. Woodbine and trans. Samuel E. Thorne, 4 vols. (Cambridge, MA: Harvard University Press, 1968), vol. II, p. 33. For the relationship between Bracton's writings and the language of the English Coronation Oath, see Fritz Schulz, "Bracton on Kingship," *EHR*, 60 (1945), 145–47.

51. Henry Knighton, *Chronicon vel Monachi Leycestrensis*, ed. Joseph Rawson Lumby, 2 vols. (London, 1889–95), vol. II, p. 219.

52. Cicero, *Tusculan Disputations* (II, 21), trans. J.E. King (Cambridge, MA: Loeb Classical Library, 1945), pp. 200–05.

53. Aquinas, *ST*, 1a2ae, q. 90, art. 1–4 ("De Essentia Legis"). For further comment, see Bourke, *Will in Western Thought*, p. 17, and Bigongiari, *Political Ideas of St.*

Conscience: "I, Conscience, knowe þis for Kynde Wit me tauȝte / That Reson shal regne and reaumes gouerne" (B. iii. 284–85). But the voluntarist tenor of fourteenth-century England encouraged men to recognize that although reason's role was essential, it was by no means exclusive. An act of royal command (*imperium*), like any other human action (*praxis*), was essentially an act of will. Writing as a political theorist, Ockham continued to elevate the power of the will but readily conceded that no act could be virtuous unless its object was approved by right reason (*recta ratio*).[54] In this regard, he accords with the Thomist doctrine of the king's *voluntas ratione regulata*, his will directed by reason.

Arguments concerning the monarch's obligation to follow reason, while suited to clerics schooled in moral philosophy, were not restricted to the realm of pure theory. In 1308 when articles were brought against Piers Gaveston, it was argued that Edward II had not been "ruled by reason in regard to the estate of the Crown" and that "if the king's will were not accordant with reason, he would obtain nothing except the maintenance and confirmation of error."[55] At the end of the century when Richard II was deposed, it was again argued that the king had exercised power without adherence to reason but rather according to his personal will. A denial of the monarch's private will and the transfer of much of the legislative will to the Commons became the price that Henry IV paid for his ascent to the throne, as evidenced by the royal declaration issued in 1399 proclaiming that the king "does not wish to be governed by his own will or by his wilful purpose, or by his own opinion, but by common advice, counsel and assent."[56]

Thomas Aquinas, p. xv. William Abel Pantin, "Grosseteste's Relations with the Papacy and the Crown" in *Robert Grosseteste*, ed. Callus, pp. 212–13, quotes the Bishop's comments on Aristotle's *Nicomachean Ethics* (V, x–xi; VIII, xii–xiii), preserved in MS. Merton 82, fol. 102ʳ.

54. Arthur Stephen McGrade, *The Political Thought of William of Ockham: Personal and Institutional Principles* (Cambridge: Cambridge University Press, 1974), p. 192, quotes from Ockham's *Super Quatuor Libros Sententiarum*, III, 12, CCC–FFF. See also Kantorowicz, p. 106, and D'Entrèves, *Medieval Contribution to Political Thought*, p. 39.

55. Richardson, "The English Coronation Oath," 67, translating from BM. Burney MS. 277, fol. 5ᵛ–6ʳ. When Edward himself was deposed in 1327, it was announced that the king "had of his own free will, and by the advice and assent of the prelates, nobles, and the whole community of the kingdom, retired from the government"; B. Wilkinson, "The Deposition of Richard II and the Accession of Henry IV," *EHR*, 54 (1939), 225. The accusation against Richard II is recorded in *Rotuli Parliamentorum*, 4 vols. (London: 1783), vol. III, p. 419: he had acted "secundum sue arbitrium voluntatis facere quicquid desideriis ejus occurrerit."

56. B. Wilkinson, "The 'Political Revolution' of the Thirteenth and Fourteenth Centuries in England," *Speculum*, 24 (1949), 504, n. 23, translating from *Rot. Par.*, vol. III,

The opening vision of the Fair Field offers us Langland's early ideal of royal conduct:

Thanne kam þer a kyng; kny3thod hym ladde;
Might of þe communes made hym to regne.
And þanne cam Kynde Wit and clerkes he made
For to counseillen þe kyng and þe commune saue.

(B. prol. 112–15)

Natural reason, here represented by Kynde Wit, had figured as a counselor to the king so often in prior political allegories that the formulation of this passage is not exceptional.[57] What is surprising is that the King later enters the poem without the guidance of *ratio* (B. iv) during particularly dangerous circumstances when the error of his judgment is shown by his desire for Conscience to marry Lady Mede. Recoiling at this suggestion, Conscience refuses to kiss Mede unless advised to do so by Reason, who is thereupon summoned to court. The King finally accepts the advice of Reason, promising to make him and Conscience his permanent counselors. In a review of various literary allegories in which Reason and Conscience fill similar roles as counselors, Atcheson Hench has shown that only in *Piers Plowman* does the allegory have truly political as well as psychological meaning; the debate normally served for instructing the individual only.[58] But in allegory as in political theory, the border between moral action and social action is narrow enough for a poet like Langland to work on both sides simultaneously. Accordingly, the King represents more than the literal *princeps*. Whereas Thomist writers thought that the "royal faculty" of man was reason, Langland has created a separate figure of Reason, thus allowing the King to be seen as the other power involved in the process of command, namely, the will itself.

To expand his analysis in the C-revision, Langland juxtaposed three remarkable scenes at the end of Passus IV and the beginning of Passus V. In the first the King, flanked by his victorious advisers Reason and Conscience, renders his verdict against Lady Mede; in the second (the so-called autobiographical addition) these same two personifications come to censure the sluggard existence of the dreamer-narrator, whose name has by this point been established as Will; and in the third scene

---

p. 415. Langland's responsiveness to the shifting trends of political theory involving the monarch's will is explored by Coleman, *"Piers Plowman" and the Moderni*, pp. 52–66.

57. Kantorowicz, pp. 107–15, speaks of this allegory from its beginnings in the eleventh century.

58. Atcheson L. Hench, "The Allegorical Motif of Conscience and Reason, Counsellors" (Charlottesville: University of Virginia Studies, vol. 4, 1951), pp. 193–201.

Reason, with Conscience as his crosier-bearer, is shown preaching before the King again. These three tableaux of action work something like a triptych's panels whose comparison discloses and amplifies their meaning. On the outer two panels, Reason and Conscience admonish the King for his negligence in enforcing justice and loving his subjects; in the central panel, they confront Will with accusations of idleness and waste.

Duns Scotus prepared the way for other political thinkers such as William of Ockham and Henry of Ghent when he wrote that every physical action was a command of the will.[59] This meant that the act of commanding could no longer be regarded as a function of the reason or law alone: to command meant *to will*. One step further led to the conclusion that to give force to the law was to will it.[60] Scotus and his successors did not exclude reason from the legislative function, but assigned to it a subordinate or fringe role in the ordering of action. The will was the central force in instituting law.[61] Though there was a growing tendency to conceive of this legislative will as embodied in the people, the early voluntarists, whose work Langland might more likely have known, located this will in the person of the king. The monarch's subjects were thought to be bound by a fiat of the legislator's will to do as he commanded. What validated a law, in theory, was the fact that the sovereign formally intended that the people obey his commands.[62] Even today when the current English monarch accepts a statute from Parliament, she gives it the official force of law by declaring "*La Reyne le veult.*"

Indeed, in her valuable analysis of Langland's evolving theory of kingship, Anna Baldwin perceives a shift away from the notion of shared sovereignty in the B-text Prologue and toward an endorsement of absolute monarchy in the C-text. A king rules better if he acts according to his own idea of justice without the encumbrances of Parliamentary advice. Such a king would rely upon his own reason and conscience, which would therefore have public as well as private roles in

59. Duns Scotus, *Ordinatio*, Prologus, pars 5, q. 2 ("Quid Sit Praxis?"), in *Opera Omnia*, vol. I, pp. 155–60. See also Francis Oakley, "Medieval Theories of Natural Law: William of Ockham and the Significance of the Voluntarist Tradition," *Natural Law Forum*, 6 (1961), 65–83.
60. Bourke, *Will in Western Thought*, p. 176.
61. *Ibid.*, p. 173. This tradition of crediting legal force to the monarch's will was so strong before Duns that even Aquinas acknowledged it: "Sed voluntas de his quae imperantur, ad hoc quod legis rationem habeat, oportet quod sit aliqua ratione regulata; et hoc modo intelligitur *quod voluntas principis habet vigorem legis*" (*ST*, 1a2ae, q. 90, art. 1).
62. Bourke, *Will in Western Thought*, p. 171. Wyclif, *Tractatus de Officio Regis* (V), ed. Alfred W. Pollard and Charles Sayle (London: Trübner, 1887), pp. 92–100, argued that as head of the kingdom, the king must compel his subjects to obey the law.

the unique manner noted by Hench, without a traditional regard for legal standards. The King of the C-text's Coronation Scene is responsible for imposing justice, not upholding the law.[63] By envisioning political solutions in terms of an individual force of will, however, Langland was pushed to the grievous extreme of absolutism: "Pragmatic rather than idealistic, he has cut his political theory according to England's lawless and unhappy cloth."[64]

Despite this extraordinary shift in favor of the Crown's power, we would do well to recall that kingship was still a rung on the social ladder, the highest above clerks and knights, but carrying with it certain prescribed duties that could be fulfilled, performed badly, or not done at all. Though the older contractual theory of feudalism had greatly deteriorated, political writers following Salisbury still conceived of the monarch and his subjects as two parties bound by an oath of fealty. The prince is God's servant, but he must also perform his sworn duty by serving faithfully his subjects, however he might decide best to do that.[65] Thus by accepting the counsel of Reason and Conscience and judging Lady Mede guilty along with her cohorts, Langland's King fulfills his sovereign duty. But when he first encountered Mede (B. iii), the King did not immediately act to punish the wrongs infesting his domain. Some tracing backwards is necessary, then, to understand this initial failure.

Though the tendency in the later Middle Ages was to scold laborers for their laziness, as the Statutes of Laborers made official in England,[66] writers on *acedia* sometimes went so far as to single out the princes themselves for criticism. In his treatment of sloth, Thomas of Chabham tells priests that at confession rulers must be admonished carefully to perform their duties diligently and without laziness.[67] Princes most often fell prey to *acedia* when they were judges who failed to mete out justice. Albertus Magnus demanded that the king be

63. Baldwin, *The Theme of Government*, pp. 50–51.

64. *Ibid.*, p. 23, with related discussion on pp. 20–21 in the chapter "The Triumph of Absolutism in the Poem as a Whole."

65. John Dickinson, "The Medieval Concept of Kingship and Some of Its Limitations, as Developed in the *Policraticus* of John of Salisbury," *Speculum*, 1 (1926), 309 and 314, discusses *Policraticus*, iv, 7, v, 6, and vi, 25.

66. Bertha Haven Putnam, *The Enforcement of the Statutes of Labourers during the First Decade after the Black Death, 1349–1359* (New York: Columbia University Press, 1908), p. 9*, shows how punishment was directed to "alii mendicare malentes in ocio quam per laborem querere victum suum."

67. Thomas of Chabham, *Poenitentiale* (BM. MS. Royal 8.F. xiii, fol. 62ʳ), transcribed by Wenzel, p. 249, with a fuller discussion of the slothfulness of princes on pp. 180–81. Among all the negligent rulers in *Purgatorio* (vii), Dante singled out Henry III of England for paying too little attention to his state duties.

the embodiment of a lively, vigilant justice and not become listless or sleepy. Showing that this complaint was not reserved only for critics from the lower estates, Henry of Lancaster (dead of the pestilence in 1361) accused himself of slothful negligence in his own activities as a judge.[68] The King in *Piers Plowman* succumbs to both these weaknesses because at first he is not vigilant to the corruption around him and, next, he makes a hasty and ill-advised decision to marry Conscience to Mede.

In a favorite passage from Shakespeare's *Henry IV, Part One* (III, i), Owen Glendower boasts "I can call spirits from the vasty deep!"—to which Hotspur replies, "Why, so can I, or so can any man; / But will they come when you do call for them?" Kings face a similar problem. They have the power to command, but their subjects must decide whether to obey. Langland acknowledges that laws can be effectively enforced only if the people consent, and yet the King's one-sided confidence is soberly qualified by Conscience:

> "I wole haue leaute in lawe, and lete be al youre ianglyng;
> And as moost folk witnesseþ wel Wrong shal be demed."
> Quod Conscience to þe Kyng, "But þe commune [wil] assente,
> It is wel hard, by myn heed, herto to brynge it,
> And alle youre lige leodes to lede þus euene."
>
> (B. iv. 180–84)

Whenever a political writer discussed the king's will, he was also obliged to consider the people's willingness to be governed by a king and to obey his legal commands.

The consent of the people is necessary for the proper operation of any society, but writers have varied in their designation of what it is the people consent to, whether the letter of the law, the reasonableness of the law, or the king's command *per se*.[69] Cicero believed that a society was determined not by a congregation of people but by their consent to just laws, and his definition was generally approved by Augustine in

---

68. Henry of Lancaster, *Le Livre de seyntz medicines*, ed. E.J. Arnould (Oxford: Anglo-Norman Text Society, no. 2, 1940), p. 23: "Et par Dame Peresce sont ensi les biens perduz. Et ausi par cele male enchanteresce ai jeo fausement jugee, comme par defaute de la verité bien et diligeaument enqueré ou seue devant de jugement rendu." For further examples of writers urging a prince to be "neither torpid nor sleepy" in his pursuit of justice, see Kantorowicz, pp. 133–34. Albertus Magnus expresses his opinions in *Enarrationes in Evangelium Matthaei (I–XX)*, VI, 10, ed. Augustus Borgnet (Paris: Vivès, 1893), vol. 20, p. 266: "rex non tantum debet esse justus . . . non torpens vel dormiens, sed viva et vigilans justitia: sicut ejus cujus voluntas auctoritas est ad omnium justorum confirmationem."

69. For a review of the contending ideas, see "The Origin and Purpose of Political Authority" in Lewis, *Medieval Political Ideas*, vol. I, pp. 140–92.

The City of God with the important proviso that the state be governed by a sense of justice embracing the spiritual as well as the practical.[70] The people's consent to the king's law was therefore tightly interconnected with their obedience to God's law. As much as they diverged on other issues, Salisbury and Aquinas concurred that the people would naturally follow laws that had an appeal to universal reason. The *Policraticus* suggests that the existence of a complete code of rational laws instituted by God practically eliminated the need for government to perform a role any greater than that of ministerial enforcement. If men can find harmony in the reasonableness of divine law, then there should be no subordination of one human will to another, and no personal allegiance of subject to king.[71] While approving this traditional emphasis on the rational, Aquinas was too insightful to ignore the fact that consent, even if it were compelled by reason, was still an act of volition, and therefore the business of government was made possible by the assertion of the people's will.[72] The more the king became the protector and embodiment of the law, the more he became the object to which the people volunteered their consent.

The theory of the king's dependence upon the people's assent was never fixed in England during the fourteenth century, and generally it varied between two poles: the insistence of Salisbury's successors that the king received his authority directly from God and therefore did not hold office from the people; and the belief, starting in the thirteenth century and most ably voiced by Marsilius, that a king's ultimate authority may come from God, but the power of government was conferred on him by the will of the people.[73] What prevailed was a "mixed theory" that combined a principle of election with the notion of the king's hereditary right.[74] Although the monarchy was weakened

70. *The City of God* (II, 21; XIX, 21), trans. Bettenson, pp. 73 and 882. The role of popular consent in Augustine's political theory is examined by Bourke in *Will in Western Thought*, p. 152. For Cicero's comment, see *De Re Publica* (I, xxv, 39), trans. Clinton Walker Keyes (New York: Loeb Classical Library, 1928), pp. 64–65.

71. Dickinson, "The Medieval Conception of Kingship," p. 335.

72. Gilby, *The Political Thought of Thomas Aquinas*, pp. 199–202.

73. Pochoda, *Arthurian Propaganda*, p. 42, discusses the view of Salisbury. For theories of "popular consent," see Bourke, *Will in Western Thought*, p. 154; D'Entrèves, *Medieval Contribution to Political Thought*, pp. 55–57; and Otto Gierke, *Political Theories of the Middle Ages*, trans. F.W. Maitland (Cambridge: Cambridge University Press, 1922), pp. 38–40 and 46–48.

74. For medieval examples of the "mixed theory," see Rymer, *Foedera*, ed. Adam Clarke and Frederick Holbrooke (London: Great Britain Public Records Com., 1816), I, i, 75; and Ivo of Chartres, "Epistola CXIV" in *Recueil des Historiens des Gaules et de la France*, rev. ed., Léopold Delisle (Paris: Victor Palmé, 1878), vol. XV, pp. 144–46. A modern discussion is offered by Dickinson, "The Medieval Conception of Kingship," p. 315.

by the debacle of Edward II, the Statute of York in 1322 reaffirmed the ideal balance between legislation by the king and consent by the people. Only eight years later, however, Edward III pushed forward his claim of absolute rule over the nation.[75] With the beginning of the Hundred Years War in 1337, the power of the Crown grew steadily stronger so that at the coronation of the ten-year-old Richard II in 1377, Archbishop Sudbury's question to the people, whether they would give their will and consent to the new king, was placed *after* the coronation oath for the first time, thereby transforming the people's ancient role to elect their sovereign and testifying to the actual as well as the symbolic power of the throne.[76] When Langland wrote in the B-text "Might of þe communes made [þe Kyng] to regne" (prol. 113), he was expressing the principle of election, already incorporated in most voluntarist theories of law, which he would reject in favor of absolutism in the C-text—but which would actually become a part of the English constitution only a quarter of a century later, when Henry Bolingbrook began making concessions to the magnates.

A.C. Spearing is mistaken, I think, when he senses that at the end of the second vision "there is still the expectation that a king will impose political solutions to society's problems."[77] Everything in the poem, as well as everything in the political theories that stand behind it, points in a different direction. Thinkers as diverse as Augustine, Salisbury, Aquinas, and Ockham agree on the fundamental proposition that man's social existence is ultimately oriented toward the ethical and the spiritual.[78] Society's moral corruption does not have a political solution; political corruption cries out for a moral remedy. If the king's will is deficient, his best counselors are not human but psychological in the form of Conscience and Reason. And what about the other participants in the social contract? How can society with all its different constituents be induced to act virtuously? In matters of practical conduct, the theory of a collective will of the people breaks down entirely. Ockham was not alone in rejecting the provisional image of the body politic. In true nominalist fashion, he insisted that the real unit of will

75. Wilkinson, "Political Revolution," p. 505.

76. McKisack, *The Fourteenth Century*, p. 399. See also Walter Ullmann, *Principles of Government and Politics in the Middle Ages* (London: Methuen, 1961), pp. 182–92; John Taylor, "Richard II's Views on Kingship," *PLPLS-LHS*, 14 (1971), 189–205; and Anthony Tuck, *Richard II and the English Nobility* (London: Edward Arnold, 1973), on the liberty given to the King's will by the judges at Shrewsbury in 1387 (pp. 116–17) and the condemnation of the King's willfulness in the articles of deposition in 1399 (pp. 222–25).

77. Spearing, *Dream-Poetry*, p. 141.

78. For the agreement of Aquinas and Salisbury on this general point, see D'Entrèves (ed.), *Aquinas: Selected Political Writings*, p. viii.

was the individual and that society was simply a multitude of such in-
dividuals.[79] Even Aquinas, realizing that consent to a ruling power was
under the control of each man's will, believed that the authority of a
prince should be carried out by inflicting punishments on singular
wrong-doers. Because this response could deal with crimes of commis-
sion only, not with crimes of omission, the Thomist remedy made no
provision for encouraging right-doers.[80] Nor did it insure that deeds
carried out according to the law were done with a good will full of the
right intentions. Moving from the first vision to the second, Langland
found himself face to face with these harder problems.

At the end of the first vision, the King has succeeded in vanquishing
False but has not discovered how to attain Truth, a concept which as-
sumes the dual meanings of the fidelity to one's ordained station in so-
ciety and the accord between a man's will and his deeds. Aquinas ob-
served that among all the different forms of government, monarchy
most encouraged men to work sluggishly toward the common good,
because laborers realized that their efforts benefited not themselves
but rather the ruler under whose power the common good had been
placed.[81] As a result, not only was the King unable to compel virtuous
acts, but his mere presence at the head of society further encouraged
slothfulness. Secondly, the King could not know or control the motives
behind actions, those inner acts of will deemed to be morally good or
bad. This consideration brought Ockham and his followers to grips
with the basic problem concerning the relations of politics, law, and
morals. If politics deals solely with overt conduct (*actus exteriores*)
and if an act's moral worth is determined by inner volition, the politi-
cal domain is rendered morally neutral, perhaps meaningless, and vir-
tue becomes a matter wholly private, internal, individual.[82] Society
might function smoothly in that the king rules, the people follow, the
peasants plow, the harvesters gather grain, and everyone eats well and
prospers. But unless these acts are done willingly with some good as
their rational object—providing "a sufficiency of material goods such
as are necessary to virtuous action"—then there is no virtue in the so-
ciety and no one has done well.

Some readers of *Piers Plowman* have had trouble deciding whether

79. Lewis, *Medieval Political Ideas*, vol. I, pp. 207–08.
80. Bigongiari, *The Political Ideas of St. Thomas Aquinas*, pp. xxviii–xxix. Aquinas'
own remarks can be read in *De Regimine*, I, xv (D'Entrèves, ed., pp. 78–83), and *ST*,
2a2ae, q. 104 (vol. 41, pp. 46–73). Also see Baldwin, *The Theme of Government*, p. 54.
81. *ST*, 1a2ae, q. 105, art. 2.
82. McGrade, *The Political Thought of William of Ockham*, p. 45. His view accords
with Aquinas and, ultimately, back to Augustine; see Lewis, *Medieval Political Ideas*,
vol. I, pp. 218–19; and Copleston, *Medieval Philosophy*, pp. 226–27.

Langland is concerned with the reform of the state or with the redemption of the individual.[83] The answer is *both*, although unlike an analyst such as Aquinas who can set politics apart as a category of morals, Langland feels the same need as Ockham to confront the two problems in the simultaneous form in which they exist in the Fair Field. I think Spearing correctly judges the ending of the first vision as "a triumph of good advice and good intentions, but with no guarantee that society can really be reformed on this basis."[84] Since true reform can be achieved only if the King's triumph of good advice and good intentions is joined by all the members of society—all those individual wills, good and bad and (mostly) in-between, eventually represented by Will the Dreamer—Langland offers little hope for the repair of the state, only for the reform of particular men in the image and likeness of God.

The second vision of *Piers Plowman* concerns the attempt to reform the common people along lines proposed by Conscience at the close of the first vision (B. iv. 180–84). In keeping with a more subjective approach, Langland has constructed the action so that it roughly follows the sacrament of penance. The separate features of the plot, as John Burrow points out, are not really confession, plowing and pardon, but rather sermon, confession, pilgrimage, and pardon.[85] Reason comes before the people and preaches a *sermo ad status* in which "he bad Wastour go werche what he best kouþe / And wynnen his wastyng wiþ som maner crafte" (B. v. 24–25). Proper conduct is urged for all the estates from merchant to king, and when Reason has ended his preaching, Repentance makes the communal Will weep tears of contrition (B. v. 59–61). After the Seven Sins have come forward to make their confessions, the people are ready to set off on a penitential pilgrimage to Truth.

Here the process breaks down. Not knowing the way to Truth, the people accept the guidance of Piers Plowman, who transforms the pil-

83. Kean, "Justice, Kingship and the Good Life," pp. 108–09.
84. Spearing, *Dream-Poetry*, p. 141.
85. Burrow, "The Action of Langland's Second Vision," p. 210. The medieval preacher who stated that confession "shuld be done afore all oþur good werkes" (*Middle English Sermons*, ed. Ross, p. 285) was following closely the belief of Augustine: "Initium operum bonorum, confessio est operum malorum" (*In Joannis Evangelium*, XII, 13—PL 35 : 1491). From the eighth century "a pilgrimage was often imposed as a penance on one who had confessed a particularly grave fault"; see E.R. Labande, "Pilgrimage," NCE, vol. XI, pp. 366–67. Carruthers, "Time, Apocalypse, and the Plot of *Piers Plowman*," 178, argues that the poem's entire action has a "modular" organization which repeats the pattern of wandering, conversion, and pilgrimage.

grimage into a season of plowing in the Half Acre and thereby, in terms of the allegory, substitutes one literal sense for another. A literal journey to a holy shrine is replaced by a life of productive labor, whose significance is established both by the prior action and by the common understanding that "al our lyuynge in þis world is a pilgrymage."[86] While showing that social problems must have a moral solution, Langland retains a tight grip on his original insistence that fulfilling one's duties in society has a value in itself. By discovering a way to examine the physical and spiritual aspects of the problem simultaneously, Langland can show the common underlying cause more graphically: *acedia* causes the pilgrim to halt his progress to a holy shrine and the laborer to stop plowing his field.[87]

The entrance of Piers, appearing suddenly but humbly in the midst of a disordered world, constitutes a true turning-point in the action of the *Visio*. His advent has almost been demanded by earlier figures deficient in the very ways that he is strong. The confession of Sloth caps the sequence of the Seven Deadly Sins and, in the C-text, is placed by itself at the beginning of Passus VII; indeed, the C-poet makes this passus a single block of unified action starting with Sloth and ending with Piers. After Sloth has passed from the scene, Repentance delivers his sermon and Hope summons the people together for their pilgrimage. The next new and colorful figure is the Palmer; in the A-text he is the very next after Sloth, without intervening characters. Reminiscent of the Dreamer, he is an idle wanderer who has visited all the sacred places of the world but cannot tell the pilgrims where to find Truth (B. v. 526–36). The Palmer is followed in all texts by Piers the Plowman, who enters as a figure of general correction. He labors diligently at his tasks, he does not wander but is satisfied to toil in the Half Acre, and while his method of pilgrimage leads to none of the Palmer's exotic shrines in Sinai and Armenia, it sets him and his companions on the road to Truth.

Manual labor, long the hermit's chief weapon against *acedia*, is what Piers prescribes for the faltering pilgrims: he wants them to help plow the Half Acre. But out of all the forms of employment in the world, why did Langland choose plowing? Why is Piers a *plowman?* There are many answers to this second question, most of them appropriate to

---

86. *Dives and Pauper,* p. 1 ("Tables"), assigns this as the title to a whole section of the work in which man's life is explained allegorically as a pilgrimage (pp. 52–54). Piers' substitution would also have had an appeal to Lollards and others who believed that men should not waste their time going on pilgrimages and should devote themselves instead to "the trewe labour that thei shulden do at home in help of hemsilf and hore neȝeboris"; see Owst, *Literature and Pulpit,* pp. 556–57.

87. Wenzel, p. 86, mentions sloth as a hindrance to the pilgrim.

one or another of Piers' roles in the poem,[88] but during his first appearance there are two ready explanations suggested by the two levels on which Langland is working. First, social commentators like Thomas Brinton designated plowmen as the last and humblest degree of laborers, those men dedicated to the works of human servitude such as plowing, digging, sowing, reaping, and working with their hands. They may occupy the lowest rung on the social ladder, but even plowmen are virtuous compared to the wasteful idlers who produce nothing and thus deprive themselves of the kingdom of God.[89] And secondly, Bishop Brinton makes clear in his sermon that manual labor of even the humblest sort had assumed a spiritual significance, so much so that the plow had become a symbol of labor whatever its physical or spiritual nature. It is not surprising, therefore, to find the plow itself figuring in discussions of the corresponding vice.

An illustration common to at least two manuscripts of *La Somme le Roy* makes this point clearly and forcefully. The illumination is divided into four panels. The top left shows Prowess, one of the virtues contrary to sloth; the bottom left shows David, typifying prowess; the bottom right dramatizes the virtue of work as a farmer sowing a large bag of seeds; and the last panel presents Idleness—"a plowman wearing a coif lies on the ground at the back. . . In center, his neglected plow, to which are harnessed two horses."[90] Somewhere behind this pictorial tradition is probably the Biblical verse that Langland knew very well: "*Propter frigus piger arare noluit*" (Prov. 20.4). Alanus de Insulis says that *acedia* makes the Christian withdraw his hand from the plow, and John Bromyard likens sloth to an unused plow and a lazy man's life to an untilled field.[91] Not only has Langland selected plowing as the archetype for all virtuous labor, but he has made the wasters' refusal to plow the Half Acre a symbolic expression of sin—a man's slothful denial of his duty as a pilgrim in this life.

Even at his initial entry into the poem, Piers assumes in his person much more than the status of a mere plowman. Besides following the plow for fifty winters, he practices a variety of other useful tasks:

88. Robertson and Huppé, pp. 18–19, produce a great deal of patristic testimony in which plowmen were interpreted as priests. While this view of Piers suits him later in the poem (B. xix), it is not very strongly supported in the second vision.

89. Brinton, *Sermons*, ed. Devlin, vol. I, p. 83.

90. *La Somme le Roy*, ed. Eric George Millar (Oxford: The Roxburghe Club, 1953), pp. 37–38, commenting on Pl. X of Millar MS., fol. 121ʳ, and Pl. XXX of BM. Add. MS. 28162, fol. 8ʳ. The latter illumination is also reproduced by Rosemond Tuve, *Allegorical Imagery*, fig. 19 (p. 96).

91. Alanus de Insulis, *Summa de Arte Praedicatoria*, "Contra Acediam" (*PL* 210: 125–26), and John Bromyard, *Summa Praedicantium*, A, viii, art. 5 (Basel, 1484).

[I dyke and I delue, I do that Treuthe] hoteþ;
Som tyme I sowe and som tyme I þresshe,
In taillours craft and tynkeris craft, what Truþe kan deuyse,
I weue and I wynde and do what Truþe hoteþ.

(B. v. 545–48)

When he assigns the men to plow and the women to spin cloth, every-
thing seems natural enough, but when he orders the knights to protect
the people and Holy Church, he immediately assumes a stature of au-
thority that transcends the sense of a literal plowman.

The C-poet adds to the company of pilgrims three new figures who
clarify the allegorical character of Piers. One is a real plowman who
steps into the literal role vacated by Piers; the second is Active who is
bound by worldly duties and therefore cannot follow the rest; and the
third is Contemplation who is willing to suffer adversity to ally himself
with Piers' quest (C. vii. 292–308). The inclusion of these three figures
helps to clarify Langland's desire to equate plowing with going on pil-
grimage. For the common laborer, the man committed to Brinton's
"works of human servitude," the faithful execution of his earthly du-
ties constitutes his pilgrimage through life, while for the man who has
chosen the path of religious contemplation, plowing becomes a dynamic
image for his spiritual employment. Both are fused in the language of
Piers' Will (B. vi. 101–04).

Yet no sooner has Piers put the pilgrims to work in the Half Acre
than certain dissident elements begin to neglect their assignments
(B. vi. 115–24). When Piers threatens them with Hunger, they feign
blindness and lameness in the hope they can secure alms without
working. Piers exercises his ability to see men's real inner intentions
and rebukes these shirkers soundly: "Ye wasten þat men wynnen wiþ
trauaille and tene" (B. vi. 133). He condemns the idlers and frauds for
living "in sleuþe," while he praises righteous hermits and anchorites
for their moderation, promising to bestow his alms upon them instead
(B. vi. 145–51). Since even the knights cannot force the wasters to
work, Piers must summon Hunger to abuse them and, sure enough,
their behavior is instantly reformed:

An heep of heremytes henten hem spades[92]
And kitten hir copes and courtepies hem maked
And wente as werkmen to wedynge and mowynge
And doluen drit and dung to ditte out hunger.

(B. vi. 187–90)

---

92. This recalls the "heremytes on an heep" (B. prol. 53) associated earlier with the
Dreamer.

Piers' action against the idlers accords strictly with the Scriptural injunction which Langland alluded to earlier: "*quoniam si quis non vult operari, nec manducet*" ("If any man will not work, neither let him eat"—2 Thess. 3.10).[93] This text had long been used to condemn *acedia* on the part of members of the lay community.[94]

This scene gives dynamic force to the work-ethic that has been developing from the poem's beginning. Holy Church, the first authoritative figure the Dreamer meets, unfolds the poem's central doctrines and resorts often to work-imagery in the process of instruction. Those who "werche wel" in the world will go to heaven, while those who "werchen with Wrong" will dwell with Satan (B. i. 128−33). This is the refrain heard throughout. Imaginatif, for example, says that God will put the saint in the highest of heaven and the penitent thief in the lowest, "*quia reddit vnicuique iuxta opera sua*" (B. xii. 213, recalling Mt. 16.27). Devotion to the Truth necessitates the performance of good works and leads toward a state of Christ-like perfection from which idlers will be excluded by the terms of the Pardon; Holy Church had taught this same lesson earlier:

> For who is trewe of his tonge, telleþ noon ooþer,
> Dooþ þe werkes þerwiþ and wilneþ no man ille,
> He is a god by þe gospel, a grounde and o lofte,
> And ek ylik to oure lord by Seint Lukes wordes.
>
> (B. i. 88−91)

She supported her sermon with a reference to the parable of the unjust steward (Lk. 16.10−13) and later, as part of her argument in favor of good works, cited another passage which confirmed their necessity for salvation (B. i. 187): "*Fides sine operibus mortua est*" ("So also faith without works is dead"—Jas. 2.26). Holy Church's sermon, placed early in the *Visio* and delivered by a figure of unimpeachable authority, drives hard at the theme of good works far in anticipation of our arrival in the Half Acre and thus helps to fix our understanding of what Langland actually means by works.

Scriptural verses quoted in the text often provide valuable insights into the meaning of a passage, especially when these verses are closely tied with major traditions of exegesis.[95] Hunger's argument with Piers

93. Skeat, II, p. 6, notes that this same verse was inserted in the margin of MS. Oriel College Oxford 79 alongside B. prol. 38.

94. Wenzel, p. 35.

95. Robertson and Huppé, p. 2, have helped us toward a fuller understanding of the kind of poem Langland wrote: "The existence of a large body of Scriptural quotations in the text of the poem furnishes a key to the ultimate source of its allegorical meaning. As we shall show, these quotations are not haphazard, decorative, or macaronic, but are

is one section heavy with such Biblical references. Hunger's main contention is that men must be forced to work:

"Go to Genesis þe geaunt, engendrour of vs alle:
In sudore and swynke þow shalt þi mete tilie
And laboure for þi liflode, and so oure lord hiȝte."

(B. vi. 232–34)

Wenzel cites this as a major Biblical text used by medieval commentators to reject slothfulness: "*In sudore vultus tui vesceris pane*" ("In the sweat of thy face shalt thou eat bread"—Gen. 3.19). It appears chief among those passages that condemn the unwillingness to work and had become "ubiquitous in late medieval discussions of sloth." [96] Owst says that English homilists from the twelfth through the fifteenth century used it to remind plowmen of their kinship with Adam and to emphasize that men of all degrees must work. [97] A tract once attributed to Richard Rolle cites this verse in a condemnation of idleness that comes even closer to Langland's:

To trauail was man bonden after he had synnid: thorugh goddis biddinge þat to him said: *In sudore uultus tui vesceris pane tuo*, . . . þou sal trauail stalwordli & noght fayntli, for he biddis þe trauail "with swete of þi face, ay til þou torne to þe erth," þat is, al þi life-tyme, þat þou lose na tyme in idelnes. [98]

Hunger quickly follows this reference with another: "*Piger propter frigus* no feeld wolde tilie; / He shal go begge and bidde and no man bete his hunger" (B. vi. 235–36). This derives from the verse "*Propter frigus piger arare noluit*" ("Because of the cold, the sluggard would not plough"—Prov. 20.4), which formed a standard accompaniment to late medieval instruction against sloth. [99] The C-text makes this point explicit: "The slowe caytif for colde a wolde no corn tylye; / In somer *for his sleuthe* he shal haue defaute" (C. viii. 244–45). After this refer-

---

connected intimately with the *sentence* of the poem." Even grander claims are made by John A. Alford, "The Role of the Quotations in *Piers Plowman*," *Speculum*, 52 (1977), 80–99, who believes that the allusions are often as central as in many sermons where "the quotations are the points *toward which* as well as from which the preacher is constantly working" (p. 86). This confidence is given elaborate expression by Ruth M. Ames, *The Fulfillment of Scriptures: Abraham, Moses, and Piers* (Evanston: Northwestern University Press, 1970). Allen, "Langland's Reading and Writing," has begun a major re-evaluation of the poet's recourse to Latin texts as part of his compositional process.
    96. Wenzel, pp. 100–01. Not otherwise heavy with Latin, the Z-text contains all of Hunger's scriptural allusions: *in sudore, piger propter frigus, seruus nequam*, and *beati omnes: / Labores manuum tuarum quia mondurabis* (vii. 216, 219, 222, 236–37).
    97. Owst, *Literature and Pulpit*, pp. 553 and 555.
    98. Rolle, "Our Daily Work," in *Yorkshire Writers*, ed. Horstmann, vol. I, p. 138.
    99. Wenzel, p. 100.

ence follows an allusion to the *servus piger* who buried his talent (Mt. 25.24 ff.), a parable that had become a recurrent exemplum against sloth since the age when Augustine wrote, "This parable was also preached on account of those who are unwilling to undertake the duty of a dispenser in the church, offering for an excuse the slothful pretext that they do not want to render an account of the sins of others."[100] Again the C-text makes explicit the passage's moral content:

> Ac he þat was a wreche and wolde nat trauaile
> The lord for his lachesse and *his luther sleuthe*
> Bynom hym al þat he hadde and ȝaf hit to his felawe
> þat leely hadde ylabored . . .
>
> (C. viii. 252–55)

Hunger's judgment accords with the impression that the pilgrims in the Half Acre are re-enacting, in familiar contemporary terms, the wandering of the Israelites in the wilderness of Sinai.[101] Like the refugees from Egypt, the pilgrims have set off for the Promised Land (Truth) but do not know the way, and when they encounter unforeseen difficulties like the season of plowing, they begin to grumble. This standard medieval interpretation of the wanderings in the desert is offered by Antoninus of Florence in his discussion "De Accidia":

> When the Israelites went through the desert by God's command in order that they might reach the Promised Land, they often suffered tedium and sadness on account of their labors, and sometimes even abhorred the manna. Therefore, they were often punished and finally kept from the Promised Land, according to Num. 14. And this signifies the *accidiosi*, who loathe going through the desert of penance or the religious life because of its labors, and who are disgusted with all spiritual things, so that finally they are deprived of everlasting life.[102]

This was a standard example of spiritual sloth in popular literature such as Dante's *Purgatorio* (xviii, 133–35), where the grumbling Israelites are used to illustrate *acedia*.[103] In this allegorical sense, the Priest who impugns the pardon fills the role of Aaron, founder of the priestly order (Num. 17), who can acknowledge the Golden Calf of indulgences without recognizing the validity of the pardon sent down from Truth.

---

100. Augustine, *Faith and Works*, 17, 32, in *Treatises on Marriage and Other Subjects*, ed. Roy J. Deferrari (Washington: Catholic University of America Press, 1955), p. 261.

101. For a similar connection between the pilgrims in the Half Acre and the wandering Israelites, see Lawlor, *Piers Plowman: An Essay in Criticism*, pp. 282–83.

102. Wenzel, p. 101, translating from Antoninus of Florence, *Summa Theologica*, I, ix (Venice: Jenson, 1480).

103. Wenzel, p. 132.

Like Moses breaking the Tablets of the Commandments, Piers tears the pardon in a fit of righteous wrath ("pure tene"—B. vii. 119).[104] The sense we get from the action of the second vision, aided by Hunger's allusions to Scripture, is that the pilgrims in the Half Acre share the same failing as the slothful Israelites and can be saved only by penance and adherence to the law, here the imperative of Dowel contained in the Pardon. The "gloss" to the Pardon shows how the virtues of labor, love, and fidelity to the law are all interconnected:

> Alle libbynge laborers þat lyuen by hir hondes,
> That treweliche taken and treweliche wynnen,
> And lyuen in loue and in lawe, for hir lowe herte
> Hadde þe same absolucion þat sent was to Piers.
>
> (B. vii. 61–64)

Piers' multiple identity—as a plowman, as Moses leading the stubborn Israelites, as a paradigm for the contemplative life, as the model Christian advancing in the pilgrimage of the life of man—goes far toward dissolving the standard distinction between physical and spiritual works, a distinction necessarily weakened by the need to see political problems (*actus exteriores*) in terms of inner acts of intention. Early in the poem Langland had divided society into two general phyla of physical and spiritual laborers: "some putten hem to þe plou3, pleiden ful selde," while "in preiers and in penaunce putten hem manye" (B. prol. 20 and 25). Later, Conscience uses the same two groupings in his advocacy of virtuous living:

> Ech man to pleye with a plow, pykoise or spade,
> Spynne or sprede donge or spille hymself with sleuþe.
> Preestes and persons wiþ *Placebo* to hunte,
> And dyngen vpon Dauid eche day til eue.
>
> (B. iii. 309–12)

The distinction between the active and the contemplative is never completely forgotten, not even during the internal wanderings of the

---

104. The parallel between Piers' tearing of the Pardon and Moses' breaking of the Tablets was noticed by Nevill Coghill, "The Pardon of Piers Plowman," p. 314; and Mary C[arruthers] Schroeder, "Piers Plowman: The Tearing of the Pardon," *PQ*, 49 (1970), 8–18. Later in the poem (B. xvii. 1 ff.) Moses appears as *Spes* bearing the Tablets which, like the Pardon, contain an unexpected two-part message: "Dilige deum et proximum tuum." The Dreamer fills the role of the Priest by asking the impertinent question, "Is here alle þi lordes lawes?" This resemblance of scenes and personages is mentioned briefly by J.A. Burrow, "Words, Works and Will," p. 122. A further connection between Piers and Moses, based on Ex. 17.6, is suggested by R. E. Kaske, "Patristic Exegesis in the Criticism of Medieval Literature: The Defense," in *Interpretations of Piers Plowman*, ed. Vasta, p. 331.

Vitae where the psychological nature of the action would lead us to expect a concentration upon spiritual works. Here the essential role of the active man that was vacated by Piers at the conclusion of the Pardon Scene is filled by *Activa-Vita*, "Peers prentys the Plouhman," who assumes Piers' adversary relation to idlers. He is inserted in part as a continuing reminder of the virtue of manual labor that opposes physical sloth.

The second vision explores the most troublesome implications of the first. Society's problems, most of them economic on the surface, cannot be solved by political means, not by the power of an ideal king counseled by Reason and Conscience, not even by the example of Piers the ideal workman. Some men will always elude the king's law, some men will always resist the example of upright living. Without forgetting the problem's broad scope, Langland focuses more and more tightly upon the individual whose duty it is to live the good life. Only on this level, which is both microscopic and microcosmic, can a remedy be found.[105] The subject of this minute examination must, of course, be someone different from Piers, someone needing remedy, someone sufficiently representative of the ills besetting mankind, and at the same time someone well enough known to the poet to be scrutinized in the closest detail. The convention of the dream-vision offered a natural candidate.

Will the Dreamer, who had been a mute witness throughout much of the *Visio*, becomes the central figure in the *Vitae*, where the workings of his psychology are carefully observed and noted, and his moral failings discovered and dramatized. Just the contrary to Tennyson's Lady of Shalott, Langland exchanges the panorama of Camelot—complete with its model King whose Merlin (Conscience plus Reason) helped expel Morgan la Fey (Lady Mede)—for a mirror in which the dominating image is the poet's own. Faithful to the evolution of *Piers Plowman* in the B-continuation, my remaining chapters will focus attention on that image in an attempt to understand better its meaning and, finally, to speculate about its resemblance to its creator. Long ago Langland the man vanished utterly from the pages of history—we cannot even be sure of his name—but in the pages of his poem, as in a mirror, he has left behind an eerie image, shadowy and protean and yet persistent, that continues to haunt our imaginations even after we have spent many hours searching for answers to the questions he poses: "Who am I? And where can I find Dowel?"

105. Wittig makes this point forcefully in "The Inward Journey," 280, and "Long Will's Pilgrimage," 53.

VI
The Question of Will in
His Waking Life

One of the unique features of *Piers Plowman* is its series of dream-visions punctuated by periods of waking. While contemporary dream-poems by Chaucer and the *Pearl*-poet are sustained under the fiction of a single uninterrupted dream, Langland chose to break Will's vision into eight separate dreams, plus two dreams-within-dreams.[1] Reasons for this episodic construction are not altogether clear. It might be argued that Langland needed to interrupt Will's visions in order to switch from one mode of allegory to another, although Chaucer felt no such need in moving between the strictly divided episodes of *The House of Fame*, and Langland himself could move in Passus XIX from divine vision to personification allegory, to historical narrative, and then to psychomachia, all without disturbing the Dreamer's sleep.

While admitting that the waking episodes often fall at appropriate moments following long and coherent stretches of action, I believe that the alternating sections of sleep and waking have a more important function. They allow Langland to establish an on-going contrast between the world of dreams and the waking life, between the Dreamer asleep and Will awake. The extra-visionary action constitutes a separate fictive world with its own moral order and rules of continuity. Langland enables his audience, as Chaucer does not, to observe the waking Dreamer over a long span of years, to share his responses to a variety of visionary experiences, and to bear witness to the broad pattern of his behavior with the possibility of a persistent vice.

1. Frank, "The Number of Visions in *Piers Plowman*," 310–11, reviews the disagreement among critics over how to divide and number the visions.

David Mills has discussed the ways that Langland generally contrasts the sinfulness of the world with the ideal advice given by figures in the dreams, and he also senses in the ambiguity of Will's character the potential for sinfulness—his idleness, his failure to do good works, his boredom in church, his inner aridity: "The physical picture may well be an image of search, but it is also an image of aimlessness and one which becomes associated increasingly with despair."[2] But Langland does not develop these negative features without coherence or pattern. All the faults that can be found in Will not only suggest an integral moral concept but also join in a concatenation of vices leading from bad to worse, from mere idleness toward—but not quite reaching—fatal despair.

The Dreamer awake is figured differently from the Dreamer asleep. The distinction is carefully rendered and is, I believe, crucial to Langland's intention. In his waking life Will is sensitized, provoked, and haunted by his dreams, as the carefree rover of the Prologue is transformed gradually into a tormented wanderer. His quest for greater religious knowledge and intellectual certainty is undercut by his failure to put into practice any of the instruction given to him. Near the poem's end in the last waking encounter between Will and Need, he can offer only one dubious piece of evidence for a life of good works: the verse transcriptions of his dreams.

But if Will's spiritual agitation and general failure to enact Dowel represent aspects of his sloth, perhaps as cause and effect, we must be sure to respect Langland's highly ambivalent treatment of him as the poem's protagonist. We must resist the urge to judge him too harshly or too quickly, because the character whose state of mind and spiritual well-being are drawn into question is also the hero-narrator, the privileged recipient of dreams attributed at times to grace, to Reason, and even to Christ. The grandest of the dreams, such as his vision of the Passion and the Harrowing of Hell (B. xviii), possess an expansiveness and spiritual might that far exceed the bluntness of those minatory dreams typical of the *acedia* tradition.[3] Whenever these exalted visions end, however, Will is returned to a waking life where his actions are again subject to our moral scrutiny, made more urgent each time by the cumulative experience of the dreams and their teachings.

---

2. David Mills, "The Role of the Dreamer in *Piers Plowman*," pp. 191–92, examines the alternation of dream and reality; on pp. 186–89, he identifies Will's possible vices.
    3. For people whose sin involves sleeping too much, it is apt that divine warnings should come through dreams. For examples, see *The Book of the Knight of La Tour-Landry*, ed. Thomas Wright, 1868; rev. 1906, EETS o.s. 33, pp. 42–44; and *An Alpha-*

In a work so deeply concerned with judging correctly—deciding between alternatives and choosing the right knowledge, the right beliefs, the right actions for the good life—it is not surprising that Langland should have made any final judgment about the poem's central character so extremely hard. Is he saint or sinner? Inspired lunatic or melancholic fool? Poet or procrastinator? Such a studied ambiguity surrounds Will that cogent arguments can be made on both sides. If in the following pages I do not always offer such a balanced view, it is because my aim is not so much to deal with ambiguity as to explore one side of that division in an effort to show how Will may be subject to slothfulness.

Jay Martin sharpens our sense of Will's ambiguity by exploring two provocative types associated with him, the wanderer and the fool. In the bad sense, a wanderer might be a fraudulent beggar or land-leaping hermit, but in the good sense, the wanderer might be a holy pilgrim or even a poet roaming the land in search of marvels to enrich his lays.[4] Like Dante's epic, *Piers Plowman* fuses the notions of pilgrimage and poetic search, although there is a moral tension in the English work lacking in the Italian: "Langland values that which is symbolized by a wandering life or what theologians call *via*, the 'way'; but when he comes to dramatize the *via* in terms of wandering, he deplores its objectification, for capricious wandering destroys the social order."[5] When discussing the fool-figure, Martin is less inclined to see the possibility of a double interpretation. He pictures the fool only as a critic of society whose visions are divinely inspired and therefore have a truthfulness beyond question.[6] He neglects to mention that some fools were indeed witless and their visions open to boundless suspicion. Though returning later to the figures of fool and wanderer—both of whom take their places in the *acedia* tradition—I shall begin

---

bet of Tales, ed. M. M. Banks, 1904–05, EETS o.s. 126 and 127, nos. 263, 284, and 285, deriving from Caesarius of Heisterbach, *Dialogus Miraculorum*, ed. Strange, vol. I, pp. 202–06 (Dist. IV, caps. xxxii–xxxviii).

4. Jay Martin, "Wil as Fool and Wanderer in *Piers Plowman*," TSLL, 3 (1962), 535–48. One homilist sums up the positive connotation of wandering in commonplace terms: "we muste nedis goye and not to stonde here in þis worlde. 3e see well þat pilgrymmes and weyfferynge men be not comonly stondynge, but euermore spedynge hem in here weyes. And þer-fore as þe gospell of Seynt Poule seyþ [2 Cor. 5; 1 Pet. 2.11] 'vocamur peregrini et aduene'—we be called pilgrymmes and comen of an-oþur contre" (*Middle English Sermons*, ed. Ross, p. 74). Frye, *Anatomy of Criticism*, p. 57, describes how the wandering poet transforms the journey into the subject of his verse.

5. Martin, 545.

6. *Ibid.*, 539–40. Siegfried Wenzel, "The Wisdom of the Fool" in *The Wisdom of Poetry*, pp. 238–39, agrees with Donaldson that Langland had a consistently negative view of the "fol sage."

by examining another standard figure represented by the protagonist: Will as sleeper.

The convention of the dream-vision required that Will fall asleep *once* in order to enter the realm of visionary search. Langland alters the convention by making Will fall asleep eight different times, in different locales, in different dress, at different times of day, and under different circumstances, so that the one consistent image offered to the reader is that of a man going to sleep. Drawing upon a rich patristic tradition, Robertson and Huppé examine each instance and judge the varying implications. For example, "the sleep of Passus XI was a sleep of the spirit as the flesh turned to concupiscence; the sleep of Passus XVI is the sleep of the contemplative, isolating himself from the world so that he may enjoy the vision of Christ."[7] These two interpretations are common enough in the exegetical tradition that is being called to witness, but they are by no means the only interpretations. Rabanus Maurus says that sleep is a mental stupor. The *Glossa Ordinaria* says it represents the forgetting of divine treasures. Augustine calls it the ignorance leading to sin. The *Allegoriae in Sacram Scripturam* gives the word *dormitio* seven distinct meanings: spiritual torpor, sickness, blindness, falling into sin, death, sexual intercourse, and the quietness of contemplation.[8] The mystical aspect of sleep is perfectly expressed by Walter Hilton in his exposition on "Ego dormio et cor meum vigilat" (Cant. 5.2):

The more I sleep from outward things, the more wakeful am I in knowing of Jhesu and of inward things. I may not wake to Jhesu but if I sleep to the world. And therefore, the grace of the Holy Ghost shutting the fleshly eyes, doth the soul sleep from worldly vanity, and opening the ghostly eyes waketh into the sight of God's majesty hid under cloud of His precious manhood.[9]

Augustine believed that a sleeper could discuss true principles in his non-mystical dream and then awake with the moral profit of remem-

---

7. Robertson and Huppé, p. 193, citing evidence found in Rabanus Maurus, *Allegoriae in Universam Sacram Scripturam* (*PL* 112:913). They earlier discuss the sleep meant "to suggest allegorically Will's state of sinful ignorance" (pp. 37–38).

8. *Allegoriae in Universam Sacram Scripturam* (*PL* 112:913); Rabanus Maurus elsewhere comments on Eph. 5.14: "Dormitionem hanc, stuporem mentis significat, quae alienatur a vera via" (*PL* 112:451); *Glossa Ordinaria* on Ps. 75.5 (*PL* 113:963); Judson Boyce Allen reviews the seven ways that Hugh of St. Cher interprets sleep in the Bible, in *The Friar as Critic: Literary Attitudes in the Later Middle Ages* (Nashville: Vanderbilt University Press, 1971), pp. 32–33.

9. Walter Hilton, *The Scale of Perfection*, ed. Evelyn Underhill (London: Watkins, 1923), pp. 424–25. Spearing, *Dream-Poetry*, p. 116, quotes Augustine and Bernard as saying that the imagery of dreams is "preliminary to genuine mystical experience."

bering these truths.[10] Late medieval scholastics questioned whether a sleeper should be held morally accountable for his thoughts and actions, and some of them suggested that since a sleeper has no free will, he cannot commit acts that are morally right or wrong.[11]

Yet alongside the profusion of Biblical interpretations, and far beneath the analyses offered by mystics and scholastics, we need to reserve a place for sleep in and of itself. No less an authority than Augustine reminds us that sleep can be nothing more than the natural process whereby the body is restored from the strains of labor.[12] V. A. Kolve offers the much-needed caveat that a sign or gesture may mean itself and nothing more:

> We must take care in our lexicography of signs to survey not merely the *full* range of demonstrable symbolic meanings, but also to allow for the *literal* meaning of things, and to respect both the possibility and the dignity of that literal meaning in our critical practice. Context governs.[13]

And when interpretation beyond the literal sense *is* called for, context guides and limits. Robertson and Huppé approach the problem of sleep in *Piers Plowman* as if each given context yielded a single definite meaning. Part of my intention in the following pages is to show that Langland has done much to preserve that sense of ambiguity inherent in the underlying tradition, with contexts allowing for more than one interpretation and more than one moral conclusion, so that we seldom form a clear impression, never know what to expect, and are always kept judging.

Langland begins his poem with a waking prologue notable for its brevity. In an age when the tendency was to lengthen and elaborate the introductions to dreams, he has stripped his prologue to a bare minimum. The landscape is reduced to a mere sketch without any of the decorative elements exploited by other poets in the Alliterative movement, although it initiates a far larger and more ambitious poem than *Wynnere and Wastoure*, *The Parlement of the Three Ages*, or even *Pearl*.[14] Its shortness, sparsity of detail, and reliance on a few selected

---

10. *The Immortality of the Soul* (14, 23), trans. Ludwig Schopp in *Writings of Saint Augustine* (New York: The Fathers of the Church, vol. 2, 1947), pp. 42–43.

11. Leff, *Gregory of Rimini*, pp. 212–13.

12. Augustine, *The Immortality of the Soul* (14, 23), p. 42.

13. Kolve, "Chaucer and the Visual Arts," p. 314.

14. The unusual briefness of this waking introduction is remarked upon by Spearing, *Dream-Poetry*, p. 138; Mills, "Role of the Dreamer," p. 184; and Burrow, "The Audience of *Piers Plowman*," 383.

features might create the impression of shallowness, if not for the remarkable details which *are* included:

> In a somer seson whan softe was þe sonne
> I shoop me into a shroud as I a sheep weere;
> In habite as an heremite, vnholy of werkes,
> Wente wide in þis world wondres to here.
> Ac on a May morwenynge on Maluerne hilles
> Me bifel a ferly, of Fairye me þoȝte.
> I was wery forwandred and wente me to reste
> Vnder a brood bank by a bourne syde,
> And as I lay and lenede and loked on þe watres
> I slombred into a slepyng, it sweyed so murye.

(B. prol. 1–10)

This exposition serves chiefly to introduce the Dreamer and his immediate circumstances—nothing of his past life, his real profession, or the places he has visited before Malvern. But the poet's restraint in executing this deft portrait has not rendered the details perfunctory, but rather charged them with the potential for signification. When the Dreamer is said to be dressed as if he were a hermit or a *sheep*, the poet raises questions meant to remain with us, to be sure, but these provocative details also sharpen our senses to the otherwise conventional elements of the opening. As I shall seek to demonstrate, these features were probably selected to suggest the Dreamer's moral condition. The simple fact that he falls asleep—an event that is, in one sense, required by the genre—takes on added significance even by the way it is staged, since his sleep comes so quickly after the poem has begun.

The Dreamer wanders "in a somer seson" and falls asleep "on a May morwenynge." Although both details are common enough in other poems, Langland makes these stock conventions work semantically. In his examination of sloth in *The Parson's Tale* (706–07), Chaucer explains that morning is "the tyme that, by wey of resoun, men sholde nat slepe" because "the morwe tyde is moost convenable a man to seye his preyeres and for to thynken on God." The notions of summertime and May return later in the poem, not to denote a season of the year but to describe the sense of false comfort felt by careless men as they lapse into sin:

> For muche murþe is amonges riche, as in mete and cloþyng,
> And muche murþe in May is amonges wilde beestes;
> And so forþ while somer lasteþ hir solace dureþ.

(B. xiv. 157–59)

Furthermore, the Dreamer who falls asleep in a suspicious season and at the wrong time of day also falls asleep in the wrong place. Unlike the courtly dreamer who lies in his bed, Will is outside "vnder a brood bank," like the slothful man in Gower's *Vox Clamantis* who is satisfied to sleep outdoors on the ground.[15] D. W. Robertson thinks that all dreamer-narrators are open to the charge of slothfulness by virtue of the fact that they fall asleep in the first place,[16] but we should recall once more V. A. Kolve's caveat that "context governs." And the context of *Piers Plowman*'s opening, largely determined by the kind of religious poem that follows, invites a far stricter moral judgment than the beginning of a poem like *The Parlement of Foules*.

Besides the circumstances of time and place that attend his sleeping, Will shows another trait frequently mentioned by writers on *acedia*: he roams and ranges about the countryside to hear wonders, and in the C-text he has already seen many "selkouthe thynges." Such roaming after curious sights connotes a mental vagrancy that would have been recognized as *curiositas*, condemned since the days of John Cassian. The slothful woman in *The Pilgrimage of the Life of Man*, for instance, is "out to ffynde thynges newe."[17] Unlike the narrator of *The Parlement of the Three Ages* who has been in the forest poaching and goes to sleep exhausted by the rigors of the hunt, Will is drawn along by no more than a vague longing for mental excitement. He wants only to *hear* marvels and does not mention a desire to participate directly. Unlike *Pearl* and other contemporary dream-poems, the vision's contents seem to arise from nothing specific in the Dreamer's waking

15. *Vox Clamantis* (VII, xiii, 821–22) in John Gower, *The Complete Works: The Latin Works*, ed. G. C. Macaulay (Oxford: The Clarendon Press, 1902): "Mollia qui dudum quesiuit stramina lecto, / Anguibus aspersa frigida terra subest" (p. 294). The reader might also be reminded of the beautiful Advent hymn, printed in *The Hours of the Divine Office in English and Latin*, 3 vols. (Collegeville, MN: The Liturgical Press, 1963), vol. I, p. 1149: "Mens iam resurgat, torpida / Non amplius iacens humi. . ."

16. Robertson, "The Doctrine of Charity in Medieval Gardens: A Topical Approach Through Symbolism and Allegory," *Speculum*, 26 (1951), 40–41. Yet Robert Henryson, for example, discourages any such interpretation of "The Lion and the Mouse" by concluding the first stanza with this couplet: "I rais and put all sleuth and sleip asyde, / And to ane wod I went allone but gyde"; *The Poems*, ed. Denton Fox (Oxford: The Clarendon Press, 1981), p. 54.

17. John Lydgate, *The Pilgrimage of the Life of Man*, ed. F. J. Furnivall and Katherine B. Locock, 1899, 1901, 1904, EETS e.s. 77, 83, 92, p. 318 (l. 11649). Curiosity, whether Cassian's *curiositas* or Gregory's *evagatio mentis circa illicita*, was long a symptom of sloth that affected both the mind and the body (Wenzel, p. 51 *et passim*). The temptation for the will to displace reality with its own curious fantasies is discussed by Russell A. Peck, "Willfulness and Wonders: Boethian Tragedy in the Alliterative *Morte Arthure*" in *The Alliterative Tradition in the Fourteenth Century*, ed. Bernard S. Levy and Paul E. Szarmach (Kent, OH: Kent State University Press, 1981), p. 155.

thoughts.[18] Thus his physical wandering and the vision of the chaotic Fair Field serve as objective correlatives for his mental disengagement, all suggesting the commonest and most easily recognized sign of one of the deadly sins—idleness.

Lack of employment was long thought to be a threat to the soul's health and was condemned in countless spiritual writings. *The Book of Vices and Virtues* summarized the general teachings on the condition, "as holy bookes tellen":

for whan a man is ydele and þe deuel fyndeþ hym ydel, he him setteþ a-swiþe to werke, and makeþ hym first þenke harm, and after to desire foule harlotries, as lecheries, and þus lese his tyme and moche good þat he myȝt doo þat he myȝt wynne þer-þorw paradis.[19]

Dame Nature gives the narrator of *Reson and Sensuallyte* a warning that leaves no doubt as to how he should proceed:

And thou, of slouthe and necligence,
Dost vnto kynde grete offence,
Of verray wilful ydelnesse,
The which ys lady and maistresse
Of vicys alle, this no drede.
Wherfore arys and take good hede,
Of wyt and of discrecion,
To do somme occupacion.[20]

Like this poem by Lydgate, *Piers Plowman* belongs to a class of works that are predominantly didactic in intent and begin by introducing a hero-narrator whose moral flaws are, at first, described in a manner both symbolic and enigmatic. *The Divine Comedy* is also such a poem. Dante starts his pilgrimage in despair, full of sleep, and in such a vulnerable condition that he is attacked by a leopard, a lion, and a wolf. These three beasts have always been interpreted as vices—sensuality,

18. Spearing, *Dream-Poetry*, p. 43, notes that one of the traits of late fourteenth-century poems is the "psychological link between the content of the dream and the dreamer's waking state of mind." If the Dreamer is curious and reckless (in the medieval sense of the word) and if the society of the Fair Field is characterized by slothful conduct—laziness or faithlessness to estate—then the link that Spearing sees in other poems may also be present here.

19. *The Book of Vices and Virtues*, p. 27. Benedict warned in his *Regula* (XLVIII, 1) that "otiositas inimica est animae." Chaucer called idleness "the yate of alle harmes" (*ParsT*, 714) and the "ministre and the norice unto vices" (*SecNT*, 1). Idleness is made the leader of vices in *The Assembly of Gods* (ll. 666 ff.), and Wyclif pronounced it "þe develis panter to tempte men to synne" in *Selected English Works*, ed. Arnold, vol. III, p. 200.

20. John Lydgate, *Reson and Sensuallyte*, ed. Ernst Sieper, 1901–03, EETS e.s. 84 and 89, p. 13 (461–68).

pride and avarice in the earliest commentaries; fraud, violence and in-continence in some modern footnotes.[21] As such, they form the figura-tive elements used to establish the allegorical mode and to provide ini-tial insights into the plight of a protagonist who is himself blind to the full significance of the beasts that attack him. Langland works just as subtly, as befits a poet describing the most stealthful of sins.[22] His im-ages are even less readily recognized as figural because they are bor-rowed from a repository of stock images not always charged with moral significance.

My discussion of the introduction ends with some comment on two details that are more powerfully charged, the Dreamer's transport into a wilderness and his suspicion that his vision is caused by fairies.

When Will crosses over the bourn between waking and dreaming, he finds himself in a wasteland: "Thanne gan I meten a merueillous sweuene, / That I was in a wildernesse, wiste I neuere where" (B. prol. 11−12).[23] Though the detail does not strictly belong to the waking prologue, its closeness to Will's waking life suggests the sort of nexus that a contemporary audience had grown to expect. No reader would have had a neutral reaction to the word *wildernesse* with its dual asso-ciations of wilderness and wildness:

Wildness meant more to the Middle Ages than the shrunken significance of the term would indicate today. The word implied everything that eluded Christian norms and the established framework of Christian society, referring to what was uncanny, unruly, raw, unpredictable, foreign, uncultured, and unculti-vated. It included the unfamiliar as well as the unintelligible. Just as the wilder-ness is the background against which medieval society is delineated, so wild-ness in the widest sense is the background of God's lucid order of creation.[24]

21. Francis Fergusson, *Dante* (New York: Macmillan, 1966), p. 98. Wenzel, p. 134, believes that Dante the pilgrim is initially impeded by *acedia*.

22. The treacherous subtlety of *acedia* was widely attested; Jonas of Orléans, *De In-stitutione Laicali* (III, vi), writes "qua peste multi clericorum et laicorum laborant, et se delinquere minime intelligunt" (*PL* 106:246).

23. Other poems use similar alliterative lines but without the forceful image of a wilderness. See *Wynnere and Wastoure* (l. 47), "Methoght I was in the world, wiste I not where"; and *Pearl* (l. 65), "I ne wyste in þis world quere þat hit wace."

24. Richard Bernheimer, *Wild Men in the Middle Ages: A Study in Art, Sentiment, and Demonology* (Cambridge, MA: Harvard University Press, 1952), pp. 19−20. The *OED*, vol. XII, W, p. 124, shows that *wilderness* is only a linguistic variant of *wildness*. Using attestations drawn from the first half of the fourteenth century, the *Dictionary* offers this definition (p. 125): "Something figured as a region of a wild or desolate char-acter, or in which one wanders or loses one's way; in religious use applied to the present world or life as contrasted with heaven or the future life." For example, *The Ancrene Riwle*, trans. M. B. Salu (London: Burns & Oates, 1955), p. 92, uses this commonplace notion of the world as "the wilderness through which you are travelling together with God's people towards the land of Jerusalem, that is, the Kingdom of Heaven."

Langland later uses the word *wilderness* with all this semantic strength to describe the life of temptation and sin through which every man passes on his way to the Heavenly Jerusalem (B. xvii. 101–04). This sense, too, stands behind the scene in which the people wander almost aimlessly in search of Truth. The spiritual sense inherent in these later scenes bears almost equal weight in the Prologue.

David Mills notes that while this wilderness may evoke the image of a desert father or prophet like John the Baptist, since Will *is* dressed as a hermit, it may also suggest his inner aridity according to the notion that "great sins are properly absolved by a life of overt wildness mirroring the sinner's moral wildness." [25] The disordered country into which Will passes (comparable to Dante's *selva oscura*) may therefore reflect something fundamentally amiss in his own spiritual life. The C-text was revised in order to incorporate a similar feeling of uncertainty, where the single correct alternative is nearly crowded out by wrong choices (prol. 10–13). This land where deceptions outnumber certainties is the one into which the Dreamer will descend to observe and live out most of his visionary experiences. It is a landscape that is also an inscape, and his lack of fear upon entering it suggests that grave problems also reside in his failure to estimate the danger of the place and to recognize the aptness of his receiving, personally, these visions of public corruption and spiritual chaos.

The last feature I wish to consider in the waking introduction is contained in the line "Me bifel a ferly, of Fairye me þoȝte" (B. prol. 6). Skeat interpreted this as meaning "due to fairy contrivance." [26] Yet in

25. Mills, "The Role of the Dreamer," p. 188; and Penelope B. R. Doob, *Nebuchadnezzar's Children: Conventions of Madness in Middle English Literature* (New Haven: Yale University Press, 1974), p. 163. The latter discussion profits from George H. Williams' study of the desert's symbolic meanings from Biblical times onward, in *Wilderness and Paradise in Christian Thought* (New York: Harper, 1962), pp. 1–64. J. A. W. Bennett (ed.), p. 82, compares the wildernesss in the Prologue to the desert through which the Israelites travelled—a recognizable sign of sin betokening the barrenness of Will's inner life.

26. Skeat, II, pp. 3–4. Bennett (ed.), p. 81, also draws attention to the connotations of this phrase. The *MED* (Part F. 1, p. 376) confirms Skeat's three definitions and adds to them the most common meaning today: a supernatural creature. The sense attributed by the *MED* to this line of *Piers Plowman* is faithful to Skeat: "supernatural contrivance; enchantment, magic, illusion; also, something supernatural or illusory, a phantom" (2.a). J. R. R. Tolkien, "On Fairy-Stories" in *Essays Presented to Charles Williams*, ed. C. S. Lewis (Oxford: The Oxford University Press, 1947), p. 43, sugggests that the word "may perhaps most nearly be translated by Magic." The various senses of this line have also been reviewed by S. T. R. O. d'Ardenne, "Me bi-fel a ferly, A Feyrie me þouhte (*PPL. A. Prol. 6*)," *English Studies Presented to R. W. Zandvoort* (Amsterdam: Swets & Zeitlinger, 1964), pp. 143–45, although her textual argument is undercut by E. J. Dobson's review in *RES*, n. s. 17 (1966), p. 72. A typical warning of the reality of fairies is offered, fittingly, at the start of the Middle English translation of Jean d'Arras' poem *Melusine* (1389), ed. A. K. Donald, 1895, EETS e.s. 68, pp. 2–6.

her study of *Sir Orfeo*, Penelope Doob offers an intriguing interpretation of Heurodis's madness that brings together much of what I feel Langland is suggesting about Will here:

We have seen that Heurodis's wandering in the orchard may be morally suspect; and her later sleep heightens the implicit condemnation. Her enjoyment of natural beauty, morally neutral in itself, yet seems to indicate her forgetfulness of other obligations; her love of sensual pleasures; her tendency, in short, to the spiritual sin of sloth, the most deceptive of sins since it often seems to be no sin at all.[27]

Doob's reading is strengthened by the argument, already offered by John Block Friedman, that the Fairy King of Heurodis's dream is meant to be recognized as the Noonday Demon long associated with *acedia* from the age of the desert fathers, and still a figure of concern to medieval mystical writers.[28] Indeed, Langland's suggestion that Will's vision had fairy causes would not have been taken lightly by his first readers. Although the contents of the vision are not especially sinister, we should not underestimate the initial impact of the reference to fairies for a first audience that did not know what kind of dream would follow.

After the vision of Lady Mede, Will is roused from his sleep for a brief encounter with the waking world:

> The Kyng and hise knyȝtes to þe kirke wente
> To here matyns and masse and to þe mete after.
> Thanne waked I of my wynkyng and wo was withalle
> That I ne hadde slept sadder and yseiȝen moore.
> Ac er I hadde faren a furlong feyntise me hente
> That I ne myȝte ferþer a foot for defaute of slepynge.
> I sat softely adoun and seide my bileue,
> And so I bablede on my bedes þei brouȝte me aslepe.
>
> (B. v. 1–8)

Nothing in the sequence of the dream-action requires this break. The poet moves from one scene in which Reason and the King have reached an accord on the proper governance of the realm, to another in which Reason in the company of the King comes to preach before the com-

---

27. Doob, p. 176.
28. John Block Friedman, "Eurydice, Heurodis, and the Noon-day Demon," *Speculum*, 41 (1966), 22–29. His point is renewed in *Orpheus in the Middle Ages* (Cambridge: Harvard University Press, 1970), pp. 188–89. For a fuller discussion of the association of the Noontide Demon with *acedia* in ˙eremitic and monastic writings, see Wenzel, pp. 5–9 and 17–19. Walter Hilton's *Exposition of Qui Habitat*, pp. 21–22, shows the continuing worry of fourteenth-century mystics over the deceptive powers of the Demon.

mon people. Elsewhere Langland is able to juxtapose far more dis-jointed actions without interrupting Will's sleep.

Just as the Dreamer had passed quickly to sleep at the poem's begin-ning, he emerges here only for a few minutes before lapsing once again into slumber. It is even possible to detect some humor when Will de-clares that he is overcome with fatigue after walking only a furlong, which is really no distance at all—about one-eighth of an English mile. Yet after walking such an inconsiderable distance, he says he is so tired that he cannot budge a foot farther for lack of sleep. This statement comes from a man who, in a strict sense, has just awakened from a morning nap. Hints of laziness and sluggishness are more direct than in the opening prologue, and later in the poem's evolution Langland makes the moment even less ambiguous by inserting the C-text's "au-tobiographical" episode, which will be discussed at length in the next chapter.

When the Dreamer awakens from his first vision, he is unhappy be-cause he has not slept sounder and seen more. Besides suggesting the sort of curiosity that was implicit in his initial desire to hear wonders, these lines give the sense that his sadness might not have an approved cause. St. Paul distinguished between two kinds of sorrow: "For the sorrow that is according to God worketh penance, steadfast unto sal-vation; but the sorrow of the world worketh death" (2 Cor. 7.10). We have seen that the sorrow of contrition was important to Langland for its power to save mankind; as Repentance says to Envy, "Sorwe for synne is sauacion of soules" (B. v. 127). Any other form of sorrow was open to the suspicion of being "the synne of worldly sorwe swich as is cleped *tristicia*" (*ParsT*, 724–25), which had originally been desig-nated by Gregory as one of the capital vices, later becoming one of the sub-vices under *acedia*.[29] Scholastic writers of the thirteenth century harkened back to Gregory in discussing *acedia* principally as the sor-row opposed to the spiritual joy of *caritas*. Aquinas further discrimi-nated between a sadness concerning a genuinely good object and the excess of a legitimate sorrow impeding the performance of good works.[30] In a discussion of penance that profits from the studies of ear-lier scholastics, Ockham decided that sorrow was exclusively within the power of the will as the result of an act of detestation, whatever its object.[31] Thus when Will is subject to sorrow here and later, we need to

29. Wenzel discusses *tristitia* throughout the theological tradition on pp. 79, 99, and 184–86.
30. U. Voll, "Acedia" in *NCE*, vol. I, p. 84.
31. Leff, *Ockham*, p. 511, citing relevant material in *Reportatio*, IV, qq. 8 and 9, N and U.

question the cause of the sorrow and to ask whether it interferes with his life of good works. Blameless sorrow could be associated with the condition of spiritual dryness over which *voluntas* has no real control, but at the beginning of Passus V, Will is sad because he has not seen enough marvels. The ambiguity of his sorrow is therefore maintained by the ambiguity of the visions—praiseworthy if the visions encourage good works, vicious if they do not—but there are other features in this waking interlude that are more definitely connected with the *acedia* tradition.

Will is last pictured in this section as a man sitting on the ground and falling asleep while muttering prayers over his beads, probably a rosary beginning with a Credo and followed by an alternating series of Pater Nosters and Ave Marias. Such an image had long formed a standard feature in complaints against *acedia*; sermons and devotional manuals constantly cited falling asleep during one's prayers as a grave symptom of sloth.[32] One preacher who delivered a sermon on the verse "*Vigilate et orate*" (Mt. 26.41) bears witness to the frequency of this fault and its grave consequences:

> For þer ben many of vs, þe more harme is, þat slepeþ when þei preye, both lered and lewde, . . . By þis slepe is vndirstond dedely synne; for like as a man semeþ dede bodely when he slepeyþ, ryght so whan a man slepeyþ in dedely synne, vhat good dede þat euere he dothe—preyinge, fastynge, almvs dede doyinge—may ne shall not profitt hym to mede of sowle in þe blisse of heven ne here in vrthe . . .[33]

Langland himself clearly associated this sleep with *acedia*, since in the Confession Scene he has the character Sloth fall asleep soon after beginning the penitential prayer Benedicite (B. v. 390–91).

The fault was more severe when one fell asleep in church. The author of *Jacob's Well* addressed the slothful man directly on this point: "þou hast slepte in holy cherche in tyme of praying."[34] Whereas in the B-text Will falls asleep outdoors, presumably still in the Malvern hills a furlong from the "brood bank" of the Prologue, the C-poet alters the circumstances so that Will goes "to þe kyrke" and falls asleep while kneeling before the cross and saying his Pater Noster (v. 105–08).

Will says he fell asleep as he "bablede" on his beads. The use of this word deserves comment. Although *babble*'s history is obscure, it meant

32. Wenzel, pp. 84–85: "This type of sinful slumber was always a very dominant aspect of the traditional notion of *acedia* and occasioned many alarming *exempla*."

33. *Middle English Sermons*, ed. Ross, p. 46. Wenzel, p. 102, says that the sleep of the Apostles was a common illustration of sloth.

34. *Jacob's Well*, p. 104.

to mumble language unintelligibly and was perhaps connected through folk-etymology with the Tower of Babel. This manner of verbal mutilation became sinful when prayers were involved. In *Ego Dormio et Cor Meum Vigilat*, Richard Rolle asks, "What gude hopes þou may come þarof, if þou lat þi tonge blaber on þe boke and þi hert ren abowte in sere stedes in þe worlde?"[35] One homilist shows that the complaint had a long and authoritative lineage:

But, frendes, þat þou spekest with þi mouthe, þou must nedis þenke itt with þin herte, for þat pleyseþ myche God. For Seynt Austyn seyþ, "What prophytes þe to prey with þi mouthe and not with þin herte?" As who sey, "No prophitt." "No, trewly," seyþ Seynte Gregori, "for þe moste stedefast preyour is to þenke with þin herte and not to speke it with þi mouthe."[36]

The author of *The Book of Vices and Virtues* paraphrases Augustine in asking, "What is it worþ to moue and to patere wiþ þe lippes, whan þe herte is al y-hid?"[37] Use of the word *patere* is also worth noting since it derives from Pater Noster—one of the prayers which Will should be saying—and meant to mumble the prayer so quickly as to render it unintelligible.

This inward failing manifests itself outwardly in Will's sleep. If he were concentrating properly on the contents of his prayers, really thinking on what it means to say "Thy will be done," he would not be able to fall asleep. Langland knew this verbal corruption was wrong because he later condemns it outright (B. xi. 303–19), and he knew also which major sin included among its sub-vices the idle execution of prayers. In the Confession Scene, it is Sloth who makes this admission: "And if I bidde any bedes, but if it be in wraþe, / That I tell wiþ my tonge is two myle fro myn herte" (B. v. 400–01). In his discussion of *acedia* as it concerned the neglect of religious duties, Wenzel says that "sinful sleep has its companion vice in 'syncopation,' the mumbling and curtailing of words in saying mass or the office."[38] Langland makes

35. *English Writings of Richard Rolle*, ed. Allen, p. 66. The *Ancrene Wisse*, ed. Tolkien, p. 29, also warns against mumbling the words of prayers or allowing one's thoughts to wander from the words. *Dives and Pauper*, p. 200, warns not to say prayers so lengthy that one cannot remain devout throughout or is encouraged to rush and say the words indistinctly. Of course the word *Lollard* was originally used as a term of abuse for people who mumbled (*lollen*) their prayers; see Leff, *Heresy*, vol. I, p. 319, n. 2, and vol. II, p. 559.

36. *Middle English Sermons*, ed. Ross, p. 155. The authorities cited are Augustine, *Enarratio in Psalmum CXVIII*, xxix (*PL* 37:1585), and Gregory, *Moralia in Job*, XXXIII, xxii (*PL* 76:701).

37. *The Book of Vices and Virtues*, p. 233.

38. Wenzel, p. 113. In *Jacob's Well*, p. 108, the slothful man is given this rebuke: "þou hast seyd rechelesly þi seruyse in rape, in syncopyng, in ouyr-skyppyng, in omyttyng."

it possible to see both these faults in Will when he falls asleep babbling his prayers, perhaps rapt by divine powers, but just as likely lulled by the mindless mutter of his own voice.

Will next awakens at the end of the Pardon Scene (B. vii. 144–viii. 67) at a moment better suited to the dramatic movement of the poem and more credibly staged than the waking of Passus V. The noise of the argument between Piers and the Priest makes a convenient stimulus for rousing the Dreamer. Since the puzzling message of the Pardon demands further consideration, we are allowed to overhear Will trying to make sense of his visions. After concluding to his own satisfaction that the dream has been truthful and that the terms of the Pardon are more certain for man's salvation than indulgences from Rome, Will sets out to seek Dowel:

> Thus yrobed in russet, I romed aboute
> Al a somer seson for to seke Dowel,
> And frayned ful ofte of folk þat I mette
> If any wiȝt wiste wher Dowel was at Inne;
> And what man he myȝte be of many man I asked.
>
> (B. viii. 1–5)

From the very outset of this quest, there is an uncomfortable feeling that Will is asking the wrong questions. It is true that Dowel is regularly described through personification, but these are nonce allegories offered by various characters, never confirmed by the poet himself, like a preacher's examples which are not meant to be understood literally. David Mills has summed up Will's mistaken assumption:

> *Dowel* is very clearly a "verb-adverb" construction suggesting a finite action, but the Dreamer, oddly, treats it as if it were a noun, . . . that is, as if it were a definite thing which could be sought out and found. . . . One cannot seek Dowel, one can only *do* well, so that the Dreamer's lack of involvement has now been turned to the pursuit of the non-existent.[39]

In addition to embarking on this dubious quest, Will is still associated with the suspicious elements of the Prologue: it is still summer, he is still roaming about, and he is still clothed in the russet color of a hermit.

The two friars whom Will encounters are not exactly characters we would expect to advance him very far along the right road, especially considering the portrayal of their brethren elsewhere in the poem, yet their advice does not lack value:

---

39. Mills, "The Role of the Dreamer," pp. 194–95.

"God wole suffre wel þi sleuþe if þiself likeþ,
For he yaf þee to yeresȝyue to yeme wel þiselue
Wit and free wil, to euery wiȝt a porcion,
To fleynge foweles, to fisshes and to beestes.
Ac man haþ moost þerof and.moost is to blame
But if he werche wel þerwiþ as Dowel hym techeþ."

(B. viii. 51–56.)

True, he must safeguard his soul by resisting the temptations of the devil and the flesh's *wille*, and he must use his intellect and free will to lead a life of good works. The Friars nonetheless mislead Will on two accounts. Faithful to the allegorizing practices of their confreres, they confirm Will in his error of imagining Dowel as a person, and they encourage him not to worry about his *sleuþe*—correctly singled out as his dominant vice—because God will tolerate it if he wishes. The air of false comfort they create can be compared to the fatal relief given by Friar Flattery's plasters just prior to the attack of Giant Sloth at the poem's conclusion.

After Will has taken his leave of the Friars, he walks alone for some distance until he finds himself "by a wilde wildernesse and bi a wode-syde,"[40] a landscape which may again be meant to reflect his state of internal disarray. He is halted in his rambling and soon lulled to sleep by the singing of the birds:

Blisse of þe briddes abide me made,
And vnder a lynde vpon a launde lened I a stounde
To lerne þe layes þat louely foweles made.
Murþe of hire mouþes made me to slepe.

(B. viii. 64–67)

Even putting aside the possibility that this enjoyment of the birds' songs may represent the same misguided pleasure for which Heurodis suffered, one can see that Will's reaction jars with what a contemporary audience might have expected. Rather than send people to sleep in the morning, the songs of birds at the opening of a *chanson d'aventure* usually aroused bodily vigor. Twittering birds were associated in medieval literature with the vernal stirrings of natural energy, particularly for regeneration, which paralleled and often stimulated a similar awakening in men, particularly in poets. Langland understood this well enough when he conceived his Vision of Kind (B. xi. 320–55). But

---

40. B. viii. 63 (Skeat). The emendation of Kane and Donaldson—"And as I wente by a wode, walkyng myn one"—goes against the overwhelming testimony of the manuscripts.

the Dreamer, who is not elsewhere stirred by fleshly love, is not moved by the songs of the "louely foweles" here. This may speak well of his character, or maybe not. The sleepy narrator in one of Lydgate's *Two Nightingale Poems* is roused from sin by the melodies of a bird; when the poet moralizes the episode, the nightingale becomes Christ and the dreamer's sleep is called sloth.[41] Whatever interpretation is given, clearly Will should be aroused rather than soothed. It had been his intention to study "þe layes þat louely foweles made" as part of a discipline natural enough for a man who will later become a poet. By contrast, the narrator of *Wynnere and Wastoure* cannot at first gratify his desire for sleep because of the "dadillyng of fewllys" (1. 44). Will's ability to fall asleep while lying outdoors in the daytime and listening to the birds suggests he may be subject to another form of *acedia*, a symptom variously called sluggishness or heaviness, "whan a man is so heuy þat he loueþ not but to lyn and reste & slepe."[42]

This quotation above from *The Book of Vices and Virtues* puts stress on a physical gesture—to *lyn* or to lean—that has special relevance to our image of Will. In the moments preceding his sleep, he is consistently pictured in a leaning position. In this episode he says of himself, "vnder a lynde vpon a launde *lened* I a stounde" (B. viii. 65). In the opening scene he "lay and *lenede* and loked on þe watres." And the word is used again later to describe his repose: I "*lened* me to a lenten, and longe tyme I slepte" (B. xviii. 5). Of course a man who must go to sleep in order to dream must also be in some sort of reclining position, but Langland's repetition of this verb is worth noting. The artist of a rare illumination from the *Piers Plowman* manuscripts provides a contemporary comment on Will's posture. In the opening scene he is not leaning against bank or a tree, but instead sits upright and rests his drooping head on his hand (see Frontispiece). Discussing this iconographic motif as a meaningful image, Gail Gibson speaks of leaning as "a stylized gesture which may suggest at once meditation and grief, creative thought or fatigue."[43] The visions that follow attest to the activity inside Will's mind, but the image of him that remains

---

41. *Lydgate's Minor Poems: The Two Nightingale Poems*, ed. Otto Glauning, 1900, EETS e.s. 80, esp. p. 3 (ll. 55–58). Rosemary Woolf, *English Religious Lyric*, pp. 232–33, relates these two poems to Pecham's *Philomena* and discusses the remarkable way in which the allegorical sense grows out of a deceptively conventional beginning.

42. *The Book of Vices and Virtues*, p. 27.

43. Gail McMurray Gibson, *The Images of Doubt and Belief: Visual Symbolism in the Middle English Plays of Joseph's Troubles about Mary* (Ph.D Dissertation, The University of Virginia, 1975), p. 100, drawing upon a discussion of this motif, with its many possible applications, in Klibansky, *Saturn and Melancholy*, pp. 286–89.

behind in the real world is virtually identical to the usual portrayal of personified Sloth. In *Jacob's Well*, for instance, the slothful man is told not "to lenyn on þin elbowe." [44]

During the long slumber of the third vision, Will has his first dream-within-a-dream (B. xi.6–405). As such, it does not properly belong to this discussion, but it deserves brief mention for two reasons: (1) amid the increasing confusion between real and visionary experience, this episode mirrors more fully and more faithfully the events of his waking life than do many of the actual waking interludes; and (2) it shows aspects of Will's character that could be signs of sloth and thus join in the concatenation of vices that leads back into his true waking life.

When rebuked by Lady Scripture for his ignorance, the Dreamer falls asleep with sorrow and anger: "Tho wepte I for wo and wraþe of hir speche / And in a wynkynge [wraþe] I weex aslepe" (B xi. 4–5). As before, his sorrow might represent a healthy regret over his past faults—"sorwe for synne is sauacion of soules"—but it is seriously qualified here by his anger. He seems to resent being accused of ignorance. Wrath, usually elevated as one of the capital vices, was sometimes considered one of sloth's symptoms—bitterness, irritability, and rancor all belonging to *acedia* [45]—and in works of the *Somme le Roi* tradition, anger comes directly after sorrow in the course of a slothful man's decline:

And so moche þis anger ouergoþ hym, þat what þat euere any good man seiþ hym . . . al it teeneþ hym; and þus he falleþ in sorwe and is euele apaied of his self, and hateþ hymself and desireþ his owne deeþ. [46]

Scripture fills the role of the "good man" whose advice makes Will sad and angry, sending him into the sleep of sin where he commits an act just short of desperation by following Recklessness, forgetting his search for Dowel, and committing himself to Fortune for forty-five years. He repents only when he is old and deserted by the flatterers Fortune, Lust-of-the-Eyes, and the Friars.

44. *Jacob's Well*, p. 103. See also E.W. Tristram, *English Wall Painting of the Fourteenth Century* (London: Routledge & Kegan Paul, 1955), p. 9: "At Syon Abbey the sign for sleep was 'to put the right hand under the cheek and forthwith close thine eyes'—a gesture often seen in paintings of Sloth as one of the Deadly Sins."

45. Bloomfield, *Seven Deadly Sins*, pp. 80–81, discusses the faculty of irascibility as the common source of *tristitia*, *acedia*, and *ira*. Wenzel, pp. 200–02, uses similar scholastic material to explain Dante's confinement of the slothful and the wrathful in the same circle of the *Inferno*. Chaucer speaks for a more popular tradition when he says, "Ire troubleth a man, and Accidie maketh hym hevy, thoghtful, and wraw" (*ParsT*, 676). Langland's Sloth confesses to paying his servants with wrath (B. v. 428).

46. *The Book of Vices and Virtues*, p. 29.

This miniature morality play, giving the audience a distinct foretaste of the poem's conclusion, suggests many of the standard features of *acedia*. Recklessness and forgetfulness were both vices belonging to sloth, and *The Book of Vices and Virtues* shows that they were traditionally connected in much the same way Langland combines them here; first, faithlessness turns a man "fro þe wille to do well":

> After þat comeþ rechelesschep, for who-so doþ vntrewely, it is no wondre þou3 he do rechelesly; for þat is a vice þat foleweþ al þe world now-a-dayes . . .
>
> After recheleshed comeþ for3etfulnesse; and for þes tweie synnes . . . falleþ ofte þat noiþer man ne womman conne ri3t wel schryue hem . . . but rechelesnesse and for3etfulnesse blynedþ so þe synful man þat he can no þing see in þe book of schrifte.[47]

Finally, to delay repentance until one is old and near death was also considered slothful. *Jacob's Well* includes this warning from Augustine under the heading "De Accidia":

> I dar no3t seyn, he seyth, þat a man schal sykerly be sauyed, 3if he take his sacramentys in his ende & deth, wyth repentauns, þat has vsyd his synne, whyl he myet, & wolde neuere leve tyl sykenes of deth com.[48]

In sum, this dream-within-a-dream and the events leading up to it contribute to the portrait of Will that otherwise emerges from the waking episodes. It is hard always to see virtue in his conduct, and the ways in which Langland has marshalled his faults—idleness and wandering that lead to sorrow, wrath, and recklessness—make it even harder not to see him as slothful.

When Will finally awakens from this long multiple dream, he is deeply agitated by the visions he has seen—his life misspent, and his notion of learning's value undercut by Imaginatyf. Langland describes his mental turmoil in much stronger terms than before:

> And I awaked þerwiþ, witlees nerhande,
> And as a freke þat fey were, forþ gan I walke
> In manere of a mendynaunt many yer after.
> And of þis metyng many tyme muche þou3t I hadde, . . .
>
> (B. xiii. 1−4)

---

47. *Ibid.*, p. 28. Forgetfulness had been a recurrent fault in Sloth's confession: he forgot his forty oaths, his debts, and all the kindnesses done him by his fellow Christians (B. v. 397, 423, 434).

48. *Jacob's Well*, pp. 107−08. Dante says that the late repentant Belacqua looked "more indolent than if Sloth were his sister," *Purgatorio*, IV, 109−11 (Sinclair, trans., pp. 62−63). In the thirteenth-century lyric "Levedi Sainte Marie, Moder and Maide," the sinner confesses that he has slept his whole life away and is now old and near death;

The chronology of this scene is very different from previous waking sections. Whereas Will was awake in Passus V only long enough to walk a couple of hundred yards, in this episode he travels about for many years, though the length of the passage does not reflect this much longer duration of time spent outside the world of dreams. There are only twenty-one lines, sixteen devoted to a synopsis of the previous vision, and virtually nothing is said of the events which befall Will during his years of wandering.

After this review of the previous dream, he lies down once more and falls asleep: "I lay doun longe in þis þoȝt and at þe laste I slept, / And as Crist wolde þer com Conscience to conforte me þat tyme . . ." (B. xiii. 21–22). Here the circumstances do little to suggest sloth; the dream continues the business of Will's waking meditation and it is said to have Christ's sanction. Earlier details are less reassuring, however.

Will says that he had awakened like a man who was *fey*, a word glossed by the *MED* as "mortally wounded, dying, doomed." It was used frequently to describe knights dying in battle, although the lyric "þe Mon þat Is" (c. 1390) shows that it also had moral overtones: "Mony mon lihþ in dedly synne / And weneþ þat he beo not *veyȝ*" (ll. 46–47).[49] But the word had another sense quite different from the ones understood by moralists. *Fey* could mean "enchanted" or "possessed of magical powers or properties."[50] The word thus recalls the phrase "a ferly of Fairye" in the Prologue, awakening once more the suspicion of supernatural contrivance. Perhaps even more provocative is the fact that the Dreamer says he was "witlees nerhande." For Will to act witlessly, or without reason, suggests psychological as well as moral chaos, since *voluntas* cannot choose a correct object unless compelled or at least guided by *ratio*.

When Will emerges from his dream of Haukyn and Patience at the beginning of Pasus XV, he is more tormented than ever, as he demonstrates by his erratic social behavior:

Ac after my wakynge it was wonder longe
Er I koude kyndely knowe what was Dowel,
And so my wit weex and wanyed til I a fool weere.
And some lakkede my lif—allowed it fewe—
And lete me for a lorel and looþ to reuerencen

---

sleep in this poem, as in this section of *Piers Plowman*, assumes two meanings: the sleep of spiritual sloth, and the sleep of a reckless life. See *English Lyrics of the XIIIth Century*, ed. Carleton Brown (Oxford: The Clarendon Press, 1932), no. 2, pp. 1–2.

49. *MED*, Part F, p. 443. Kane and Donaldson have decided in favor of *fey*, the reading found in the C-text and a few B-manuscripts.

50. *MED*, Part F, pp. 365–66.

Lordes or ladies or any lif ellis,
As persons in pelure wiþ pendaunt3 of siluer;
To sergeaunt3 ne to swiche seide no3t ones,
"God loke yow, lordes," ne loutede faire,
That folk helden me a fool; and in þat folie I raued
Til Reson hadde ruþe on me and rokked me aslepe,
Til I sei3, as it sorcerie were, a sotil þyng wiþ alle.

(B. xv. 1–12)

Jay Martin believes that Will is the fool of conscience who stands up as society's critic and speaks with the voice of satire,[51] although another way of looking at the evidence also presents itself. Whereas the sage critic merely poses as an idiot to gain a fool's immunity, Will admits that he actually did become a fool after his wit "weex and wanyed," a verbal formula usually applied to lunar cycles and here suggesting lunacy.[52] Furthermore, Will's discourtesy to his social superiors does not take the form of broad social complaint. He is simply rude. Anticipating the vision in which Anima expounds the doctrine of love and prepares the Dreamer to envisage the Tree of Charity, Will's unkind treatment of his fellow Christians is perhaps meant to show that he is uncharitable, has violated the Golden Commandment of *Dilige proximum tuum*, and is therefore much in need of the instruction that Anima will offer.

If *fool* cannot be taken simply as court jester and critic—Martin goes so far as to place Will the Dreamer in the honored tradition of Will Somers—we must explore a wider range of meanings. The principal dictionaries agree that *fool* has two important senses besides jester: one who is destitute of reason, and one who is a sinner.[53] The first of these senses is compelled here by the fact that his wit waned, as well as by his urgent admission "in þat folie I raued," while the second meaning of sinner is worth keeping in mind as a possible implication of the first.

Awake and asleep, the Dreamer is unsettled by his intense search after a knowledge of Dowel. Every reader of *Hamlet* knows what can happen to a man who broods too long on a disturbing problem, and

---

51. Martin, "Wil as Fool and Wanderer," 539–40.

52. Donaldson, *The C-Text and its Poet*, p. 152, calls attention to the similarity between the lunatic Dreamer and the "lunatyk lollares" who "arn meuynge aftur þe mone; moneyeles þei walke, / With a good will, witteles, mony wyde contreyes . . ." (C. ix. 110–11). Wittig, "Long Will's Pilgrimage," 62, equates witlessness with being "stripped of false intellectual refuge."

53. *MED*, Part F, p. 673, defines *fool* as a jester, a dazed man, and a sinner. In addition, the *OED*, vol. IV, p. 398, offers a more precise definition: "one who is deficient in, or destitute of reason or intellect."

these results were even more familiar to an age in which meditation formed an important part of religious practice. Mystical writers and even the author of the *Somme le Roi* warned that prolonged or unwise spiritual zeal could lead to the slothful symptom of languor that deprived a man of all desire to do good. More scientific than moral in his approach, Guillaume d'Auvergne cautions that too profound a probing into spiritual matters and too burning a desire for deeper understanding might cause a melancholy temperament—the humor best suited to contemplation, according to Aristotle—to develop into the melancholy disorder of true madness. His warning is an echo from the days of John Cassian when the desert fathers suffered from spiritual dryness and *tristitia* after long periods of solitary meditation.[54] The Aristotelian-Thomistic analysis of passions made it difficult to think of *acedia* any longer as a vice freely chosen, since an imbalance in the humors could cause sloth-like symptoms without the consent of the will. Alexander of Hales offered this apology for the vice's "natural" causes:

In this respect [*acedia*] is not the greatest sin or incurable, because it occurs in many people who are disposed to it, as to melancholy. Hence, it often arises from the infirmity of *melancholia* or another weakness, and thus is not said to be the greatest sin or incurable.[55]

Even if a man's native humor predisposed him to sin, he still had the obligation to resist it, to seek a cure, and to make certain that the venial passion was not transformed by habit into a mortal sin. Roger Bacon gave this prescription for relieving a man unsettled by too much mental concentration:

. . . it is necessary for the mind's tranquility that our human weakness sometimes turn away our mind from its attention to inner and outer cares and turn it toward comforts and recreations that are necessary for our body. Because otherwise our spirit becomes anxious, dull, *accidiosus*, sadder than it ought to be, weary with disgust of the good, querulous, and ready to frequent movements of impatience and anger.[56]

Bacon's warning anticipates the advice given to Thomas Hoccleve by his friend—"To muse longe in an hard mateere, / The wit of man

---

54. A medieval writer like Guillaume d'Auvergne could describe the same set of symptoms in either way: in *De Universo* he attributes them to melancholy, in *De Virtutibus* to sloth. Klibansky, *Saturn and Melancholy*, pp. 74 and 78, writes concerning the common signs that linked melancholy with *acedia*.

55. Alexander of Hales, *Summa Theologica*, II–II, 566, trans. Wenzel, p. 59.

56. Roger Bacon, *Moralis Philosophia*, III, vii, 8, ed. F. Delorme and E. Massa (Turin: In Aedibus Thesauri Mundi, 1953), p. 181.

abieth it ful deere"[57]—and should remind us also of Will, especially in his querulous behavior towards his fellow men.

If melancholy was not blameworthy when caused by an imbalance in the humors, madness too might be forgiven when caused by the loss of reason. Ockham, for example, made allowance for the willfulness of lunatics, because when the will acts without reason as among the demented and mad, that act is considered to be without moral value.[58] But Will the Dreamer does not seem to qualify for this exemption. His wit waxes as well as wanes, and his sleep is brought on by Reason.

Rather than a morally neutral affliction, madness was viewed as Heaven's chastisement inflicted on individuals partly to punish past sins and partly to avert future ones.[59] The relationship between sin and madness is not simply causal; to the Christian sensibility, vice is by definition a derangement of the mind's faculties. Doob is right to say that "sin is the worst madness, the only madness that really matters."[60] But not all madness was sinful or even morally neutral. Langland himself takes special care to set apart the divinely inspired lunatic who is in fact virtuous. In a striking addition to the C-text's gloss to Piers' Pardon, he mentions this class of "lunatyk lollares" who will share in the rewards of the Pardon despite their failure to work; they are "Godes munstrals and his mesagers and his mery bordiours" (C. ix. 105–38). The distinction accords with what Doob sees as the standard medieval division of lunatics into two types: the Unholy Wild Man "who goes mad because of his own sin and who lives in the wilderness as a beast until his guilt is purged"; and the Holy Wild Man "whose flight to the desert and whose primitive, superficially bestial life there are usually inspired by the desire for sanctity and spiritual perfection."[61]

The question immediately arises as to which group should Will be assigned? Is he the holy hermit dedicated to the ascetic life of John the Baptist and the desert fathers? Or is he the unholy lunatic driven mad by God's grace so that he may suffer and eventually be saved? Careful not to allow any simple conclusion, Langland leaves open the sugges-

---

57. *Hoccleve's Works: The Minor Poems*, ed. Frederick J. Furnivall and I. Gollancz, 1892 and 1897, rev. Jerome Mitchell and A. I. Doyle, 1970, EETS e.s. 61 and 73, "Dialogus cum Amico," p. 127 (ll. 496–97).

58. Leff, *Ockham*, p. 486, drawing from *Quodlibeta Septem*, I, q. 20, and *Reportatio*, III, q. 13, F.

59. *Saturn and Melancholy*, p. 78.

60. Doob, p. 230. See also Judith S. Neaman, *Suggestion of the Devil: Insanity in the Middle Ages and the Twentieth Century* (New York: Octagon Books, 1978). At least one critic alleges that the poet himself was actually unhinged by the calamities of his age: Stanley B. James, "The Mad Poet of Malvern: William Langland," *Month*, 159 (1932), 221–27.

61. Doob, pp. 138–39.

tion that Will belongs to the tribe of Unholy Wild Men, a figure who is prone to the persistent sin of *acedia*—its symptoms so bewilderingly like madness itself—but who repeatedly receives visions from grace that offer the instruction essential for his salvation and release. In the meantime he must suffer.

When Will wakes after his vision of Faith, Hope, and Charity, he reaches the nadir of his decline. If Langland has arranged for a concatenation of vices leading from idleness and somnolence to sorrow and finally madness, he now suggests that the Dreamer approaches a state of desperation in which he has no concern for physical pain and turns a blind eye to the outside world:

> Wolleward and weetshoed wente I forþ after
> As a reccheless renk þat reccheþ of no wo,
> And yede forþ lik a lorel al my lif tyme
> Til I weex wery of þe world and wilned eft to slepe
> And lened me to a lenten, and longe tyme I slepte;
> Reste me þere and rutte faste til *Ramis palmarum*
>
> (B. xviii. 1–6)

It would be easy enough to agree with Robertson and Huppé that Will has undergone a virtuous transformation. He has exchanged the hypocritical garb of a hermit for the sackcloth of a true penitent; he has made himself callous toward mere physical suffering; he is weary of a world that represents one member of the unholy trinity of *Mundus*, *Caro*, and *Diabolus*; and his Lenten anticipation of Easter sends him into a sacred trance of contemplation.[62] Even his appearance sets him apart from the slothful man who hated to go barefoot, to wear rough clothes on his body, and to fast or abstain from dainty food and drink.[63] Perhaps his idleness and abnegation of worldly values even make him receptive to the direct apprehension of God as described by Meister Eckhart and other mystics in the tradition of Pseudo-Dionysius:

Thus to reach God is to turn inward to this divine element: it is to cast off all desire and aspiration (even those toward sanctity and God Himself), and to attain to a state of sheer abnegation and nothingness. Hence a man's highest attainment is Poverty: to do nothing, to own nothing, to know nothing; thereby he is open to God.[64]

62. See Robertson and Huppé, p. 212.
63. Wenzel, p. 86.
64. Leff, *Medieval Thought*, p. 301, summarizes ideas such as those expressed by Eckhart.

But to view the passage in this way, the reader must ignore evidence which points in another direction. Will resembles a *lorel*—a rogue, beggar, fool, or one of the damned[65]—and he again falls into the posture of leaning that characterizes the slothful man. In his wanderings he shows recklessness, which Augustine says can result from sorrow: "unhappy men do not attain what they want, namely, the happy life, for they do not also will what must be its companion, and without which no one can deserve to attain it, namely, an upright life."[66] Far from the life of high sanctity preached by Meister Eckhart, Will may have become so distracted that he strays further and further from the enactment of Dowel.

Even more troubling is Will's statement "I weex wery of þe world," which is an admission quite different from having been "wery forwandred" in the Prologue. We are perhaps justified in recalling Petrarch's sense of disgust toward the world's turbulence and filth—"*vite mee tedia et quotidianum fastidium!*"[67] When the seven deadly sins were distributed among the Three Enemies of mankind—Flesh, World, and Devil—sorrow was associated with *Mundus*.[68] Speaking in the last accents of the Middle Ages, Robert Burton offers these observations on a slothful man's weariness:

An idle person . . . knows not when he is well, what he would have, or whither he would go. He is tired out with everything, displeased with all, weary of his life: neither well at home nor abroad, he wanders, and lives beside himself.[69]

A fourteenth-century reader might have recognized this emotional weariness as *langure*, so commonly numbered among the sub-vices of *acedia* that *Jacob's Well* places it immediately before wanhope.[70] As a

65. *MED*, Part L, p. 1224.
66. Augustine, *The Free Choice of the Will* (I, 14, 30), trans. Russell, p. 101.
67. Wenzel, p. 158, quotes from Petrarch's *Secretum*.
68. *Ibid.*, pp. 166–67.
69. Robert Burton, *The Anatomy of Melancholy*, ed. Floyd Dell and Paul Jordan-Smith (New York: Farrar and Rinehart, 1927), p. 213.
70. *Jacob's Well*, p. 112. See also p. 106 in the same work and p. 29 in *The Book of Vices and Virtues*. Wenzel, pp. 34 and esp. 218–19, lists *languor* among the "characteristic definitions often found in treatises of the twelfth, thirteenth, and fourteenth centuries." Illuminating studies on the history and causes of wanhope are provided by Rose Bernard Donna, *Despair and Hope: A Study of Langland and Augustine* (Washington, DC: The Catholic University of America Press, 1948); and Susan Snyder, "The Left Hand of God: Despair in Medieval and Renaissance Tradition," *SRen*, 12 (1965), 18–59. Arieh Sachs, "Religious Despair in Mediaeval Literature and Art," *MS*, 26 (1964), 253, notes that "an important aspect of this connection between despair and madness is the fact that desperate persons were supposed to be particularly prone to nightmares."

signal that Will might be only one step away from despair, this weariness has considerable importance.

The dream of Christ's Passion that follows Will's world-weary travels has an effect perfectly suited to his psychological needs. From the thirteenth century onward, *acedia* had been understood among scholastic circles as an affective or emotional defect,[71] and to intensify one's affective life, meditating on Christ's suffering was considered an important means, perhaps the best. Rosemary Woolf makes this comment about Middle English lyrics: "meditation on the Passion brings tears to the eye and sweetness to the heart; the meditator grieves and loves."[72] Since this is the same love necesary for good works, it is significant that Sloth admits in the Confession Scene that "Goddes peyne and his passion pure selde þenke I on" (B. v. 404). Bearing witness to the power of meditation to relieve *acedia*, the anonymous *Tretyse of Loue* offers this prescription:

> Who is it þat by slouthe sholde leue to lerne or to labour to doo wel, . . . beholde how in the ende of his lyfe [Christ] was trauelyd, whanne he prayed soo that wyth his swette ranne from hym droppes of blood, rennyng down on his blessid body to therthe. And after beholde whan he was at the pyler, how sorowfully he was scorged of the felon Iewes, not oonly on his legges but ouerall his fayr body. And at the last beholde how he vpon the harde crosse was sore traueylled the daye of his letyng blood.[73]

And yet it is not safe to assume that Will's visionary experience in Passus XVIII has been earned by merit. The high majesty and spiritual power of the dream in which Will envisages Christ's entry into Jerusalem and Harrowing of Hell, as well as the Passion and Crucifixion, may come more as remedy than reward. Augustine had noted centuries earlier that the gifts of grace were often bestowed upon men who were not deserving. If grace abounds to the chief of sinners, there is surely enough for a man whose vice is so subtle that it often appears to be no vice at all.

When Will awakes after his vision of the Harrowing, he is filled with the zeal of sudden understanding. He has sensed the enormity of Christ's sacrifice and the miracle of the Resurrection. His spiritual excitement contrasts optimistically with his previous woe and despondency, and this rekindled vigor shows itself in the way he urges his wife and daughter to wake up for the Easter service:

---

71. Wenzel, pp. 64–65.
72. Woolf, *English Religious Lyric*, p. 21.
73. *The Tretyse of Loue*, ed. John H. Fisher, 1951, EETS o.s. 223, p. 96.

That men rongen to þe resurexion, and riȝt wiþ þat I wakede
And callede Kytte my wif and Calote my doghter:
"Ariseþ and reuerenceþ Goddes resurexion,
And crepeþ to þe cros on knees and kisseþ it for a Iuwel
For Goddes blissede body it bar for oure boote;
And it afereþ þe fend, for swich is þe myȝte
May no grisly goost glide þere it shadweþ."

(B. xviii. 425−31)

His advice to Kitte and Kalote even indicates some measure of his
moral recovery, since the slothful husband typically failed to correct
his wife and instruct his children in their religious duties.[74] Going to
the cross was itself a penitential act recommended in monastic writ-
ings as a cure for *acedia*,[75] although Will's explanation of its signifi-
cance leaves the reader with an uneasy feeling that he may not fully
grasp the meaning of the gesture. *Dives and Pauper* devotes a whole
chapter to the proper reasons for crawling to the cross,[76] but Will's
explanation—that the Devil is afraid of it and no ghost will glide
through its shadow—smacks of primitive fetishism, Christianity as
folkish superstition unworthy of a man whose dreams have opened to
him such a treasury of theological riches.

Will writes down his dream after awakening. Keeping this poetic
record of his visions further suggests that he is better oriented toward
the life of Dowel, although this sense of accomplishment is undercut
when he goes to Mass and falls asleep during the Offertory:

Thus I awaked and wroot what I hadde ydremed,
And dighte me derely and dide me to chirche
To here holly þe masse and to be housled after.
In myddes of þe masse þo men yede to offryng
I fel eftsoones aslepe, and sodeynly me mette
That Piers þe Plowman was peynted al blody
And com in wiþ a cros bifore þe comune peple,
And riȝt lik in alle lymes to oure lord Iesu.

(B. xix. 1−8)

This awesome vision of Piers as the Man of Sorrow is reminiscent of
Christ's appearance in the Gregorian Mass, but whereas Christ ap-
peared for Gregory to affirm His real presence in the Host,[77] the

74. *Jacob's Well*, p. 108; the confession of Sloth in *Cursor Mundi*, p. 1554 (Cotton,
ll. 28276−85); and John Myrc, *Instructions for Parish Priests*, ed. Edward Peacock,
1868, EETS o.s. 31, ll. 1195−97 (p. 37).
75. Fleming, "*The Dream of the Rood* and Anglo-Saxon Monasticism," 64.
76. *Dives and Pauper*, pp. 87−89.
77. For a further discussion of the Gregorian Mass, its origin, and various artistic

bloody Piers is meant to teach the meaning of Christ's sacrifice in human terms, as Conscience shortly afterwards explains to the Dreamer (B. xix. 63–68). This lesson on the willing acceptance of suffering, coming so late in the poem, should make us wonder whether Will understood its proper function when *he* suffered and sorrowed earlier. At the very least, we should be suspicious of a man who announces that he goes to take communion and to hear the whole Mass, but then falls asleep midway through the ceremony before receiving the sacrament and without taking part in the service. The Offertory, during which the people bring their gifts forward to the celebrant, is the one part meant to involve the congregation as participants and not simply passive witnesses.[78] David Mills has enumerated the variety of questions raised by this scene:

Does religious observance inspire a divine revelation, or is the dream a rejection of a meaningless ritual? Does the Dreamer fall asleep in church through boredom, or conveniently because he must make his offering, or in revolt against the worldly church, or because the worldly offering leads him naturally to think of God's offering for Man, the subject of his vision?[79]

This array of questions can be reduced to form two general alternatives: does the vision represent a natural extension of Will's meditation on the meaning of the Mass, or does the vision come unexpectedly as a gift of grace to a man who may not have deserved it? The appearance of the Man of Sorrow follows logically in the affective mode that had governed the two previous visions and is beautifully suited to the Offertory, that moment in the Mass signifying Christ's sacrifice upon the cross.[80] What remains unclear is whether Will has his mind intent upon this or any other significance at the time he falls asleep. He seems different from other persons, fictional and real, who experienced similar mystical visions in church. Margery

treatments, see Louis Réau, *Iconographie de l'Art Chrétien: Iconographie des Saints* (Paris: Presses Universitaires de France, 1958), vol. III, part ii, pp. 614–16; also, "Gregoriusmesse" in *Lexikon der Christlichen Ikonographie,* begun by Engelbert Kirschbaum (Freiburg: Herder, 1970), vol. II, col. 199–202.

78. Joseph A. Jungmann, *The Mass of the Roman Rite, Its Origins and Development,* trans. F. A. Brunner, 2 vols. (New York: Benziger, 1951–55), vol. II, pp. 4–17; and O. B. Hardison, Jr., *Christian Rite and Christian Drama in the Middle Ages* (Baltimore: The Johns Hopkins University Press, 1965), pp. 59–64 from "The Mass as Sacred Drama."

79. Mills, "The Role of the Dreamer," p. 189. For examples of the punishments visited upon those who fell asleep during church, see Caesarius of Heisterbach, *Dialogus Miraculorum,* vol. I, pp. 202–06 (IV, xxxii–xxxviii).

80. Rudolf Peil, *A Handbook of the Liturgy,* trans. H. E. Winstone (London: Nelson, 1960), pp. 76–86; for a discussion more closely allied to the medieval service and its interpretation, see Hardison, *Christian Rite and Christian Drama,* pp. 59–64.

Kempe, for example, received her vision of the wounded Christ only after meditating on His Passion:

> . . . as þe creatur lay in hir contempplacyon in a chapel of owr Lady, hir mynde was ocupijd in þe Passyon of owr Lord Ihesu Crist, & hyr thowt verily þat she saw owr Lord aperyn to hir gostly syght in hys manhod with hys wowndys bledyng as fresch as þow he had ben scorgyd be-forn hir.[81]

Walter Hilton says that in addition to praying and thinking on God, a man must have a clean conscience, free of doubt and sin: "þen schalt þou be-holden with þin eiȝe—what?—soþly, God."[82] Commentators on the Mass wrote that the priestly celebrant praying quietly during the Offertory fuses with the figure of Christ meditating on the events of the Passion that will follow shortly, a figure that might serve as a model of meditation for individuals watching from the congregation.[83]

Like students of mysticism and actual recipients of mystical visions, poets agreed that there should be a link between a narrator's waking thoughts and the contents of the dream that follows. In Dunbar's "The Passioun of Christ," the narrator who is kneeling before a crucifix while remembering the sufferings of Jesus is suddenly overcome by a sleep in which he has a painfully detailed vision of the Passion.[84] And the narrator of the anonymous debate-poem "In þe Ceson of Huge Mortalite" is also in a church kneeling before a crucifix when he notices the statue of a woman on a recent tomb. Fixing his mind "to ane ymage with gret deuocione," he is ravished by a slumber and dreams that he overhears a dialogue between this woman and her worms.[85] In both poems the waking narrators have their minds focused upon the subjects that will be explored within their dreams. This is probably not the case with Will. Unlike other poets, Langland tells us nothing of Will's thoughts at the moment he falls asleep, and the Dreamer's confusion over what he sees suggests that his mind was somewhere else entirely. Any conclusion must be approached carefully —and here only provisionally—but I believe that Langland leaves ample room to suggest that Will, bored through inattention, might be

81. *The Book of Margery Kempe*, ed. Sanford Brown Meech and Hope Emily Allen, 1940, EETS o.s. 212, p. 207.

82. Hilton, *An Exposition of Qui Habitat*, ed. Wallner, p. 26.

83. Hardison, p. 61.

84. Dunbar, *Poems*, ed. Mackenzie, pp. 155–59.

85. Karl Brunner (ed.), "Mittelenglische Todesgedichte," *Archiv für das Studium der neueren Sprachen*, 167 (1935), 30–35. For a commentary, see Woolf, *Religious Lyric*, pp. 328–30, and Kathleen Cohen, *Metamorphosis of a Death Symbol: The Transi Tomb in the Later Middle Ages and the Renaissance* (Berkeley: University of California Press, 1973), pp. 29–30.

one of the "sleperys in cherche" frequently condemned in expositions on *acedia*.

After the vicar has departed for home, the Dreamer wakes up and writes down his vision (B. xix. 480–81). His work as a poet again suggests that he pursues this occupation according to some understanding of Dowel, although his emotional response to the vision of Pentecost and the founding of Holy Church leaves us with a feeling of uneasiness, especially when it is compared to the spiritual exhilaration of a mystic like Margery Kempe, whose visionary experiences were followed by "a newe gostly joye & a newe gostly comfort, wheche was so meruelyows þat sche cowde neuyr tellyn it as sche felt it." [86] Will is once again possessed by a despondency reminiscent of the spiritual dryness felt by mystics after long periods of contemplation:

> Thanne as I wente by þe wey, whan I was thus awaked,
> Heuy chered I yede and elenge in herte.
> I ne wiste wher to ete ne at what place,
> And it neghed nei3 þe noon and wiþ Nede I mette
> That afrounted me foule and faitour me called.
>
> (B. xx. 1–5)

The atmosphere of exaltation that imbued the last waking episode has vanished, as Will has returned to a state of *tristitia* unlike that of the meditator who grieves and loves. *Jacob's Well* is careful to discriminate among the different kinds of heart-ailing. If this anguish has natural causes and does not work against *caritas*, it is not sin. If the sorrow is a form of spiritual dryness that results from one's appetite for "gostly trauayle," it is only a venial sin. But if a man is so sluggish and distracted that he neglects things necessary for his physical or spiritual welfare—as Will seems to have done when confronted by Need— "þanne is it dedly synne." [87]

Although Langland is typically vague about the causes of Will's heaviness and heart-sickness, he does not altogether foreclose the possiblity that Need comes to upbraid someone who is so immobilized by *tristitia* that he does not understand the true ascetic way, with its allowance for moderate food and drink, that is, for those temporal necessities required for sustaining each man in his life of virtue. [88] Nor do

86. *The Book of Margery Kempe*, p. 209.
87. *Jacob's Well*, p. 114.
88. Leff, *Medieval Thought*, p. 45, discusses how Augustine's *City of God* sanctions the Earthly City as a place where men must live and care for their physical needs—food, clothing, shelter, and so on—until the two cities are divided on the Day of Judgment. The fullest treatment of this encounter is offered by Robert Adams, "The Nature of Need in *Piers Plowman* XX," *Traditio*, 34 (1978), 273–301.

the circumstances preceding Will's final dream offer any definite clues to his moral condition:

> Whan Nede hadde vndernome me þus anoon I fil aslepe
> And mette ful merueillously þat in mannes forme
> Antecrist cam þanne, and al þe crop of Truþe
> Torned it tid vp so doun and ouertilte þe roote,
> And made Fals sprynge and sprede and spede mennes nedes.
>
> (B. xx. 51–55)

Unlike earlier dreams, the initial contents of this vision do spring directly from the previous topic of conversation, although an allegorical substitution has taken place. The crops that provide for man's physical needs have been replaced by the "crop of Truþe" and the offshoots of False that appeal to man's spiritual needs, both good and bad. If we are to learn something of the Dreamer's psychological and moral being, we must search instead in the sermon of Need, a figure who would not have been introduced here if he did not bring some instruction required by Will.

Standing outside the realm of dream-allegory, this personification appears to Will in his waking life. The boundaries between dream and reality are thus fitfully confused. Is it any wonder that Will has become so distraught when his dreams impinge upon the nightmare of this world, affording him no escape? Need begins by addressing Will with terms such as *foule* and *faitour* that the narrator has already applied to him in his waking life. He then explains that food, drink, and clothing are three of life's necessities, so long as their use is governed by *spiritus temperantiae*. At the end of his instructional speech, he tells Will about the wise men who had "woneden in [wildernesse] and wolde noʒt be riche" (B. xx. 39), and he reminds him that Christ had endured privation in order to "suffre sorwes ful soure þat shal to Ioye torne" (B. xx. 47). The inclusion of Need's lecture suggests that Will has never heard these subjects before or, more likely, has forgotten them.

Almost nothing that Need says is new to the poem. In one of his earliest lessons, the Dreamer was told by Holy Church that three things—clothing, food, and drink—are held in common and must be consumed in measure (B. i. 23–26). Patience had told him much the same thing concerning Christ's decision to endure the life of poverty for mankind's sake, and had added a warning that Sloth sometimes used the example of Christ's poverty as an excuse for idleness:

> And þouʒ Sleuþe suwe pouerte and serue noʒt God to paie,
> Meschief is ay a mene and makeþ hum to þynke

That God is his grettest help and no gome ellis,
And he his seruaunt, as he seiþ, and of his sute boþe.

(B. xiv. 254–57)

And in Passus XIX, Grace had explained the *spiritus temperantiae* and applied it to the use of food, drink and clothing (281–88). If Need comes to tell Will things he ought to have in mind, things he has already been taught more than once, then it is likely he has forgotten these lessons by failing to review them as Holy Church had ordered from the start: "rekene hem by reson, reherce þow hem after" (B. i. 22).

Among the mental faculties that operate in Langland's psychological allegory, including Reason, Wit, Imaginatyf, and in some sense Will, it is remarkable that the power of *Memoria* is omitted. Whether in Augustine's three-part division of the soul or in the more elaborate medical and scholastic divisions of the mind—with chambers of the brain allotted variously to *imaginatio*, *aestimativa*, and *memoria*[89]—special emphasis was laid upon the power of the memory to store away the images, intentions, and wisdom gathered by the other powers for future use. A traditional definition is given by Bartholomaeus Anglicus, quoted here in John Trevisa's late fourteenth-century translation: "*memoratiua* . . . holdiþ and kepiþ in þe tresour of mynde þingis þat beþ apprehendid and iknowe bi þe ymaginatif and *racio*."[90] Even those who credited imagination with certain powers of recollection thought it retained only images and sense impressions. The ideas and intentions that are essential to man's spiritual education are stored only by the *vis memorativa*, the power specifically omitted from the psychomachia of *Piers Plowman*.[91] Moral writers like Langland were

---

89. A contemporary explanation of these faculties can be found in *On the Properties of Things: John Trevisa's Translation of Bartholomaeus Anglicus "De Proprietatibus Rerum"*, gen. ed. M. C. Seymour, 2 vols. (Oxford: The Clarendon Press, 1975), p. 98. Valuable for its pictorial evidence is Edwin Clarke and Kenneth Dewhurst's *An Illustrated History of the Brain Function* (Oxford: Sandford, 1972), pp. 10–48.

90. *On the Properties of Things*, ed. Seymour, p. 98.

91. *Memoria* is mentioned only as one of the duties of Anima: "And whan I make mone to God, *memoria* is my name" (B. xv. 26). Murray Wright Bundy, *The Theory of Imagination in Classical and Medieval Thought* (Urbana: University of Illinois Studies in Language and Literature, no. 12, 1927), pp. 179–80, says that the *vis memorativa* was thought to be the storehouse of ideas rather than images, and that the imagination simply retained sensations. Judith H. Anderson shares my reservations about equating Imaginatyf with *memoria* as a "storehouse of ideas and past events" in *The Growth of a Personal Voice: "Piers Plowman" and "The Faerie Queene"* (New Haven: Yale University Press, 1976), pp. 84–85, as does Britton J. Harwood, "Imaginative in *Piers Plowman*," *MÆ*, 44 (1975), 249–63. Against this testimony stand Bloomfield, *Apocalypse*, pp. 171–72, and Carruthers, *The Search for St. Truth*, p. 101, who maintain that Imaginatyf is "almost synonymous with memory."

especially alert to the role played by memory, not only at the moment of instruction but throughout a man's earthly life. In Lydgate's *Pilgrimage of the Life of Man*, for instance, Grace Dieu gives the Pilgrim a servant named Memoyre who will carry the various pieces of his moral armor until needed in the battle against the Vices.[92]

Yet in ways known to the most humble Christian as well as the most learned, a full remembrance of one's wrong-doings was a vital part of confession leading to the repair of man's fallen nature. Forgetfulness, on the other hand, led the way back into sin:

> . . . for whan a man or a womman rekkeþ not to schryue hem, þei forȝeteþ here defautes and synnes, and þat is wel gret perel. For þer may no man haue forȝeuenesse wiþ-out verrey schrifte þat bereþ repentaunce in herte, knowlechyng in mouþ, buxumnesse in deede, þat is amendement and fulfillyng in deede.[93]

This passage from *The Book of Vices and Virtues* is excerpted from a larger discussion of sloth, the vice to which forgetfulness was attached. If Will's lack of memory is demonstrated by his inability to retain important lessons and by the absence of Memorativa from the poem's psychological allegory—since *voluntas* was never credited with an independent power of recollection—then this failure contributes to our general impression of where Will's main trouble lies.

But how guilty is a man if he happens to have been born with a bad memory? He does not willfully thrust things out of his mind. He simply forgets. Moral ambiguity again surrounds Will's conduct. We have seen that volitional acts, the only acts to which blame can be attached, were traditionally divided into two types. Elicited acts are accomplished by the will itself as a power of the soul (wishing, intending, consenting), but commanded actions are carried out in some other human power under the direction of the will (walking, talking, focusing the senses, disguising one's self as a hermit). Yet so many of Will's actions in his waking life which ought to be classified as "commanded" actions—wandering idly, leaning against a bank, growing fatigued, and going to sleep—belong to a twilight region not under the immediate control of an active will.[94] In an earlier chapter we saw that *acedia*,

92. Lydgate, *Pilgrimage of the Life of Man*, pp. 241–45.
93. *The Book of Vices and Virtues*, p. 28. See also *Pilgrimage of the Life of Man*, p. 114 (l. 4340), and Dan Michel's *Ayenbite of Inwyt*, ed. Richard Morris, 1866, rev. Pamela Gradon, 1965, EETS o.s. 23, p. 32.
94. Even physical roaming, which would seem to require a persistent effort of the will, was not necessarily voluntary. Aelred of Rievaulx, for instance, said that overwhelming disquiet forced him to yield to "inordinate wandering, a sign of emptiness and dangers"; see his *Sermones de Oneribus*, XVI (*PL* 195:424).

to which these acts usually belong, had itself become morally ambiguous in scholastic analyses that conceived of it as a passion not sinful unless confirmed by the will. Since Will the Dreamer is not confirmed in this habit—he does undergo a change after the affective vision of Passus XVIII—it is possible to view his *acedia* as a mere passion influencing his behavior, his speech, even the workings of his mind. In this way, recognizing this passion and understanding its influences on the body and mind should provide valuable insights into Will's personality, explaining also a great deal about the formal progress of the poem offered to us as the journal of this mental wanderer.

In *The Parson's Tale* (676), Chaucer gives the standard description of sloth as the vice that makes a man "hevy, thoghtful, and wraw"; by this we can better understand Will's unabating seriousness, dark brooding, and biting irascibility. The poem may not be devoid of humor, but Will almost never participates except as the butt. Besides characteristics of temperament and mood, the *homo accidiosus* tended to have other mental habits in conjunction with sorrow.[95] Concluding his major treatment of *acedia*, Aquinas used Gregory's *evagatio mentis circa illicita* as a general rubric under which he gathered other traits of the sloth-ridden mind:

All the other five which he reckons as effects of spiritual apathy are included in the straying of the mind after illicit things. When this reaches the peak of the mind itself, importunately desirous of rushing after this or that without rhyme or reason, it is called uneasiness of mind (*importunitas mentis*); if it is in the knowing faculty it is called idle curiosity (*curiositas*); if in speech, it is called loquaciousness (*verbositas*); and if in the body not staying put, then it is called bodily restlessness (*inquietudo corporis*), as when a person's rambling mind is shown through inordinate movement of the limbs. If he moves from place to place it is called instability (*instabilitas*). Or maybe instability refers to fluctuation of purpose.[96]

Will's bodily roaming can thus be understood as the outward reflection of an inward condition. His loquaciousness distracts and annoys his instructors, like Holy Church, and the uneasiness of his mind sends his conversation off on tangents that sometimes cloud the issue, sometimes draw into discussion subjects of no central importance, and sometimes stray so far from the main topic that the coherence of the

---

95. *Moralia in Job*, XXXI, xlv, 88 (*PL* 76:621), is discussed by Wenzel, pp. 23–24.
96. Aquinas, *ST*, 2a2ae, q. 35, art. 4 (vol. 35, pp. 34–35). Other authors who condemned the slothful *evagatio mentis* include Rabanus Maurus, *De Ecclesiastica Disciplina*, III (*PL* 112:1251–53); Jonas of Orléans, *De Institutione Laicali*, III, vi (*PL* 102:246); Alcuin, *De Virtutibus et Vitiis Liber*, xxxii (*PL* 101:635); and Hugh of St. Victor, *De Sacramentis Christianae Fidei*, XIII, i (*PL* 176:526).

lesson is all but lost. His desire to pursue questions that are better left unasked—why is Aristotle damned and Trajan saved? Why should men try to live a holy life if they are predestined to Heaven or Hell?—represents an unwholesome curiosity that not only completes his depiction as *homo accidiosus* but, what is more, nearly cripples the progress of the poem throughout the *Vita de Dowel* and much of the *Vita de Dobet.* Langland's steady concern to explore the psychological aspects of sloth makes his poem representational in form as well as diagnostic in method. In ways astonishingly modern, its structure *is* its meaning, and our response as audience to that structure—our occasional confusion, impatience, even boredom—is made to conform to the mental state of the protagonist whose inner experiences we are forced to share vicariously.

This is not the place to examine in detail the intellectual digressions, detours, and dead-ends that constitute Will's mental wandering in the *Vitae*, nor to inquire as to what extent his journey is given true direction and purpose by the grand visions in the later part of the *Vita de Dobet.* But we do need to remind ourselves that all of Will's inward travels were initially in quest of something quite specific: to learn what Dowel means. Next, the knowledge found in dreams was to be translated by Will into actions in the waking life. The essence of Dowel is *doing.* This is why our crucial judgment must come to bear upon Will in the waking world, the place where actions finally can be counted. By constantly withdrawing into the realm of visions, the Dreamer cuts himself off from most possibilities of doing well—feeding the hungry, clothing the naked, visiting the sick, and so on—and in the brief interludes when he is awake, his conduct is described in ways permitting us to conclude that many occasions for good works are missed because he is preyed upon by the vice which *Cursor Mundi*, backed by patristic and scholastic traditions concerning sloth, defined as the "vn-stedefastnes of wille wandring."[97]

Jay Martin does well to remind us that Will's character is informed by two recognizable but ambiguous types, the wanderer and the fool, and I have sought in this chapter to add another type no less ambiguous: the sleeper. My discussion was designed partially to show that all of these types belong also to the *acedia* tradition and partially to suggest the impossibility of any simple moral interpretation. While I have sometimes stressed the Dreamer's similarity to the personification of Sloth, I hope also to have conveyed the impression of his immense superiority, his complexity, his real human worth. Here we have the dif-

---

97. *Cursor Mundi*, p. 1540 (l. 27,793).

ference, so to speak, between Emma Bovary and a bored housewife from Scarsdale: the former suffers from a metaphysical malady of tragic proportions, the latter only feels a vague anxiety which can be eased with a martini and a Valium. It is a difference in dimension that makes the one of them an endlessly fascinating literary figure, the other a colorless and uninteresting representative of a type.

Toward the end of *Piers Plowman* (B. xix. 1 and 481), Will has begun to write down accounts of his visions. He has become a poet, in short. The full-time writer has always been the target for suspicion, most especially in the Middle Ages when imaginative literature was often considered worthless if not dangerous. The poet's prolonged mental struggles had none of the sanction granted to the monk's spiritual exercises or the mystic's contemplation, and his work with pen and ink struck many men as an excuse for idleness, for sitting comfortably all day long while others lived by the sweat of their brows. Although my final chapter is devoted to Langland's ambivalent attitude toward his own work as a poet, the topic is worth raising at the close of this chapter, because Will's identity as poet has served critics since the nineteenth century in their argument that *Piers Plowman* is a truthful record of the life and times of Will Langland. Part of my intention implicit in this chapter, and explicit in the one that follows, is to suggest that the slothfulness of Will's character, so often based on features standard to writings on *acedia*, argues against any strict autobiographical reading.

VII

The Image in the Glass: The C-Text Autobiography

The "autobiographical" section of the C-text (v. 1–108) has long been admired as the most personal disclosure in any of the three versions of *Piers Plowman*. We are granted our fullest look at the Dreamer in his waking life and are allowed to hear him speak of himself at greater length than anywhere else in the poem's non-visionary action. Langland seems to present the passage as a remembrance of past life and a critique of past experience. By describing it as "a brilliant portrait of the personality of a man who knew himself well,"[1] E. Talbot Donaldson summarizes widespread critical opinion endorsing this passage as factual autobiography.

Much of the best twentieth-century criticism of the poem is likewise based on the assumption that the seemingly autobiographical references are true and factually undistorted. John Lawlor, for example, offers the following outline of Langland's life based upon the account of the poet's livelihood in C v:

From certain passages in the poem it has been inferred that the author was born about 1332 near the Malvern hills, perhaps educated at the monastery of Great Malvern, took minor clerical orders (which did not require celibacy), and came to London where he lived with his wife Kit and his daughter Nicolette on Cornhill, making a living by saying prayers for the souls of his benefactors. Other details concern his dress, his scant respect for the self-important, his reluctance to work manually, his persistence in writing verse, and his admission that he had led an unprofitable life.[2]

---

1. Donaldson, *The C-Text and Its Poet*, p. 226.
2. Lawlor, *Piers Plowman: An Essay in Criticism*, pp. 12–13. Supporters include

Others have tried to avoid biographical comment on the Dreamer as one means of avoiding any judgment upon the reliability of these references.[3] Yet the question of authenticity persists and must be addressed by any critic who would increase our understanding of the Dreamer, his relationship to the poet, and the meaning of the poem at large.

Even the first modern critics were divided on the issue of the biographical references, with the consensus shifting back and forth almost from one generation to the next. In 1813 the editor T.D. Whitaker arrived at the conclusion that the William who dreams all these dreams is a purely "imaginary personage."[4] Thomas Wright later maintained that Langland had been a monk, thus ignoring the evidence of C v which indicates other forms of religious employment.[5] Walter Skeat, on the other hand, used the prestige of his edition of 1886 to establish firmly the practice of inferring Langland's biography from references which the Dreamer makes about himself. In "The Author's Life," he renders a lengthy *vita* later passed along faithfully from critic to critic; Lawlor's biographical sketch quoted above is simply a précis of Skeat's. In 1901 A.S. Jack tackled the problem anew and launched an important attack on the literal reading of these references.[6] He was followed by a line of critics such as H.W. Wells who similarly focused their attentions upon the Dreamer as an independent figure, using "biographical" evidence to learn more about his character, not about Langland's.[7]

This shifting consensus reflects a more general movement of opinion throughout recent medieval studies. George Kane offers this much-needed caveat to students of Langland and Chaucer directly:

R.W. Chambers, *Man's Unconquerable Mind* (London: Jonathan Cape, 1939), esp. pp. 167–69; George Kane, *Middle English Literature*; and Bloomfield, *Apocalypse*, p. 97.

3. Among these are T.P. Dunning, *Piers Plowman: An Interpretation of the A-Text* (London: Longmans, 1937); Robert Worth Frank, *Piers Plowman and the Scheme of Salvation* (New Haven: Yale University Press, 1957); and to some extent Robertson and Huppé, *Piers Plowman and the Scriptural Tradition*.

4. Robert Langland, *Visio Willi de Petro Plouhman, Item Visiones ejusdem de Dowel, Dobet, et Dobest,* ed. Thomas Dunham Whitaker (London: John Murray, 1813), p. xix, as well as the title page and p. v for a separate description of Langland as an Oxford-trained priest.

5. *The Vision and Creed of Piers Ploughman,* ed. Thomas Wright, 2 vols., 2nd. ed. rev. (London: J.R. Smith, 1856), vol. I, p. ix.

6. A.S. Jack, "The Autobiographical Elements in *Piers the Plowman*," *JGPh*, 3 (1901), 393–414.

7. Harry W. Wells (trans.), *The Vision of Piers Plowman* (New York: Sheed and Ward, 1935), pp. 285, 290 *et passim*; his introductory remarks on the poet draw inferentially on the contents of the poem. Jack's argument is scrutinized by Donaldson,

Whatever sense of reality a dreamer or narrator awakens in us, we have no historical authorization, just as we have no good logic, for imputing that dreamer's particular attributes and circumstances and attitudes to the actual poet.[8]

The temptation to commit this error with Langland is forever strong since, unlike Chaucer whose life-records span 549 pages in a modern edition,[9] the author of *Piers Plowman* remains a man of absolute mystery. No reliable information whatsoever exists outside the poem to sharpen, alter, or cancel the impression we form of our poet-narrator. Lacking external evidence, the reader has only the contents of the poem to justify or disqualify equating the poet with the Dreamer. Langland does, I believe, afford us evidence that does disallow any *simple* equation. As Kane correctly observes, "the poets invite us to identify the narrators with themselves, and then, by the character of what is narrated, caution us not to carry out the identification."[10] Mary Riach has gone further in suggesting that the Dreamer's description of himself might be a joke and mean exactly the opposite.[11] Langland may have depicted himself as lazy and rude in the same ironic vein as Chaucer claiming to have no knowledge of love.

At least two considerations complicate our efforts to equate Will with Langland: (1) the moral discrepancy between what the poet preaches and what the Dreamer practices and (2) the casting of the action in C v in the conventional form of a debate between traditional rivals—Wit and Will.

Skeat notes the curious departure between doctrine and autobiography, especially in C v: "the poet seems to confess that he lived just such an idle and blameworthy life as did those against whom he directs his satire."[12] The narrator condemns beggars, but he begs; he criticizes clerics for going to London to earn a better living, but he does his own churchly work in London; he inveighs against "long" lay-abouts who will not work, but he claims to be "too long" to do any work himself. The Dreamer's failings are in fact scrupulously delineated to form a pattern of moral misconduct. And after the elaborate expositions of

pp. 220–21, in his illuminating survey of the critical tradition concerning the autobiographical problem.

8. George Kane, *The Autobiographical Fallacy in Chaucer and Langland Studies* (London: H.K. Lewis, 1965), p. 17.

9. *Chaucer Life-Records*, ed. Martin M. Crow and Clair C. Olson (Oxford: The Clarendon Press, 1966).

10. Kane, *Fallacy*, p. 15.

11. "Langland's Dreamer and the Transformation of the Third Vision," *EIC*, 19 (1969), 6 and 11.

12. Skeat, II, p. xxxvii.

the preceding three chapters, we should recognize, as I am confident Langland's audience did, that these faults were condemned under the broad banner of *acedia*.

In his careful and erudite analysis of C v, Donaldson issues this challenge: "the rejection of the poet's account of himself entails one great responsibility that no one has ever attempted to meet: that is, to explain what purpose the autobiographical passage was meant to serve if it is fictional."[13] The confusion felt by Skeat and others disappears, however, as soon as the Dreamer is seen as an entity distinct from a poet writing with no steady care for autobiographical accuracy, with no desire to offer a realistic portrait of his *outward* self. The discrepancy is not between what the poet preaches and the poet practices, but between what Langland advocates and the Dreamer demonstrates. Thus Will is rendered as a character whose moral flaws, like those of so many others in the poem, serve to instruct. The "autobiography" of C v takes the form of a debate or *altercatio* between psychological faculties and is, therefore, no less artificially staged than the confession of Sloth.

Much of Donaldson's final chapter in *The C-Text and Its Poet* is dedicated to a close examination of C v, and I have chosen in the following pages to respond directly to his argument because it is the most learned and logically persuasive of all those voiced in favor of autobiographical authenticity. Donaldson's powers of mind and breadth of scholarship have combined to produce what remains the most illuminating work on the C-text, and yet I believe that he has not been well served by the assumption that "Langland was telling the truth about himself and not whimsically devising an elaborate fiction."[14] Without pausing long enough to consider whether a fiction might not accord with some serious didactic end, he embarked in search of the truth he believed Langland was divulging about himself.

On the assumption that the C-poet has assembled stray facts from the B-text and augmented them into a full and accurate account of his past life, Donaldson sets about to determine the exact nature of that religious occupation. Concentrating largely upon the descriptions of the clerical orders in Bishop William Lyndwood's *Provinciale seu Constitutiones Anglia* (1433), Donaldson decides that Langland could have occupied any order below that of sub-deacon, since married men were normally allowed to rise no higher. He thinks that Langland might well have been an acolyte who would have been expected to

13. Donaldson, p. 220.
14. *Ibid.*

serve the altar in church. Already two difficulties arise, as he is quick to admit. Married clerks seldom attained the position of acolyte, and if Will had done so, "for one reason or another he was not performing his office."[15]

Donaldson next examines the long-standing idea that Langland might have earned his living by saying prayers for the souls of the dead. The text lends some support for this theory (C. v. 48), but Donaldson has doubts: "Certainly we should expect a beneficed clerk to be static rather than peripatetic and to employ the officially sanctioned service book of the altar to which he was attached, rather than a Primer."[16] He then fixes his interest upon a minor order of chantry clerks whose numbers are thought to have been rather large during the fourteenth century. Their duty was to serve chantry priests as acolytes and choristers in offering prayers for the souls of the living as well as the dead. Yet this identification is hard to press because almost nothing is known about these clerks, except that they were cited by Parliament for the neglect of their duties.[17] Although the Dreamer says, "This y segge for here soules of suche as me helpeth," it is unclear whether his prayers were said for the living or the dead. Donaldson decides that he probably did both, or either, as the need required. The conclusion Donaldson reaches, however, is rather curious: that Langland was neither priest, nor monk, nor acolyte, nor regular member of a chantry; he was instead "a sort of itinerant handy man" whose "odd jobs were prayers."[18] Still, Will seems to be sensitive to the irregularity of his profession.

All these rational contortions are required by the assumption of a true autobiographical content. The difficulties and inconsistencies are multiplied if one considers—as Donaldson promises to, but does not—other biographical elements elsewhere in the poem which in terms of his argument have no less authority and yet do not always accord with C v. In the opening lines of the Prologue, the Dreamer says that he is dressed as a hermit roving the Malvern Hills, at some distance from the London setting of the autobiographical section. He

---

15. *Ibid.*, pp. 201–06.

16. *Ibid.*, p. 211.

17. *Ibid.*, p. 214, citing Jusserand, *A Contribution to the History of English Mysticism*, p. 89, n. 1. See also McKisack, pp. 304–05.

18. Donaldson, pp. 218–19. Rosalind Hill, "'A Chaunterie for Soules': London Chantries in the Reign of Richard II" in *The Reign of Richard II*, ed. DuBoulay and Barron, p. 245, admits to the difficulty of tracing the activities of such a "free-lance mass-priest"; Bertha Putnam, "Wage-laws for Priests after the Black Death," *AHR*, 21 (1915/16), 12–32, had already demonstrated that chantry priests were an all too typical target for criticism during the period.

later calls himself a beggar, a wanderer, and a lunatic, without further reference to religious vocation. Indeed, in the waking interlude of Passus XVIII and XIX where the Dreamer hastens to Mass with his wife Kitte and daughter Kalote (the latter not mentioned in C v), he takes no part in the ceremonies and apparently enjoys no privileged place in the congregation often ceded to clerical orders.

In short, it is not enough to say that Langland has "assembled, expanded, augmented, and made explicit in the C-passage" references to his life scattered throughout the B-text.[19] The poet has created a new scene with a figure of indeterminate nature who metamorphoses even in the process of being described. Such a figure, if divorced from the notion of autobiography, takes his place comfortably alongside characters such as the Seven Deadly Sins of the Confession. The shrift of Avarice is illustrative of this method. He first announces that he is a seller at fairs, then a draper, then a taverner, and finally a prominent moneylender. To try reconciling all these jobs to some single worldly occupation is to miss the point. Avarice is a composite figure, as was Sloth, embodying the many species of the sin he represents.

The depiction of Avarice is a fair paradigm for examining the creation of the Dreamer's self-portrait. Both are introduced as unrepentant sinners and both move from one point of self-characterization to another with little regard for logical consistency. Thus the Dreamer can have been an acolyte *and* a married man, the son of a well-to-do family *and* a beggar, a peripatetic priest *and* a stationary member of a chantry. As in the case of Avarice, the portrait of Will lacks mimetic unity; it is not meant to imitate any single person or even a particular type. Both these figures have, instead, an overlying moral coherency reflecting the didactic impulses behind their creation.

Donaldson states his case in extreme terms, leading his reader to believe that C v must be judged as either the truth or a whimsical fiction. These alternatives are too stark, because they exclude the sort of purposive fiction which readers of moral allegory naturally expected. To Donaldson, however, the only other choice is to consider the passage as "an obscurely motivated description of no one in particular."[20] After reviewing several of the crucial points upon which the Dreamer's conduct is in conflict with the moral sanctions of the poem, however, Donaldson is compelled to agree in part with earlier critics such as Jack and Manly, who were unable to reconcile the poet's preachings elsewhere with his confession here. But still he concludes that C v rep-

19. Donaldson, p. 201.
20. *Ibid.*, p. 202.

resents, truthfully, an *apologia pro vita sua* offered by Langland to show the sinfulness of his past life.[21] It is impossible for us to discard this contention for the same reason it is impossible for Donaldson to prove it conclusively, because we simply know nothing about Langland outside his poem.

However, four questions are perhaps more pressing than the one which Donaldson addresses. (1) What exactly *is* sinful in the record of the Dreamer's life contained in C v? (2) In what way might this major addition, even without strict factual accuracy, form an important part of the poet's *spiritual* autobiography? (3) Why did Langland see fit to insert this self-portrait at such an early point in his final version? And (4) what does this section suggest to us about Langland's "public image" created by the A-version, which had already been circulating for perhaps two decades?

Although Donaldson begins his examination of Langland's career with the statement "on none of these matters, probably, would a fourteenth-century reader have required commentary,"[22] the twists and turns of his subsequent discussion lend little support to that statement. True, a contemporary audience would not have experienced great confusion over many of the literal details, but their concern with these matters would not have been so tightly restricted to the literal. We would do well to recall the tenor of Kane's argument, that a fourteenth-century audience would not have expected any honest, factual account of the poet's livelihood. Far from it. What convention demanded was a fictional pose granting insight into the Dreamer's moral predicament, which was perhaps—but only *perhaps*—shared by the poet.

Skeat says of C v that Will "describes his own laziness in amusing terms."[23] This comment strikes at the heart of the passage. Not only has Skeat registered the dominant moral theme, but he also notes the comical manner in which the poet launches the "autobiography." Comical tone in a religious work does not detract from a particular moral lesson but rather fortifies and sharpens it, as we are reminded by V.A. Kolve in his examination of the Corpus Christi dramas:

Laughter was respectable in the Middle Ages partly because it could teach. Notwithstanding its value as entertainment, it seldom neglected this other function, as even genres less obviously didactic than the cycle-plays can testify.[24]

21. *Ibid.*, pp. 219–20 and 226.
22. *Ibid.*, p. 202.
23. Skeat, II, p. 60.
24. V.A. Kolve, *The Play Called Corpus Christi* (Stanford: Stanford University Press,

The comedy of C v is clear enough to any audience as the age-old farce of the liar caught in his own lies, but the modern reader must work toward a fuller appreciation of the lesson which the comedy teaches.

The passage begins with five lines describing how the Dreamer awakens after his first vision, no longer in the Malvern Hills but on Cornhill, and how he has become unpopular among the idlers of London:

> Thus y awakede, woet God, whan y wonede in Cornehull,
> Kytte and y in a cote, yclothed as a lollare,
> And lytel ylet by, leueth me for sothe,
> Amonges lollares of Londone and lewede ermytes,
> For y made of tho men as resoun me tauhte.
>
> (C. v. 1−5)

Will speaks out of the historical moment at which the C-revision is being written, a time when he enjoys some reputation as a moralist for "making" poetry as Reason once taught him. In the lines that follow, the Dreamer recollects the instructions that Reason gave him at some undetermined time in the past. Upon a first reading, the opening lines seem to indicate that the Dreamer has reformed his life in accordance with these teachings, but this impression is not altogether supported, since among all the many useful occupations prescribed by Reason, the writing of poetry is never mentioned. What is more, Will is still dressed as a *lollare*, which Skeat glosses as "a lounger, an idle vagabond." [25]

Whatever else the opening hundred lines of C v do to make us uncomfortable about Will, they frustrate any sense we might have of linear chronology. Will has awakened from his first vision and proceeds to tell us of a previous experience that could only have occurred before he fell asleep in the Malvern Hills—his meeting with Reason and Conscience—after which he falls asleep and has another vision that continues the allegory of the first. That is, the second vision of the C-text takes place chronologically *before* the first—if, that is, we try to fit the events into a normal time-sequence. But we are not meant to. Instead, we are supposed to conceive of events in the order they are told to us, an order that has its own specific purpose, since what comes last is what Langland wishes his audience to remember best. And what

---

1966), p. 129. Donaldson, p. 226, has a similar sense that the passage's "humor implies a greater depth of understanding."

25. Skeat, II, pp. 60−61.

comes last in this scene of C v is the description of the Dreamer as a lazy and arrogant shirker.

Will's recollection begins as he meets with Conscience and Reason during a warm harvest season when he was in good health (C. v. 6–8). The warm weather suggests both the "somur sesoun" of the Prologue and the season of complacency for those ignorant of their sins. The Dreamer is not long allowed to remain comfortable in his slothfulness but is quickly reprimanded by Reason:

> In an hot heruest whenne y hadde myn hele
> And lymes to labory with and louede wel fare
> And no dede to do but to drynke and to slepe.
> In hele and in inwitt oen me apposede;
> Romynge in remembraunce, thus Resoun me aratede.
>
> (C. v. 7–11)

Stated more forthrightly than in the Prologue, the Dreamer's moral condition is affected by laziness and a tendency to daydream and sleep. Reason interrupts him in the midst of his mental roaming, demanding to know why he cannot serve in church, why he cannot cook, mow hay, rise early to reap, stay awake at night guarding against thieves, or perform *any* physical labors. The Dreamer responds with a series of feeble excuses:

> "Y am to wayke to worche with sykel or with sythe
> And to long, lef me, lowe to stoupe,
> To wurche as a werkeman eny while to duyren."
>
> (C. v. 23–25)

Since Will has already described himself as a man in good health with strong limbs, this brief speech places him solidly among that group of shirkers with whom he was obliquely identified earlier when he travelled abroad in a hermit's disguise.[26] Reason sees through these lies, forcing the Dreamer to consider himself in terms already familiar in the poem's rhetoric of condemnation:

> . . . "For an ydel man þow semest,
> A spendour þat spene mot or a spille-tyme,

26. In the Z-text, Robert also complains: "For *fodere non valeo*, so feble ar my bones: / Caucyon, ant Y couthe, *caute* wolde Y make, / That Y ne begged ne borwed ne in despeyr deyde" (v. 142–44). Transparent excuses of this sort are common to the sloth tradition. In *Ayenbite of Inwyt*, Dan Michel says that the slothful man uses this strategy to avoid hard labors: "me him hat zomþing / þet him þingþ hard. he him excuseþ: þet he hit ne may do. oþer yef he hit onderuangþ: he hit deþ / oþer litel / other naʒt" (p. 33).

> Or beggest thy bylyue aboute at men hacches
> Or faytest vppon Frydayes or feste-dayes in churches,
> The which is lollarne lyf, þat lytel is preysed."

(C. v. 27–31)

The Dreamer responds to Reason's indictment with a lengthy speech amounting to an admission of guilt. He says that in his youth his father and friends had sent him to school to learn the Scriptures and religious lore, but since his patrons have died, he finds no life attractive except in his "longe clothes," whether the unholy hermit's habit or the *lollare's* clothes he is wearing at the beginning of this passus.

This portrait of a man who has wasted his education by becoming a beggar is similar to something Sloth says in the Confession: "I yarn aboute in youþe and yaf me nauȝt to lerne, / And euere siþþe be beggere by cause of my sleuthe" (B. v. 439–40; C. vii. 53–54). This parallel between Sloth and the Dreamer is too close to have been accidental and is supplemented by later information: the Dreamer says he makes a monthly tour of various houses where he begs "withoute bagge or botel but my wombe one" (C. v. 52). At the end of Will's confession, Conscience enters the debate and chooses to criticize him principally for his life of beggary: "Ac it semeth no sad parfitnesse in citees to begge" (C. v. 90). This accent upon the Dreamer's life as a beggar helps to clarify the basis for his unholiness in the Prologue, as the association of him with the "heap of hermits" had hinted. The self-portrait marks indelibly in our minds the image of a false beggar, which is invoked again later and defined with no moral ambiguity in the Confession of Sloth.

After Reason has brushed aside the Dreamer's excuse of physical weakness, Will assumes another pose and frames a new, more clever argument against indulging in manual labor. He enumerates at some length his various clerical duties, which seem intentionally muddled in definition, perhaps by Will in an effort to baffle Reason, or perhaps by the poet in order to show the confusion of someone who makes up his lies as he goes along. But Will's conclusion is stated loud and clear:

> "Me sholde constrayne no clerc to no knaues werkes,
> For by þe lawe of *Levyticy* þat oure lord ordeynede,
> Clerkes ycrouned, of kynde vnderstondynge,
> Sholde nother swynke ne swete . . ."

(C. v. 54–57)

The Scriptural foundation for this contention is sound (Lev. 21), and other fourteenth-century writers voiced similar statements supporting the exemption of clerics from physical works.[27] Such excuses were valid when sincerely meant by a bona-fide cleric, but the Dreamer soon reveals an arrogance of tone that undercuts his position, especially if he is not actually performing the church offices that he claims:

> "Hit bycometh for clerkes Crist for to serue
> And knaues vncrounede to carte and to worche.
> For sholde no clerke be crouned but yf he come were
> Of frankeleynes and fre men and of folke ywedded.
> Bondemen and bastardus and beggares children,
> Thyse bylongeth to labory, and lordes kyn to serue
> God and good men, as here degre asketh, . . ."
>
> (C. v. 61–67)

Conscience is not deceived by Will's argument and sweeps aside his excuses with the remark that his actual livelihood bears little resemblance to any pious occupation. He is simply a beggar, Conscience points out, and not obedient "to prior or to mynistre" (C. v. 89–91). The Dreamer's defense collapses and he submits to all the allegations. His sudden transition from sinful *acedia* to repentance is similar to the movement noted by Wenzel between the Confession of Sloth and the speech of Robert the Robber in the B-text. But submitting to criticism and waiting for grace are not enough; Will's real obligation, as Conscience insists, is to make an act of restitution.

Reason prescribes a compensatory discipline—"the lyif þat is louable" (C. v. 103)—and the Dreamer, like Sloth at the end of his confession, begins his act of penance, but does not see it through to the end:

> And to þe kyrke y gan go, God to honoure,
> Before þe cross on my knees knokked y my brest,
> Syȝing for my synnes, seggyng my *pater-noster*,
> Wepyng and waylyng til y was aslepe.
>
> (C. v. 105–08)

This passage undercuts our sense of optimism by suggesting the failure of the Dreamer's best intentions, because he does not complete the penitential ritual while corrupting the Pater Noster (which he had cited earlier as an authority—C. v. 87) by falling asleep in the midst of his prayer. While he had argued that clerics should be exempted from physical labor, he proves himself inattentive to even his churchly tasks. More important, he loses the benefit of his penance by failing to fulfill its terms either in act or in spirit. Just as Sloth knocks himself on the

---

27. *The Cloud of Unknowing*, p. 50, responds also to those people in the secular world who object to the apparent idleness of those in the contemplative life.

breast and falls asleep while saying his Benedicite (B. v. 390–91), Will knocks himself on *his* breast and then goes to sleep while saying the Pater Noster and "wepyng and waylynge." A fourteenth-century audience would have required no elaborate commentary in order to understand that falling asleep in church during one's prayers was sinful, a sign of deadly sloth.[28] The unflattering portrait of Will is therefore consistent throughout: he excuses himself from physical labor, but then falls asleep in the midst of his religious exercise.

So far, the discussion of biographical authenticity has focused on two main topics: (1) the careful delineation of the Dreamer's character along lines laid down by traditional writings on *acedia* and (2) the muddled connection between the livelihood that Langland describes for Will and any documented religious profession of the fourteenth century. But there is at least one more important consideration. The C-text identifies the Dreamer as "Will" almost immediately when he enters the poem's visionary action; Lady Holy Church's first words to him are "Wille, slepestou?" (C. i. 5). After his interview with Holy Church, he becomes again a purely passive spectator, until the opening section of C v when he is drawn back to center stage, this time with the faculties of Reason and Conscience as his fellow performers. The episode is an important one, since it invites the audience for the first time to read the poem's allegory psychologically in such a way that Will represents, to some extent, the faculty *Voluntas*. As if to insure that this occasion not be missed, the C-poet has chosen a simple, recognizable format—a debate between Wit and Will.

Before we can properly assess the importance of that choice, we must take notice of another scholarly problem that impinges on our discussion of Will the Dreamer. Closely related to the debate over the truthfulness of the autobiographical references is the controversy over authorship. For those such as Manly and Fowler who have argued in favor of multiple authorship, the problem never arises; for them there is no single poet with whom to equate Will, because the hand that drew him "yclothed as a lollare" in C v was different from the hand that had first sketched him "in abite as an ermyte."[29] While Kane's monograph on authorship has satisfied most readers that a single poet is responsible for all three versions of *Piers Plowman*, we are left with

28. A slothful man's preference for sleep instead of spiritual activity or religious ceremonies is ascribed to *hevynesse* in *The Book of Vices and Virtues*, p. 27.

29. John M. Manly, "The Authorship of *Piers Plowman*," MP, 7 (1909), 83–144, used the poet's self-contradictory portrayal of Will as evidence of multiple authorship. See also Fowler, *Literary Relations of the A and B Texts*, pp. 185–86.

the question of what name he bore. For our present purposes, it is less important to know whether his last name was Langland than to decide what first name he went by. For over ninety years, readers have been swayed by Skeat's decision in favor of William, and Kane's study asserts once more the reasonableness of that view.[30]

I would like to draw attention to one further point that has been overlooked: in the manuscript titles, marginalia, and colophons, the author is never called simply Will, but rather William or Wilhelmus. Yet inside the poem, the Dreamer is always called Will, never William. The point is small, but not so small that it should be ignored by those who would equate Langland with the Dreamer on the basis of the practice, common among fourteenth-century poets, of giving their own correct names to their first-person narrators.[31] At the very least, William Langland gave his Dreamer a shortened form of his first name, and until a better explanation can be offered, I suggest he did so to allow "Will" to take upon himself the role of *Voluntas* at certain important moments, such as the opening of C v.

Our understanding of Will's debate with Reason can be deepened if we know something of the native tradition that stands behind it. The word *reason* was a fairly recent arrival in Middle English from Latin,[32] but the moral and psychological confrontation that Langland describes was by no means a novelty. The human will had often been placed in opposition to wit, the lexical equivalent of reason and a faculty whose function would be difficult to distinguish from that of *ratio*.[33] Worth noting is a textual note in Skeat's edition in which *wit* is cited as a significant manuscript variant for *Reson* in the opening of C v.[34] Here we have the testimony of at least one medieval witness, and perhaps several more, who felt that the two words were interchangeable in this context.

30. Skeat, II, pp. xxvii–xxxii; and Kane, *Authorship*, Chapter III, pp. 26–51.
31. *Ibid.*, pp. 56–57.
32. *OED*, vol. VIII, R, p. 212, "reason," III. 10: "That intellectual power or faculty . . . which is ordinarily employed in adapting thought or action to some end; the guiding principle of the human mind in the process of thinking." The earliest attestation is from *The Ancrene Riwle* (c. 1225): "Wummon is þe reisun, þet is, wittes skile." From the beginning *reason* was defined by the native word "wit."
33. *OED*, vol. XII, W, p. 201, "wit," I. 2: "The faculty of thinking and reasoning in general; mental capacity, intellect, reason." For the joining of *intellectus* and *ratio* in opposition to *voluntas*, see Alexander, *Theories of Will*, pp. 136–39, and Gilson, *History*, pp. 463–64. In a study intended to clarify Langland's psychological terms, Randolph Quirk concludes that by *wit* the poet meant *ratio particularis*; "Langland's Use of *Kind Wit* and *Inwit*," *JEGP*, 52 (1953), 182–88. Robertson and Huppé, p. 106, argue Wit's affinity with Reason.
34. Skeat, I, p. 118.

As we saw in Chapter II, reason and will were commonly thought to be linked in the enactment of good works—the reason discriminated between right and wrong, and the will chose to exert itself—but when the will acted against the edicts of reason, that action was sinful.[35] Writers of moral literature interested themselves in the inter-dependence of these two powers of the soul, warning of the dangers inherent in the independent action of the will. In one of the earliest Middle English examples, the author of *Sawles Ward* speaks of wit and will as a husband and wife working together to safeguard the welfare of their home, the human body.[36] A thirteenth-century lyric puts the warning more directly:

> Hwenne-so wil wit ofer-stieþ   [surmounts
> þenne is wil and wit for-lore,
> Hwenne-so wil his hete hieþ   [hastens
> þer nis nowiht wit icore.
> Ofte wil to seorȝe sieþ,
> Bute ȝif wit him wite to-fore,
> Ac hwenne-so wil to wene wrieþ,   [turns aside
> þe ofo of wisdom is to-tore.[37]   [coif

A longer treatment entitled "Wyt & Wille" is offered in MS. Digby 102, where each of the lyric's nine stanzas ends with a stern reminder such as "Gostely and bodily hym self he shendes, / þat leueþ wyt and worcheþ by wille."[38] Wit and will naturally invited alliterative treatment, and at some time during the fourteenth century a poet of no remarkable gifts executed a work that goes under the modern title *The Conflict of Wit and Will*.[39] Though the poem survives only as a series of mutilated fragments, it is worth considering not only because it attests to a keen fourteenth-century awareness of the precarious hierarchy of wit over will, but also because one of the central figures in the

---

35. Even voluntarists like Ockham could admit that the will required the direction of reason in order to reach virtue; Leff, *Ockham*, pp. 482–83 and 505. The voluntarists also held to the old belief that "to sin is voluntarily to violate right reason, either by omitting to do what should be done or committing what should not be done. In both cases, as St. Augustine said, it means going against God's will and His eternal law" (Leff, *Gregory of Rimini*, p. 207).

36. *Early Middle English Verse and Prose*, ed. J.A.W. Bennett and G.V. Smithers (Oxford: The Clarendon Press, 1968), esp. pp. 247–49.

37. *English Lyrics of the XIIIth Century*, ed. Brown, no. 39, p. 65.

38. *Twenty-Six Political and Other Poems*, ed. J. Kail, 1904, EETS o.s. 124, pp. 22–24.

39. *The Conflict of Wit and Will: Fragments of a Middle English Alliterative Poem*, ed. Bruce Dickins (Kendal: Leeds School of English Language Texts and Monographs, no. 4, 1937), pp. 15–19.

poem is a mysterious character named Angus, whom the editor identifies as the "angwissh of troubled herte" caused by *acedia*.[40]

The pairing of wit and will can be found throughout *Piers Plowman*, both in short didactic passages and in larger dramatic action. The walls of Truth's castle are made of wit to keep out will (B. v. 587). Janglers have wit to work what they will (B. prol. 37). Eld and Holiness lament that wit is torn to pieces for the pleasure of will (B. xi. 45). The Rat says that his fellow rodents must use their wit to withstand the Cat's will (B. prol. 156–57). And Covetise confesses that he never had a will to use wit in asking for God's mercy (B. xiii. 383–86). Examples of this sort are common.[41] They serve as a periodic reminder of Langland's special interest in these two faculties, with will having the active power to confound wit.

The Dreamer is not often called Will outright in any version of the poem, but Langland does so on at least two important occasions in order to establish specifically his relationship with Reason or Wit. While Skeat maintains that Will is first named in the B-text after Reason has delivered the sermon that "made Wille to wepe water wiþ hise eiȝen" (B. v. 61), there is some doubt that this is anything other than the collective *voluntas* of the people.[42] Yet the Dreamer is certainly the one later named Will by the figure Thought, who has taken him in search of Wit: "Wher Dowel and Dobet and Dobest ben in londe / Here is Wil wolde wite if Wit koude hym teche" (B. viii. 128–29). In the B-text, Wit's sermon represents the first expansion upon the teachings of Holy Church since Passus I, placing important emphasis on the internal rather than external reality of the good life. The C-poet, knowing that the action of the poem would eventually focus upon the Dreamer and his inner quest, inserts the personal allegory of C v and uses it to signal future difficulties by pitting Will against Reason, the faculty that should be his partner and guide, in an informal but recognizable debate.

Debates of one kind or another, sometimes a heated argument, sometimes a reasoned Boethian dialogue, constitute a remarkably large portion of *Piers Plowman*. The Dreamer has a contentious interview with Holy Church; Conscience and Lady Mede debate before the King; Piers and Hunger disagree over the treatment of laborers; Piers

---

40. *Ibid.*, p. 7, taking the language of Chaucer, *ParsT*, 677.
41. For instance, B. ii. 153–55, v. 184–87, x. 170–71, xiv. 126–27, and xix. 367–71.
42. Skeat, II, p. 71; and Kane, *Authorship*, p. 59, maintaining that A. v. 43–44 should be read allegorically, not biographically.

and the Priest argue over the validity of the Pardon; and so on. Debate is so prominent a feature that several medieval scribe-editors were persuaded in their judgment of the poem's "genre," since an impressive number of manuscripts bear as their title *Dialogus Petri Plowman*.[43] Although some of these disputes, such as the debate over the Pardon, have conclusions so ambiguous that they are still being argued about today, the debate between Will and Reason has a clear and definite ending. Will admits that he is wrong and has behaved badly.

This was a foregone conclusion. Even before he accepts Reason's criticism, Will's position appears untenable, judged either according to an external set of moral values—he defends the life of slothfulness—or on the basis of its internal logical inconsistencies. He starts off boasting of his good health, but when Reason urges him to engage in manual labor, he complains that he is too tall and too weak to endure the work (C. v. 7–10 and 23–25). Elsewhere in his defense he says that clerks should serve and sing at Mass instead of doing menial chores (C. v. 60 and 68–69), although Reason has already rebuked him for not singing in church (C. v. 12). Besides other insights provided by C v, we find that a medieval author, rather than framing arguments equally poised on both sides of a question as in *The Owl and the Nightingale*, could exercise his ingenuity in constructing an argument so feeble that it was bound to collapse.

The burden of evidence that overcomes Will is provided by Conscience, a curious figure who remains silent throughout most of the debate. From Aristotle onward, the conscience was thought to be responsible for advising which alternatives to choose, and this function as proctor over the will earned for Conscience a prominent role in Langland's poem, right up to the end when it is Conscience who sets off in a final search for Piers the Plowman. Conscience is the accuser of sin and works to weigh down the soul with guilt over past misdeeds, but it also shows the soul beforehand what is right, teaching it what is learned from reason—what is pleasing to God and what is best for its future spiritual welfare—although a seminal treatise by Philip the Chancellor distinguished between *synderesis* and *conscientia* in that

---

43. Bodl. MS. Laud. Misc. 581; Cambr. Univ. Lib. MSS. Dd 1.17, Gg 4.31, Ll 4.14; BM. Add. MS. 35287; Trin. Col. Cambr. MS. B 15.17; and Oriel Col. Oxon. MS. 79. For further discussion of medieval confusion over the genre of Langland's poem, see Kane, *Authorship*, p. 47, and Bloomfield, *Apocalypse*, p. 8. And for a guide to further reading on debate writings, consult Francis Lee Utley, "Dialogues, Debates, and Catechisms" in *A Manual of the Writings in Middle English, 1050–1500*, gen. ed. Albert E. Hartung (New Haven: The Connecticut Academy of Arts and Sciences, 1972), vol. III, pp. 669–745 and 829–902.

the latter involved free choice and therefore could make mistakes.[44] In the scholastic division of the rational soul, conscience served as an intermediary between the intellect (reason) and will, and its function was to enforce upon the will the syllogistic evidence for right conduct rendered by the intellect.[45]

In the debate of C v, Conscience performs in strict accordance with this tradition. Will encounters Reason only when he passes by way of Conscience, just as Conscience had summoned Reason to advise the King in the previous scene. And it is in the presence of Conscience that Reason lays bare the record of Will's lazy and profitless life. The terms of Will's defense are not without independent merit, however, since there *was* a sound argument to be made in favor of exempting the clergy from manual labor. In the face of this logic, Reason falls silent. It is here that Conscience enters the debate for the first time. Will had used part of the Pater Noster at the close of his defense—"*Fiat voluntas tua*" (88)—but by charging that Will has done wrong to beg in cities, Conscience is accusing him of acting *against* God's will, the standard definition of sin. Will accepts the truth of this charge and admits that he has misspent his time, although his proposal for future living does not please his interlocutors. Will says that he must wait for God's grace before he begins to make amends,[46] but Reason objects that this is just another excuse for inaction. He urges Will to begin a praiseworthy life at once, and when Conscience adds the weight of his office, Will sets off for the church where, alone, he falls asleep during his prayers. Without the constant aid of Conscience and Reason, Will is not able to persevere long in his new life of penance and spiritual regeneration.[47] He lapses back into his habitual vice.

Once Will has fallen asleep, he dreams that he sees Reason and Conscience again, this time standing before the King. The persistence of these two allegorical characters suggests motives for the insertion of the C v debate in this particular spot. Reason and Conscience appear in three consecutive scenes: in the first and third they advise the King;

---

44. For more on conscience, see Gilson, *History*, p. 77, and Priscilla Jenkins, "Conscience: The Frustration of Allegory" in *Critical Approaches*, ed. Hussey, pp. 125–42. Philip the Chancellor's *Summa de Bono* (c. 1235) is discussed by Timothy C. Potts, *Conscience in Medieval Philosophy* (Cambridge: Cambridge University Press, 1980), pp. 12–31, with translations from the text, pp. 94–109.

45. Robertson and Huppé, p. 158, citing Godfrey of Fontaines.

46. Peter Lombard, *Sententiarum Libri Quatuor*, II, xxxix (*PL* 192:746), gave support for will requiring grace: "Sed voluntas haec semper caret effectu, nisi gratia Dei adjuvet et liberet."

47. Bourke, *Will*, pp. 35–36, cites various commentators who held that the will, when separated from the other powers of the soul, could do nothing by itself.

in the central one they argue with Will. The King comes to represent *voluntas* both as the beneficiary of their counsel and as the force that enacts what is right for the realm. As I have sought to demonstrate in Chapter V, the King is the embodiment of monarchal will as the active power behind the enforcement of just laws. By contrast, Will in C v is a personal will responsible for executing what is right in a man's life. But the King solicits and then submits to the advice of Reason and Conscience, whereas Will runs into the two almost by accident, resists their counsel, and probably falls short in his enactment of the good life they recommend. Yet the relation of C v to these bracketing scenes does not leave Will in a wholly unflattering light. While portraying the King as monarchal will, Langland depicts his Will as the monarch of the soul, the essential force to whom other mental powers gather and upon whom all moral actions depend. This aggrandizement of *voluntas* is, as we saw in Chapter II, consonant with the major developments in fourteenth-century theology.[48]

John Burrow has remarked upon the aptness of Will as dreamer-narrator in a Boethian allegory in which the protagonist is the learner, since the will is psychologically the object of instructive agents such as reason and conscience.[49] The question remains whether this was a happy accident, the result of Stacy de Rokayle christening his son William, or whether Langland took pains to generalize the character of the protagonist by rendering him a willful Everyman whose mistakes, triumphs, and recurrent lapses reflect the collective Christian experience. Kane believes that in naming the protagonist Will, "the poet was not merely publishing his own baptismal name but also implying that the Dreamer was—to some indeterminable extent—made in his own image."[50] That phrase *to some indeterminable extent* lingers, more a challenge than a qualification.

Opposition to the autobiographical interpretation has drawn up behind Robertson and Huppé, who have contended that psychological personifications like Wit and even Will stand for the faculties as such, generalizations applied *to* the individual but not themselves representing the faculties *of* an individual. As Elizabeth Kirk has noted, "the

---

48. Augustine had spoken of the will as "a ruler and kind of judge" (*The Free Choice of the Will*, trans. Russell, p. 122), and the fourteenth-century voluntarists made even grander claims. Bourke, *Will*, p. 179, provides this later testimony from St. Francis de Sales: "Among the numberless multitudes and varieties of action, movements, sentiments, inclinations, habits, faculties and powers that are in man, God has established a natural monarchy, and it is the will that commands and dominates over all that is found in this little world."

49. Burrow, "Words, Works and Will," p. 116.

50. Kane, *Authorship*, p. 65.

name *Will* is thus almost too appropriate to be autobiographical."[51] A compromise position has been taken by others such as Bloomfield, who believes that the "I" of the poem is both Langland and every Christian man, "both species and individual at the same time."[52] Such a compromise has a clear appeal, because opposing arguments make claims equally convincing in the absence of any solid biographical information outside the poem. But even a compromise cannot render a satisfactory account for everything we find in Will's character. Not every Christian shared in his spiritual anxieties and suffered from his peculiar flaws. As I have tried to show, Will is the victim of a particular sin, not all seven. Langland may have seen sloth behind much of the corruption in his world, but this choice was not unanimous with all moral poets; Chaucer bears witness that many of Langland's contemporaries found their special trouble with lechery, a sin that makes few inroads into the Dreamer's moral life. Even viewed as a psychological faculty, as it is in the C-text "autobiography," Langland's Will is not representative of all the wills of every man, woman, and baptized child in Christendom. He does not choose evil or a lesser good and thus fall prey to cupidity; if anything, he chooses not to choose, only to drink, daydream, and sleep.

All this particularity suggests that Langland created Will upon a single model—himself—though without steady interest in mirroring his own image in any literal manner. To acknowledge his own lazy temperament, he drew generously upon traditional teachings on sloth; and whether or not the poet was known to his friends as Will, the protagonist who bears that name is drawn in ways responsive to what the poet knew about the theology of *voluntas*. If Langland's true personal image can never be recovered in confident detail, we can at least begin to attribute the distortions in the mirror to definite pressures and purposes from within his didactic work.

This notion of "the image in the mirror" has not been introduced solely as a product of personal fancy. Langland uses it at least twice in contexts whose implications, taken by themselves, bear upon my present point. The reflection is probably much less attractive than the

51. Robertson and Huppé, pp. 34 and 121; and Kirk, *Dream Thought*, pp. 49–50. See also Spearing, *Dream-Poetry*, p. 153; Carruthers, *The Search for St. Truth*, p. 94; Wittig, "Long Will's Pilgrimage," 280; and Martin, *The Field and the Tower*, p. 6.

52. Bloomfield, *Apocalypse*, p. 7, borrowing the phrase from Kantorowicz, p. 493. Woolf, "Non-Medieval Qualities," pp. 120–21, strikes this compromise: "Whilst his intention may have been to show Everyman seeking a solution to the moral corruption and philosophical problems of his own age, in fact he was exploring the perplexities of his own mind."

original was, and the reflected image, thus distorted, requires some attempt by the reader to interpret its meaning. At the beginning of Passus XI when Will is accused by Scripture of having no knowledge of himself—"*Multi multa sciunt et seipsos nesciunt*"—he falls into a deeper sleep and has a dream-within-a-dream in which Fortune fetches him into the Land of Longing. Once there, she makes him look "in a Mirour þat hiȝte Middelerþe" where he sees wonderful things that he will desire and briefly possess (B. xi. 1–11). As if absorbed into the landscape of the Mirror, Will surrenders to the temptations pictured in it, and for forty-five years he abandons his quest for Dowel, trusts in the Friars, and dedicates himself to the company of Fortune. He is finally abandoned by his false comforters when he is old and worried about where he will be buried.

The chronology of this deeper dream and, even more, Will's wholesale submission to a life of vice represent something different from his actual life, something offered not even as a premonition, but rather as an inward look at his worst *potential* for wrong-doing. The "Will" enchanted by the Mirror is a second will such as Augustine discovered in his own introspective quest for self-knowledge in his *Confessions*: "So these two wills within me, one old, one new, one the servant of the flesh, the other of the spirit, were in conflict and between them they tore my soul apart."[53] In the spiritual frenzy that led toward his conversion experience, Augustine proposed that it was the will's nature to double itself, one *voluntas* tending toward the life of carnal sin, the other striving for the life of spiritual purity.[54] By creating a second Will in the mirror of this dream-within-a-dream, Langland portrays his own worse will, the corrupt nature that Scripture had said he must learn about. It is likely Augustine was specifically in the poet's mind, since at the end of Passus X, just before the appearance of the second Will, Langland had quoted from exactly the same section of the *Confessions* (VIII, 8–10) in which Augustine discussed the doubleness of *voluntas*.[55]

The Will of Passus XI is not, of course, the second Will but the *third*, the alter ego of the protagonist, who is himself the alter ego of the poet. I raise this perplexity only to suggest that the Augustinian principle of doubleness might apply to the poem at large, with Will the

53. Augustine, *Confessions* (VIII, 5), trans. Pine-Coffin, p. 164.
54. *Ibid.* (VIII, 8–10), pp. 171–75. Arendt, *Willing*, pp. 87 and 94, discusses Augustine's theory of the two contending wills.
55. Skeat, II, p. 163, notes that the line Will quotes—"Ecce ipsi ydiote rapiunt celum vbi nos sapientes in inferno mergimur" (B. x. 460)—is adapted from the *Confessions* (VIII, 8): "Surgunt indocti et coelum rapiunt, et nos cum doctrinis nostris sine corde, ecce ubi uolutamur in carne et sanguine" (*PL* 32:757).

Dreamer standing as the worse half or wavering mirror-image of William Langland the man.

During Anima's explanation of charity in Passus XV, Langland again has occasion to mention the magical properties of the mirror. Will says that he has searched all over the land without finding perfect charity, and he wonders if it might be secretly locked away inside, as Christ is mystically innate within all objects of divine creation:

> Clerkes kenne me þat Christ is in alle places
> Ac I seiȝ hym neuere sooþly but as myself in a Mirour:
> *Hic in enigmate, tunc facie ad faciem.*
>
> (B. xv. 161–62)

He explains the *vestigia Dei* by reference to a familiar passage from Paul—"We see now through a glass in a dark manner, but then face to face" (1 Cor. 13.12)—but in doing so, he compares the symbolic images of this world to the image which he himself casts in a mirror, as if making of Will a literary image seen *per speculum in aenigmate* which demands some manner of interpretation.[56] Not wishing to put too much weight on my own provisional images—the poem as a mirror and Will as an enigma—I would simply emphasize that Will is indeed a very puzzling figure, one who bodies forth the age-old mystery of the hero as once described by Huizinga:

> Another set of tension-producing themes hinges on the hidden identity of the hero. He is incognito either because he is deliberately concealing his identity, or because he does not know it himself, or because he can change his shape at will. In other words, he is wearing a mask, he appears in disguise, he carries a secret. Once more we are close to the old and sacred game of the hidden being who will only reveal himself to the initiated.[57]

We might assume that the initiates in this case were the people who knew Langland personally, those who knew the answers to so many of the questions that vex modern critics. Was he married or monkish? Did he live in London or Malvern, or travel all over the country? How did he earn his livelihood? Was he a railer and a public nuisance to some? But even the people who knew Langland the man perhaps might not have offered confident answers to other serious questions raised by the poem: was he melancholy? was he *accidiosus*? was he mad? did he really have visions?

---

56. Carruthers, *The Search for St. Truth*, pp. 94–95 and 116, connects the Mirror of Middle-Earth with Paul's *speculum in aenigmate* as the medium by which the Dreamer recognizes himself and then profits from the image's dissimilarity to himself.

57. Johan Huizinga, *Homo Ludens: A Study of the Play-Element in Culture* (1950; rpt. Boston: The Beacon Press, 1955), p. 133.

Partially in response to nineteenth-century critics, whose desire to hear medieval poets speaking in their own unmuffled voices is shared by Donaldson, many critics of the past two decades have swung to the opposite extreme in preferring Leo Spitzer's view that these poets addressed their audiences with an impersonality that encouraged easier identification with the author and thereby readier access to his experience:

> I submit the theory that, in the Middle Ages, the "poetic I" had more freedom and more breadth than it has today: at that time the concept of intellectual property does not exist because literature dealt not with the individual but with mankind: the "ut in pluribus" was an accepted standard. . . . And we must assume that the medieval public saw in the "poetic I" a representative role of mankind, that it was interested only in this representative role of the poet.[58]

Although Spitzer's appraisal is satisfying enough for many poets of the twelfth and thirteenth centuries, he is less convincing when he states that a fourteenth-century poet like Dante was interested in himself only as "an example of the generally human capacity for cognizing the supramundane" that can only be experienced by the particular man.[59] The concentration by an author like Juan Ruiz upon a special vice such as lechery, like Dante's exile from the particular city of Florence and his love for an individual woman named Beatrice, suggests a true self-interest that accords with a more general recognition, often credited to the influence of the Franciscans, of the uniqueness of each individual being.[60] Noting that in Langland's century "personality emerges as the final human perfection, the one most godlike," Judith H. Anderson finds in the last six passus of *Piers Plowman* a deepening interest in personality involving in the broadest sense "the reality—metaphysical, psychological, verbal, and actual—that a person might have."[61] The most profitable approach therefore must lie in considering Will as a *stylized* reflection of Langland himself, bent and molded into an image better suited to the poem's didactic ends.

Passus V of the C-text provides other topics for speculation, provoca-

58. Leo Spitzer, "Note on the Poetic and Empirical 'I' in Medieval Authors," *Traditio*, 4 (1946), 415–16.

59. *Ibid.*, 417, with the discussion of Juan Ruiz on 418.

60. Oberman, "Fourteenth-Century Religious Thought," 82. For a discussion of Franciscanism and the rise of science as well as naturalistic art during the thirteenth and fourteenth centuries, see Lynn White, Jr., "Natural Science and Naturalistic Art in the Middle Ages," *Amer. Hist. Rev.*, 52 (1947), 421–35; and Fleming, *An Introduction to the Franciscan Literature*, pp. 235–62.

61. Anderson, *The Growth of a Personal Voice*, p. 127.

tive but more tenuous by far, which nonetheless belong to our discussion of the autobiographical element. Will begins by saying that he lived in London and dressed as a beggar, but was resented by practicing beggars and hermits because he wrote about those lay-abouts. This passage makes sense only if we understand that in the years preceding the C-revision, when the A-text and perhaps the B-text too were circulating, *Piers Plowman* had won for Langland a reputation as society's critic, a sharp-tongued censor crying out against faithless hermits, false beggars, and corrupt clergy, so that when he added to the poem late in life, he took advantage of his "public image" as it had been projected by his poetry. Apparently many medieval readers made the same mistake as nineteenth-century critics, believing that the poet was the selfsame person as his protagonist-narrator. This confusion was not uncommon. Scribes copying the *Libro de Buen Amor* were shocked when they believed they had learned of Archpriest Juan Ruiz' sexual exploits, and some women who saw the dark-skinned Dante in the streets of Verona concluded that his face had been scorched during his journey through Hell.[62] In his spurious continuation of the A-version of *Piers Plowman*, for instance, John But makes no clear distinction between Will the protagonist and Will the author of the poem. In context, then, Will's remark about his success as a poet may involve a certain irony that I intend to explore in the next (and final) chapter, but it is worth asking here whether anything else might lie behind the reference other than the poet's sly encouragement to gullible readers.

The role-playing of the poet, his skill at assuming masks and striking exaggerated poses, is a modern rediscovery made possible by scholarly biographies throwing light on the discrepancy between poetic myth and breakfast-table reality. For instance, these biographies tell us that the priapic Byron, whose reputation as a latter-day Don Juan was trumpeted throughout Europe, spent his whole life recalling that his best love had been a choirboy at Cambridge.[63] The modern discovery is a *re*-discovery because the discrepancy would have been clear enough in most earlier societies, those smaller and more familiar communities of "the initiated" where the poet was a public figure seldom sufficiently

62. Spitzer, 418–19, discusses titles and marginalia in early manuscripts of the *Libro de Buen Amor* as evidence that the scribes interpreted "the incidents narrated as if they were events that had actually happened to the author." Boccaccio's *Life of Dante*, trans. G.R. Carpenter (New York: The Grolier Club, 1900), pp. 84–85, recalls how the women of Verona whispered their suspicions that Dante had actually visited Hell—and how Dante, overhearing the gossip, was amused by their credulity.

63. Leslie A. Marchand, *Byron: A Portrait* (New York: Knopf, 1970), p. 38. On the poet's use of his work to create a personal myth, see Jerome J. McGann, *Fiery Dust: Byron's Poetic Development* (Chicago: Chicago University Press, 1968), pp. 287–99.

distant from his audience to maintain any convincingly fabricated literary-self. Chaucer's original audience knew him too well as the shrewd diplomat to foreign courts, able administrator of the Wool Custom, and masterful versifier to be anything but amused by his poetic posturing as a hopeless naif in *The House of Fame* and tedious balladeer in *The Canterbury Tales*. While allowing for a comparable amusement among Langland's coterie—as well as the poet's own bemusement, like Dante's, at the uninitiated who accepted his poem as literally true—we might also entertain the further possibility that Langland actually grew to resemble the image he had created for himself in the poem.

Along with acknowledging an author's role-playing, we must also allow the medieval poet the same potential as a modern writer like Edgar Allen Poe for confusing his persona with himself, for believing his self-made myth so deeply that he became unable to know the dancer from the dance. It is possible to see in Dante's career, for example, the poet becoming entranced with the ever more exalted vision of himself as the lover of Beatrice, so that the early sonnets and canzoni (most of them spoken with a non-personal voice epitomizing Spitzer's theory) grew into the highly personal narrative of the *Vita Nuova* and beyond into the *Comedy*, which took whatever personal reality had ever existed as a husk and discovered therein a whole universe of spiritual values. Similarly, it is possible to imagine that during Langland's life-long struggle with *Piers Plowman*, he grew entranced with his own image in the glass, already a stylized reflection of the poet as censor and sinner, so that the longer he was engaged in the enterprise of fashioning that image, the more he began to resemble it—perhaps for a purpose that was completely rational, and no less profitable to the Christian community than Dante's incorporation of the personal element into his *Comedy*.

I wish to end this chapter by indulging in one final speculation, asking whether Langland might have had some such sane and serious motive for taking upon himself—or at least not actively discouraging those who would see in him—the image of Will the Dreamer. Putting aside the possibility that he actually confused himself with his persona, as well as the suggestion that he merely enjoyed tricking naive readers, I would like to entertain the notion that Langland might have manipulated his outward behavior and appearance as an extension of his poem's didactic intent. Years of work had made the C-poet wiser, more aware of his personal temperament and, in short, more self-conscious. Having conquered sin by knowing its nature, he may have proceeded to make his conduct a form of exterior confession and penance, as if to say "This is what I had the *potential* to become!" and at the same time asking insistently, "Is this not what you really *are*?"[64]

This would help explain how the poet who criticized the "lollares of Londone" could speak of himself "yclothed as a lollare." If his intentions were virtuous, his appearance made no difference except in its power to shock, to disturb, to warn. A distant precursor of Byron and Baudelaire, Langland may have used his poetry to create of himself a myth of vice that eventually subsumed, outwardly at least, much that had been real and quotidian and mother-born, not in order to champion vice by holding forth as its spokesman, but to ridicule vice by standing up as a living parody—as Will appears to do in the C-text "autobiography"—and mocking *acedia* by offering himself as a comical example against it. If so, he may have been as holy a Wild Man as could be found in legend or romance, and as fine a Fool as was ever conjured up by Shakespeare.

64. Donald R. Howard, *The Idea of the Canterbury Tales* (Berkeley: University of California Press, 1976), p. 374, views the Pardoner as a figure who "exists to reveal to the society its own evil and to the 'good citizen' the evil in himself. He makes us question all cultural values and suspect all moral discourse of being cant." What is more, Howard perceives the Pardoner as "a grotesque mirror-image of Chaucer himself" (p. 376), as an ironic spirit who plays roles to manipulate illusions for instruction—Chaucer knowingly, the Pardoner unwillingly.

VIII
The Poet as Worker

The utter originality of *Piers Plowman* quickens our desire to know more about the strange genius who wrote it. While the preceding chapter ended with speculation about Langland's outward conduct, this chapter brings my study to its conclusion with further speculation, this time about the poet's artistic temperament.

Because history has denied us even the minimal details of Langland's life and looks, our guesses about his resemblance to his narrator-protagonist must be always tentative and unsure, forever couched in the uneasy language of hypothesis. Yet on one point we can be absolutely certain: like Will the Dreamer, William Langland was a poet. Largely on the basis of the *Visio*, we can envisage him as a medieval avatar of the wandering Orpheus, driven by the need to speak forth in his own voice and bring forth verses calculated to threaten what was most unstable and sinful in his society. In return, he earned the hatred of those representing the true threat within the frail unity of that society, the "lollares of Londone and lewede ermytes." The English poet addressed a religious community that was too often content with the easiest if not the surest route to salvation. Men could give alms to false beggars, they could support unholy hermits, and they could confess to friars and pay silver for light penance. Unable to close his eyes to the implications of these practices, Langland sought to shock the folk out of their communal complacency—itself a form of pandemic sloth— into a keener perception of the Giant Sloth that reckoned to destroy true Unity as soon as Friar Flattery succeeded in putting Contrition to sleep.

At the same time, there is a cross-current running throughout the poem, intensifying in the B and C versions, which is created by the sense that Langland felt no deep confidence in the merit of working as a poet. Whatever the causes of this uncertainty—perhaps criticism from onlookers who mistook his occupation as an excuse for idleness, perhaps his own intense awareness that words often fail to achieve the intentions of a writer—Langland's ambivalent attitude bespeaks a wavering of will in the face of the challenge. This ambivalence also shows itself in the kind of poetry he wrote. Unlike a mystic such as Richard Rolle who struggled with the problem of *how* to communicate a nearly ineffable experience, Langland's difficulty lay in deciding *what* to communicate, which topics to exclude, which answers to prefer, how to distinguish the greater from the lesser good in the pursuit of the perfect life.

If Langland indeed shared the Dreamer's slothful temperament, but recognized his native infirmity well enough to explore it in his characterization of Will, then it is reasonable to assume that he also sought other remedy, no doubt finding part of it in a regimen proven effective for centuries: the act of writing. Thus by acknowledging Langland's personal inclination to sloth, we can reconcile the two conflicting impressions we get of him as a poet, his anxiety over the value of his work and yet his life-long persistence in that craft—the one of which is *acedia*'s symptom, the other its cure.

Respect for the power of language runs very deep in Langland's poem. He has taken special care to describe all the important events of sacred history as miracles of speech or writing.[1] Wit interprets the act of divine creation as a linguistic process under the control of God: "And al at his wil was wrou3t wiþ a speche, / *Dixit & facta sunt*" (B. ix. 32–46). The word of prophecy in the Old Testament is fulfilled in Christ (B. xix. 80–82), and because the Virgin "conceyued þoru3 speche" of the Holy Ghost, the Incarnation is also transformed into a linguistic act: "*Verbum caro factum est*" (B. xviii. 129; v. 499). Just as Moses had received the Old Law through the letters engraved upon the Tablets (B. v. 566–91), Christ inaugurated the New Law by saving the adulterous woman through the characters he wrote in the dust: "Holy kirke knoweþ þis, þat Christes writyng saued" (B. xii. 76–84). Even the first act of salvation is described as a result of language, when the gates of Hell are broken with the uttering of the words *Rex glorie* and Christ marshals a phalanx of texts against the speechless Satan—"I

---

1. Curtius, *European Literature*, pp. 310–11, catalogues "the religious metaphorics of the book" as offered by the Bible itself. Langland's attitudes toward language will come as no surprise to readers of more recent criticism, especially the first and final chapters of Northrop Frye's *The Great Code: The Bible and Literature* (New York: Harcourt Brace Jovanovich, 1982), pp. 3–30 and 199–233.

may do mercy þoruȝ my rightwisnesse and alle my wordes trewe" (B. xviii. 389). Langland never misses an opportunity to look beyond the evocative and even the hieratic powers of language to elevate it as the supreme instrument of God's work on earth.

When Langland accents the role of God's word in the act of creation, he also emphasizes man's likeness to the divine maker—"*Faciamus hominem ad imaginem nostram*" (Gen. 1.26; B. ix. 42)—with the clear implication that man's capacity for language sets him apart from all other creatures as perhaps the foremost element in his God-like nature. Since Christ's verbal miracle at Cana stands as the first instance of Dowel, the use of language must somehow be involved in living the good life and repairing man's divine image. It is therefore not surprising that the Tree of Charity bears leaves of "lele wordes" and blossoms of "buxom speche" (B. xvi. 6–7) and that various definitions of the Three Do's involve the correct uses of language. The figure Thought explains that Dowel is practiced by anyone who is "meke of his mouþ, milde of his speche" and "trewe of his tunge"; Dobet is someone "louelich of speche" who has preached to the people and translated the Bible (B. viii. 78–95). Wit later adds that Dobest means not wasting any speech "þat spire is of grace / And Goddes gleman and a game of heuene" (B. ix. 99–106).

This point is dramatized later when the Holy Ghost descends to divide the gifts of grace, bestowing the first blessing on those men who will use language faithfully to preach, instruct, and otherwise aid their fellow Christians (B. xix. 229–33). The definitions offered by Thought and Wit are really elaborations of a lesson given much earlier by Holy Church herself. When Will asked the question of central importance to the whole poem—"How may I save my soul?"—she explained that the surest treasure was Truth:

> For who is trewe of his tonge, telleþ noon ooþer,
> Dooþ þe werkes þerwiþ and wilneþ no man ille,
> He is a god by þe gospel, a grounde and o lofte,
> And ek ylik to oure lord by Seint Lukes wordes.
> The clerkes þat knowen it sholde kennen it aboute
> For cristen and vncristen cleymeþ it echone.
>
> (B. i. 88–93)

This is the first passage in the poem to suggest the alliterative trio of *words, works* and *will* that develops into such an important interlocking theme.[2] Holy Church says that to gain salvation a man must speak

2. J.A. Burrow, "Words, Works and Will," in *Critical Approaches*, ed. Hussey, pp. 111–24.

true words, perform works accordingly, and bear an ill will toward no man. She adds that it is the duty of clerics to spread the gospel (Thought's definition of Dobet), although beneath the placid surface of her advice lurk problems that Langland would discover later when he began to plumb deeper. Cannot a man speak true words arising from a false will? And cannot a well-intended cleric write a long allegorical poem but lose the merit of his work through the inability of his audience to understand its hard meaning?

A man's work with literature is useful, says Langland, when the words are inspired by God and are therefore valuable to Christian readers. Writers of saints' lives give comfort to the poor, Cato's "stories" teach men how to bestow alms, and compilers of bestiaries offer their audiences examples both instructional and pleasing.[3] The Angel appeared "to pastours and to poetes" to announce Christ's birth (B. xii. 148–50), and the Holy Ghost continues to inspire men to write the books without which clerics would be like blind men: "Alþouȝ men made bokes, þe maister was God, / And Seint Spirit þe samplaries, & seide what men sholde write" (B. xii. 101–02). The philosopher Plato is called a "poete," and Lady Scripture praises the "patriarkes and prophetes and poetes" who condemned wealth while preaching poverty (B. x. 178 and 344–45).

But Will draws into question the value of writing when he recalls the fate of Solomon and Aristotle:

> Maistres þat of Goddes mercy techen men and prechen,
> Of hir wordes þei wissen vs for wisest as in hir tyme,
> And al holy chirche holdeþ hem boþe in helle!
> And if I shal werche by hir werkes to wynne me heuene
> That for hir werkes and wit now wonyeþ in pyne,
> Thanne wrouȝte I vnwisly, whatsoeuere ye preche.

(B. x. 389–94)

If Will raises doubts about the writer's profession by summoning up the examples of pre-Christian authors whose good words did not compensate for their deficient works, Langland himself frames a disturbing scene just prior to the Harrowing of Hell in which Book (the Bible) appears to bear witness to the truth of these sacred events and, what is more, to swear that unless things happen as he says, he should be burned. The syntax of this passage is sufficiently ambiguous to have elicited articles from distinguished scholars, but the general implication is clear. Even a text as sacred as the Bible can be trusted only as

---

3. B. vii. 87; vii. 74; xii. 235–36. Martin, *The Field and the Tower*, pp. 56–70, chooses the interlude with Imaginatif (B. xii. 16–29) to discuss language's usefulness.

long as its message is confirmed by events, and whenever it fails as a repository of truth, it should be rejected.[4] Langland has generated such an atmosphere of doubt concerning even moral literature that his poem cannot take for granted the merit of its own existence. He is therefore acutely aware of the need, if not always the means, to justify that existence.

Since the Bible offered the surest words for belief, the search for Holy Church's "best treasure" involved the understanding of this and related Latin texts through a variety of exegetical methods. Working in the shadow of a lengthy tradition of theological commentary, however, a vernacular poet must have felt wary about the limitations of his more modest enterprise. Not only did his mother-tongue lack the allusiveness and sacramental power of Latin, but his culture at large had no adequate literary theory allowing intrinsic value to the creations of the human mind. Spearing has summed up the difficulty in this manner:

A fiction might be seen as an allegory or parable, in which case it could be said to convey the truth in a veiled form . . . Or again a fiction might claim to be a true history, an account of what really happened as set down in authentic sources. But there was no way of saying that a fiction possessed an imaginative truth or validity even though it did not correspond to any literal truth . . . In these circumstances, to present a literary fiction as a dream—one imaginative product as an analogue or metaphor for another imaginative product—offered a medieval poet an extremely useful way out of his dilemma.[5]

This assessment may apply well enough to Chaucer and other secular poets such as the satirists of the Alliterative tradition, but when a religious poem is offered as a work of the human imagination, even *sub specie visionis*, it is laid open to all the suspicion attached to that unreliable mental faculty. Since Will is not steadily guided by an authority such as Lady Holy Church, and since he simply transcribes his dreams without due regard for their interpretation or inquiry into their trustworthiness, *Piers Plowman* incorporates in itself the limitations as well as the resources of poetry as a product of imagination.

As if to compensate for the shortcomings of a vernacular dream-vision, Langland seems at first to have sought justification for his poem

---

4. B. xviii. 255–60 (Skeat, I, B. xviii. 252–57) has been discussed by R.E. Kaske, "The Speech of 'Book' in *Piers Plowman*," *Anglia*, 77 (1959), 117–44; Richard L. Hoffman, "The Burning of 'Boke' in *Piers Plowman*," *MLQ*, 25 (1964), 57–65; and Carruthers, *The Search for St. Truth*, pp. 141–42. All agree generally that Book (the Bible) means he should be burned if he does not fulfill his duty as an accurate witness to sacred history.

5. Spearing, *Dream-Poetry*, p. 74. Gabriel Josipovici, *The World and the Book* (London: Macmillan, 1971), pp. 52–56, discusses the folly of fiction for any medieval writer seriously committed to Truth.

by using many of the truth-seeking methods practiced at the universities, namely, the scholastic disputation as well as the methods of Scriptural commentary so ably discussed by Robertson and Huppé. Bloomfield's claims are less far-reaching but no less positive: "This use of Biblical (and Patristic) citation, besides giving Langland the authority he seeks for, reveals a remarkable sense of the power of language."[6] This would be more comforting if Langland were the only speaker, but his poem contains many voices, each trying to exploit the power of language to its own best advantage. The Pardon Scene, for example, is heavily encrusted with Scriptural citations which do not really serve the central topic of the debate. At bottom, the argument has to do as much with texts and their interpretation as with the validity of the pardon. The Priest, who misses its message through his hollow sophistry, is so distracted by outward show that he never consults the Bible itself; and Piers, who seeks value beyond formalism, prefers the simple wisdom of the Bible to the distorted and confusing interpretations of clerics. Thus the Pardon Scene dramatizes one of the poem's most disturbing realizations about language by showing how even sacred texts can be abused by willful men whose intentions are corrupt, although their methods enjoy the full sanction of clerical tradition.

Suspicion that language has the potential to corrupt mankind runs as deep in Langland's poem as his respect for its power to effect divine miracles. Just as the crucial events of sacred history are enacted through language, so too does Langland find the abasement of language at work behind most of the evil in the world. The bad angels fell because they believed Lucifer's lies (B. i. 116–18), and Imaginatyf says that Adam possessed Eden only as long as he refrained from talking, but was driven out when he grumbled about his food and sought forbidden knowledge (B. xi. 417–19). Satan's continuing presence in the world is represented at the beginning of the poem by the Dungeon of the Father of Falsehood, who had urged Adam and Eve to disobey, counseled Cain to murder his brother, tricked Judas into betraying Christ, and continued to spread his lies throughout the land. When Will asks to know more about Falsehood, Holy Church summons his daughter Lady Mede, who is about to marry False Fickle-tongue: "Fauel þoruȝ his faire speche haþ þis folk enchaunted, / And al is Lieres ledynge þat lady is þus ywedded" (B. ii. 42–43).

Indeed, the desire for *mede* or material reward lies behind much of

6. Bloomfield, *Apocalypse*, p. 37.

the perversion of speech. Lawyers will not open their mouths unless they can expect a large fee (B. prol. 211–14; vii 40–52). The corrupt friars are singled out for special comment because they gloss the Bible in any manner necessary to elicit money from the people (B. prol. 58–61); in the end, Friar Flattery enters Unity through "hende speche" and lulls Contrition to sleep with his false guarantees. Again, the twisting of Scriptural citations can be traced back to Lady Mede:

> "I leue wel, lady," quod Conscience, "þat þi latyn be trewe.
> Ac þow art lik a lady þat radde a lesson ones
> Was *omnia probate*, and þat plesed hire herte
> For þat lyne was no lenger at þe leues ende.
> Hadde she loked þat left half and þe leef torned
> She sholde haue founden felle wordes folwynge þerafter:
> *Quod bonum est tenete*; Truþe þat text made."
>
> (B. iii. 337–43)

As usual, not all practices fall solidly on one side of the line dividing good from evil, Truth from Falsehood. As part of his sermon against the corrupt priesthood, Anima criticizes university dons and doctors for not knowing their material, as well as clerics for "overhopping" parts of the Mass and Divine Office:

> Doctours of decrees and of diuinite maistres,
> That sholde konne and knowe alle kynnes clergie
> And answere to Argumentʒ and assoile a *Quodlibet*—
> I dar noʒt siggen it for shame—if swich were apposed
> Thei sholde faillen of hir Philosophie and in Phisik boþe.
> Wherfore I am afered of folk of holy kirke,
> Lest þei ouerhuppen as ooþere doon in office and in houres.
>
> (B. xv. 380–86)

The failure to learn the skills appropriate to one's profession and the careless syncopation of a prayer or liturgical text may not spring from the same malice of intent as the hypocritical friar's distortion of a text for his own selfish ends, but both faults would have been viewed as the idle use of language and, as we have seen in previous chapters, were grouped together under a single moral rubric.

The phrase "idle speech" itself is not carelessly used in Langland's poem. The spirit of temperance teaches men not to waste "wordes of ydelnesse" (B. xix. 286), and Conscience instructs Peace to close the gates of Unity against "titeleris in ydel" (B. xx. 299). The adjective "idle" itself suggests a particular vice, and in the Confession Scene the personification Sloth admits that he is occupied every day "wiþ ydel tales at þe Ale and ouþerwhile in chirches" (B. v. 402–03). Although speech can figure in the enactment of many different vices, Langland takes special notice of its involvement in *acedia*. Among "þe braunches þat bryngen a man to sleuþe" are the instances in which a man prefers "an harlotes tonge" and grows angry if he hears anything except "wordes of murþe" (B. xiii. 414–19). Immediately following these branches, Langland launches into a sermon on the good and evil uses of language:

> Patriarkes and prophetes, prechours of Goddes wordes,
> Sauen þoruȝ hir sermon mannes soule fro helle;
> Riȝt so flatereris and fooles arn þe fendes disciples
> To entice men þoruȝ hir tales to synne and harlotrie.
>
> (B. xiii. 427–30)

Though Haukyn has confessed to all seven deadly sins, Langland leaves the odd impression that the "foule wordes" of flatterers and entertainers have done the most to soil his coat and leave him in a state of near desperation; his tirade against unholy minstrels is prefaced with the line "This ben þe braunches, beþ war, þat bryngen a man to wanhope" (B. xiii. 420–57).[7] At the end of the poem, Langland again makes this peculiar connection between deceitful speech and the severest form of *acedia* when he says that Wanhope, the bride of Sloth, is the daughter of Tom Two-tongue, "þat neuere swoor truþe" (B. xx. 159–62). If vitiating speech and sloth are intricately bound up with one another in Langland's sensibility, then we can see why he might have worried that his hard poem, so confusing in places and so open to misunderstanding, might have made him appear like one of those who enticed men into sin or wasted their time on "ydel tales."

As with so many other self-criticisms, Langland's personal misgivings about his work as a poet are projected onto Will the Dreamer, in his conduct as a Christian writer and in the ways he chooses to justify his "making." Early in the poem Holy Church advises Will to compose a lesson that will express the message of Truth: "Lereþ it þus lewed men, for lettred it knoweþ, / That Trueþe is tresor þe trieste on erþe" (B. i. 136–37). In the A-text she clearly wants this instruction to take

---

7. Donaldson, *The C-Text and Its Poet*, pp. 142–43, comments on the movement from Sloth into the branches leading to it (which include "wordes of murthe") and then to the poet's attempt to clarify his idea of minstrels, but he does not discover any coherence in this transition of topics. Carruthers, *The Search for St. Truth*, offers the most far-reaching analysis of Langland's attitudes toward debased language as the cause of the world's corruption and a true rhetoric, representing an epistemological tool, as the means for restoration: "language needs redemption before society can be repaired" (p. 52).

the form of poetry,[8] although in all versions Will tries to beg off with the plea that he lacks "kynde knowyng," which Holy Church impatiently defines as every man's fundamental instinct to love God and avoid sin (B. i. 138–46). Much later, Will is still wondering whether he dares to make his dreams known among men. The figure Good Faith (Lewtee) guarantees him that it is permissible for laymen to make public their moral observations in order to reprove sin, but is quick to add the following qualifications:

Ac be þow neueremoore þe first þe defaute to blame;
Thou3 þow se yuel seye it no3t first; be sory it nere amended.
Thyng þat is pryue, publice þow it neuere;
Neiþer for loue looue it no3t ne lakke it for enuye.

(B. xi. 103–06)

Seconded by Lady Scripture, Good Faith's restrictions raise several questions about Will's literary efforts. Is he sincerely reluctant to point the accusing finger? Does he publish some things that are better kept secret? And is he moved always by intentions free of spite, anger, and resentment? In this passage, for example, Will wants to publish his dream abroad because he is angry at the friars who concern themselves more with burials than with baptisms.

The best known passage dealing with Will's work as a poet (deleted from the C-text) comes early in his interview with Imaginatyf, who criticizes him for wasting his time "wiþ makynges" when there are already enough books explaining Dowel:

And þow medlest þee wiþ makynges and my3test go seye þi sauter,
And bidde for hem þat 3yueþ þee breed, for þer are bokes ynowe
To telle men what Dowel is, Dobet and Dobest boþe,
And prechours to preuen what it is of many a peire freres.

(B. xii. 16–19)

This rebuke is especially surprising since it comes from the mental faculty responsible for the creation of literary fictions. Moreover, Will's defense is not strong enough to allay the suspicion that these criticisms might be justified. He says that his "making" is identical to the relaxation used by saints to reach perfection and that even stern Cato pre-

8. Agreeing with the wording of the Z-text—"preche hit in thyn harpe" (i. 86)—the A-text makes clear that the lesson should be poetic:

For þus wytnessiþ his woord, werche þou þeraftir,
þat loue is þe leuest þing þat oure Lord askiþ,
And ek þe plante of pes; *preche it in þin harpe*
þer þou art mery at mete, 3if men bidde þe 3edde.
[For bi kuynge knowynge in herte *comseth ther a fitte*.]   (A. i. 135–38)

scribed amusement as a relief from care: *"Interpone tuis interdum gaudia curis."* But like the text-cropping Lady Mede, Will overlooks the next line—*"Ut possis animo quemuis sufferre laborem"* [9]—which makes it clear that periods of enjoyment should be used only to counterbalance labors of the sort he himself has not pursued. The solace of the saints that he mentions is the *occupatio* prescribed by Cassian for ascetics whose arduous spiritual exercises left them vulnerable to spiritual dryness. In short, Will's excuses do not form a convincing response to the charges, since he has performed none of the physical or spiritual labors that earned relaxation.

Although this passage must be read as part of the characterization of Will and not Langland, it no doubt expresses something of the poet's concern over his own literary endeavors. As Nevill Coghill suggests, Langland may have worried that he had chosen a worthless employment and "let himself play about with poetry, only to form an incurable and time-consuming habit that led nowhere." [10] John Burrow further enumerates the questions that might have burdened his mind:

Was it legitimate for him to write such a poem? Was it necessary? Were there not already sufficient books on the Good Life? How could more words help, when what mattered were works and, above all, the secret will itself? Was he not perhaps brother under the skin to his chief enemies—the glib and hypocritical friars? [11]

As a projection of Langland's own worst fears about himself, Will does not share this sense of anxiety. He says that if someone would explain the meaning of the Three Do's, he would stop wasting his time and devote himself entirely to churchly duties. Imaginatyf responds with definitions of faith, hope, and charity that are reliable enough to generate long sections of the allegory in the *Vita de Dobet* (B. xvi–xvii). And how does Will react? He continues to wander about, writing poetry.

Langland offers little further comment about Will's "making" in the B-text. In the first and last lines of Passus XIX, Will does say that he

9. *The Distichs of Cato: A Famous Medieval Textbook*, ed. and trans. Wayland Johnson Chase (Madison: University of Wisconsin Studies in the Social Sciences and History, no. 7, 1922), p. 30 (III, 6). Significantly, these lines follow immediately another proverb in which the Latin poet warned against the dangers of sloth: "Segnitiem fugito, quae uitae ignauia fertur; / Nam cum animus languet, consumit inertia corpus."

10. Nevill Coghill, "God's Wenches and the Light That Spoke (Some Notes on Langland's Kind of Poetry)," *English and Medieval Studies Presented to J.R.R. Tolkien*, ed. Norman Davis and C.L. Wrenn (London: Allen & Unwin, 1962), p. 200.

11. Burrow, "Words, Works and Will," p. 118. Peck, "Chaucer and the Nominalist Questions," 760, says that the fourteenth-century poet shared with the philosopher an extraordinary sensitivity to the abuses of language in man's quest for truth.

wrote down his dreams as soon as he woke up, although in neither case is there any indication that he questioned their source or tried to interpret their contents. He appears to write as an uncritical transcriber who does not examine and perhaps does not fully understand the substance of his dreams. During the vision in this same penultimate passus, Will kneels as the Paraclete descends in the form of grace to bestow diverse gifts upon the followers of Piers. Yet it is unclear whether the Dreamer is among the recipients and whether poetry is one of the sanctioned labors. The men who receive the gift of words are "prechours and preestes and prentices of lawe" (231); the alliteration invites "poetes" as well, but Langland declined to include them.

The poet's final estimation of the Dreamer's poetic trade is locked away inside the C-text "autobiography," a section whose announced intention is to explain how Will became a satiric poet after his encounter with Reason. The logic of the passage is as riddling as its chronology. Will says that he has launched broadsides against London beggars and hermits as Reason had instructed, but later we find among Reason's wide-ranging catalogue of professions no mention of poetry, only a condemnation of the idle life which Will seems to continue following. We are given only hints that his occupation may be worthwhile. Recalling the parable of the woman who searched for the lost coin (Lk. 15.8−10), Will says that he will wait to find grace before making amends for his past life (C. v. 99−101). If one concludes that Will is indeed among those who receive this gift of the Holy Ghost, then his "making" may be labor according to grace. Otherwise, it is hard to see how his activity at the beginning of the passage constitutes any reform of his past life. As Anne Middleton puts it, "if the activity he intends is 'making,' its nature, subject, and place among other human crafts and estates are left maddeningly unclear."[12] Writing the C-version later in his own life, Langland seems to have become more self-critical of his work as a poet and to have vented his anxiety in the depiction of Will, who appears much guiltier of both sloth *and* poetic misconduct in C than in A or B.

If Langland explores his personal anxiety over "making" through the characterization of Will, he exposes his misgivings about the literary profession at large through his varied treatments of minstrelsy.[13] Despite the abundance of references in Langland's work and in other

12. Anne Middleton, "The Idea of Public Poetry in the Reign of Richard II," *Speculum*, 53 (1978), 104.

13. Donaldson, *The C-Text and Its Poet*, pp. 147−48, discusses the profusion of minstrel imagery in the poem and, pp. 136−55, offers a splendid treatment of Langland's attitudes toward minstrelsy.

writings of the period, however, it is hard to reconstruct any clear picture of what fourteenth-century minstrels actually did, what roles they played as performers, and what contributions they made to the transmission and even the creation of literature. Although a bias against the sort of bardic hero popularized by Sir Walter Scott has led recent critics like Dieter Mehl to dismiss the "romantic fiction" and to claim for the minstrel a role no greater than that of musician, John Burrow offers a more balanced and historically accurate picture of an entertainer who sang, recited stories, and even contributed to the creative process.[14] Thus we must understand that the distinction between poet and performer was much less rigid than in modern times: poets performed their own works in public, and minstrels freely altered, deleted, and added. It is therefore fitting that *Piers Plowman* presents the minstrel as the archetype for men engaged in the full enterprise of poetry, both the recitation and the process of composition, as well as some of the least savory chores of the profession such as farting and fiddling. It is my intention to explore Langland's divided opinion of these performers—a few of whom were inspired by God, but most of whom were money-grubbing entertainers—as well as his grave doubts about whether even a good minstrel like Haukyn could lead a life free of the inherent excesses and temptations of his trade.

In the opening panorama of the Fair Field, Langland brings special attention to bear on two classes of minstrels, one blameless and the other described as the children of Judas, the embodiment of wanhope:

> And somme murþes to make as Mynstralles konne,
> And geten gold with hire glee giltless, I leeue.
> Ac Iaperes and Iangeleres, Iudas children,

14. Burrow, *Richardian Poetry*, pp. 12–14. Dieter Mehl, *The Middle English Romances of the Thirteenth and Fourteenth Centuries* (London: Routledge & Kegan Paul, 1968), p. 7 and generally pp. 7–13, had diminished the literary contributions of the minstrels. A variety of evidence can be produced to indicate that "minstrels were normally the professional purveyors of romances" and other forms of popular literature; see Albert C. Baugh, "The Middle English Romance: Some Questions of Creation, Presentation, and Preservation," *Speculum*, 42 (1967), 1–31. See, for example, *The Romance of Emaré*, re-ed. Edith Rickert, 1906, EETS e.s. 99, p. xxviii; *Firumbras and Otuel and Roland*, ed. Mary Isabelle O'Sullivan, 1935, EETS o.s. 198, p. xxv; and *Mandeville's Travels*, ed. M.C. Seymour (Oxford: The Clarendon Press, 1967), p. 158. Baugh, pp. 29–30, concludes that minstrels not only inserted occasional couplets and brief passages, but were accustomed to altering, reshaping, and transforming a poem into a new utterance. Robert M. Longsworth, "*Sir Orfeo*, the Minstrel, and the Minstrel's Art," *SP*, 79 (1982), 1–11, endorses this view, while Richard Firth Green, *Poets and Princepleasers: Literature and the English Court in the Late Middle Ages* (Toronto: University of Toronto Press, 1980), especially "The Court of Cupid," pp. 101–34, traces the fourteenth-century decline, so keenly registered by Langland, of the minstrel's status from a courtly man of letters to a lowly music-maker.

Fonden hem fantasies and fooles hem makeþ,
And han wit at wille to werken if hem liste.

(B. prol. 33–37)

These lines set up the lop-sided judgment that runs throughout the poem. Evil minstrels are easy to find. They shelter Liar when he flees from court (B. ii. 230–31); they have common access to Lady Mede (B. iii. 131–33); and they are welcome at the tables of clerics, where they make blasphemous jokes whenever the conversation turns to theology —and are paid better for their dirty stories than men who always have Holy Scripture on their lips (B. x. 30–58).[15]

Good minstrels are much harder to locate in the B-text. The strongest defense comes near the end of Passus XIII where three non-literal entertainers are designated "Goddes minstrales" to replace the fool, the jester, and even the king's minstrels:

The *pouere* for a fool sage sittyng at þi table,
And a *lered man* to lere þee what our lord suffred
For to saue þi soule from Sathan þyn enemy,
And fiþele þee wiþoute flaterynge of good friday þe geste,
And a *blynd man* for a bourdeour, or a bedrede womman
To crie a largesse bifore oure lord, youre good loos to shewe.
Thise þre maner minstrales makeþ a man to lauȝe,
And in his deeþ deyinge þei don hym gret confort
That bi his lyue liþed hem and loued hem to here.

(B. xiii. 443–51)

By granting charity to the poor, the sick, and the pious, a patron can receive in return the ultimate entertainment that exists only in Heaven. But this passage, absent in the majority of B-manuscripts and otherwise wedged between two forthright denunciations of real minstrels, offers little consolation to a poet like Langland unless he concentrates on purely religious subjects, as the "lered man" does, without the complications of the dreams and allegories that might well be criticized as frivolous distractions from Truth. Perhaps because the subject-matter moves in this direction in the *Vita de Dobet*, or because Langland simply became more scrupulous in his treatment of the Dreamer, the B-revisor became increasingly sensitive about identifying Will as a musical entertainer and took pains to dissociate him from the more suspicious forms of minstrelsy.[16]

15. Curtius, pp. 471–72 ("The Mode of Existence of the Medieval Poet") notes that self-respecting authors had a standing complaint against the buffoons who were rewarded so handsomely for their low entertainments.

16. The B-poet cut out two passages from the A-text (i. 135–38 and viii. 43–45) that had made Will appear to be a minstrel.

There is large agreement among critics that Langland confronted the debased profession of minstrelsy most boldly in his portrayal of Haukyn the Active Man.[17] Haukyn introduces himself as a wafer-baker providing the food men eat physically as cakes and spiritually as the Eucharist, but his primary occupation is that of minstrel. It has long been argued that he represents the sort of guiltless minstrelsy delineated in the Prologue,[18] although he is an unqualified failure as a purveyor of honest entertainment. Rich lords withhold their patronage, and no wonder, as Donaldson points out: "the list of things Haukyn cannot do forms one of the most inclusive catalogues of the functions of a fourteenth-century minstrel in Middle English poetry:"[19]

> Couþe I lye and do men lauȝe, þanne lacchen I sholde
> Ouþer mantel or moneie amonges lordes Mynstrals.
> Ac for I kan neiþer taboure ne trompe ne telle no gestes,
> Farten ne fiþelen at festes ne harpen,
> Iape ne Iogele ne gentilliche pipe,
> Ne neiþer saille ne sautrie ne synge wiþ þe gyterne,
> I haue no good giftes of þise grete lordes . . .
>
>   (B. xiii. 228–34)

If Haukyn is meant to be seen as another stylized reflection of Will and thus of the poet as well, he forms yet another outlet for Langland's self-suspicions and not a means of showing that "the minstrel at his highest is the ideal man of God," since "the corruption of the highest is also the worst."[20] His Coat of Baptism is stained with all the seven deadly sins, and the idle words of Gluttony cause him to veer toward despair (B. xiii. 399–408). Langland proceeds from the "branches that lead a man to sloth" into a steady condemnation of minstrels, even the "kynges minstrales," concluding with these lines:

> There flateres and fools þoruȝ hir foule wordes
> Leden þo þat liþed hem to Luciferis feste
> Wiþ *turpiloquio*, a lay of sorwe, and Luciferis fiþele.
>
>   (B. xiii. 454–56)

Langland quickly adds "Thus Haukyn þe Actif man hadde ysoiled his cote" (457), thereby leaving the strong impression that the abuses of minstrelsy—here defined as any manipulation of language to distract men with hollow conceits that cannot sustain hope—is the immediate

---

17. Donaldson, pp. 140–42 and 150–51; Bloomfield, *Apocalypse*, pp. 151–52; and Spearing, *Dream-Poetry*, p. 157.
18. Chambers, *Man's Unconquerable Mind*, p. 151.
19. Donaldson, p. 141.
20. Bloomfield, *Apocalypse*, p. 152.

cause of Haukyn's sinfulness in general and his *acedia* in particular. Far from the ideal man of God, Haukyn is left vulnerable to all the vices attached to minstrelsy so that we are left with the unsettling impression that Langland imagined no way for a man, even with hard work and the best of intentions, to pursue a poetic career without the stain of sin.

Since older men tend to grow more conservative in their politics and morals, it is understandable that the C-poet grew sterner in his disapproval of minstrels, a group he may have been identified with by others despite his own sense of a higher calling. It is true that the C-text's description of Haukyn leaves out all mention of his stained coat, but the tirade against sinful entertainers is preserved immediately after the confession of Sloth, where the juxtaposition of subjects renders the moral ramifications of minstrelsy less ambiguous (C. vii. 70–119). The C-poet furthermore withdraws the initial suggestion that there are *any* good minstrels in the Fair Field. Whereas the B-text allowed that some performers were at least guiltless, the C-version drops this exception and elaborates instead upon the sinfulness of the craft:

> And summe murthes to make as mynstrels conneth,
> Wolleth neyther swynke ne swete, bote sweren grete othes,
> Fyndeth out foule fantasyes and foles hem maketh
> And hath wytt at wille to worche yf þei wolde.
> That Poule prechede of hem preue hit y myhte;
> *Qui turpiloquium loquitur* is Luciferes knaue.
>
> (C. prol. 35–40)

Donaldson wrestles with the question involved in this alteration: why does the C-text preserve the same attitude as the previous two versions toward all occupations except minstrelsy?[21] He feels that Langland's campaign against lewd minstrels was aggravated by a crisis in terminology, by the inability of words to define people and professions adequately. Just as the security of the kingdom is threatened by the lack of two separate terms to distinguish good meed from evil meed, the integrity of Langland's own enterprise is jeopardized for want of two words to distinguish the many bad minstrels who cracked jokes about the Trinity from the one good minstrel who wrote a serious poem about the Three Do's.

Donaldson concludes that the logic of majority rule influenced the way in which the crisis was in one sense resolved. Since most entertainers belonging to the profession were dishonest and threatened mo-

---

21. Donaldson, p. 136.

rality, their opprobrium was transferred to all the practitioners of the trade and to almost the whole body of entertainment arts.[22] Langland offers no defense that would protect himself from the same blame that he casts upon minstrels, except (in the C-text only) the vague suggestion that he is one of the "lunatyk lollares" who prophesy under the direct inspiration of God (ix. 105–38).[23] In this sense the crisis created within the poem is never wholly resolved. We are left with the feeling that Langland was never fully convinced that his work as a "maker" could be vindicated before the court of public opinion or in the consistory of his conscience before God.

What do we conclude, then, about a man who spent much of his life writing and revising a poem that he refused to defend as anything more than a dream-journal written as a form of recreation? I believe that some minimal answers to that question—I stress the word *minimal* and add *provisional*—will come by first recognizing the Dreamer's slothfulness and then inferring that this temperament was most likely shared self-consciously by Langland himself. Thus we can detect throughout *Piers Plowman*, in all versions and divisions, the poet's response to an image of himself as a man given to idleness, pensiveness, impatience, anxiety, and indecision.

Did Langland use poetry simply as an escape from idleness? Curtius documents a centuries-old tradition in which writers praised poetry as a means of avoiding idleness (*otium*) and in the Middle Ages as a cure for sloth.[24] Seneca offered the warning "Otium sine litteris mors est et hominis vivi sepultura," which the didactic poet Cato put into his *Disticha* (III, 6) in a verse immediately preceding the one quoted by Will in his self-acquittal before Imaginatyf. Chaucer knew the topos well enough to have used it in *The Book of the Duchess* (1155–58) and the Prologue to *The Second Nun's Tale*:

> And for to putte us fro swich ydelnesse,
> That cause is of so greet confusioun,
> I have heer doon my feithful bisynesse
> After the legende, in translacioun. . .

>   (*CT*, VIII, 22–25)

Since a poet's work required a certain amount of physical stasis—the longer the poem, the more time spent sitting—a writer's efforts always

---

22. *Ibid.*, pp. 141–42.
23. Curtius, pp. 474–75 ("The Poet's Divine Frenzy"), explains how the notion of poetic madness came down to the Middle Ages from the Roman authors and ultimately from Plato.
24. *Ibid.*, pp. 88–89 and 468–69.

occupied a dubious middle ground *inter labores et ocia* (to use Gower's expression)[25] so that the quality of his labor depended on the ways in which his mind filled the hours of idleness.

Reinhard Kuhn offers an interpretation of one of Dante's more obscure allegories that seems to address exactly this point.[26] On the Terrace of Sloth in *Purgatorio* (xix, 7–33), Dante dreams that he sees a Siren with many enigmatic attributes. Her cross-eyes suggest a warped view of the outside world; her garbled speech, the difficulty of communication; her pale face, a melancholic temperament; her maimed feet, a lack of physical movement; and the absence of hands, a sign that she is incapable of good works. But then she is transformed into something very lovely, because out of *acedia* may arise a beautiful and haunting song. Yet when Virgil reveals the Siren's foul belly, she reverts to ugliness. Dante seems to have detected an inspiration within idleness that created a causal relationship between ennui and art, but he realized also that the resultant art could not be morally neutral. Idleness may be the necessary condition for producing poetry, but the poetry itself determines whether the time spent *inter labores et ocia* has been worthwhile.[27] This line of thought would have led Langland back in a full circle and left him once again in a state of uncertainty.

Idleness may have been "the ministre and norice unto vice" in the view of Chaucer's Nun and many others who wrote in an effort to avoid *otium*, but within the range of sloth's species it is the least severe and easiest to remedy. If we assume that Langland's slothful temperament presented a far more serious problem than the improper enjoyment of leisure, we must suspect that he occupied himself with writing his vast allegory for reasons more complicated than simply eluding idleness. Insight into his reasons is provided by one of the first poets of the Western tradition, as Hesiod in his *Theogony* praises poetry as an escape from *taedium vitae*:

For though a man have sorrow and grief in his newly-troubled soul and live in dread because his heart is distressed, yet when a singer, the servant of the

25. Gower ends the *Confessio Amantis* with a Latin commendation to Henry of Lancaster in which he offers an account of his literary corpus: "inter labores et ocia ad aliorum noticiam tres libros doctrine causa forma subsequenti propterea composuit"; *The English Works*, ed. G.C. Macaulay, 1900–01, EETS e.s. 81 and 82, vol. II, p. 479.

26. Kuhn's interpretation as a whole can be found in *The Demon of Noontide*, p. 58. The Italian poet is probably recalling Horace's Satire II, iii, 14–15, "Vitanda est improba Siren Desidia," in *Satires, Epistles and Ars Poetica*, trans. Fairclough, pp. 152–53.

27. In a famous passage from *The Fates of Illustrious Men*, trans. Louis Brewer Hall (New York: Ungar, 1965), pp. 104–07, Boccaccio defends leisure as the necessary condition for a poet who fills his idleness with great diligence. At the same time, he warns

Muses, chants the glorious deeds of men of old and the blessed gods who inhabit Olympus, at once he forgets his heaviness and remembers not his sorrows at all, but the gifts of the goddesses soon turn him away from these.[28]

Hesiod had the listener's response first in mind, but it is possible that relief from despondency came also to the singer, the audience of his own poem, from the active process of performance and the business of making verses.

The Hellenic tradition deriving from Hesiod mingled with the early Christian tradition represented by the desert fathers of Egypt, so that the works of John Cassian suggest a prescription against *acedia* not far removed from that of the *Theogony*. In *De Institutis* he speaks repeatedly of the need for physical labor as *occupatio*, while elsewhere he concentrates upon the monk's duty to regulate his inner disposition by cultivating fortitude.[29] Taken together, these pieces of advice serve as a defense for the kind of writing that is both pleasant labor and penetrating self-analysis designed to root out *acedia* by cultivating the contrary virtue. The efficacy of the prescription is witnessed centuries later when Robert Burton offers this justification for his vast anatomy:

> If any man except against the matter or manner of treating of this my subject, and will demand a reason of it, I can allege more than one. I writ of melancholy, by being busy to avoid melancholy, . . . I writ therefore, and busied myself in this playing labour, *otiosaque diligentia ut vitarem torporem feriandi* . . . *atque otium in utile verterem negotium* [to escape the ennui of idleness by a leisurely kind of employment . . . and turn idleness into a useful enterprise].[30]

Penelope Doob offers a provocative study suggesting that the troubled poet Thomas Hoccleve followed a regimen similar to those prescribed by Cassian and Burton when he turned to the business of poetry to distract himself from his own melancholy.[31] With Hoccleve as with Langland, we can never be sure to what extent the account of his life represents factual autobiography, but whether his madness was real or a metaphorical way of describing man's life of sin, he considered his poetry as a weapon for countering the affliction.[32] For example, at the

---

against fraudulent men who affect the leisure of a poet in order to enjoy idleness for its own sake. Outside appearances are seldom reliable, as Langland was so acutely aware.

28. Hesiod's *Theogony* (98–103) is included in *The Homeric Hymns and Homerica*, trans. Hugh G. Evelyn-White (Cambridge, MA: Loeb Classical Library, 1914), pp. 84–85.

29. *De Institutis*, ed. Petchenig, X, 7–25, and *Conlationes XXIV*, ed. Petschenig, V, 23.

30. Burton, *The Anatomy of Melancholy*, pp. 20–21.

31. Doob, pp. 30 and 208–31.

32. Doob, pp. 210–11 and 229, leaves open the question of autobiographical authenticity. Jerome Mitchell argues that Hoccleve presents an accurate account of his own

beginning of the *Regement of Princes* (c. 1412) Hoccleve described the morbid anxiety that drove him to wander aimlessly outside the city, until he was urged to write down his troubles so that he might be diverted from his melancholy.[33] After this and several other attempts at relief failed, he set about translating some worthwhile work for Henry of Lancaster, and through this therapy he cured both his poverty and desperation, like Burton two centuries later.

Hoccleve also took the advice to talk aloud about his problems when he undertook to write his *Complaint* (c. 1421). He had felt so weighed down with languor and sorrow that he could hardly go on living, until he decided to open his heart and divulge his emotional troubles (ll. 22–35).[34] Hoccleve next wrote the *Dialogus cum Amico* in which he announced his intent to translate the Latin treatise *Lerne to Dye*. His Friend, however, worried that these mental labors might precipitate the same problems he had suffered in the past and serve rather as a strain than a remedy:

Of studie was engendred thy seeknesse,
And þat was hard / woldest thow now agayn
Entre into þat laborious bisynesse,
Syn it thy mynde and eek thy wit had slayn?
Thy conceit is nat worth a payndemayn:
Let be / let be / bisye thee so no more,
Lest thee repente / and reewe it ouersore.

(379–85)

The Friend's fears were based on a common belief that the hard concentration required to write poetry could cause rather than cure a mental disorder such as melancholy, a psychological affliction which, as illustrated in the works of Guillaume d'Auvergne, was often indistinguishable from *acedia*.

Offering an observation that would have been confirmed by Cassian, Boccaccio remarked that too much studious repose is "the mother of dullness and the enemy of creativity." In a minatory dream of the sort

---

life and character, in *Thomas Hoccleve: A Study in Early Fifteenth-Century English Poetic* (Urbana: University of Illinois Press, 1968), pp. 1–19. On the other hand, Eva M. Thornley has judged Hoccleve's *Male Regle* (c. 1406) more conventional than autobiographical on the basis of the number of features it shares with penitential lyrics of the period; "The Middle English Penitential Lyric and Hoccleve's Autobiographical Poetry," *NM*, 68 (1967), 295–321.

33. Doob, p. 217, draws upon *Hoccleve's Works: The Regement of Princes*, ed. Frederick J. Furnivall, 1897, EETS e.s. 72, pp. 1–11. She notes, p. 28, that Chaucer uses a similar method to exorcise the Black Knight's grief in *The Book of the Duchess* (ll. 548–51).

34. *Hoccleve's Works: The Minor Poems*, ed. Furnivall and Gollancz, p. 96. This volume also includes the text of *Dialogus cum Amico*, pp. 110–39.

common in the *acedia* tradition, the phantom of Petrarch appears to the lethargic Boccaccio and delivers this advice:

> . . . too much severity sometimes breaks the lazy person rather than refreshes him, and I think that it is best by far to use mildness, so that I may inspire shame for your slothfulness rather than ill will in your spirit.[35]

The long, taxing labor involved in writing and constantly revising *Piers Plowman* may have benefited Langland as a means for exploring his slothful temperament by combining self-analysis and confession with the act of penance, but we cannot know what, if any, safeguards he might have taken—whether alternating his writing with some other occupation as Cassian would have prescribed, or cutting short his work whenever the burden became too great. Considering the grave concerns of Hoccleve's Friend, added to the fact that Langland's ongoing dissatisfaction with his poem makes it unlikely that the task was an easy one, we should allow for the possibility that the work itself may have posed dangers nearly equal to its benefits.

Realizing that a slothful temperament was an infirmity readily provoked by hard discipline, men like Roger Bacon concluded that people who suffered from *acedia* were often better helped by finding outlets for relaxation.[36] It should come as no surprise, therefore, that Will's only explicit excuse for his "making" relies totally on Cato's advice to relieve care with some enjoyment; many holy men "pleyden þe parfiter to ben" (B. xii. 20–24). The holy men Will has in mind were probably the desert fathers who used relaxation to thwart *ariditas spiritualis*, or simply monks for whom Benedict allowed a varied discipline and even moderate laughter.[37] The author of *An Alphabet of Tales*, quoting the same line as Langland from Cato's *Disticha*, tells a story in which the great desert father Anthony defended recreation as a necessary means for protecting the unity of a religious order. To make his point, the saint had ordered an archer to keep pulling back on his bow until the man refused for fear of breaking it:

> Than Saynt Anton sayd vnto hym agayn, "loo! son, þus it is in þe werke of allmyghtie God; ffor and we draw it oute of mesur, we may sone breke itt; þat is to say, and we halde our brethir so strayte in aw þatt þai com to no myrth nor no sporte, we may lightlie cauce þaim to breke þer ordur. And herefor vs muste som tyme lowse our pithe, & suffre þaim hafe som recreacion & dis-

---

35. Boccaccio, *The Fates of Illustrious Men*, trans. Hall, pp. 202 and 206.
36. Wenzel, pp. 59–60.
37. Benedict, *Regula* (vii), Doyle, trans., pp. 27–28.

porte emang all þer other chargis, as Caton says, *Interpone tuis interdum gaudia curis.*"[38]

Robert Henryson uses this same image in the Prologue to the *Fables*:

> For as we se, ane bow that ay is bent
> Worthis vnsmart and dullis on the string;
> Sa dois the mynd that is ay diligent
> In ernistful thochtis and in studying.[39]

He thus confirms Will's assertion that writing poetry, whatever its moral service, might afford the poet with healthy relaxation. As Johan Huizinga has observed, "all poetry is born of play."[40]

Despite the general medieval acceptance of poetry's recreative function, Langland stands as an unremitting advocate of work and, in his own voice, makes hardly any allowance for relaxation. In the opening vision of the Fair Field, he praises the laborers who "putten hem to plouȝ, *pleiden ful selde,* / In settynge and sowynge swonken ful harde" (B. prol. 20–21). Even his kind of verse bears witness to the minimizing of what we might call "play-elements"—rhyme, fixed meter, stanzaic composition, decorative imagery.[41] Not tempted by the elaborate stanzas that caught the fancy of the author of *Pearl* and *Sir Gawain*, Langland chose instead to write in a plain but serviceable meter which the great artificer Chaucer dismissed as "rum, ram, ruf." Even if we consider personification and allegory as manifestations of the mind at play, Langland's dissatisfaction with images and his tendency to discard the allegorical in favor of the literal betray an underlying disdain for the game-elements inherent in the poetic tradition in which he worked. In his hands, language becomes a working and workman-like instrument that moves against the normal intent of poetry to cultivate the artificial and the playful.

Langland's neglect of game-elements, I believe, has much to do with his conception of his role as a true *vates* or religious poet. Examining the history of literature in various cultures, Huizinga has noted that the play-elements in poetry increase in direct proportion as belief in a sacred myth diminishes.[42] The inverse corollary is not invariably

---

38. *An Alphabet of Tales*, ed. Banks, pp. 5–6. Kolve, *The Play Called Corpus Christi*, pp. 128–29, quotes this passage as an illustration that "the Middle Ages frequently used images of breaking or bursting to express this need for relaxation into laughter."
39. Henryson, *The Poems*, ed. Fox, p. 4 (ll. 22–25).
40. Huizinga, *Homo Ludens*, p. 129.
41. *Ibid.*, p. 132.
42. *Ibid.*, p. 130.

true—speeches in the devout Corpus Christi plays were often composed in highly elaborate stanzas consonant with their pervasive game-spirit—but it seems to apply well enough to Langland as a poet who believed so totally in the divine story of Christ that he saw no need to obscure it permanently with ornaments. The play-elements that are included—the discarded images, the shape-shifting personifications, the disintegrating allegories—bear witness to the difficulty and frustration of understanding, *really* understanding, the ultimate Truth whose existence is never questioned. Thoreau once wrote that "unconscious despair is concealed even under what are called the games and amusements of mankind." [43] Had he made allowance for men as sensitive and resourceful as himself, he might have realized that in literary endeavors the writer might discover a game that could be used, consciously and skillfully, as a firm bulwark against despair.

Escaping idleness, analyzing the pathology of his dominant vice, and granting relaxation to body and spirit: not one of these can be discounted as part of Langland's motive for writing so doggedly at his poem. Nor, taken all together, do they provide a complete account to satisfy our sense of his obsessiveness. That sense is sharpened not so much by familiarity with a single text but rather by a view of his entire career, in sequence and as process. G.H. Russell, an expert by way of his work as the editor of the new C-text, believes that Langland applied himself hard to his business, often striving against a feeling of dissatisfaction and frustration evident in all three versions. The A-text "seems to have ended in dissatisfaction, even in something approaching despair," [44] and despite the mammoth effort invested in the B-continuation, there are signs everywhere that work proceeded fitfully, with impatience over the limitations of genre, with the begrudging resignation of "that was a way of putting it—not very satisfactory," and with the beleaguered hope that what came later would redeem what had already passed. There *would* be time for visions and revisions.

Besides an attempt to correct and polish, the C-text was another huge task requiring a great deal of time and a great deal of labor. Again the work seems to have been spurred on by relentless dissatisfaction, but without clear motives. [45] Since Langland busied himself not only with major additions and deletions but also with the alteration of hundreds of small details, not always with happy results, the final version

43. Henry David Thoreau, *Walden, or Life in the Woods* (New York: Collier Books, 1962), p. 18.
44. G.H. Russell, "Some Aspects of the Process of Revision in *Piers Plowman*," in *Critical Approaches*, ed. Hussey, p. 30.
45. Several distinguished critics have felt that the word "dissatisfaction" best describes Langland's attitude toward his poem; see for example Bloomfield, *Apocalypse,*

of the poem has gained a "well-deserved reputation for fussiness."[46] So many passages were arbitrarily and pointlessly changed that one is tempted, as Manly once remarked, "to think they were rewritten for the mere sake of rewriting."[47]

My own final impression is not so absurdist. Langland had a great deal to say to his audience, and part of his goal was to mirror the whole history of a spiritual life—his own—in a dream-poem transformed from an objective to a reflexive medium. Having determined its structural outlines in the B-text, "he could proceed only by going back, rewriting his poem from the beginning, incorporating in it his subsequent experience, and making its next topic precisely the difficulties he had in continuing it at all."[48] With these praiseworthy intentions, Langland betrays none of Boccaccio's desire for reputation either in his own time or among subsequent generations of readers.[49] Fame was not the spur. There is no sense of artistic immortality such as one finds in *The House of Fame*—though rejected by Geoffrey the dreamer (ll. 1873–82)—and no awareness that vernacular literature survives to be read by some future audience, as Chaucer notes in Book II of *Troilus* (ll. 22–28). Langland does not even speak of his work as a poem that can be finished and released as a self-contained entity; it is as if "making" itself were a never-ending process, "a continuous action rather than a finite production, which *as a mode of life* must be justified before God and man."[50] This concept of poetry as process rather than product, evidenced by an almost unending series of revisions in the C-text, accords beautifully with one of the central tenets of the poem—that a man's intentions count more than the outward results of those intentions—so that together they provide the most comprehensive explanation for Langland's "making." To write poetry took an assertion of the poet's will, and to persevere meant that his will con-

p. 37; Burrow, "Words, Works and Will," p. 120; and Martin, *The Field and the Tower*, p. 1. Russell, pp. 38–39, suggests some motives for the C-revision, but also shows that many prior explanations are unsatisfactory. Carruthers, *The Search for St. Truth*, pp. 171–72, feels that there would have been a D-text, an E-text, and so on, since the poem insists constantly on the partialness of its meaning.

46. Russell, p. 44.

47. J.M. Manly, "*Piers the Plowman* and Its Sequence" in *The Cambridge History of English Literature*, ed. Sir A.W. Ward and A.R. Waller, 15 vols. (Cambridge: The University Press, 1907–33), vol. II (1908), p. 30.

48. Spearing, *Dream-Poetry*, p. 151.

49. Boccaccio, *The Fates of Illustrious Men* (Bk. VIII), pp. 204–05, urges poets to subdue sloth with a fervent desire for renown. Curtius, pp. 476–79, offers a valuable discussion of "Poetry as Perpetuation." The opposing Christian view is outlined by B.G. Koonce's *Chaucer and the Tradition of Fame: Symbolism in "The House of Fame"* (Princeton: Princeton University Press, 1966), pp. 13–45.

50. Middleton, "The Idea of Public Poetry," 103.

tinued to work in the service of God, whatever men might think of the poem's contents or artistic merits.

Efrem Bettoni has offered the following illustration of voluntary commitment according to Duns Scotus: "By one act of the will I can determine myself to write, and by another act I can decide not to write, but I cannot be simultaneously in act in regard to both things together."[51] Because Langland made his decision to write, any decision not to write would have represented a willful trespass. As a mental activity involving willing and thinking, the poetic process would have been regarded by Scotistic thinkers as an act cut off from the outside world—like the act of dreaming itself—and therefore more nearly perfect perhaps, because it was not subject to earthly transcience. Such voluntary activities ceased not because they had reached their own end, but only because man is a mortal creature who cannot sustain any action indefinitely. Since the last two passus of the C-version are virtually identical to the corresponding sections of the B-text, Russell believes that the process of revision was cut short by the poet's death.[52] If that is true, we might conclude that Langland sustained his efforts as long as he was humanly able.

Considering the poet's willing commitment in favor of work *per se*, without total concern for the visible fruits of this labor, we can detect an elusive brotherhood between Langland the writer and Piers the humble plowman, based not on the outward dignity of labor according to social status but on their shared devotion to *doing*. The nexus is strengthened because plowing had been invoked since classical times as a metaphor for writing. Cicero wrote to his friend Atticus, "Hoc litterularum exaravi—I plowed out this little letter," and Isidore transmitted the metaphor to the Middle Ages in his *Etymologiae* (VI, 9, 2 and 14, 71).[53] The equation of writing with plowing is made by Jean de Meun in *Le Roman de la Rose* (ll. 21,181−82) and by Chaucer in *The Knight's Tale*: "I have, God woot, a large feeld to ere, / And wayke been the oxen in my plough" (*CT*, I, 886−87). Perhaps the most remarkable example for our purposes is found in *Ackermann aus*

51. Efrem Bettoni, *Duns Scotus: The Basic Principles of His Philosophy*, trans. Bernardino Bonansea (Washington: The Catholic University of America Press, 1961), p. 158, with reference to the *Commentaria Oxoniensia*, Lib. I, dist. xxxix, art. 3, sect. 2 (vol. I, pp. 1216−21).

52. Russell, "The Process of Revision," pp. 47−48. This view runs counter to the suggestion made by Carruthers, p. 173, that the poet, like Aquinas, might have been halted in his work by an epiphany convincing him that all he had written was mere straw.

53. Curtius, pp. 313−14, and D. Wilfred Abse, *Speech and Reason*(Charlottesville: University Press of Virginia, 1971), p. 84.

Böhmen, whose third part begins with the riddling line "*Ich bins gen-annt ein ackerman, von vogelwat is mein pflug*," the second half of which means "the quill is my plow."[54] This scribal adage was too well known to have been far from Langland's mind. Although the poetic process was basically mental, a poem the size of *Piers Plowman* would have demanded a great many hours at the quill-plow.[55]

Writing thus becomes another way of plowing the Half Acre in a more profound sense than understood perhaps by Chaucer and most members of scriptoria. In the mystical meaning explored in Passus XIX, the plowman is an image of the preacher and the conveyer of God's message —work that conforms to Thought's definition of Dobet (B. viii. 78–95) —although Langland never wholly forgets the origi-nal image of Piers as a humble laborer pursuing the most basic form of Dowel which leads simply but surely to Heaven. "Jesus said to him: No man putting his hand to the plough and looking back is fit for the kingdom of God" (Lk. 9.62): this metaphor, too, must have weighed upon Langland's artistic life. Like Piers' plowing, the poet's "making" became a form of pilgrimage and an act of penance, but without ever losing its fundamental meaning as an assertion of the will in the ser-vice of God.

Langland's unspoken attitude toward his writing can be illustrated by the scene from Lydgate's *Pilgrimage of the Life of Man* in which the Pilgrim encounters the figure Labor, who is engaged in the task of weaving and unweaving nets. At first the Pilgrim is puzzled:

> "Yt wer merveyl thow sholdest the
> So symple a crafft on the to take,
> To make nattys & vnmake;
> The wyche crafft (whan al ys souht)
> Ys so pore, yt wynneth nouht."

> (ll. 11,340–44)

Like the poet who offers nothing essential to the maintenance of so-ciety, Labor explains that he continues to "make & vnmake" in order to avoid idleness and erase the rust of vice with continual diligence: "Swych as I kan, swych I acheue."[56] Lydgate, like Deguilleville before

54. Curtius, p. 314, credits the right interpretation to Arthur Hübner.
55. Curtius, pp. 468–69, reviews the tradition in which the writing of poetry was regarded as hard, sweat-producing labor, so that it was believed that "he upon whom lies such a task has renounced sloth." Stephen A. Barney, "The Ploughshare of the Tongue: The Progress of a Symbol from the Bible to *Piers Plowman*," MS, 35 (1973), 261–93, traces the plow-imagery to 1 Cor. 9.10–12 as the source of Langland's notion of spiri-tual labor.
56. Lydgate, *Pilgrimage of the Life of Man*, ed. Furnivall and Locock, pp. 310–13 (l. 11,349).

him, must have understood that Labor's making and unmaking were analogous to the poet's work of writing and revising, and at the same time reminiscent of the Christian tradition's greatest champion of work for its own sake. Deguilleville's Labor and the poet Langland can both be compared to Paul the Hermit, who from one point of view is an archetypally absurd character spending his solitary life in the wastes of Egypt weaving baskets, burning them at the end of each year, and then beginning all over again to weave another mountain of wattle.[57] Yet these figures differ from an absurd hero like the Sisyphus of Camus in two crucial ways: their drudgery was voluntary in the fullest sense of the word, and the ordeal had a conclusion far beyond itself—to reach a Heaven whose glories were so transcendent as to equalize the worldly trades of poet and plowman, basket-weaver and king.

We must take care, then, not to number Langland among the mass of men who endure lives of quiet desperation. He was forever vocal over the corruption that he found in society and the possibility that his own poem could do little to stem the decline, and might even contribute to the atmosphere of doubt and confusion. Yet it would be equally wrong to envisage him as a sort of fourteenth-century William Cowper toiling obsessively at *The Task* while haunted by the belief that whatever he did, he was damned below Judas. Langland tried hard to dissociate himself from the "Iaperes and Iangeleres, Iudas children," but what really set him apart were most likely his trust in God's mercy and his hope of eternal reward.

It is sometimes possible to glimpse the Kierkegaardian catch-image in this apparent willingness to take a step forward and to prize that step above the fear of uncertainty, so that not to step forward signified the crime of inaction and despair, even if a man strayed into error and stumbled, and even if he discovered his step needed to be withdrawn. But for Langland these were uncertainties of means only, not of ends. Truth remained eternally aloft in the Tower. It was a matter of finding one's way out of the labyrinth of the Fair Field where so many deceitful voices were bent on making a man take a step backwards. Though the roads were many, and some preferred above others, those that led uphill eventually brought the pilgrim home to the Tower. It was Good Faith who first encouraged Will to speak out against the corruption of

---

57. The saint's labor was imitated by others such as St. Arsenius and thus became a standard mode of religious *occupatio*, one shunned by Chaucer's Pardoner (*CT*, VI, 444–46). The popularity of the story can probably be attributed to Cassian's inclusion of the saint's example in *De Institutis* (X, 24). Langland himself praises this hermit's work: "Poul after his prechyng paniers [baskets] he made" (B. xv. 290). See again Hemingway, "The Two St. Pauls," 57–58.

the friars, and in the end it was probably *lewtee* that sustained Langland in his endeavors: faith in a loving and merciful God, and confidence that "making" with words was the one form of Dowel that he did best.

The leading British philosophers of the early fourteenth century had speculated that human perception, including the poet's visions, might be nothing other than unprovable and untrustworthy opinion, no matter how carefully the writer tried to set down his experiences.[58] The link between the mind and reality was forged by words whose meanings were instituted by the voluntary assent of the speaker and his listeners alike, so that the individual mind with its shifting imagistic-linguistic processes became a place for boundless exploration, but also a place for inevitably getting lost.[59] The poet's last refuge was not aesthetics or intellectual theology. It was simple fideism. There remained only one absolute—the will of a loving God—but that would have been enough.

Since Langland's poem ends just short of Will's death and the Day of Judgment, we must go to Revelations 20.12 for the final unwritten scene in his spiritual life:

And I saw the dead, great and small, standing in the presence of the throne. And the books were opened; and another book was opened, which was the book of life. And the dead were judged by those things which were written in the books, according to their works.

The author of Revelations probably conceived of these books as records kept in Heaven as part of the mystery of the Doom, but there was a belief in the Middle Ages that each man brought with him his own account book or register of his good and bad works:[60] "At þe dredful dome, [the] dede shulle rise / And comen alle before Crist, acountes to yelde" (B. vii. 193–94).

For Langland, the book of his life would not have been only a vast

58. Gardner, *Life and Times of Chaucer*, pp. 292–93.

59. Peck, "Chaucer and the Nominalist Questions," 747 *et passim*, has more to say about the ways in which a fourteenth-century poet responded to new, startling speculation about the nature of language.

60. In *Everyman*, for instance, the account book is a literal stage prop which the protagonist is trying urgently to prepare for presentation; see V.A. Kolve, "*Everyman* and the Parable of the Talents," *Medieval English Drama*, ed. Jerome Taylor and Alan H. Nelson (Chicago: University of Chicago Press, 1972), p. 317. Behind the passage in Revelations stands the image of the book in Malachi 3.16–18. Thomas of Celano's hymn *Dies Irae* gave terrible prominence to the role of this book at the Last Judgment:

Liber scriptus proferetur
In quo totum continetur
Unde mundus iudicetur.

manuscript bearing the title *Visio Willi de Petro Plouhman* but the book as symbolic evidence of a life spent laboring faithfully in the Lord's vineyard, with aches and strains and sweat of the brow. Even Boccaccio acknowledged that fame was only a secondary reward: "if all trace of a person is lost among mankind, his memory is not lost to God for whose glory he worked."[61] It probably would not have mattered greatly to Langland that mankind has lost virtually all memory of his mundane existence, because he would have been comforted by the fundamental assurance that every labor willingly undertaken and loyally endured would be rewarded in the end—an assurance given powerful voice here by Thomas à Kempis, speaking in the person of God:[62]

One houre shal come whan all labour shal cesse & all noyse. Litel it is & short, all þat passiþ wiþ tyme. Do þat þou dost; labore treuly in myn vyneȝerde; I shal be þy rewarde. Write, rede, synge, morne, kepe silence, pray, suffre manly contrariousnes. For euerlastyng lif is worþe all þese & moche more & muche gretter bateiles.

61. Boccaccio, *The Fates of Illustrious Men*, p. 205.
62. *The Earliest English Translation . . . of the "De Imitatione Christi"* (III, 52), ed. John K. Ingram, 1893, EETS e.s. 63, p. 124.

Bibliography

The following list constitutes a bibliography only of the books and articles actually referred to in the body of this work. It is divided into four parts: I. References Works; II. Editions and Translations; III. Other Primary Sources; IV. Scholarly Studies. Titles are alphabetized within each part, except the second which is in chronological order. All primary works are arranged according to the name of their author, or if anonymous, by the title of the work.

I. Reference Works

Lexikon der Christlichen Ikonographie. Ed. Engelbert Kirschbaum, *et al.* Freiburg: Herder, 1970.

Middle English Dictionary. Ed. Hans Kurath, Sherman M. Kuhn, and John Reidy. Ann Arbor: University of Michigan Press, 1956–.

New Catholic Encyclopedia. Ed. The Editorial Staff at The Catholic University of America. New York: McGraw-Hill, 1967.

The Oxford English Dictionary. Ed. James A. H. Murray, Henry Bradley, W. A. Craigie, C. T. Onions. 12 vols. and Supplement. Corr. ed. Oxford: The Clarendon Press, 1933.

II. Editions and Translations

Langland, Robert. *Visio Willi de Petro Plouhman, Item Visiones eiusdem de Dowel, Dobet, et Dobest.* Ed. Thomas Dunham Whitaker. London: John Murray, 1813.

[Langland, William.] *The Vision and Creed of Piers Ploughman.* Ed. Thomas Wright. 2 vols. 2nd. ed. rev. London: J. R. Smith, 1856.

Langland, William. *Piers the Plowman.* Ed. Walter W. Skeat. 2 vols. London: Oxford University Press, 1886.

[Langland, William.] *The Vision of Piers Plowman.* Trans. Henry W. Wells. New York: Sheed and Ward, 1935.

[Langland, William.] *Piers the Plowman: A Critical Edition of the A-Version.* Ed. Thomas A. Knott and David C. Fowler. Baltimore: The Johns Hopkins Press, 1952.

Langland, William. *Piers the Ploughman.* Trans. J. F. Goodridge. Harmondsworth: Penguin, 1959.

[Langland, William.] *Will's Visions of Piers Plowman and Do-Well.* Ed. George Kane. London: The Athlone Press, 1960.

Langland, [William.] *Piers Plowman: The Prologue and Passus I–VII of the B Text as Found in Bodleian MS. Laud Misc. 581.* Ed. J. A. W. Bennett. Oxford: The Clarendon Press, 1972.

[Langland, William.] *Will's Visions of Piers Plowman, Do-Well, Do-Better and Do-Best.* Ed. George Kane and E. Talbot Donaldson. London: The Athlone Press, 1975.

Langland, William. *Piers Plowman: An Edition of the C-text.* Ed. Derek Pearsall. Berkeley: University of California Press, 1979.

[Langland, William.] *Piers Plowman: The Z Version.* Ed. George Rigg and Charlotte Brewer. Toronto: Pontifical Institute of Mediaeval Studies, no. 59, 1983.

III. Other Primary Sources

Aelred of Rievaulx. *Sermones de Oneribus. PL* 195:361–502.

Alanus de Insulis. *Regulae de Sacra Theologia. PL* 210:621–84.

———. *Summa de Arte Praedicatoria. PL* 210:109–98.

———. *De Virtutibus et De Vitiis et De Donis Spiritus Sancti.* Ed. Odon Lottin. *MS,* 12 (1950), 20–56.

Albertus Magnus. *Opera Omnia.* Ed. Auguste Borgnet. 38 vols. Paris: Vivès, 1890–99.

Alcuin. *De Virtutibus et Vitiis Liber. PL* 101:613–38.

Aldhelm. *De Octo Prinicipalibus Vitiis. PL* 89:281–90.

An Alphabet of Tales. Ed. M. M. Banks. 1904–05, EETS o.s. 126 and 127.

The Ancrene Riwle. Trans. M. B. Salu. London: Burns & Oates, 1955.

Ancrene Wisse. Ed. J. R. R. Tolkien. 1962, EETS o.s. 249.

Andreas Capellanus. *De Amore.* Ed. E. Trojel. Copenhagen: Libraria Gadiana, 1892.

Anecdotes Historiques d'Etienne de Bourbon. Ed. Albert Lecoy de la Marche. Paris: Renouard, 1877.

Anselm. *Cur Deus Homo?. PL* 158:359–432.

Antoninus of Florence. *Summa Theologica.* Venice: Jenson, 1480.

The Apocryphal New Testament. Trans. M. R. James. Oxford: The Clarendon Press, 1924.

Aristotle. *De Anima.* Trans. W. S. Hett. Cambridge, MA: Loeb Classical Library, 1957.

Les Arts Poétiques du XIIe et XIIIe siècles. Ed. Edmond Faral. Paris: Champion, 1924.

Augustine. *Concerning the City of God against the Pagans.* Trans. Henry Bettenson. Intro. David Knowles. Harmondsworth: Penguin, 1972.

———. *De Civitate Dei. PL* 41:13–804.

———. *Confessions.* Trans. R. S. Pine-Coffin. Harmondsworth: Penguin, 1961.

———. *De Duabus Animabus. PL* 42:93–112.

———. *Enarratio in Psalmum CXVIII. PL* 37:1501–96.

———. *Epistola. PL* 33.

———. *The Immortality of the Soul.* Trans. Ludwig Schopp. *Writings of Saint Augustine.* New York: Fathers of the Church, vol. 2, 1947.

———. *In Joannis Evangelium Tractatus CXXIV. PL* 35:1379–1976.

———. *De Libero Arbitrio. PL* 32:1221–1310.

———. *De Opere Monachorum. PL* 40:547–82.

———. *In Psalmum CI. PL* 37:1293–1316.

———. *In Psalmum CXXIX. PL* 37:1696–1703.

———. *Retractationum. PL* 32:583–656.

———. *The Teacher, The Free Choice of the Will, and Grace and Free Will.* Trans. Robert P. Russell. Washington: The Fathers of the Church, vol. 59, 1968.

———. *Treatises on Marriage and Other Subjects*. Ed. Roy J. Deferrari. Washington: The Fathers of the Church, vol. 27, 1955.

———. *De Trinitate. PL* 42:819–1098.

Bacon, Roger. *Moralis Philosophia*. Ed. F. Delorme and E. Massa. Turin: In Aedibus Thesauri Mundi, 1953.

———. *Opus Maius*. Ed. John Henry Bridges. 2 vols. Oxford: The Clarendon Press, 1897.

[Bartholomaeus Anglicus.] *On the Properties of Things: John Trevisa's Translation of Bartholomaeus Anglicus "De Proprietatibus Rerum"*. Gen. ed. M. C. Seymour. 2 vols. Oxford: The Clarendon Press, 1975.

Bede. *In Matthaei Evangelium Expositio. PL* 92:9–132.

Benedict. *Regula*. Ed. Rudolphus Hanslik. Vienna: Corpus Scriptorum Ecclesiasticorum Latinorum, vol. 75, 1960.

[———.] *St. Benedict's Rule for Monasteries*. Trans. Leonard J. Doyle. Collegeville, MN: The Liturgical Press, 1948.

[———.] *Three Middle-English Versions of the Rule of St. Benet*. Ed. Ernst A. Kock. 1902, EETS o.s. 120.

Bernard of Clairvaux. *De Diligendo Deo. PL* 182:973–1000.

———. *On the Necessity of Loving God*. Ed. Anton C. Pegis. *The Wisdom of Catholicism*. New York: Random House, 1949.

———. *Sermones super Cantica Canticorum. Opera*. Ed. J. Leclercq, C. H. Talbot, and H. M. Rochais. 3 vols. Rome: Editiones Cistercienses, 1957.

Biblia Sacra. Madrid: Biblioteca de Autores Christianos, 1965.

Boccaccio, Giovanni. *The Fates of Illustrious Men*. Trans. Louis Brewer Hall. New York: Ungar, 1965.

———. *Life of Dante*. Trans. G. R. Carpenter. New York: The Grolier Club, 1900.

The Book of the Knight of La Tour-Landry. Ed. Thomas Wright. 1868; rev. 1906, EETS o.s. 33.

The Book of Vices and Virtues: A Fourteenth Century English Translation of the "Somme le Roi" of Lorens d'Orléans. Ed. W. Nelson Francis. 1942, EETS o.s. 217.

Brinton, Thomas. *Sermons, 1373–1389*. Ed. Mary Aquinas Devlin. Camden Third Series, nos. 85–86, 1954.

Bromyard, John. *Summa Praedicantium*. Basel, 1484.

Burton, Robert. *The Anatomy of Melancholy*. Ed. Floyd Dell and Paul Jordan-Smith. New York: Farrar and Rinehart, 1927.

Caesarius of Heisterbach. *Dialogus Miraculorum*. Ed. Josephus Strange. 2 vols. Cologne: Lempertz, 1851.

Cassian, John. *Conlationes XXIV*. Ed. Michael Petschenig. Vienna: Corpus Scriptorum Ecclesiasticorum Latinorum, vol. 13, 1886.

———. *De Institutis Coenobiorum et De Octo Principalium Vitiorum Remediis Libri XII*. Ed. Michael Petchenig. Vienna: Corpus Scriptorum Ecclesiasticorum Latinorum, vol. 17, 1888.

[———.] *The Works of John Cassian*. Trans. Edgar C. S. Gibson. *A Select Library of the Nicene and Post-Nicene Fathers*. Gen. eds. Philip Schaff and Henry Wace. New York: The Christian Literature Company, 1894. Vol. 11, pp. 161–641.

[Cato.] *The Distichs of Cato: A Famous Medieval Textbook*. Trans. Wayland

Johnson Chase. Madison: University of Wisconsin Studies in the Social Sciences and History, no. 7, 1922.

Chartularium Universitatis Parisiensis. Ed. H. Denifle and E. Chatelain. Paris: Delalain, 1889.

[Chaucer, Geoffrey.] *The Works of Geoffrey Chaucer.* Ed. F. N.Robinson. 2nd. ed. Boston: Houghton Mifflin, 1957.

Chaucer Life-Record. Ed. Martin M. Crow and Clair C. Olson. Oxford: The Clarendon Press, 1966.

Cicero. *De Re Publica.* Trans. Clinton Walker Keyes. New York: Loeb Classical Library, 1928.

———. *Tusculan Disputations.* Trans. J. E. King. Cambridge, MA: Loeb Classical Library, 1945.

The Cloud of Unknowing and The Book of Privy Counselling. Ed. Phyllis Hodgson. 1944, EETS o.s. 218.

The Conflict of Wit and Will: Fragments of a Middle English Alliterative Poem. Ed. Bruce Dickins. Kendal: Leeds School of English Language Texts and Monographs, no. 4, 1937.

Cursor Mundi. Ed. Richard Morris. 1874–93, EETS o.s. 57, 59, 62, 66, 68, 99, 101.

Dante Alighieri. *The Divine Comedy.* Trans. John D. Sinclair. 3 vols. 1939; rpt. Oxford: Oxford University Press, 1961.

Denis le Chartreux. *Summa de Vitiis et Virtutibus. Opera Omnia.* Montreuil, 1910.

Dives and Pauper. Ed. Priscilla Heath Barnum. 1976, EETS o.s. 275.

Dunbar, William. *Poems.* Ed. W. Mackay Mackenzie. 1932; rpt. London: Faber and Faber, 1970.

Early Middle English Verse and Prose. Ed. J. A. W. Bennett and G. V. Smithers. Oxford: The Clarendon Press, 1968.

English Lyrics of the XIIIth Century. Ed. Carleton Brown. Oxford: The Clarendon Press, 1932.

Epictetus. *The Discourses.* Trans. W. A. Oldfather. 2 vols. New York: Loeb Classical Library, 1926–28.

Erthe upon Erthe. Ed. Hilda M. R. Murray. 1911, EETS o.s. 141.

"Die Evangelien-Geschichten der Homiliensammlung des Ms. Vernon." Ed. Carl Horstmann. *Archiv für das Studium der Neueren Sprachen und Literaturen*, 57 (1877), 241–316.

Firumbras and Otuel and Roland. Ed. Mary Isabelle O'Sullivan. 1935, EETS o.s. 198.

Fortescue, Sir John. *De Laudibus Legum Angliae.* Trans. Francis Gregor. London: Sweet and Maxwell, 1917.

Geoffrey of Vinsauf. *Poetria Nova.* Trans. Margaret F. Nims. Toronto: Pontifical Institute of Mediaeval Studies, 1967.

Giraldus Cambrensis. *Gemma Ecclesiastica.* Ed. J. S. Brewer. 2 vols. London: The Rolls Series, 1862.

Glossa Ordinaria. PL 113 and 114.

Gower, John. *The Complete Works: The Latin Works.* Ed. G. C. Macaulay. 2 vols. Oxford: The Clarendon Press, 1902.

———. *The English Works.* Ed. G. C. Macaulay. 1900–01, EETS e.s. 81 and 82.

Gregory the Great. *Moralia in Job. PL* 75 : 509–1162 and 76 : 9–782.

[Grosseteste, Robert]. *Roberti Grosseteste Epistolae.* Ed. H. R. Luard. London: The Rolls Series, 1861.

Guillaume de Lorris and Jean de Meun. *Le Roman de la rose.* Ed. Félix Lecoy. 3 vols. Paris: Champion, 1970.

Henry of Bracton. *De Legibus et Consuetudinibus Angliae.* Ed. George E. Woodbine. Trans. Samuel E. Thorne. Cambridge, MA: Harvard University Press, 1968.

Henry of Lancaster. *Le Livre de seyntz medicines.* Ed. E. J. Arnould. Oxford: Anglo-Norman Text Society, no. 2, 1940.

Henryson, Robert. *The Poems.* Ed. Denton Fox. Oxford: The Clarendon Press, 1981.

Hesiod. *The Homeric Hymns and Homerica.* Trans. Hugh G. Evelyn-White. Cambridge, MA: Loeb Classical Library, 1914.

[Hilton, Walter.] *An Exposition of Qui Habitat and Bonum Est in English.* Ed. Björn Wallner. Lund Studies in English, no. 23, 1954.

———. *The Scale of Perfection.* Ed. Evelyn Underhill. London: Watkins, 1923.

[Hoccleve, Thomas.] *Hoccleve's Works: The Minor Poems.* Ed. Frederick J. Furnivall and I. Gollancz. 1892–97, rev. Jerome Mitchell and A. I. Doyle, 1970, EETS e.s. 61 and 73.

———. *Hoccleve's Works: The Regement of Princes.* Ed. Frederick J. Furnivall. 1897, EETS e.s. 72.

The Holy Bible: Translated from the Latin Vulgate [Douay-Rheims]. London: Catholic Truth Society, 1956.

Horace. *Satires, Epistles and Ars Poetica.* Trans. H. Rushton Fairclough. Cambridge, MA: Loeb Classical Library, 1926.

The Hours of the Divine Office in English and Latin. 3 vols. Collegeville, MN: The Liturgical Press, 1963.

Hugh of St. Victor. *De Sacramentis Christianae Fidei.* PL 176:173–618.

Huon de Mery. *Li Tournoiemenz Antecrit.* Ed. Georg Wimmer. Marburg: Ausgaben und Abhandlungen aus dem Gebiete der Romanischen Philologie, no. 76, 1888.

Hymns to the Virgin and Christ. Ed. Frederick J. Furnivall. 1867, EETS o.s. 24.

Innocent III. *De Contemptu Mundi.* PL 217:701–46.

Ivo of Chartres. *Recueil des Historiens des Gaules et de la France.* Rev. ed. Léopold Delisle. Paris: Victor Palmé, 1878. Vol. 15.

Jacob's Well: An English Treatise on the Cleansing of Man's Conscience. Ed. Arthur Brandeis. 1900, EETS o.s. 115.

[Jean d'Arras.] *Melusine.* Ed. A. K. Donald. 1895, EETS e.s. 68.

Jean de Joinville. *Histoire de Saint Louis. Recueil des Historiens des Gaules et de la France.* Paris: Daunou and Naudet, 1840. Vol. 20.

John of the Cross. *Dark Night of the Soul.* Trans. E. Allison Peers. New York: Doubleday, 1959.

———. *Noche Oscura. Vida y Obras de San Juan de la Cruz.* Ed. Crisogono de Jesus. Madrid: Biblioteca de Autores Cristianos, 1964.

[John of Salisbury.] *Ioannis Saresberiensis Episcopi Carnotensis Policratici siue de Nugis Curialium et Vestigiis Pilosophorum Libri VIII.* Ed. C. C. I. Webb. Oxford: The Clarendon Press, 1909.

John Duns Scotus. *Opus Oxoniense [Commentaria Oxoniensia]*. Ed. M. F. Garcia. 3 vols. Quaracchi: Collegium S. Bonaventurae, 1912–14.

Jonas of Orléans. *De Institutione Laicali. PL* 106:121–278.

[Julian of Norwich]. *A Book of Showings of the Anchoress Julian of Norwich*. Ed. Edmund Colledge and James Walsh. Toronto: Pontifical Institute of Medieval Studies, no. 35, 1978.

———. *Revelations of Divine Love*. Trans. and intro. Clifton Wolters. Harmondsworth: Penguin, 1966.

[Kempe, Margery.] *The Book of Margery Kempe*. Ed. Sanford Brown Meech and Hope Emily Allen. 1940, EETS o.s. 212.

[Knighton, Henry.] *Chronicon vel Monachi Leycestrensis*. Ed. Joseph Rawson Lumby. London: Rolls Series, 1895.

The Liber Albus of the Priory of Worcester. Ed. James Maurice Wilson. London: Worcestershire Historical Society, 1919.

Liber de Modo Bene Vivendi. PL 184:1199–1306.

Love, Nicholas. *The Mirrour of the Blessed Lyf of Jesu Christ*. Ed. Lawrence F. Powell. Oxford: The Clarendon Press, 1908.

Lydgate, John. *The Assembly of Gods*. Ed. Oscar Lovell Triggs. 1896, EETS e.s. 69.

———. *Lydgate's Minor Poems: The Two Nightingale Poems*. Ed. Otto Glauning. 1900, EETS e.s. 80.

———. *The Pilgrimage of the Life of Man*. Ed. F. J. Furnivall and Katherine B. Locock. 1899–1904, EETS e.s. 77, 83 and 92.

———. *Reson and Sensuallyte*. Ed. Ernst Sieper. 1901–03, EETS e.s. 84 and 89.

The Macro Plays. Ed. Mark Eccles. 1969, EETS o.s. 262.

Macrobius. *Commentary on the Dream of Scipio*. Trans. W. H. Stahl. New York: Columbia University Press, 1952.

Mandeville's Travels. Ed. M. C. Seymour. Oxford: The Clarendon Press, 1967.

Matthew Paris. *Chronica Majora*. Ed. Henry Richards Luard. 7 vols. London: The Rolls Series, 1872–83.

Dan Michel. *Ayenbite of Inwyt*. Ed. Richard Morris, 1866, rev. Pamela Gradon, 1965, EETS o.s. 23.

Middle English Sermons. Ed. Woodburn O. Ross. 1940, EETS o.s. 209.

"Mittelenglische Todesgedichte." Ed. Karl Brunner. *Archiv für das Studium der neueren Sprachen*, 167 (1935), 30–35.

Mum and the Sothsegger. Ed. Mabel Day and Robert Steele. 1936, EETS o.s. 199.

[Myrc, John.] *Myrc's Duties of a Parish Priest*. Ed. Edward Peacock. 1868, EETS o.s. 31.

Pecock, Reginald. *The Folewer to the Donet*. Ed. Elsie Vaughan Hitchcock. 1924, EETS o.s. 164.

Peraldus, William. *Summa de Vitiis et Virtutibus*. Antwerp, 1587.

Peter John Olivi. *Quaestiones in Secundum Librum Sententiarum*. Quaracchi: Collegium S. Bonaventurae, 1922–26.

Peter Lombard. *Sententiarum Libri Quatuor. PL* 192:519–962.

[Petrarca.] *Petrarch's Secret, or The Soul's Conflict with Passion*. Trans. William H. Draper. London: Chatto & Windus, 1911.

Philippe de Navarre. *Les Quatre Ages de l'homme*. Ed. Marcel de Fréville. Paris: Firmin Didot, 1888.

Rabanus Maurus. *Allegoriae in Universam Sacram Scripturam*. PL 112: 849–1088.

——. *De Ecclesiastica Disciplina*. PL 112:1191–1262.

Rhetorica ad Herennium. Trans. Harry Caplan. Cambridge, MA: Loeb Classical Library, 1954.

Rolle, Richard. *English Prose Treatises of Richard Rolle de Hampole*. Ed. George G. Perry. 1866, rev. 1921, EETS o.s. 20.

——. *English Writings of Richard Rolle, Hermit of Hampole*. Ed. Hope Emily Allen. Oxford: The Clarendon Press, 1931.

——. *Yorkshire Writers: Richard Rolle of Hampole and His Followers*. Ed. C. Horstman. 2 vols. London: Swan Sonnenschein, 1895.

The Romance of Emaré. Re-ed. Edith Rickert. 1906, EETS e.s. 99.

Rotuli Parliamentorum. 4 vols. London, 1783.

Ruysbroeck, John. *Love's Gradatory*. Trans. Mother St. Jerome. London: Washbourne, 1915.

Rymer. *Foedera*. Ed. Adam Clarke and Frederick Holbrooke. London: Great Britain Public Records Com., 1816.

Simon de Tournai. *Disputationes*. Ed. Joseph Warichez. Louvain: Spicilegium Sacrum Lovaniense, 1932.

La Somme le Roy. Ed. Eric George Millar. Oxford: The Roxburghe Club, 1953.

Songe du Castel. Ed. Roberta D. Cornelius. *PMLA*, 46 (1931), 321–32.

Suso, Henry. "*Orologium Sapientiae*, or The Seven Poyntes of Trewe Wisdom." Trans. William Caxton. Ed. Karl Horstmann. *Anglia*, 10 (1888), 323–89.

[Teresa of Jesus.] *The Life, Relations, Maxims and Foundations*. Ed. John J. Burke. New York: Columbus Press, 1911.

Tertullian. *On Prescription against Heretics. The Ante-Nicene Fathers*. Ed. Alexander Roberts and James Donaldson. Buffalo: The Christian Literature Publishing Co., 1885.

[Thomas Aquinas.] *Aquinas: Selected Political Writings*. Ed. A. P. D'Entrèves. Trans. J. G. Dawson. Oxford: Blackwell, 1954.

——. *Opera Omnia*. 25 vols. Parma, 1852–73.

——. *The Political Ideas of St. Thomas Aquinas: Representative Selections*. Ed. Dino Bigongiari. New York: Hafner, 1953.

——. *Summa Theologiae*. 60 vols. New York: McGraw-Hill, 1964.

Thomas à Kempis. *The Earliest English Translation of the First Three Books of the "De Imitatione Christi"*. Ed. John K. Ingram. 1893, EETS e.s. 63.

Thoreau, Henry David. *Walden, or Life in the Woods*. New York: Collier, 1962.

Tractatus de Ordine Vitae. PL 184:559–84.

The Tretyse of Love. Ed. John H. Fisher. 1951, EETS o.s. 223.

Twenty-Six Political and Other Poems. Ed. J. Kail. 1904, EETS o.s. 124.

Walsingham, Thomas. *Historia Anglicana*. Ed. Henry Thomas Riley. 2 vols. London: The Rolls Series, 1863–64.

[Wimbledon, Thomas.] *Wimbledon's Sermon "Redde Rationem Villicationis Tue": A Middle English Sermon of the Fourteenth Century*. Ed. Ione Kemp Knight. Pittsburgh: Duquesne University Press, 1967.

Winner and Waster. Ed. Israel Gollancz. London: Oxford University Press, 1930.

Wyclif, John. *Selected English Works.* Ed. Thomas A. Arnold. 3 vols. Oxford: The Clarendon Press, 1869–71.

——. *Tractatus de Officio Regis.* Ed. Alfred W. Pollard and Charles Sayle. London: Trübner, 1887.

——. *Trialogus.* Ed. Gotthard Lechler. Oxford: The Clarendon Press, 1869.

IV. Scholarly Studies

Abse, D. Wilfred. *Speech and Reason.* Charlottesville: University Press of Virginia, 1971.

Adams, Marilyn McCord. "Intuitive Cognition, Certainty, and Scepticism in William Ockham." *Traditio,* 26 (1970), 389–98.

Adams, Robert. "The Nature of Need in *Piers Plowman* XX." *Traditio,* 34 (1978), 273–301.

Aers, David. *Chaucer, Langland and the Creative Imagination.* London: Routledge & Kegan Paul, 1980.

Alexander, Archibald. *Theories of Will in the History of Philosophy.* New York: Charles Scribner's Sons, 1898.

Alford, John A. "The Role of the Quotations in *Piers Plowman.*" *Speculum,* 52 (1977), 80–99.

——. "Some Unidentified Quotations in *Piers Plowman.*" *MP,* 72 (1974/75), 390–99.

Allen, Judson Boyce. *The Friar as Critic: Literary Attitudes in the Later Middle Ages.* Nashville: Vanderbilt University Press, 1971.

——. "Langland's Reading and Writing: *Detractor* and the Pardon Passus." *Speculum,* 59 (1984), 342–62.

Ames, Ruth M. *The Fulfillment of Scriptures: Abraham, Moses, and Piers.* Evanston: Northwestern University Press, 1970.

Anderson, Judith H. *The Growth of a Personal Voice: "Piers Plowman" and "The Faerie Queene".* New Haven: Yale University Press, 1976.

Anson, Peter F. *The Call of the Desert: The Solitary Life in the Christian Church.* London: S.P.C.K., 1964.

Arbesmann, Rudolph. "The *Daemonium Meridianum* and Greek and Latin Patristic Exegesis." *Traditio,* 14 (1958), 17–31.

Arendt, Hannah. *The Life of the Mind. Volume II: Willing.* New York: Harcourt Brace Jovanovich, 1978.

Arnheim, Rudolf. *Entropy and Art: An Essay on Disorder and Order.* Berkeley: University of California Press, 1971.

Arway, Robert J. "A Half-Century of Research on Godfrey of Fontaines." *New Scholasticism,* 36, 2 (1962), 192–218.

Baker, Denise N. "From Plowing to Penitence: *Piers Plowman* and Fourteenth-Century Theology." *Speculum,* 55 (1980), 715–25.

Baldwin, Anna P. *The Theme of Government in "Piers Plowman".* Cambridge: Brewer, 1981.

Barney, Stephen A. "The Ploughshare of the Tongue: The Progress of a Symbol from the Bible to *Piers Plowman.*" *MS,* 35 (1973), 261–93.

Baugh, Albert C. "The Middle English Romance: Some Questions of Creation, Presentation, and Preservation." *Speculum,* 42 (1967), 1–31.

Bennett, J. A. W. *Chaucer at Oxford and at Cambridge*. Oxford: Oxford University Press, 1974.

Benson, C. David. "An Augustinian Irony in *Piers Plowman*." *N&Q*, n.s. 23 (1976), 51–54.

Benson, Larry D. *Art and Tradition in "Sir Gawain and the Green Knight"*. New Brunswick, NJ: Rutgers University Press, 1965.

——— and Siegfried Wenzel (eds.). *The Wisdom of Poetry: Essays in Early English Literature in Honor of Morton W. Bloomfield*. Kalamazoo: Medieval Institute, 1982.

Berndt, David E. "Monastic *Acedia* and Chaucer's Characterization of Daun Piers." *SP*, 68 (1971), 435–50.

Bernheimer, Richard. *Wild Men in the Middle Ages: A Study in Art, Sentiment, and Demonology*. Cambridge, MA: Harvard University Press, 1952.

Bettoni, Efrem. *Duns Scotus: The Basic Principles of His Philosophy*. Trans. Bernadino Bonansea. Washington: The Catholic University of America Press, 1961.

Blanch, Robert J. (ed.). *Style and Symbolism in Piers Plowman: A Modern Critical Anthology*. Knoxville: University of Tennessee Press, 1969.

Bloomfield, Morton W. *Essays and Explorations*. Cambridge, MA: Harvard University Press, 1970.

———. *Piers Plowman as a Fourteenth-Century Apocalypse*. New Brunswick, NJ: Rutgers University Press, 1962.

———. *The Seven Deadly Sins: An Introduction to the History of a Religious Concept with Special Reference to Medieval English Literature*. East Lansing: Michigan State College Press, 1952.

———. "Was William Langland a Benedictine Monk?". *MLQ*, 4 (1943), 57–61.

Bourke, V. J. "Will." *New Catholic Encyclopedia*, Vol. 14, pp. 909–13.

———. *Will in Western Thought: An Historico-Critical Survey*. New York: Sheed and Ward, 1964.

Bruyne, Edgar de. *Etudes d'esthétique médiévale*. 3 vols. Brugge: De Tempel, 1946.

Bundy, Murray Wright. *The Theory of Imagination in Classical and Medieval Thought*. Urbana: University of Illinois Studies in Language and Literature, no. 12, 1927.

Burdach, Konrad. "Der Dichter des Ackermann aus Böhmen und seine Zeit." *Vom Mittelalter zur Reformation: Forschungen zur Geschichte der Deutschen Bildung*. Berlin: Weidmannsche, 1932.

Burrow, John A. "The Action of Langland's Second Vision." *Style and Symbolism in Piers Plowman*. Ed. Blanch, pp. 209–27.

———. "The Audience of *Piers Plowman*." *Anglia*, 75 (1957), 373–84.

——— (ed.). *Geoffrey Chaucer: A Critical Anthology*. Baltimore: Penguin, 1969.

———. "Langland *Nel Mezzo Del Cammin*." *Medieval Studies for J. A. W. Bennett*. Oxford: The Clarendon Press, 1981, pp. 21–41.

———. *Richardian Poetry*. New Haven: Yale University Press, 1971.

———. "Words, Works and Will: Theme and Structure in *Piers Plowman*." *Piers Plowman: Critical Approaches*. Ed. S. S. Hussey, pp. 111–24.

Caillois, Roger. "Les Démons de midi." *Revue de l'Histoire des Religions*, 115 (1937), 142–72; 116 (1937), 54–83 and 143–86.

Callus, Daniel A. (ed.). *Robert Grosseteste: Scholar and Bishop.* Oxford: The Clarendon Press, 1955.

Cantor, Norman F. *Medieval History.* New York: Macmillan, 1963.

Cargill, Oscar. "The Date of the A-Text of *Piers Plowman.*" *PMLA,* 47 (1932), 354–62.

Carlyle, R. W. and A. J. *A History of Mediaeval Political Theory.* 6 vols. Edinburgh and London: William Blackwood, 1903–36.

Carruthers, Mary. *The Search for St. Truth: A Study of Meaning in Piers Plowman.* Evanston: Northwestern University Press, 1973.

——— and Elizabeth D. Kirk. (eds.). *Acts of Interpretation, The Text in Its Context 700–1600: Essays in Honor of E. Talbot Donaldson.* Norman, OK: Pilgrim, 1982.

Chadwick, Owen. *John Cassian.* 2nd ed. Cambridge: Cambridge University Press, 1968.

Chambers, R. W. *Man's Unconquerable Mind.* London: Jonathan Cape, 1939.

Clark, David W. "William of Ockham on Right Reason." *Speculum,* 48 (1973), 13–36.

Clarke, Edwin and Kenneth Dewhurst. *An Illustrated History of the Brain Function.* Oxford: Sandford, 1972.

Clay, Rotha Mary. *The Hermits and Anchorites of England.* London: Methuen, 1914.

Coghill, Nevill K. "God's Wenches and the Light That Spoke (Some Notes on Langland's Kind of Poetry)." *English and Medieval Studies Presented to J.R.R. Tolkien.* Eds. Norman Davis and C. L. Wrenn. London: Allen & Unwin, 1962, pp. 200–18.

———. "The Pardon of Piers Plowman." *Proceedings of the British Academy,* 30 (1944), 303–57.

Cohen, Kathleen. *Metamorphosis of a Death Symbol: The Transi Tomb in the Later Middle Ages and the Renaissance.* Berkeley: University of California Press, 1973.

Cohn, Norman. *The Pursuit of the Millennium: Revolutionary Millenarians and Mystical Anarchists of the Middle Ages.* Rev. ed. New York: Oxford University Press, 1970.

Coleman, Janet. *Medieval Readers and Writers, 1350–1400.* New York: Columbia University Press, 1981.

———. *Piers Plowman and the "Moderni".* Rome: Edizioni di Storia e Letteratura, 1981.

Copleston, F. C. *A History of Medieval Philosophy.* New York: Harper & Row, 1972.

———. *A History of Philosophy.* 8 vols. Rev. ed. Westminster: Newman, 1950.

Coulton, G. G. "Theological Schools in Medieval England." *Church Quarterly Review,* 118 (1934), 98–101.

Courtenay, William J. *Adam Wodeham: An Introduction to His Life and Writings.* Leiden: Brill, 1978.

———. "Covenant and Causality in Pierre d'Ailly." *Speculum,* 46 (1971), 94–119.

———. "The Critique on Natural Causality in the Mutakallimum and Nominalism." *HTR,* 66 (1973), 77–94.

———. "The Effect of the Black Death on English Higher Education." *Speculum*, 55 (1980), 696–714.

———. "John Mirecourt and Gregory of Rimini on Whether God Can Undo the Past." *Recherches de Théologie ancienne et médiévale*, 39 (1972), 224–56 and 40 (1973), 147–74.

———. "Nominalism and Late Medieval Religion." *The Pursuit of Holiness*. Ed. Trinkaus and Oberman, pp. 26–59.

———. "Nominalism and Late Medieval Thought: A Bibliographical Essay." *Theological Studies*, 33 (1972), 716–34.

Crombie, A. C. *Robert Grosseteste and the Origins of Experimental Science, 1100–1700*. Oxford: The Clarendon Press, 1953.

Cross, Claire. "'Great Reasoners in Scripture': The Activities of Woman Lollards, 1380–1530." *Medieval Women*. Ed. Derek Baker. Oxford: Blackwell, 1978, pp. 359–80.

Curry, Walter Clyde. *Chaucer and the Mediaeval Sciences*. 2nd. ed. rev. London: Allen & Unwin, 1960.

Curtius, Ernst Robert. *European Literature and the Latin Middle Ages*. Trans. Willard R. Trask. New York: Pantheon, 1953.

D'Ardenne, S.T.R.O. "Me bi-fel a ferly, A Feyrie me þouhte (*PPL*. A. Prol. 6)." *English Studies Presented to R. W. Zandvoort*. Amsterdam: Swets & Zeitlinger, 1964, pp.143–45.

Darwin, Francis D.S. *The English Mediaeval Recluse*. London: S.P.C.K., n.d.

Day, Mabel. "Duns Scotus and *Piers Plowman*." *RES*, 3 (1928), 333–34.

Delaney, Sheila. *Chaucer's "House of Fame": The Poetics of Skeptical Fideism*. Chicago: University of Chicago Press, 1972.

Denomy, A. J. "The *De Amore* of Andreas Capellanus and the Condemnation of 1277." *MS*, 8 (1946), 107–49.

D'Entrèves, Alexander Passerin. *The Medieval Contribution to Political Thought: Thomas Aquinas, Marsilius of Padua, Richard Hooker*. Oxford: Oxford University Press, 1939.

D'Evelyn, Charlotte. "Instructions for Religious." *A Manual of the Writings in Middle English, 1050–1500*. Ed. J. Burke Severs. New Haven: The Connecticut Academy of Arts and Sciences, 1970, pp. 458–81 and 650–59.

Dickinson, John. "The Medieval Conception of Kingship and Some of Its Limitations, as Developed in the *Policraticus* of John of Salisbury." *Speculum*, 1 (1926), 308–37.

DiMarco, Vincent. *Piers Plowman: A Reference Guide*. Boston: G. K. Hall, 1982.

Donaldson, E. Talbot. *Piers Plowman: The C-Text and Its Poet*. 1949; rpt. London: Frank Cass, 1966.

Donna, Rose Bernard. *Despair and Hope: A Study in Langland and Augustine*. Washington: The Catholic University of America Press, 1948.

Doob, Penelope B. R. *Nebuchadnezzar's Children: Conventions of Madness in Middle English Literature*. New Haven: Yale University Press, 1974.

Du Boulay, F. R. H. *An Age of Ambition: English Society in the Late Middle Ages*. London: Nelson, 1970.

——— and Caroline M. Barron (eds.). *The Reign of Richard II*. London: Athlone, 1971.

Dunning, T. P. *Piers Plowman: An Interpretation of the A-Text*. London: Longmans, 1937.

Edwards, Kathleen. *The English Secular Cathedrals in the Middle Ages.* 2nd ed. rev. Manchester: Manchester University Press, 1967.

Emden, A. B. *A Biographical Register of the University of Oxford to A.D. 1500.* 3 vols. Oxford: The Clarendon Press, 1957–59.

Empson, William. *Seven Types of Ambiguity.* 3rd ed. rev. London: Chatto and Windus, 1953.

Erickson, Carolly. *The Medieval Vision: Essays in History and Perception.* New York: Oxford University Press, 1976.

Erzgräber, Willi. *Neues Handbuch der Literatur Wissenschaft.* Vol 8: *Europäisches Spätmittelalter.* Wiesbaden: Athenaion, 1978, pp. 231–39.

———. *William Langlands "Piers Plowman": Eine Interpretation des C-Textes.* Heidelberg: Carl Winter, 1957.

Faral, Edmond. "Jean Buridan." *Histoire Littéraire de la France,* 38 (1949), 462–605.

Fergusson, Francis. *Dante.* New York: Macmillan, 1966.

Fleming, John V. "*The Dream of the Rood* and Anglo-Saxon Monasticism." *Traditio,* 22 (1966), 43–72.

———. *An Introduction to the Franciscan Literature of the Middle Ages.* Chicago: Franciscan Herald Press, 1977.

Fowler, David C. *Piers the Plowman: Literary Relations of the A and B Texts.* Seattle: University of Washington Press, 1961.

———. "Poetry and the Liberal Arts: The Oxford Background of *Piers the Plowman.*" *Arts Libéraux et philosophie au moyen âge.* Paris: Vrin, 1969, pp. 715–19.

Frank, Robert W., Jr. "The Conclusion of *Piers Plowman.*" *JEGP,* 49 (1950), 309–16.

———. "The Number of Visions in *Piers Plowman.*" *MLN,* 66 (1951), 309–12.

———. *Piers Plowman and the Scheme of Salvation.* New Haven: Yale University Press, 1957.

Friedman, John Block. "Eurydice, Heurodis, and the Noon-day Demon." *Speculum,* 41 (1966), 22–29.

———. *Orpheus in the Middle Ages.* Cambridge, MA: Harvard University Press, 1970.

Frye, Northrop. *Anatomy of Criticism: Four Essays.* 1957; rpt. New York: Atheneum, 1969.

———. *The Great Code: The Bible and Literature.* New York: Harcourt Brace Jovanovich, 1982.

Gaffney, Wilbur. "The Allegory of the Christ-Knight in *Piers Plowman.*" *PMLA,* 46 (1931), 155–68.

Gibson, Gail McMurray. *The Images of Doubt and Belief: Visual Symbolism in the Middle English Plays of Joseph's Troubles about Mary.* Diss. University of Virginia, 1975.

Gierke, Otto. *Political Theories of the Middle Ages.* Trans. F. W. Maitland. Cambridge: The University Press, 1922.

Gilby, Thomas. *The Political Thought of Thomas Aquinas.* Chicago: University of Chicago Press, 1958.

Gilson, Etienne. *History of Christian Philosophy in the Middle Ages.* New York: Random House, 1955.

———. *The Mystical Theology of Saint Bernard*. Trans. A.H.C. Downes. London: Sheed and Ward, 1940.

———. *Reason and Revelation in the Middle Ages*. New York: Scribner, 1938.

Glorieux, P. *La Littérature Quodlibétique*. Paris: Vrin, 1925.

Gray, Douglas. *Themes and Images in the Medieval English Religious Lyric*. London: Routledge & Kegan Paul, 1972.

Green, Richard Firth. *Poets and Princepleasers: Literature and the English Court in the Late Middle Ages*. Toronto: University of Toronto Press, 1980.

Hardison, O. B., Jr. *Christian Rite and Christian Drama in the Middle Ages*. Baltimore: The Johns Hopkins University Press, 1965.

Harvey, Barbara F. "The Monks of Westminster and the University of Oxford." *The Reign of Richard II*. Ed. F.R.H. Du Boulay and Caroline M. Barron. London: The Athlone Press, 1971.

Harwood, Britton J. "Imaginative in *Piers Plowman*." *MÆ*, 44 (1975), 249–63.

———. "*Liberum-Arbitrium* in the C-Text of *Piers Plowman*." *PQ*, 52 (1973), 680–95.

———. "*Piers Plowman*: Fourteenth-Century Skepticism and the Theology of Suffering." *Bucknell Review*, 19, 3 (1971), 119–36.

Hemingway, Samuel B. "The Two St. Pauls." *MLN*, 32 (1917), 57–58.

Hench, Atcheson L. "The Allegorical Motif of Conscience and Reason, Counsellors." Charlottesville, VA: University of Virginia Studies, 4 (1951), 193–201.

Hieatt, Constance B. *The Realism of Dream Visions: The Poetic Exploitation of the Dream-Experience in Chaucer and His Contemporaries*. Paris: Mouton, 1967.

Highfield, Roger. *The Early Rolls of Merton College*. Oxford: The Clarendon Press, 1964.

Hoffman, Richard L. "The Burning of 'Boke' in *Piers Plowman*." *MLQ*, 25 (1964), 57–65.

Hort, Greta. *Piers Plowman and Contemporary Religious Thought*. London: S.P.C.K., 1938.

———. *Sense and Thought: A Study in Mysticism*. London: Allen & Unwin, 1936.

———. "Theological Schools in Medieval England." *Church Quarterly Review*, 116 (1933), 201–18.

Howard, Donald R. *The Idea of the Canterbury Tales*. Berkeley: University of California Press, 1976.

———. *The Three Temptations: Medieval Man in Search of the World*. Princeton: Princeton University Press, 1966.

Huizinga, Johan. *Homo Ludens: A Study of the Play-Element in Culture*. 1950; rpt. Boston: The Beacon Press, 1955.

———. *The Waning of the Middle Ages*. Trans. F. Hopman. 1924; rpt. Harmondsworth: Penguin, 1955.

Hussey, S.S. (ed.). *Piers Plowman: Critical Approaches*. London: Methuen, 1969.

Jack, A. S. "The Autobiographical Elements in *Piers the Plowman*." *JGPh*, 3 (1901), 393–414.

James, Stanley B. "The Mad Poet of Malvern: William Langland." *Month*, 159 (1932), 221–27.

Jenkins, Priscilla. "Conscience: The Frustration of Allegory." *Critical Approaches*. Ed. Hussey, pp. 125–42.

Jones, Rufus M. *The Flowering of Mysticism: The Friends of God in the Fourteenth Century*. New York: Macmillan, 1939.

Jordan, Robert M. *Chaucer and the Shape of Creation: The Aesthetic Possiblities of Inorganic Structure*. Cambridge, MA: Harvard University Press, 1967.

Josipovici, Gabriel. *The World and the Book*. London: Macmillan, 1971.

Jungmann, Joseph A. *The Mass of the Roman Rite, Its Origins and Development*. Trans. F. A. Brunner. 2 vols. New York: Benziger, 1951–55.

Jusserand, J. J. *Piers Plowman: A Contribution to the History of English Mysticism*. Trans. and rev. by the author. London: Unwin, 1894.

Kane, George. *The Autobiographical Fallacy in Chaucer and Langland Studies*. London: H. K. Lewis, 1965.

————. *Middle English Literature: A Critical Study of the Romances, the Religious Lyrics, "Piers Plowman"*. London: Methuen, 1951.

————. *Piers Plowman: The Evidence for Authorship*. London: The Athlone Press, 1965.

Kantorowicz, Ernst H. *The King's Two Bodies: A Study in Mediaeval Political Theology*. Princeton: Princeton University Press, 1957.

Kaske, R. E. "Patristic Exegesis in the Criticism of Medieval Literature: The Defense." *Interpretations of Piers Plowman*. Ed. Vasta, pp. 319–38.

————. "The Speech of 'Book' in *Piers Plowman*." *Anglia*, 77 (1959), 117–44.

Katzenellenbogen, Adolf. *Allegories of the Virtues and Vices in Mediaeval Art from Early Christian Times to the Thirteenth Century*. London: The Warburg Institute, 1939.

Kean, P. M. "Justice, Kingship and the Good Life in the Second Part of *Piers Plowman*." *Critical Approaches*. Ed. Hussey, pp. 76–110.

————. "Love, Law, and *Lewte* in *Piers Plowman*." *Style and Symbolism*. Ed. Blanch, pp. 132–55.

Keen, Maurice. "Huizinga, Kilgour and the Decline of Chivalry." *Medievalia et Humanistica*. Ed. Paul Maurice Clogan. Cambridge: The University Press, 1977, pp. 1–20.

Kermode, Frank. *The Sense of an Ending: Studies in the Theory of Fiction*. New York: Oxford University Press, 1967.

Kirk, Elizabeth D. *The Dream Thought of "Piers Plowman"*. New Haven: Yale University Press, 1972.

Klibansky, Raymond, Erwin Panofsky and Fritz Saxl. *Saturn and Melancholy: Studies in the History of Natural Philosophy, Religion and Art*. London: Thomas Nelson, 1964.

Knowles, David. *The Evolution of Medieval Thought*. Baltimore: Helicon Press, 1962.

Kolve, V. A. *Chaucer and the Imagery of Narrative: The First Five Canterbury Tales*. Stanford: Stanford University Press, 1984.

————. "Chaucer and the Visual Arts." *Writers and Their Background: Geoffrey Chaucer*. Ed. Derek Brewer. Athens, OH: Ohio University Press, 1975, pp. 290–320.

————. "*Everyman* and the Parable of the Talents." *Medieval English Drama*.

Ed. Jerome Taylor and Alan H. Nelson. Chicago: University of Chicago Press, 1972.
————. *The Play Called Corpus Christi*. Stanford: Stanford University Press, 1966.
Koonce, B.G. *Chaucer and the Tradition of Fame: Symbolism in "The House of Fame"*. Princeton: Princeton University Press, 1966.
Kuhn, Reinhard. *The Demon of Noontide: Ennui in Western Literature*. Princeton: Princeton University Press, 1976.
Labande, E. R. "Pilgrimage." *New Catholic Encyclopedia*, Vol. 11, pp. 362–72.
Lagorio, Valerie Marie, and Ritamary Bradley. *The Fourteenth-Century English Mystics: A Comprehensive Bibliography*. New York: Garland, 1981.
Lawlor, John. *Piers Plowman: An Essay in Criticism*. London: Edward Arnold, 1962.
Leff, Gordon. *Bradwardine and the Pelagians*. Cambridge: The University Press, 1957.
————. *Gregory of Rimini: Tradition and Innovation in Fourteenth Century Thought*. Manchester: Manchester University Press, 1961.
————. *Heresy in the Later Middle Ages: The Relation of Heterodoxy To Dissent, c. 1250–c. 1450*. 2 vols. Manchester: Manchester University Press, 1967.
————. *Medieval Thought: St. Augustine to Ockham*. Harmondsworth: Penguin, 1958.
————. *Paris and Oxford Universities in the Thirteenth and Fourteenth Centuries: An Institutional and Intellectual History*. New York: John Wiley, 1968.
————. *William of Ockham: The Metamorphosis of Scholastic Discourse*. Manchester: Manchester University Press, 1975.
Lerner, Ralph, and Muhsin Mahdi (eds.). *Medieval Political Philosophy: A Sourcebook*. New York: Free Press, 1963.
Lerner, Robert E. *The Age of Adversity: The Fourteenth Century*. Ithaca: Cornell University Press, 1968.
Lewis, C. S. *The Allegory of Love: A Study in Medieval Tradition*. Oxford: Oxford University Press, 1936.
————. *The Discarded Image: An Introduction to Medieval and Renaissance Literature*. Cambridge: The University Press, 1970.
Lewis, Ewart. *Medieval Political Ideas*. New York: Knopf, 1954.
Little, A. G. and F. Pelster (eds.). *Oxford Theology and Theologians, c. A.D. 1282–1302*. Oxford: The Clarendon Press, 1934.
Longsworth, Robert M. "*Sir Orfeo*, the Minstrel, and the Minstrel's Art." *SP*, 79 (1982), 1–11.
Lot-Borodine, M. "L'Aridité ou 'siccitas' dans l'antiquité chrétienne." *Etudes Carmélitaines Mystiques et Missionaires*, 22, 2 (1937), 191–205.
Lottin, Odon. "Le Libre Arbitre chez Godefroid de Fontaines." *Revue Néoscolastique de Philosophie*, 40 (1937), 213–41.
————. "Libre Arbitre et liberté depuis Saint Anselme jusqu' à la fin du XIIIe siècle." *Psychologie et morale aux XIIe et XIIIe siècles*. Louvain: Abbaye du Mont César, 1942, Vol. 1, pp. 11–389.

————. "La Psychologie de l'acte humain chez Saint Jean Damascène et les théologiens du XIIIe siècle occidental." *Revue Thomiste*, 36 (1931), 631–61.

MacCulloch, J. A. *Medieval Faith and Fable*. Boston: Marshall Jones, 1932.

McDavid, Raven, and Audrey Duckert (eds.). *Lexicography in English*. New York: New York Academy of Sciences, 1973.

McEvoy, James. *The Philosophy of Robert Grosseteste*. Oxford: The Clarendon Press, 1982.

McFarlane, K.B. *Lancastrian Kings and Lollard Knights*. Ed. G.L. Harriss and J.R.L. Highfield. Oxford: The Clarendon Press, 1972.

McGann, Jerome J. *Fiery Dust: Byron's Poetic Development*. Chicago: Chicago University Press, 1968.

McGrade, Arthur Stephen. *The Political Thought of William of Ockham: Personal and Institutional Principles*. Cambridge: The University Press, 1974.

McKisack, May. *The Fourteenth Century, 1307–1399*. Oxford: The Clarendon Press, 1959.

McNamara, John F. "Responses to Ockhamist Theology in the Poetry of the *Pearl*-Poet, Langland, and Chaucer." Diss. Louisiana State University, 1968.

Mallet, Charles Edward. *A History of the University of Oxford*. 3 vols. New York: Longmans, 1924–28.

Manly, J. M. "The Authorship of *Piers Plowman*." MP, 7 (1909), 83–144.

————. "The Lost Leaf of *Piers Plowman*." MP, 3 (1906), 359–66.

————. "*Piers Plowman* and Its Sequence." *The Cambridge History of English Literature*. Ed. Sir A. W. Ward and A. R. Waller. 15 vols. Cambridge: The University Press, 1907–33, vol. 2 (1908), pp. 1–42.

Marchand, Leslie A. *Byron: A Portrait*. New York: Knopf, 1970.

Marrone, Steven P. *William of Auvergne and Robert Grosseteste: New Ideas of Truth in the Early Thirteenth Century*. Princeton: Princeton University Press, 1983.

Martin, Jay. "Wil as Fool and Wanderer in *Piers Plowman*." TSLL, 3 (1962), 535–48.

Martin, Priscilla. *Piers Plowman: The Field and the Tower*. New York: Barnes and Noble, 1979.

Mathew, Gervase. *The Court of Richard II*. London: Murray, 1968.

Mehl, Dieter. *The Middle English Romances of the Thirteenth and Fourteenth Centuries*. London: Routledge & Kegan Paul, 1968.

Michalski, Konstanty. "Le Problème de la volonté à Oxford et à Paris au XIVe siècle." Studia Philosophica: Commentarii Societatis Philosophicae Polonorum, 2 (1937), 233–365.

Michaud-Quantin, Pierre. "La Classification des puissances de l'âme au XIIe siècle." *Revue du Moyen-Age Latin*, 5 (1949), 15–34.

Middleton, Anne. "The Idea of Public Poetry in the Reign of Richard II." *Speculum*, 53 (1978), 94–114.

————. "Two Infinities: Grammatical Metaphor in *Piers Plowman*." ELH, 39 (1972), 169–88.

Mills, David. "The Role of the Dreamer in *Piers Plowman*." *Critical Approaches*. Ed. Hussey, pp. 180–212.

Miner, John Nelson. "Schools and Literacy in Later Medieval England." *British Journal of Education Studies*, 11 (1962/63), 16–27.

Mitchell, Jerome. *Thomas Hoccleve: A Study in Early Fifteenth-Century English Poetic.* Urbana: University of Illinois Press, 1968.

Molinari, Paul. *Julian of Norwich: The Teaching of a Fourteenth Century English Mystic.* London: Longmans, 1958.

Monahan, Edward J. "Human Liberty and Free Will According to John Buridan." *MS,* 16 (1954), 72—86.

Moody, Ernest A. "A Quodlibetal Question of Robert Holcot, O.P., on the Problem of the Objects of Knowledge and of Belief." *Speculum,* 39 (1964), 53—74.

Mulhern, P. F. "Practice of Penance." *New Catholic Encyclopedia,* Vol. 11, p. 73.

Murtaugh, Daniel Maher. *Piers Plowman and the Image of God.* Gainesville: University Press of Florida, 1978.

Muscatine, Charles. "Locus of Action in Medieval Narrative." *Romance Philology,* 17 (1963), 115—22.

—————. *Poetry and Crisis in the Age of Chaucer.* Notre Dame: University of Notre Dame Press, 1972.

Neaman, Judith S. *Suggestion of the Devil: Insanity in the Middle Ages and the Twentieth Century.* New York: Octagon Books, 1978.

Oakley, Francis. "Medieval Theories of Natural Law: William of Ockham and the Significance of the Voluntarist Tradition." *Natural Law Forum,* 6 (1961), 65—83.

Oberman, Heiko A. *Archbishop Thomas Bradwardine, A Fourteenth Century Augustinian.* Utrecht: Kemink & Zoon, 1957.

—————. " 'Facientibus Quod In Se Est Deus Non Denegat Gratiam': Robert Holcot, O.P., and the Beginnings of Luther's Theology." *HTR,* 55 (1962), 317—42.

—————. *Forerunners of the Reformation: The Shape of Late Medieval Thought.* Trans. Paul L. Nyhus. New York: Holt, Rinehart and Winston, 1966.

—————. "Fourteenth-Century Religious Thought: A Premature Profile." *Speculum,* 53 (1978), 80—93.

—————. *The Harvest of Medieval Theology: Gabriel Biel and Late Medieval Nominalism.* Cambridge, MA: Harvard University Press, 1963.

—————. "Some Notes on the Theology of Nominalism, with Attention to Its Relation to the Renaissance." *HTR,* 53 (1960), 47—76.

Orme, Nicholas. *Education in the West of England, 1066—1548.* Exeter: University of Exeter, 1976.

Orsten, Elizabeth M. " 'Heaven on Earth': Langland's Vision of Life within the Cloister." *ABR,* 21 (1970), 526—34.

Owst, G. R. *Literature and Pulpit in Medieval England.* 1933; rev. Oxford: Blackwell, 1961.

—————. *Preaching in Medieval England: An Introduction to Sermon Manuscripts of the Period c. 1350—1450.* Cambridge: The University Press, 1926.

Painter, Sidney, and Brian Tierney. *Western Europe in the Middle Ages, 300—1475.* New York: Knopf, 1970.

Palmer, Barbara. "The Guide Convention in *Piers Plowman.*" *LSE,* n.s. 5 (1971), 13—28.

Palmer, P., and P. E. McKeever. "Sacrament of Penance." *New Catholic Encyclopedia,* Vol. 11, pp. 73—83.

Pantin, W.A. (ed.). *Documents Illustrating the Activities of the General and Provincial Chapters of the English Black Monks, 1215–1540.* 3 vols. London: Camden Third Series, nos. 45, 47, 54, 1931–37.

———. "Grosseteste's Relations with the Papacy and the Crown." *Robert Grosseteste.* Ed. Callus.

Peck, Russell A. "Chaucer and the Nominalist Questions." *Speculum,* 53 (1978), 745–60.

———. "Numerology and Chaucer's *Troilus and Criseyde.*" *Mosaic,* 5 (1972), 1–29.

———. "Willfulness and Wonders: Boethian Tragedy in the Alliterative *Morte Arthure.*" *The Alliterative Tradition in the Fourteenth Century.* Ed. Bernard S. Levy and Paul E. Szarmach. Kent, OH: Kent State University Press, 1981, pp. 153–82.

Peil, Rudolf. *A Handbook of the Liturgy.* Trans. H. E. Winstone. London: Nelson, 1960.

Pelzer, Auguste. "Les 51 Articles de Guillaume Occam censurés en Avignon en 1326." *Revue d'Histoire Ecclésiastique,* 18 (1922), 240–70.

Pernoud, Marie Anne. "Innovation in William of Ockham's References to the 'Potentia Dei'." *Antonianum,* 45 (1970), 65–97.

Pochoda, Elizabeth T. *Arthurian Propaganda: "Le Morte Darthur" as an Historical Ideal of Life.* Chapel Hill: The University of North Carolina Press, 1971.

Pollard, Graham. "The *Pecia* System in the Medieval Universities." *Medieval Scribes, Manuscripts and Libraries: Essays Presented to N.R. Ker.* Ed. M.B. Parkes and Andrew G. Watson. London: Scolar Press, 1978.

Potter, G.R. "Education in the Fourteenth and Fifteenth Centuries." *Cambridge Medieval History.* Ed. J.B. Bury *et al.* New York: Macmillan, 1936.

Potts, Timothy C. *Conscience in Medieval Philosophy.* Cambridge: The University Press, 1980.

Powicke, Frederick Maurice. *The Medieval Books of Merton College.* Oxford: The Clarendon Press, 1931.

Putnam, Bertha Haven. *The Enforcement of the Statutes of Labourers during the First Decade after the Black Death, 1349–1359.* New York: Columbia University Press, 1908.

———. "Wage-laws for Priests after the Black Death." *AHR,* 21 (1915/16), 12–32.

Quirk, Randolph. "Langland's Use of *Kind Wit* and *Inwit.*" *JEGP,* 52 (1953), 182–88.

Rauch, Rufus William. "Langland and Mediaeval Functionalism." *Review of Politics,* 5 (1943), 441–61.

Réau, Louis. *Iconographie de l'Art Chrétien: Iconographie des Saints.* Paris: Presses Universitaires de France, 1958.

Riach, Mary. "Langland's Dreamer and the Transformation of the Third Vision." *EIC,* 19 (1969), 6–18.

Richards, R.C. "Ockham and Skepticism." *New Scholasticism,* 42 (1968), 345–63.

Richardson, H. G. "The English Coronation Oath." *Speculum,* 24 (1949), 44–75.

———. "An Oxford Teacher of the Fifteenth Century." *Bulletin of the John Rylands Library,* 23 (1939), 436–57.

Robertson, D. W., Jr. "The Doctrine of Charity in Medieval Gardens: A Topical Approach Through Symbolism and Allegory." *Speculum,* 26 (1951), 24–49.

———— and Bernard F. Huppé. *Piers Plowman and Scriptural Tradition.* Princeton: Princeton University Press, 1951.

————. *A Preface to Chaucer: Studies in Medieval Perspectives.* Princeton: Princeton University Press, 1962.

Robson, J.A. *Wyclif and the Oxford Schools.* Cambridge: Cambridge University Press, 1966.

Rousseau, Philip. *Ascetic, Authority, and the Church in the Age of Jerome and Cassian.* Oxford: Oxford University Press, 1978.

Russell, Bertrand. *The Conquest of Happiness.* 1930; rpt. London: Unwin, 1975.

Russell, G. H. "The Salvation of the Heathen: The Exploration of a Theme in *Piers Plowman.*" *JWCI,* 29 (1966), 101–16.

————. "Some Aspects of the Process of Revision in *Piers Plowman.*" *Critical Approaches.* Ed. Hussey, pp. 27–49.

Russell, Jeffrey Burton. *Medieval Civilization.* New York: John Wiley, 1968.

Ryan, John K., and Bernardino M. Bonansea (eds.). *John Duns Scotus, 1265–1965.* Washington, DC: The Catholic University of America Press, 1965.

Sachs, Arieh. "Religious Despair in Mediaeval Literature and Art." *MS,* 26 (1964), 231–56.

St-Jacques, Raymond. "Langland's Christ-Knight and the Liturgy." *Revue de l'Université d'Ottawa,* 37 (1967), 146–58.

Salter, Elizabeth. *Piers Plowman: An Introduction.* Oxford: Blackwell, 1962.

————. "*Piers Plowman* and the Visual Arts." *Encounters: Essays on Literature and the Visual Arts.* Ed. John Dixon Hunt. New York: Norton, 1971.

San Cristóbal-Sebastián, Antonio. *Controversias acerca de la voluntad desde 1270 a 1300.* Madrid: Editorial y Librería, 1958.

Sanderlin, George. "The Character '*Liberum Arbitrium*' in the C-text of *Piers Plowman.*" *MLN,* 56 (1941), 449–53.

Schmidt, A.V.C. "Langland and Scholastic Philosophy." *MÆ,* 38 (1969), 134–56.

Schroeder, Mary C[arruthers]. "Piers Plowman: The Tearing of the Pardon." *PQ,* 49 (1970), 8–18.

Schulz, Fritz. "Bracton on Kingship." *EHR,* 60 (1945), 136–76.

Scott, T.K., Jr. "Nicholas of Autrecourt, Buridan, and Ockhamism." *Journal of the History of Philosophy,* 9 (1971), 15–41.

Seesholtz, Anna Groh. *Friends of God: Practical Mystics of the Fourteenth Century.* New York: Columbia University Press, 1934.

Smalley, Beryl. "The Bible and Eternity: John Wyclif's Dilemma." *JWCI,* 27 (1964), 73–89.

————. *English Friars and Antiquity in the Early Fourteenth Century.* Oxford: Blackwell, 1960.

————. "Robert Holcot, O.P." *Archivum Fratrum Praedicatorum,* 26 (1956), 5–97.

Snyder, Susan. "The Left Hand of God: Despair in Medieval and Renaissance Tradition." *SRen,* 12 (1965), 18–59.

Southern, R. W. *Western Society and the Church in the Middle Ages*. Harmondsworth: Penguin, 1970.

Spearing, A. C. *Medieval Dream-Poetry*. Cambridge: The University Press, 1976.

———. "Verbal Repetitions in *Piers Plowman* B and C." *JEGP*, 62 (1963), 722–37.

Spender, Stephen (ed.). *W.H. Auden: A Tribute*. New York: Macmillan, 1975.

Spitzer, Leo. "Note on the Poetic and the Empirical 'I' in Medieval Authors." *Traditio*, 4 (1946), 414–22.

Stebler, Vinzenz. "Die *Horae Competentes* des Benediktinischen Stundengebetes." *Studia Anselmiana*, 42 (1957), 15–24.

Steinmetz, David C. "Late Medieval Nominalism and the *Clerk's Tale*." *ChauR*, 12 (1977/78), 38–54.

Taylor, John. "Richard II's View on Kingship." *PLPLS-LHS*, 14 (1971), 189–205.

Thomas, Mary Edith. *Medieval Skepticism and Chaucer*. New York: William-Frederick, 1950.

Thompson, S. Harrison. "Pro Saeculo XIV." *Speculum*, 28 (1953), 801–07.

Thornley, Eva M. "The Middle English Penitential Lyric and Hoccleve's Autobiographical Poetry." *NM*, 68 (1967), 295–321.

Tolkien, J. R. R. "Of Fairy-stories." *Essays Presented to Charles Williams*. Ed. C. S. Lewis. Oxford: Oxford University Press, 1947, pp. 38–89.

Trapp, Damasus. "Augustinian Theology in the Fourteenth Century: Notes on Editions, Marginalia, Opinions and Book-Lore." *Augustiniana*, 6 (1956), 146–274.

Trinkaus, Charles, and Heiko A. Oberman (eds.). *The Pursuit of Holiness in Late Medieval and Renaissance Religion*. Leiden: Brill, 1974.

Tristram, E. W. *English Wall Painting of the Fourteenth Century*. London: Routledge & Paul, 1955.

Tuchman, Barbara W. *A Distant Mirror: The Calamitous Fourteenth Century*. New York: Knopf, 1978.

Tuck, Anthony. *Richard II and the English Nobility*. London: Edward Arnold, 1973.

Tuma, George Wood. *The Fourteenth Century English Mystics: A Comparative Analysis*. 2 vols. Salzburg: Institut für Englische Sprache und Literatur, 1977.

Tuve, Rosemund. *Allegorical Imagery: Some Mediaeval Books and Their Posterity*. Princeton: Princeton University Press, 1966.

———. "Notes on the Virtues and Vices." *JWCI*, 26 (1963), 264–303 and 27 (1964), 42–72.

Ullmann, W. "The Influence of John of Salisbury on Medieval Italian Jurists." *EHR*, 59 (1944), 384–92.

———. *Principles of Government and Politics in the Middle Ages*. London: Methuen, 1961.

Underhill, Evelyn. *Mysticism*. London: Methuen, 1930.

Utley, Francis Lee. "Dialogues, Debates, and Catechisms." *A Manual of the Writings in Middle English, 1050–1500*. Gen. ed. Albert E. Hartung. Vol. 3. New Haven: The Connecticut Academy of Arts and Sciences, 1972, pp. 669–745 and 829–902.

Vasta, Edward (ed.). *Interpretations of Piers Plowman*. Notre Dame: University of Notre Dame Press, 1968.

————. "Truth, the Best Treasure, in *Piers Plowman*." *PQ*, 44 (1965), 17–29.

Verbeke, Gérard. "Le Développement de la vie volitive d'après S. Thomas." *Revue Philosophique Louvain*, 56 (1958), 5–34.

Vogel, Claude L. (ed.). *Psychology and the Franciscan School*. New York: Bruce, 1932.

Voll, U. "Acedia." *New Catholic Encyclopedia*, Vol. 1, pp. 83–84.

Walsh, James J. "Nominalism and the *Ethics*: Some Remarks about Buridan's *Commentary*." *Journal of the History of Philosophy*, 4 (1966), 1–13.

Weisheipl, James A. "Curriculum of the Faculty of Arts at Oxford in the Early Fourteenth Century." *MS*, 26 (1964), 143–85.

————. "Developments in the Arts Curriculum at Oxford in the Early Fourteenth Century." *MS*, 28 (1966), 151–75.

Wenzel, Siegfried. "Acedia, 700–1200." *Traditio*, 22 (1966), 73–102.

————. "Petrarch's *Accidia*." *StudR*, 8 (1961), 36–48.

————. *The Sin of Sloth: Acedia in Medieval Thought and Literature*. Chapel Hill: The University of North Carolina Press, 1967.

White, Lynn, Jr. "Natural Science and Naturalistic Art in the Middle Ages." *AHR*, 52 (1947), 421–35.

Whitworth, Charles W., Jr. "Changes in the Roles of Reason and Conscience in the Revisions of *Piers Plowman*." *NQ*, n.s. 19 (1972), 4–7.

Wilkinson, B. "The Deposition of Richard II and the Accession of Henry IV." *EHR*, 54 (1939), 215–39.

————. "The 'Political Revolution' of the Thirteenth and Fourteenth Centuries in England." *Speculum*, 24 (1949), 502–09.

Williams, George H. *Wilderness and Paradise in Christian Thought*. New York: Harper, 1962.

Wittig, Joseph S. "The Dramatic and Rhetorical Development of Long Will's Pilgrimage." *NM*, 76 (1975), 52–76.

————. "*Piers Plowman*, B, Passus IX–XII: Elements in the Design of the Inward Journey." *Traditio*, 28 (1972), 211–80.

Woolf, Rosemary. *The English Religious Lyric in the Middle Ages*. Oxford: The Clarendon Press, 1968.

————. "Some Non-Medieval Qualities of *Piers Plowman*." *Essays in Criticism*, 12 (1962), 111–25.

————. "The Theme of Christ the Lover-Knight in Medieval English Literature." *RES*, n.s. 13 (1962), 1–16.

Yates, Frances A. *The Art of Memory*. 1966; rpt. Harmondsworth: Penguin, 1969.

Index